NOVEMBER 1918

THE MAKING OF THE MODERN WORLD

This group of narrative histories focuses on key moments and events in the twentieth century to explore their wider significance for the development of the modern world.

PUBLISHED

The Fall of France: The Nazi Invasion of 1940, Julian Jackson
A Bitter Revolution: China's Struggle with the Modern World, Rana Mitter
Dynamic of Destruction: Culture and Mass Killing in the First World War,
  Alan Kramer
Sharpeville: An Apartheid Massacre and its Consequences, Tom Lodge
Algeria: France's Undeclared War, Martin Evans

SERIES ADVISERS

PROFESSOR CHRIS BAYLY[†], University of Cambridge
PROFESSOR RICHARD J. EVANS, University of Cambridge
PROFESSOR DAVID REYNOLDS, University of Cambridge

NOVEMBER 1918

THE GERMAN REVOLUTION

ROBERT GERWARTH

OXFORD
UNIVERSITY PRESS

Great Clarendon Street, Oxford, OX2 6DP,
United Kingdom

Oxford University Press is a department of the University of Oxford.
It furthers the University's objective of excellence in research, scholarship,
and education by publishing worldwide. Oxford is a registered trade mark of
Oxford University Press in the UK and in certain other countries

First Edition published in 2020

Impression: 1

Published in the United States of America by Oxford University Press
198 Madison Avenue, New York, NY 10016, United States of America

British Library Cataloguing in Publication Data

Data available

Library of Congress Control Number: 2019953826

ISBN 978-0-19-954647-3

Printed and bound in Great Britain by
Clays Ltd, Elcograf S.p.A.

For Gundi and Helga –
Daughters of the Weimar Republic

Preface

November 1918 has a special resonance and place in German history. It marks not one but two momentous and closely intertwined events that profoundly transformed the fate of Europe's largest state: Germany's defeat in the Great War *and* the subsequent revolution that swept away the monarchy and transformed the country into one of the most progressive democracies in the world, the Weimar Republic. Yet the November Revolution, born out of defeat and ideological conflict, does not feature prominently on the list of events that are commemorated with pride by German democrats today. On the contrary: commonly referred to in the existing historical literature, political speeches, and journalistic op-ed pieces as a 'failed' or 'half-hearted' revolution, the events of late 1918 have long been viewed as part of Germany's 'special path' towards the abyss of the Third Reich. Because the revolution did not bring about a sufficiently radical break with Germany's imperial past, it failed, or so the story goes, to inspire genuine allegiance to democracy among German citizens and allowed radicals like Hitler to exploit the alleged weaknesses of the system.

This book suggests an alternative interpretation of the November Revolution—one that does more justice to the achievements of the events of 1918–19, which constituted both the first and the last revolution in a highly industrialized country worldwide prior to the peaceful revolutions in Eastern and Central Europe in 1989–90. Other revolutions that preceded 1918 or followed in later years—the French Revolution of 1789, the pan-European revolutions of 1848, the Bolshevik Revolution in Russia, or Mao's Chinese Revolution—took place in non- or partially industrialized societies, or they were imposed from outside, as was the case in much of Eastern Europe in 1945–9 where 'revolutions' were not backed by the masses, but imported by the Red Army. This was at odds with Karl Marx's materialist conception of history as a sequence of stages, in which bourgeois revolutions—replacing monarchic rule with liberal constitutions and capitalist economies—would occur *before* the age of communist revolutions. By the beginning of the twentieth century, however, the debate about how to achieve a communist utopia had evolved with the Marxist camp. For some, like Lenin, industrialization was not a prerequisite for a proletarian revolution which could be achieved even in partially industrialized countries like Russia with a 'vanguard' of professional revolutionaries who would subsequently spread class consciousness and drive forward the industrialization of their country. Others, such as the influential German theorist and Social Democratic politician Eduard Bernstein, argued that in highly industrialized countries like Germany the economy had become too complex for a revolution—socialism could be realized without a violent revolution and through incremental legislative reforms.

Debates such as these underpinned many of the tensions within the Left—tensions which grew further in 1914 when the outbreak of war in Europe and the support of socialist parties in all European countries (with the exception of Italy) for their respective countries' war efforts showed the fragility of international class solidarity in the face of nationalist mobilization. We will return to these important rifts and debates within the European Left in the book, even though the chronological focus lies on the events unfolding from 1917 onwards.

Starting in 1917, the year in which America's entry into the war and two revolutions in Russia prompted a revolution of expectations both for the war itself and for the post-war order, and ending in late 1923, when the revolutionary years ushered in a more stable period in German history, this book seeks to achieve two things: first, it aims to offer a new narrative analysis of the turbulent events that led to the military collapse of Imperial Germany and the establishment of the first German democracy. Second, it strives to do so without falling into the trap of reading German history backwards and viewing the events of November 1918 through the prism of Hitler's rise to power after the onset of the Great Depression in 1929 and Weimar's eventual 'failure' in 1933. To achieve these aims, the book takes more seriously than is often the case the perspectives of those Germans who lived through the end of the Great War and the early years of the Weimar Republic. Instead of taking for granted the retrospectively imposed narrative of the 'doomed Republic' that has become a staple of history school books and public discourses about interwar Germany, I suggest that the future of Weimar was wide open in the early years of the republic's existence, with failure as likely as success, and optimism about the future as common as pessimism. Furthermore, by placing the events that led to the German Revolution within the broader Central–Eastern European context in which they belong, I argue that the November Revolution was one of the more successful revolutions of the period 1917–23. After all, between 1917 and 1923, there were more than thirty attempts at violent regime change across Europe, some of them more successful than others. Similar to the Austrian and Czech(oslovak) revolutions, the German November Revolution achieved its principal aims—peace and democratization—in an initially non-violent way, thus avoiding anything comparable to the unimaginably brutal civil war that followed Lenin's October Revolution.

As the German Revolution of 1918 has often been portrayed as a 'minor revolution', it is worth reflecting on what the term actually means. Given the very varied nature of revolutions across time and space, historians have debated endlessly how to define it. Most agree that revolutions involve mass participation, and—if successful—a significant change to the pre-existing political system. However, some have argued that revolutions also need to be violent to qualify as such. According to this somewhat romanticized 'maximalist' interpretation of revolution, promoted, in very different ways, by Thomas Paine, Jules Michelet, Karl Marx, and others, revolutions had to be violent to destroy the old regime and its supporters. Yet such an interpretation overlooks that, in reality, there is no 'standard revolution' and that some of the most transformative revolutions—such as the ones that ended Communist regimes across Eastern and Central Europe in 1989–90—were largely non-violent (with the notable exception of Romania).

Other aspects that are often emphasized as quintessentially revolutionary are 'suddenness' and radical change in the distribution of wealth. Yet, in the case of China, Mao had to fight a variety of opponents for more than two decades before taking power in 1949 without anyone doubting that the Chinese Revolution was indeed a revolution. Similarly, the American Revolution lasted from 1765 to 1783, and while it resulted in very significant political change, it led to no redistribution of wealth. Suddenness was certainly not a characteristic of either the American or Chinese revolutions, though violence clearly was. The same can be said about the Mexican revolution and the subsequent civil war (1913–20). Generally speaking, revolutions tend to be more violent when one of the core demands of the revolutionaries goes beyond political change and touches on the redistribution of wealth, land, and the 'means of production' as any such redistribution is likely to be implemented through the use of force and set to trigger a violent response from those about to be dispossessed.

If revolutions take very different forms, they can also produce fundamentally different outcomes: post-revolutionary regimes can be democracies—as was the case in 1918–19, and again in 1989–90, across East–Central Europe—or they can replace brutal dictatorships with new totalitarian regimes, as in Russia (1917), Cuba (1959), or Iran (1979).

Given the huge range of causes, forms, and results of events we view as 'revolutions', it might be best to adopt a more sober, minimalist definition that centres on popular radical change of an existing political system. In Germany (as in Russia in the spring of 1917), the initial core demand that triggered the November Revolution of 1918 was to immediately end the war. The state's failure to do so swiftly turned the *Kriegsbeendigungsrevolution* (the revolution to end the war) into something much bigger, as sailors, soldiers, and demonstrating workers demanded that the Kaiser—now seen as an obstacle to immediate peace—should abdicate. The Kaiser's refusal to do so led to calls for more significant systemic change even though there remained significant disagreements among the revolutionaries as to whether Germany should become a Councils' Republic or a parliamentary democracy. The war and the Central Powers' increasingly likely defeat were thus the main triggers of revolution. Without it, none of the revolutions that occurred in places like Germany, Austria, or Hungary would have happened. In all of these cases (and the same may be said of Russia in 1917 and China after 1945), the revolutions stemmed from a major crisis of legitimacy of the existing political order, not so much from the condition of society as predicted by Marx.

Herein also lies the reason for starting this book in 1917. It is impossible to understand Germany's revolution and indeed the wide range of contemporary expectations for an as yet unknown future in 1918 without acknowledging that the Great War, which was transformed in various ways in 1917, became the unintentional enabler of the different social or national revolutions that unfolded across Europe in and around 1918. In its final stages, from 1917 onwards, the war changed in nature, as the Bolshevik revolution of 1917 and the threat of imminent defeat led to Russia's withdrawal from the war while the Western Allies, strengthened by America's entry into the conflict that same year, forced Germany to begin a decisive offensive in the West before US troops arrived in large numbers—a move that would ultimately prove to be the beginning of the end for Imperial Germany. Meanwhile events in Russia had a dual effect: Petrograd's admission of defeat heightened expectations of imminent victory in Germany (only months before the ultimate defeat led to the search for the 'internal enemies' who had allegedly caused that collapse), while simultaneously injecting powerful new energies into the German far Left at a time when German society (like many other combatant societies) was longing for peace and political change after four years of fighting.

Finding an appropriate end date for this book was considerably more difficult. It was possible to choose from a variety of events that, to contemporaries at least, seemed either to bring to an end the German Revolution, or change its course and character: the murder of Rosa Luxemburg and Karl Liebknecht by Freikorps soldiers in Berlin in January 1919, the fall of the Munich Soviet Republic at the beginning of May 1919, the signing of the Versailles Peace Treaty in June 1919, the ratification of the Weimar constitution in August 1919, and the failure of the extreme Left and Right to topple the republican system on several occasions between 1920 and 1923. Eventually, November 1923—which marks the failure of Hitler's beer hall putsch in Munich, the end of the Franco-Belgian occupation of the Ruhr, and the beginning of Weimar's political and economic stabilization—seemed a logical end-point for a book of this kind, which is more concerned with the events, aftermath, and legacies of the November Revolution than with the Nazi rise to power.

In offering an alternative narrative analysis of the tumultuous events that transformed Germany from a semi-authoritarian empire into a democratic nation-state, and by highlighting the ways in which they were remembered and instrumentalized in subsequent years, the book follows the general direction of other titles in OUP's 'Making of the Modern World' series, from Rana Mitter's *A Bitter Revolution: China's Struggle with the Modern World* (2004) to Alan Kramer's *Dynamic of Destruction* (2007).

Since I first signed the contract for this book well over a decade ago, I have been side-tracked by other projects, notably my biography of Reinhard Heydrich (*Hitler's Hangman*, Yale UP, 2011) and my most recent book, *The Vanquished: Why the First World War Failed to End* (Allen Lane, 2016). Yet, in the end, these 'distractions' helped me to re-think my views on the events that unfolded in Germany in November 1918, and to see them in a much broader geographical and chronological context and brighter light.

Working on this book has been an enjoyable task, partly because the format of the book series has allowed me to draw on a wide range of important specialist studies (the authors of which, I hope, will recognize the huge intellectual debt I owe to their archival and conceptual works), but also because of the many conversations I have had about the book with a number of inspiring colleagues and friends, all of whom contributed to its completion in one way or another. Thanking some of the people who have helped me along the way is no more than a public acknowledgement of gratitude. For the past decade I have been fortunate to live and work in Dublin, which has become a major intellectual hub for German and European history in the period covered by this book. Countless conversations with my brilliant Ireland-based colleagues and friends—notably John Horne, Mark Jones, Alan Kramer, Stephan Malinowski, Tony McElligott, William Mulligan, and Jennifer Wellington—have helped me enormously to sharpen some of my arguments, and to abandon others. Needless to say, all remaining errors of fact or judgement in this book are entirely attributable to me.

The work on this book has taken me to a great number of libraries, and I am thankful to the staff of all of them. At the Herder Institut in Marburg, where I had the privilege to spend a semester as an Alexander von Humboldt Senior Research Fellow, I benefited greatly from the hospitality of the Institute's Director, Peter Haslinger, who provided excellent working conditions and space to think. And although this book is not primarily the result of extensive archival research, but a work of synthesis, I would like to acknowledge the crucial assistance in identifying some key archival sources of Jan Bockelmann and Ursula Falch, who collated large numbers of documents and literature in various archives and libraries across Germany and Austria.

I am fortunate in having a long-standing and productive relationship with Oxford University Press, with whom I am now publishing my seventh book, two of them as the sole author. I am particularly grateful to Sir Richard Evans as the general editor of the 'Making of the Modern World' series, and to Christopher Wheeler (then OUP's commissioning editor for history), for initially suggesting that it would be a good idea to write a book of this sort. Richard's feedback on the manuscript draft was also invaluable. After Christopher's retirement in 2013, Robert Faber took over as editor of the history list at OUP, and it is a sign of how long it has taken me to finish this book that Robert, too, retired before its completion. Matthew Cotton oversaw the final editing process while Sathiya Krishnamoorthy was in charge of the book's smooth production and I am indebted to the entire OUP team, including the indexer Judith Acevedo, for showing remarkable patience throughout the process. I am also grateful to the National University of Ireland for awarding me a publication grant. Various anonymous peer reviewers took time from their very busy schedules to read through the draft manuscript and made immensely helpful comments, for which I wish to thank them.

My final thanks, as always, go to my family. My parents offered all sorts of support during my frequent visits to Berlin. My mother, Evelyn Gerwarth, who always showed huge interest in my work, sadly passed away as I was finishing this book. In Dublin, my wife Porscha, despite her own busy schedule as a Professor of Romantic Literature, found time to offer critical feedback and stylistic advice on various occasions. Happy moments away from the desk were usually spent in her company and that of our two sons, Oscar and Lucian, who—now 8 years of age—have shown a healthy indifference to the subject of this book, but provided the author with wonderful and plentiful distractions throughout the process of writing it. Last but not least, I wish to thank my two oldest living relatives, my grandmother Gundi Arndt and my aunt Helga Fennig—two strong women who were both born in the Weimar Republic. As eyewitnesses of Germany's turbulent twentieth century, they taught me a great deal about the contingency of the future and the need to judge the past on its own terms. This book is dedicated to them.

Robert Gerwarth,
Dublin, January 2020

Contents

List of Maps

List of Illustrations

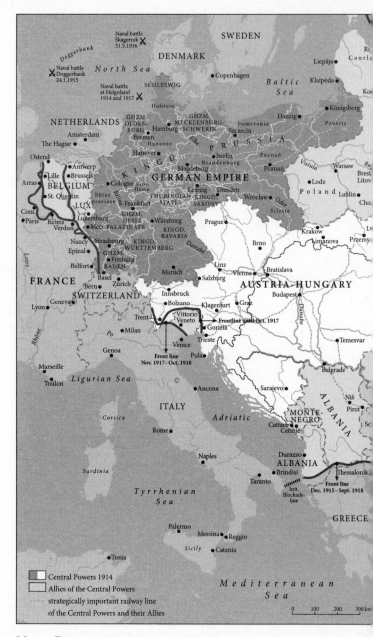

Map 1 Europe, 1914

 onia

●Dünaburg

Moscow●

Simbirsk●

s

●Smolensk

●Tula

●Penza

●Minsk

Volga

Saratov●

Pinsk
●

●Orel

RUSSIA

●Voronezh

→ Border of the German-Austrian sphere of influence in 1918

●Rovno

Kiev●

Kharkov●

Tsaritsyn●

→ Frontline, end of 1917

Dnieper

●Choczim

Dniester

Bug

Ekaterinoslaw●

Don

Rostov a.D.

Chernivtsi

Taganrog●

●Nikolaev

Odessa●

●Ekaterinodar
(from 1920 Krasnodar)

Crimea

●Kronstadt

ROMANIA

Sevastopol●

Bucharest

Danube

●Constanta

Black Sea

Batumi

Front line Spring/Summer 1918 ←●

●Tutrakan

Nicosia

Kars●

LGARIA

●Trabzon

●Adrianople

Constantinople
●●Skadar

Kızıl-Irmak

Front line 1916/17 ←

Erzurum

Archindjan●

●Gallipoli

ean

●Angora

Tigris

OTTOMAN EMPIRE

Nusaybin●

●Smyrna

Baghdad Railway

Adana●

Euphrates

s

●Aleppo

Dodecanese
(ital.)

Cyprus

ARABIA

Crete

Map 2 Europe, 1918

Legend:

········ Austria-Hungary border, of the Ottoman Empire until 1918 and the Russian Empire until 1917

········ Border of the countries of the Austrian crown until 1918

········ Turkey after the Peace of Sèvres in 1920
▓▓▓ Turkey after the Peace of Lausanne in 1923

·······Curzon Line December 8, 1919

0   100   200   300

ATVIA
(independent)

Daugavpils

Moscow ●

Ulyanovsk ●

Smolensk ●

● Tula

Vilnius
('23)

Minsk ●
Belarussian SSR.
(1919)

● Orel

Saratov ●

Volga

olish)

Pinsk ●

wel

UNION OF THE SOVIET
SOCIALIST REPUBLICS (USSR)

Voronezh ●

vno ●

Kiev ●

Kharkov ●

Tsaritsyn ●
(from 1925 Stalingrad)

Dnieper

ern
iaa
'23)

Chernivtsi

Dniester

Ukrainian SSR.
(1917–19)

Dnepropetrovsk ●

Don

● Rostov a.D.

Moldovan
ASSR.
(1924)

Bug

Taganrog

Bessarabia
(1918/20 rom.)

Nikolayev ●

OMÂNIA

Brusso

● Odessa

Ekaterinodar
(from 1920 Krasnodar)

Bucharest ●

Constanta ●

Crimea
Crimea ASSR.
(1921)

Novorossiysk ●

Danube

Sevastopol ●

Sochi ●

Transcaucasian
SFSR.
Georgian SSR.
(1922–36)

leyen

Varna ●

Black Sea

Batumi ●

LGARIA

Burgas ●

Sinope ●

(1920/21
Turk.)
Kars ●

div

Edirne ●
(1920–22
Greek occupied)

Constantinople ●

Skadar ●

Trabzon ●

Erzurum ●
ARMENIA
(1918–20 independent)

(1919/20
Greek)

Mudania ●

Bursa ●

Kizil-Irmak

Ankara ●

Gallipoli

Diyarbekir ● Tigris

Pergamon ●
(1919–22 Greek.)

TURKEY
(1923 Republic)

Mardin ●

gean

Smyrna ●

● Urfa

Gaziantep ●
1919–21 French occupied)

Adana ●
Mersin ●

Euphrates

Antalya ●

Iskenderun
(Alexandretta)
S. A

Aleppo ●
Syria
(1920 French Mandate)

s

Dodecanese
(ital.)

Latakia ●
Alawite
State
(1924–30)

● Hama

Nicosia ●
Cyprus
(brit.; 1925 colony)

● Homs

Crete

Tripoli ●
Lebanon

'Like a beautiful dream'

Introduction

In the early morning hours of 10 November 1918, a small convoy of cars crossed the Belgian–Dutch border near the village of Eijsden, carrying the last German Kaiser and King of Prussia, Wilhelm II, into exile. The previous day, his head of government, Chancellor Max von Baden, had publicly announced, without the Kaiser's authorization, that Wilhelm had abdicated. Only a few hours later, Philipp Scheidemann, one of the leaders of Germany's largest political party, the Majority Social Democrats (MSPD), had proclaimed the German Republic from a balcony of the parliament building, the Reichstag. Later that night, upon receiving confirmation that the Queen of the Netherlands and the Dutch government had granted him political asylum, an anxious Wilhelm and his closest entourage fled the Army High Command's Field Headquarters in the German-occupied Belgian city of Spa in his royal train. Fearing his imminent arrest by revolutionary soldiers, Wilhelm assumed that he was bound to suffer the same fate as his distant relative, Tsar Nicholas II of Russia, who had been brutally murdered along with his family by the Bolsheviks less than four months earlier—an incident that may have influenced the Dutch government's decision to grant Wilhelm political asylum in the Netherlands.[1]

Hoping to remain unrecognized as he crossed the border, Wilhelm swapped the royal train for an unmarked car as he approached the Dutch frontier. His hopes for anonymity were quickly dashed as members of the local population recognized the Kaiser and started to abuse him verbally as a war criminal. Wilhelm was eventually able to continue his journey into the Netherlands by train. Two weeks later, almost unnoticed by a German public that no longer cared what the former

Figure 0.1 Visibly shaken by the revolutionary situation in Germany, Wilhelm II waits with his staff at a station on the Dutch border, on the train journey into exile. The day before, Reich Chancellor Max von Baden had announced the Kaiser's abdication without waiting for his consent.

Kaiser had to say, he formally renounced—'once and for all'—his claim to the German and Prussian thrones.[2]

It was an inglorious end to the rule of Queen Victoria's first grand-child, a man who had been on the German throne since 1888. His fate over the subsequent thirty years—or so it must have seemed to him as he reflected on his life in the Dutch castle of Doorn, his home until his death in 1941—mirrored that of the country he had led for three decades: a tale of rapid rise and dramatic fall. The contrast between the increasingly prosperous German Empire of the late nineteenth century—the hegemonial power on the European continent—and the country's military collapse in 1918 could not have been greater. Back in 1871, when the German nation-state was founded by Otto von Bismarck, it had been set up as a federal constitutional monarchy, a union of twenty-five larger and smaller states, most of which continued to be ruled by sovereign kings, princes, and dukes, who accepted the supremacy of the Prussian king as German Kaiser. In political terms, Imperial Germany was not a parliamentary democracy like Britain, France, or the United States, but it was certainly not an unpopular autocratic state like tsarist Russia either. Imperial Germany had a constitution, an active national parliament, and independent state parliaments that controlled the respective states' budgets. Despite its semi-authoritarian political regime (the government was not dependent on a parliamentary majority but on royal consent), and a three-tier electoral system in its largest state (Prussia), the country had a flourishing civil society and an increasing number of people participated in political life through elections or involvement in the growing trade union movement. In the decades leading up to 1914, the German Reich, the youngest of the major nation-states in Europe, had also become the most culturally and economically dynamic country on the continent. Its population had increased massively, from 49 million in 1890 to 67 million in 1913; its cities grew exponentially, and life expectancy, literacy rates, and living standards improved significantly.[3] In economic terms, Germany displaced Britain as Europe's premier industrial power at the turn of the century, leading the way in the so-called 'second industrial revolution' that brought huge advances in the chemical and electrical industries. Income per capita and the country's GDP also grew exponentially, leading to noticeably rising living standards, while the state offered its citizens legal security and an increasingly tight net of social benefits. Glaring socio-economic inequalities persisted, but by 1914 it was equally clear that the working classes were in danger of losing much more than just their chains if they attempted, and failed to bring about, a violent overthrow of the existing system. The largest political party to represent workers' interests, the Social Democratic Party (SPD), acknowledged this reality by gradually moving away from the orthodox Marxist mantra of revolution. Instead of a political revolution, the SPD's leadership increasingly advocated gradual change through reforms in order to improve the working conditions and living standards of their main supporters: the ordinary working people.[4]

For all these reasons, Germany on the eve of the First World War was a remarkably stable state—certainly a lot less 'nervous' or plagued by 'perpetual crisis' than has sometimes been suggested.[5] To be sure, Imperial Germany was not without political and social tensions, but it was by no means a hotbed of revolutionary activity or agitation either.[6]

The outbreak of the Great War changed everything. Back in 1914, Kaiser Wilhelm II, who had done much to escalate the local conflict between Austria-Hungary and Serbia into a pan-European war, believed that the war would inevitably cement his country's hegemony on the Continent. Most of his subjects shared that optimistic sentiment in August 1914 and entered the war in a confident—though not always enthusiastic—mood.[7] Many Germans fully anticipated a swift victory. The Kaiser famously promised them that the war would be over by the autumn. Some public intellectuals even hailed the war as a 'cleansing storm' that would pave the way for a bright future.[8]

The mood of invincibility was encouraged by the early stunning victories of the German army. In the West, a military triumph initially seemed feasible—at least until the German advance towards Paris was halted on the Marne River in early September 1914. This severe set-back meant the failure of the 'Schlieffen Plan'—the German tactical plan to win a decisive and swift victory over Britain and France in the West before fighting the Russian armies in the East, leading to a stale-mate on the Western front. From now on, and for much of the rest of the war, some eight million troops were facing each other along a front of 700 kilometres, from the North Sea to the Swiss border, unable to penetrate the enemy lines to a meaningful degree. Meanwhile in the East an early Russian invasion of East Prussia was repelled by General Paul von Hindenburg, a veteran of the Franco–Prussian war of 1870–1, and his talented Chief of Staff Erich Ludendorff. Over the coming years, these two men, now in charge of the Army High Command (OHL), would gradually turn Germany into a military dictatorship—one in which the wishes of the parliamentary majority, most notably their 1917 Peace Resolution which demanded an end to the war and a peace without indemnities or annexations, were either sidelined or altogether ignored. While war-weariness and discontent were growing in Germany, the military leadership managed to appease large parts of the population with an unexpected victory in the East. Aided by the two revolutions that occurred in Petrograd in 1917, but also prompted by the ill-fated Kerensky offensive that summer, German troops rapidly advanced towards the Russian capital, making it necessary for Lenin to seek a negotiated surrender which took the form of the draconian Treaty of Brest-Litovsk signed in early 1918.[9]

Germany's victory in the East was important for two reasons. First, it heightened expectations of an imminent military triumph in the West within the German military elite and large parts of the population. Second, it prompted the mastermind of Germany's war effort, Quartermaster-General Erich Ludendorff, to gamble on an all-out spring offensive on the Western front, designed to knock Britain and France out of the war before significant numbers of US troops arrived in Europe and altered the balance of power on the battlefield.[10]

If, after Russia's exit from the war, there had still been widespread optimism in Germany that the war would be won, the failure of Ludendorff's offensives on the Western front in the summer of 1918 and the military collapse of Berlin's allies—Bulgaria, as well as the Austro-Hungarian and Ottoman empires—made a German defeat inevitable. Exhausted from four years of fighting and faced with the prospect of military collapse, the German home front decisively turned against a continuation of the war and indeed against the monarchy itself. The regime's last-minute attempts to democratize the political system by introducing constitutional reforms and installing a new, more liberal government under Prince Max von Baden in October 1918 proved insufficient to save the Kaiser. Within days, in Kiel a sailors' mutiny against orders for the German High Seas Fleet to confront the Royal Navy in a desperate last-minute battle spread across the country's twenty-six constituent states and toppled all ruling houses, culminating in the proclamation of a republic on 9 November and Wilhelm's flight into exile the following morning.[11]

The remarkably swift political transformation of Germany in the autumn of 1918 stunned contemporary observers, as did the largely bloodless course of the first phase of the revolution. On 10 November 1918, the day of Kaiser Wilhelm II's flight into exile, the prominent editor-in-chief of the liberal daily *Berliner Tageblatt*, Theodor Wolff, famously published an enthusiastic commentary eulogizing the unfolding events: 'Like a sudden driving windstorm, the greatest of all revolutions has toppled the imperial regime together with all it comprised, from top to bottom. One can call it the greatest of all revolutions since never before was such a solidly built and walled Bastille taken at one go ... Yesterday morning, at least in Berlin, everything was still there. Yesterday afternoon, all of it had vanished.'[12] Wolff found it particularly praiseworthy that the imperial regime had been swept away almost without violence. 'Every people that aspires to rise to true freedom must see this example before it. Among us, symbols of the old spirit were lined up like the marble statues on the Siegesallee. A mature, sensible people swept them aside without breaking anything.'[13]

Wolff's enthusiastic appraisal of the November events may appear surprising, considering that in standard history books, the Revolution of 1918 is generally portrayed as an 'incomplete' revolution at best. It is certainly not among the events that German democrats today remember with pride. Instead it is frequently referred to as a 'half-hearted' revolution that failed to create a democracy strong enough to with-stand the onslaught of Nazism in the early 1930s. Yet such a verdict seems highly unbalanced and only makes sense from the perspective of 1933. Instead, it could be argued that the achievements of the November Revolution—the only successful revolution in a highly industrialized country before 1989—were thoroughly remarkable: within days, Germany peacefully transformed itself from a constitutional monarchy with restricted political participation by the parliament to what was probably the most progressive republic of the era. Germany became a democracy which, despite massive domestic and foreign policy chal-lenges (most of them the consequences of a lost war), lasted for fourteen years and thus survived longer than nearly all of the other European democracies founded in 1918. In recent years, more positive, or at least more open-ended, narrative histories of Weimar have been published, but, in the general perception, the republic's foundational event, the November Revolution, remains overshadowed by tragic shortcomings and wasted opportunities that allegedly proved fateful for the demise of democracy fourteen years later.[14]

The dramatic transformation of Germany in this period also becomes more visible when it is acknowledged that 1918 was as much a cultural and social revolution affecting gender relations and citizenship rights as it was a political one.[15] The revolution signified not merely the collapse of the Hohenzollern regime and all other aristocratic rulers in Germany, but also the politicization and mobilization of large parts of the population, notably of women, who had previously been excluded from the right to vote, and who suddenly—because of the death of more than two million German men in the war—constituted a signifi-cant majority of the overall electorate. Although the history of the Weimar Republic has often been written from a very male perspective, women played a prominent role in the revolutionary events that led to the creation of a democracy. This in itself should hardly come as a sur-prise given that the war had created a significant female demographic 'surplus' of more than two million compared to the male population. In 1918, Germany was the first highly industrialized country in the world to introduce universal suffrage for women. The swift introduction of female voting rights was somewhat surprising even if calls for suffrage equality had become louder during the war. However, the MSPD's support had been somewhat lukewarm—the party's priority was firmly on reforming the Prussian three-class suffrage laws and still as late as October 1918 it seemed as if the MSPD leadership had been willing to ditch demands for female suffrage in exchange for the introduction of universal male suffrage in Prussia which would have further strengthened their position in elections.[16] As the crisis of the imperial regime deepened and the revolution overturned the existing regime, however, an opportunity arose for an even more radical rethinking of citizenship rights.

When women first had the right to participate in national elections—in this case for the January 1919 elections for the National Assembly—female voters exceeded male voters by 2.8 million.[17] The structural transformations of state and society caused by the war and its outcome thus opened spaces for participatory rights that would have been unthinkable before 1914.[18]

The year 1918 also brought the Germans additional freedoms that no one would have thought possible before 1914 and that went far beyond the end of official censorship.[19] Alongside the political reforms that guaranteed equal participation rights to all adult Germans, there were now greater sexual freedoms and better access to birth control for heterosexual women. Simultaneously, there was—at least initially—a moment of hope among the gay community that homosexuality would be decriminalized. Even if the much discussed removal of Article 175 (which criminalized sex between two men) from the German criminal code never happened, there was broad consensus among gay rights activists that greater freedoms of expression existed after the war.[20] Gay rights activists immediately responded to the November Revolution with considerable enthusiasm, and viewed it as the dawn of a new era of sexual liberation heralding the decriminalization of homosexuality. 'The great revolution of the past weeks must be welcomed with joy from our point of view', wrote Magnus Hirschfeld, leader of the world's first LGBT rights organization, the Berlin-based Scientific-Humanitarian Committee, in November 1918. 'The new era brings us freedom of speech and publication, and with the liberation of all who were formerly oppressed, we may with certainty assume that those on whose behalf we have worked for many years'—that is, homosexuals and other 'sexual intermediaries'—'will also receive an equitable assessment'.[21]

Not everyone, of course, shared Wolff's or Hirschfeld's enthusiasm. Contemporary reactions to the events of November 1918 in Germany were, as one would expect, extremely varied. While many former front-line officers and NCOs resented the revolution, the vast majority of soldiers, relieved at having survived four years of a historically unprecedented war, returned home as pacifists and welcomed the revolution as an event that brought an end to the horrible experiences they had been subjected to between 1914 and 1918. Others, notably sailors on the ships of the High Seas Fleet that had been sitting idly in Germany's North Sea ports for most of the war, and soldiers who had served in the rear areas, actively participated in the revolution that toppled the German monarchy.[22]

On the home front, too, opinions were deeply divided, mostly along party political lines. The conservative Heidelberg-based medievalist Karl Hampe described the revolution of 9 November from the perspective of a middle-class intellectual, for whom Bismarck's nation-state of 1871 had been the high point of Germany's national history. For Hampe 9 November marked the 'most wretched day of my life! What has become of the Kaiser and the Reich? From the outside, we face mutilation [...and] a sort of debt servitude; internally we face...civil war, starvation, chaos.'[23] His Berlin-based colleague Hans Delbrück, one of the most influential historians in Imperial Germany and a strong believer in the monarchy, also shared this sentiment. When, on 11 November 1918, he celebrated his seventieth birthday in the company of other eminent intellectuals, the mood was uniquely sombre, as one of those present recalled: 'It was an odd celebration, more like a funeral. One spoke in muffled tones.' Delbrück himself expressed his deep regret over the end of the monarchy, 'with which all his political beliefs and his faith in Germany's future were inseparably intertwined'.[24]

The arch-conservative politician Elard von Oldenburg-Januschau (who would play an active and unfortunate role in the political events of January 1933, when he advised his old friend President Paul von Hindenburg to appoint Hitler as Chancellor) also resented the revolution and spoke for many German aristocrats when he wrote that he 'could not find words to express my sorrow over the events of

November 1918; to describe how shattered I was. I felt the world collapsing, burying under its rubble all that I had lived for and all that my parents had taught me to cherish since I was a child.'[25] Others went even further in their despair. Distraught at the collapse of Imperial Germany and faced with an uncertain financial future, Albert Ballin, the Jewish shipping magnate and personal friend of Wilhelm II, committed suicide on 9 November 1918. Ballin, the head of Hapag—once the world's largest shipping company—was simply unable to cope with the perceived bleakness of the present and future.[26]

At the same time it is worth bearing in mind that—at least in the autumn and winter of 1918—the revolutionary transformation of Germany from a constitutional monarchy with limited parliamentary participation rights into a modern republic enjoyed the backing of an overwhelming majority of Germans, either out of conviction or because they felt that the country's internal democratization would be rewarded with more lenient peace terms at the upcoming Peace Conference in Paris.[27] The women's rights activists Anita Augspurg and Lida Gustava Heymann, who became supporters of Kurt Eisner's socialist revolution in Munich, were full of enthusiasm for the 'new life' they experienced after November 1918: 'the following months seemed like a beautiful dream, so surreal and glorious! The heavy burden of the war years was lifted, and people walked with a spring in their step, full of optimism for the future! Time was flying, meal times were ignored, nights became days, no sleep was needed; a glowing flame burnt in us, fuelling our desire to help with the creation of a better society... Those winter months were full of hard work, hope, and happiness...'[28]

Hermann Müller, the Social Democrat and future two-term Reich Chancellor, also recalled the widespread enthusiasm for the revolution on 9 November: 'When I arrived at Lehrter Train Station in Berlin around 9 p.m. on 9 November 1918...the masses were still surging through the streets in the dark. On their faces you could see their joy that the revolution had been accomplished, a revolution that would bring the sorely tested German people an eagerly desired peace.'[29]

The optimism of the moment is also well captured in Leonhard Frank's autobiographical novel *Links, wo das Herz ist* (1952). Here, the pacifist Frank, whose open criticism of the war had forced him into exile in Switzerland in 1915, describes how his literary alter ego, Michael Vierkant, and his Austrian wife Lisa, first learn about the revolution in Bavaria over a meal in a Berlin restaurant: 'A newspaper seller came in and called out: "Bavaria a free socialist republic! Kurt Eisner is minister-president!" "Now everything will be different, now everything will be good," Michael said with excited joy. "Everything will be great. And we're in the midst of it." He pressed Lisa's hand. She said: "Why did millions of people have to die beforehand?" He tried to console her. "At least they did not die in vain. Now everything will be good." '[30] Even the otherwise often sceptical anarchist theorist Gustav Landauer enthusiastically wrote to his friend Fritz Mauthner on 28 November 1918 that he had only been able to bear the recently ended 'horror war' because of 'hope for that which has now come [...] glowing and profound life, the fulfilment of centuries, living through history in the making.'[31]

Irrespective of whether one perceived the events of November 1918 as a threat or an opportunity, there was one thing on which all contemporary observers agreed: that the events of November 1918 constituted a proper revolution, or, in the words of the monarchist newspaper *Kreuzzeitung*, a 'cataclysm such as history has never seen'.[32] From the extreme Right to the communist Left, no one in autumn 1918 seriously questioned whether a major revolution had occurred in Germany—a judgement that differs significantly from that of subsequent generations of political commentators and historians.[33] The latter two groups have been significantly more hostile in their assessment of the events of November 1918 than contemporaries, labelling it as a 'failed', 'incomplete', or even 'betrayed' revolution—a judgement primarily informed by their retrospective knowledge about how Weimar's future ended.[34] Because the new political leaders in 1918 left pre-existing economic and social relations, state bureaucracies, and the judiciary relatively untouched, and because of Weimar's eventual demise in 1933, the November Revolution is frequently seen as an 'incomplete' revolution of secondary importance that lacked the drama and ideological overtones of the 'great' European revolutions of 1789 and 1917.[35] Some have even doubted whether the events of November 1918 qualify as a revolution at all.[36]

How did this remarkable redefinition of the events that occurred in Germany in late 1918 come to be? The changing perception of the revolution in fact began in 1919 when the overwhelming initial support for the democratic revolution of 1918 was weakened for a number of reasons, not least because many Germans had harboured unrealistic and unmanageable expectations, both in terms of what a revolution could achieve and how the democratization would impact on the peace treaty that was drawn up by the victorious Allies in Paris from January 1919 onwards. While those on the far Left had been longing for a revolution, it was not *this* revolution to which they had aspired. Like their leaders in 1918, Karl Liebknecht and Rosa Luxemburg, many people on the far Left perceived the military collapse of Imperial Germany in November 1918 as a historically unique opportunity to create a socialist state run by the workers' and soldiers' councils that had sprung up all over the country as the old imperial system disintegrated. Although not altogether uncritical of Lenin's Bolshevik Revolution in Russia, they desired a more encompassing political and social revolution that would break radically with the old elites and hierarchies of Imperial Germany. Ebert's unshakable determination to hold a general election for a constituent National Assembly to answer the question of Germany's future form of government was perceived and portrayed by the far Left as a fundamental 'betrayal' because it prevented the realization of their own, more radical ambitions for the reorganization of German society and its political systems.

However, in late 1918 and early 1919, their position was only supported by a small minority. The events of 1918–19 thus marked a climax in the long and turbulent history of divisions within the German (and indeed international) labour movement, from the early twentieth-century 'revisionism' conflict between orthodox Marxist proponents of revolution and Social Democratic reformists through to the clash between those socialists supporting the war effort and those opposing it, culminating in the formal split between the MSPD and the more left-leaning Independent Social Democrats (USPD) in 1917. The 'betrayal' of 1918–19 took the conflict one step further, as the far Left felt that the MSPD had prevented a 'real' revolution at a time when it was allegedly feasible. The shadow of these accusations continues to linger even today. As late as 2008, the then chairman of *Die Linke*, the far Left heir to the GDR's ruling party, the SED, openly declared that Ebert's 'betrayal' of the workers' movement in 1918 had 'set the course for the disastrous history of the Weimar Republic'.[37]

The MSPD leadership under Friedrich Ebert also had high expectations in the autumn of 1918: if demobilization and democratization could be achieved without resistance from the old elites, Germany would be offered moderate peace conditions, so they believed, that would allow the country to emerge from the war as a strong democracy and an equal partner in the post-war international order. This was a hope that was shared by many bourgeois liberals, even if they had not initially been supportive of a political revolution.[38] Many of them were positively surprised by the lack of radicalism and the relative absence of violence in November 1918, and noted with relief that neither chaos nor civil war spread immediately after the takeover of 9 November. The revolution's very lack of radicalism, its pragmatism, was frequently emphasized as laudable by contemporaries. This 'elasticity', as the director of the Berlin-based Kaiser-Wilhelm-Institute for Physics, Albert Einstein, formulated in a thoroughly favourable assessment for a Swedish colleague on 14 November, was 'the most surprising experience among all the surprises' of the previous days.[39]

For the prominent theologian and philosopher Ernst Troeltsch, whose 'Spectator Letters' offer a glimpse into liberal perceptions of the revolution, the greatest uncertainties had already disappeared by 10 November: 'After a troubled night, the morning newspapers presented a clear picture: the Kaiser was in the Netherlands, the revolution had been victorious in most centres (...). Not a man died for Kaiser and Reich! All civil servants are now working for the new government! All duties of the state will be carried out and there has been no run on the banks!'[40] The famous novelist Thomas Mann had a similar impression when he strolled through Munich in the sunshine of 10 November while reflecting on the events of the previous day: 'The German Revolution is a very German one, even if it is a proper revolution. No French savagery, no Russian Communist excesses', he noted with relief.[41]

What changed this perception, and contemporaries' retrospective assessment of the November Revolution more generally, was the further course of the revolution, notably its radicalization and violent escalation in early 1919. The far Left's 'Spartacist Rising' of January 1919, the Munich Soviet Republic later that spring, and the brutal backlash by right-wing Freikorps volunteers seemed to many contemporaries to be an unwelcome echo of the Russian Civil War. Similarly disappointing for many of those people who had initially supported the democratization of Germany was that the expectations for a negotiated peace treaty clashed brutally with the actual conditions of peace imposed on the young democracy by the victorious allies in the Versailles Peace Treaty in the summer of 1919. The fact that the Allies maintained the economic blockade beyond the official end of hostilities to ensure German 'good behaviour' while the peace treaty was drawn up further alienated starving Germans from the Western powers. Although everyone was aware that a non-acceptance of the peace terms would result in the resumption of hostilities, the nationalist Right was quick to portray this as 'proof' of the republic's inability to negotiate a better future for Germany. In the collective memory, the revolution, military defeat, and its principal consequence—the peace treaty of Versailles—gradually merged into one narrative in which the revolution, an act of betrayal of the fighting men on the front, had caused an unnecessary military defeat and bore full responsibility for the harshness of the Paris Peace Settlement.

No one exploited this soon-to-be widely shared narrative of betrayal and failure more persistently and successfully than Adolf Hitler. Exactly five years after the proclamation of the German Republic, on 9 November 1923, Hitler first attempted his 'national revolution' in the unsuccessful Munich 'beer hall putsch'. He had deliberately chosen this date for his futile bid to revise the result of 'November 1918' and to instigate a 'rebirth' of the German people. During his subsequent imprisonment in the Bavarian fortress of Landsberg, Hitler penned *Mein Kampf*, in which his stylized memory of 9 November 1918 featured prominently as his moment of political awakening: unconscious and temporarily blinded by poison gas in the last weeks of the war, he awoke on 12 November 1918 in his military hospital bed in the Prussian town of Pasewalk, and felt that the world around him had changed beyond recognition. The once mighty Imperial German Army, in which he had served as a dispatch runner, had collapsed. The Kaiser had abdicated in the face of revolutionary turmoil. His homeland, Austria-Hungary, no longer existed. Upon receiving the news of the Central Powers' military defeat, Hitler experienced a meltdown: 'I threw myself on my bed, and buried my burning head in my pillow and the duvet. I had not cried since the day I had stood at my mother's grave. Now I couldn't do anything else.'[42] For the Nazis, 9 November became a date of annual mobilization against the republic, a date on which Hitler's followers were called upon to 'honour the fallen' of the failed putsch by working towards the replacement of the hated system established in 1918 with a mythical Third Reich.[43]

In the 1920s, Alfred Rosenberg, Hitler's 'chief ideologue', thus spoke of 9 November as a 'day of destiny', a 'most passionately fought over' date that was intimately connected with the burning question of Germany's future: was this future, he asked, to be shaped by the 'November criminals' or by the 'national revolutionaries' around Hitler?[44] Both before 1933 and after Hitler's appointment as Reich Chancellor, the Nazis' political discourse remained intimately linked to the November Revolution and their ambition to revise its outcomes. In countless speeches, the 'Führer' proclaimed that 'November 1918' would never be repeated and that those responsible for the 'November crime'—the political Left and, of course, 'the Jews'—had to be punished. Hitler himself remained obsessed with the 'treason' he associated with 9 November 1918 right up until his death. In his final orders of May 1945, he insisted that there would be no repeat of the 'crimes' of November 1918, no 'stab-in-the-back' by 'internal enemies'. Even the complete annihilation of the entire German nation and its people was preferable, to Hitler, to a disgraceful surrender.[45]

Nazi Germany's total defeat in the Second World War did not bring an end to the history battles over the meaning of the events of 9 November. Even though these battles changed in nature over time, they continued to be fierce. In fact, they tell us more about changing political cultures in Germany than about the revolution itself. In the East German 'Democratic Republic' or GDR, the 'November Revolution' featured very prominently in both political discourse and historiography, mainly because it seemed to legitimate the existence of a powerful party of 'socialist unity'—the ruling SED—which emerged from the forced 1946 merger of the SPD and KPD (German Communist Party) in the Soviet-occupied eastern half of the country. Precisely because such a united working-class party had been missing in 1918, so went the GDR's official reading of the past, a genuine 'proletarian revolution' had been doomed to fail. Instead of a serious and open-ended historical engagement with the events of 1918, the Marxist-Leninist historiography of the GDR unsurprisingly supported this interpretation, labelling the November Revolution as a bourgeois uprising. In this narrative, the leaders of the Majority Social Democrats assumed the role of the traitors who abandoned and betrayed a proletarian revolution. Only the Spartacus League and the KPD featured as progressive heroes, whose visionary revolutionary ambitions were thwarted by Ebert, Noske, and their bourgeois-reactionary thugs.[46]

Although scholarship in the West German Federal Republic (FRG) was much more free of state interference, historical judgements about the November Revolution were also fundamentally shaped by the prevailing *Zeitgeist*. The major historiographical controversies of the years after 1945 were conditioned by both the search for the root causes of the 'German catastrophe' that was Nazism *and* the intellectual climate of the Cold War. The fact that a mere fourteen years separated the revolution of 1918 from the advent of the Third Reich in 1933 prompted the tempting (but misleading) interpretative meta-narrative of the 'doomed' republic, a hastily improvised democratic state sitting uncomfortably between the Kaiserreich and Hitler's dictatorship.[47] 'Weimar' was portrayed as a warning from history that democracies can fail, but also as a dark template against which the Federal Republic compared favourably as a much more stable, more Westernized, and more economically successful democracy.[48]

Yet there were also noticeable differences in opinion and changing assessments of '1918' in the Federal Republic. The main historiographical and public controversy post-1945 revolved around whether or not alternative options had been available to the leading historical actors of November 1918, notably the MSPD.[49] The different positions in that debate curiously mirrored those of the MSPD and the USPD during the Weimar Republic. While some argued that the only alternative to Ebert's decision to establish a parliamentary democracy (through compromises with the old non-democratic elites of Imperial Germany) was a Bolshevik dictatorship along Russian lines (the MSPD position in 1918–19),[50] more left-leaning commentators saw a great deal of democratizing potential in the Workers' and Soldiers' Councils, which was apparently left untapped by Ebert (the USPD's position).[51] Mirroring the accusations of the far Left against Ebert and the Majority Social Democrats in the 1920s and early 1930s, the events of 1918 were characterized by some, in Sebastian Haffner's famous words, as a 'revolution betrayed'.[52]

The accusation that Ebert and the MSPD had failed to provide Germany with a stable democratic foundation went hand in hand with the supposition that Germany and the world might have been spared Hitler if the Revolution of 1918–19 had not been 'incomplete'.[53] The fact that, up until the outbreak of the Great Depression in late 1929, Weimar democracy successfully survived several attempts by the extreme Left and Right to violently assume power was consciously ignored in this interpretation, largely because it stood in the way of the narrative of the Social Democrats' 'betrayal' of a 'true' revolution.

While the public debates about '9 November 1918' and the Weimar Republic's place in German history have become considerably less

heated in recent times, prompting some to speak of the November
Revolution as a now 'forgotten revolution',[54] historical research on the
period has been anything but stagnant, with some major paradigm
shifts changing our perspective on the events of November 1918. A
new consensus, for example, has emerged among historians that the
history of the first German democracy should not be viewed in terms
of its outcome, but explored in an open-ended fashion. While fruitful,
this consensus has not yet led to a new general study of the November
Revolution that has been able to fulfil its promise.[55] The one hundredth
anniversary of the Revolution offers an opportunity for a sober exam-
ination of the events of 1918, and a new historical narrative that takes
more seriously the ways in which contemporaries perceived, experienced, and narrated both the world around them and their future. If
many of them used the term 'crisis' to describe the result of Germany's
military defeat, they did so to express a state of uncertainty or ambiguity
about the future—a future which contemporaries continuously speculated about but were naturally unable to foresee.[56]

A second historiographical trend that should have had a much
stronger impact on our perception of the events in Germany in
November 1918 is the rise of transnational history. Conventionally, the
November Revolution has only ever been considered in a strictly
national context, or with casual references to simultaneous events in
Western Europe. However, it is debatable whether German history in
this period can be meaningfully explored within the context of the
history of 'the West', most notably the supposedly normative development of France and Great Britain. The two latter societies were long-
established democracies that emerged victoriously from the First
World War, while Germany was not. German history in this period
instead followed an East-Central European pattern of military defeat,
revolution, imperial collapse, and democratic rebirth. Compared with
the other imperial successor states and new democratic states in Europe
after 1918—such as Hungary or the Baltic States—the Weimar Republic
was not only particularly stable but also relatively long-lived. After all,
from the early 1930s onwards, democracy was increasingly perceived
by many Europeans as an outdated and inadequate form of government, incapable of dealing with the socio-economic and political fall-
out of the Great Depression. Of all the parliamentary democracies
created in East-Central Europe after 1918 (with the notable exceptions
of Finland and Czechoslovakia), the Weimar Republic was one of the

last of the post-imperial democratic successor states founded after the
Great War to give way to totalitarianism.

In order to appreciate just how radically transformative the events of
November 1918 were, one also needs to take more seriously the idea
of Wilhelmine Germany as an 'empire'—an empire that collapsed in
1918 and gave way to a republican nation-state that was much less
ethnically diverse than its predecessor. Imperial Germany was, in fact,
an empire in more than one sense: first, the term German Empire (or
Kaiserreich) described the ethnically mixed and hierarchically structured
territory within the post-1871 boundaries of the nation-state founded
by Otto von Bismarck and Wilhelm I.[57] Yet, despite its name and its
self-perception as an ethnically homogeneous nation-state, the German
Empire comprised large non-German ethnic minorities, notably some
3.5 million Poles, 1.8 million Alsace-Lorrainers, and some 150,000
Danes in North Schleswig, who were technically full German citizens,
but who were often portrayed and perceived by German nationalists as
potentially disloyal and secessionist.[58]

Second, the term referred to Germany as a global empire with overseas territories in Africa, Asia, and the Pacific, territories that had been
colonized primarily in the late nineteenth century. Since the 1880s,
influential private organizations such as the German Colonial Society
or the Pan-German League had lobbied for the Kaiser's government
to acquire overseas colonies to turn Germany into a global empire
similar to those of Britain and France. Although Chancellor Otto von
Bismarck had never been a supporter of Germany's global expansion,
he ultimately succumbed to public pressure on this matter, leading to
colonial acquisitions in China, the Pacific, and Africa.[59]

Third, and related to the second point, Germany became a major
European land empire after 1914, when its armies annexed large territories in East-Central Europe. Russia's exit from the war and the Treaty
of Brest-Litovsk in early 1918, expanded that imperial rule further by
giving Germany control over huge swathes of territories that had previously been ruled by the Romanovs. The German defeat in November
1918 brought an abrupt end to Berlin's multiple imperial engagements
in Europe and the wider world, though not, of course, to imperial
fantasies in which East-Central Europe in particular played a very
prominent role as a space for future colonial conquest.[60]

Viewed from this broader geographical perspective, it becomes
clearer that the historical trajectory of Britain and France—the two

main European victor states of the Great War—was in no way normative, but rather highly exceptional. The German Revolution of 1918–19 was part of a much larger moment of European political change, including the multiple violent transformations taking place in the vast 'shatter-zones' left by the collapse of the Russian, Austro-Hungarian, and Ottoman empires as well as an era of revolution that began in Petrograd in 1917 and did not end until the territorial revolution that trans-formed the remnants of the Ottoman Empire into a republican Turkish nation-state in 1923. Between 1917 and 1920 alone, Europe experi-enced some twenty-seven violent transfers of political power, many of them accompanied by latent or open civil wars.[61] Russia in particular experienced two revolutions within less than twelve months, eventu-ally resulting in a civil war that cost the lives of well over three million people. In neighbouring Finland, formerly an autonomous duchy in the Romanov Empire and a non-combatant during the Great War, a brief but extremely bloody civil war in 1918 killed off more than 1 per cent of the country's population within little more than three months. During the years 1918–23, well over four million people—more than the combined wartime casualties of Britain, France, and the United States—died as a result of armed conflicts in post-war Europe. In addition, millions of impoverished refugees from Central, Eastern, and Southern Europe roamed the war-torn landscapes of Western Europe in search of safety and a better life.[62] It is with good reason that some historians have classified the years immediately after 1918 as a time of 'extended European civil war'.[63]

Compared to the revolutionary regime changes that occurred else-where in Europe, and the subsequent civil wars triggered by revolu-tions in places such as Russia, Ukraine, Finland, and even Hungary, the German Revolution was remarkably bloodless. Yet, the broader European context had a profound impact on how contemporary Germans perceived events inside Germany: older cultural anxieties about the threat of revolution, for example, were intensified and trans-formed by news of events in revolutionary Russia from 1917 onwards, leading to fears (or hopes) that Germany was about to become the next country for a Bolshevik takeover.[64] Such fears were by no means confined to the far Right. The very measured left-leaning artist Käthe Kollwitz, for example, expressed her disgust over the 'terrible conditions in Russia' in her diary in late 1918 while reflecting on her country's potentially bleak future: 'Is Germany facing the threat of similar anarchy to Russia?'[65] The widespread contemporary notion that Germany was on the verge of experiencing 'Russian conditions'—an impression that also guided Ebert's decisions in 1918–19—can only be understood if we place the German experience in a broader (Central and Eastern) European context.

A broader perspective is also important when it comes to determining the 'place' of the German Revolution in modern European history. Both the great European revolution of the West (the French Revolution of 1789) and the great European revolution of the East (the Russian Revolution of 1917) quickly led to civil wars and dictatorships without anyone denying their historical significance. Even compared to other European revolutions—those in Finland and Hungary in 1918 and 1919—the revolutionary events in Germany were not only relatively bloodless but also remarkably successful when measured against their objectives: the restoration of peace and the replacement of the monarchy with a democratic regime. While the counter-revolution triumphed in Finland and Hungary, and levels of violence soared, the Ebert government succeeded in channelling revolutionary energies, maintaining public order in the face of a historically unprecedented defeat, and peacefully demobilizing several million heavily armed soldiers. Within just a few days, Germany transformed itself from a constitutional monarchy with limited political participation rights into a republic that, despite extreme internal and external challenges, survived for fourteen years.

In view of the enormous challenges that the emerging Weimar Republic faced, Theodor Wolff's already cited comment that the German Revolution of 1918 was the 'greatest' of all revolutions may appear daringly optimistic, perhaps even naive. Nevertheless, it is an important example of a widespread contemporary sentiment that is often omitted or ignored in teleological readings of the November Revolution. Instead of pondering the 'lost opportunities' of 1918 or reading history backwards, this book will instead reconstruct the perspectives of contemporaries, thereby attempting to do justice to an exciting, open-ended period in German history that—at least initially—was filled with great hopes and expectations. In order to understand these hopes and optimistic perspectives, it is necessary to turn first to the year 1917, a year which profoundly transformed the character of the First World War and shaped Germans' expectations for the future.

I

1917 and the revolution of expectations

On 19 January 1917, a remarkable telegram signed by the German Foreign Minister, Arthur Zimmermann, arrived in Mexico City. In that telegram, Zimmermann instructed the German envoy in the capital, Heinrich von Eckardt, to explore the possibility of a military alliance with the Mexican authorities. As part of the deal, Berlin would back Mexico financially and logistically if the Mexican government waged an attack on the United States, supporting its efforts to recapture those formerly Mexican territories lost to the USA in 1848, namely Texas, New Mexico, and Arizona. Besides the highly provocative war proposal to Mexico, the telegram also offered military support through 'ruthless employment of our submarines' in the Atlantic. In a follow-up message of 5 February, Zimmermann urged his envoy in Mexico City to contact the Mexican President, Venustiano Carranza, immediately.[1]

This seemingly absurd offer—an idea proposed by a junior Foreign Ministry official, Hans Arthur von Kemnitz, and subsequently endorsed by the highest political and military authorities in Germany—deserves some further explanation. For it was the 'Zimmermann Telegram', coupled with Germany's declaration of unrestricted submarine warfare a few days earlier, that was to lead to US military intervention in the Great War.[2] Zimmermann, a career diplomat who had been appointed German Foreign Minister in November 1916, had recommended himself for the job as a strong advocate of inciting imperial insurrections in the territories of the Allied states since 1914. Ever since the outbreak of war in 1914, the German Foreign Office had developed secret plans to destabilize the Allied home fronts by supporting revolutionary movements of different political complexions: Irish republicans aiming to sever ties with London, jihadists in the British and French empires, and Russian revolutionaries conspiring against the tsar's autocratic regime in Petrograd.[3] Although largely indifferent to the political ambitions of each of these movements, Berlin saw them as temporary strategic partners in an effort to weaken the Allies from within.[4] Zimmermann had been at the very heart of these efforts, meeting with the human rights activist and Irish republican Roger Casement as early as 1914 to discuss the possibility of arming republican revolution-aries in a bid to violently end British rule over Ireland. Much to the regret of the strategists in the German Foreign Office, however, none of their efforts seemed to deliver the desired results. The roughly 3,000 Muslim PoWs who were first interned in a special 'Half Moon Camp' in Zossen near the German capital, before being dispatched to the Mesopotamian and Persian fronts for propaganda purposes, never managed to mobilize large numbers of jihadists. In the spring of 1916, the German Foreign Office suffered a further setback when the German-backed Easter Rising failed to ignite a general revolution in Ireland. Casement, who had spent the first two war years in the Reich trying to set up an 'Irish Brigade' from PoWs in German captivity, was arrested for treason shortly after disembarking from a German U-boat off the coast of Kerry.[5]

Despite these setbacks, Zimmermann was appointed to succeed Gottlieb von Jagow as Foreign Minister in late November 1916. Jagow had stepped down in protest against the German military leadership's plans to escalate submarine warfare—a subject of considerable contro-versy throughout the war. Ever since the sinking of the British pas-senger ship *Lusitania* by a German U-boat in May 1915, with the loss of 1,200 lives, the German navy had reluctantly limited the use of U-boats in order not to provoke Washington's entry into the war. The issue remained a bone of contention between Chancellor Bethmann Hollweg and Germany's admiralty in 1915 and 1916, but for the time being Bethmann Hollweg kept the upper hand. For Bethmann Hollweg, American neutrality was politically and militarily desirable, not least because the United States was the only major Western power that could potentially facilitate a negotiated peace to unlock the stale-mate in which the Western front powers found themselves in 1916.

Yet, as the prospects of a negotiated peace were decreasing in late 1916, the pressure of the German army and naval leadership was mounting to use the U-boats for a decisive blow against Britain.

On 9 January 1917, Bethmann Hollweg finally succumbed to the Army High Command's (OHL) pressure and agreed that unrestricted submarine warfare should be resumed. Foreign Minister Zimmermann had supported the OHL's plans for some time and made his own preparations for the event of Washington's declaration of war on Germany. The Zimmermann Telegram was part of these preparations.

Unfortunately for Zimmermann, however, his telegram to Mexico was intercepted by British intelligence and immediately shared with the American Ambassador to London, Walter Hines Page, who in turn sent it on to US President Woodrow Wilson.[6] The intelligence on Germany's offer of a military alliance hit Washington like a bombshell for two reasons. First, in Wilson's view, the telegram confirmed that Germany's government was being dishonest: while pretending to be open to American mediation in finding a compromise peace, the Germans were secretly plotting an anti-American alliance.[7] Instead of actively trying to find a compromise peace, Germany clearly aimed to add fuel to the fires of the diplomatic hotspot that was Mexico, a state in revolutionary turmoil between 1910 and 1917, and one in which US troops had intervened twice—in 1914 and again in 1916—to safeguard US interests in the region.[8] The second reason why the Zimmermann Telegram was so important and explosive was its unfortunate timing. British intelligence about the telegram arrived in Washington just as Germany resumed unrestricted submarine warfare on 1 February 1917, pushing US public opinion further in favour of US military intervention.

Germany's decision to escalate submarine warfare had a longer prehistory. When on 24 March 1916, the British steamer *Sussex* was torpedoed in the English Channel with some eighty casualties and several Americans injured, Washington responded sternly. The Germans had recently intensified their submarine attacks on British ships, many of which they rightly suspected of carrying war materials as cargo. In response to the sinking of the *Sussex*, Wilson now issued an ultimatum to Berlin to either stop submarine attacks on passenger ships and merchantmen or face an end of US–German diplomatic relations—a step that came close to a declaration of war. Chancellor Bethmann Hollweg responded by calling off the intensified submarine warfare. Furthermore, on 4 May, he made the '*Sussex* pledge' to follow 'cruiser rules' which stipulated that submarines had to surface and their crew had to search merchant ships for contraband and place the 'enemy' crews in safety before sinking a vessel—unless the ship in question refused to stop and allow the search. The Germans had stopped following cruiser rules when Britain introduced so-called Q-ships with concealed deck guns in order to lure submarines to the surface before attacking them. In total, these Q-ships were to destroy an estimated fourteen U-boats and damage sixty over the course of the war. But Bethman Hollweg also insisted on 4 May that the USA should act on the illegal British naval blockade, which in German eyes was viewed much more leniently by Washington than the U-boat issue.[9]

When the Chief of Staff of the OHL, Falkenhayn, was replaced with the popular 'victor of Tannenberg', Paul von Hindenburg, at the end of August 1916 after the former had failed to achieve a decisive break-through in the West, the strategic priorities changed again. Hindenburg and his right-hand man Erich Ludendorff soon intervened more directly in government matters, establishing a de facto military dicta-torship. One area where they imposed their will against the wishes of the civilian government was the more extensive use of submarines to break the naval blockade, which was causing severe hunger on the German home front. In Hindenburg's and Ludendorff's view, unre-stricted submarine warfare would put enormous pressure on Britain, ultimately forcing London out of the conflict.[10]

The continuing blockade and the prospect of more synchronized Allied offensives in early 1917 thus encouraged the new leadership of the German OHL—Hindenburg as Chief of Staff and Erich Ludendorff as his Quartermaster General—to look for ways to break the deadlock. One of them, or so it seemed, was unrestricted submar-ine warfare, which the German navy's aggressive leadership under Admiral Reinhard Scheer had advocated for some time. The number of German submarines rose from forty-one in January 1916 to 103 in January 1917, peaking at 140 in October that year.[11] The Allies at this point controlled most of the seas and could draw upon their empires and on the neutrals—above all the United States—for manufactured goods, food, raw materials, even if their efforts to stifle their enemies' imports worked slowly. The only way to cripple this traffic, or so the navy leadership argued, was for Germany to unleash its submarines, untrammelled by the international convention that they should sur-face and give warning before sinking their victims. American President Wilson insisted on his interpretation of maritime law. This infuriated the Germans because American economic support for the Allies meant added pressure for the German army on the Western front.[12]

The German naval leadership estimated that their U-boats could sink some 600,000 tons of cargo per month, severely crippling British supplies and forcing London out of the war within five months. In this highly optimistic estimate, a US entry into the war would not matter because it would be over before American troops could be fully mobilized and dispatched to Europe. Failing to use unrestricted submarine warfare, by contrast, would lead to Germany's slow strangulation. Hindenburg, Ludendorff, and the Kaiser agreed to take the gamble against the wishes of the civilian leadership including Foreign Minister von Jagow and Bethmann Hollweg, who both considered the risk of bringing the USA into a then unwinnable conflict as too high.[13]

On 31 January 1917 news broke around the world that Germany would recommence unrestricted submarine warfare the following day. In a 'prohibited zone' around the British Isles and France almost all vessels risked being torpedoed without warning. On 1 February 1917, Germany began unrestricted submarine warfare against all ships in the Atlantic bearing the American flag, both passenger and merchant ships. Two ships were sunk in February, and most American shipping companies held their ships in port.[14]

Many contemporaries in Germany were fully conscious that the German declaration of unrestricted submarine warfare would make the US entry into the war inevitable, or at least highly likely. The Australian musician Ethel Cooper, who lived in Leipzig during the war, wrote to her sister Emmie in Adelaide in a letter she managed to get smuggled through Switzerland: 'The first of February has come and gone, the submarine war has been declared, and we, like the rest of the world, are waiting for further developments.' Her American neighbours, she noted, had 'packed for the fourth time and given notice to their landlords, and the two Dutch and Danish families I know are discussing whether they shouldn't do the same, and they all regard the current moment as the most critical one since 1 August 1914. The Americans are saying that they would perish of shame if Mr Wilson were to make another compromise.'[15] Uncertainty gave way to anxiety. The always well-informed Harry Count Kessler, observing events unfold from Bern in neutral Switzerland, noted in his diary on 1 February 1917: 'Most concerns revolve around America's stance . . . In general, the mood among us is sombre but we remain determined; mood of a man heading for a life-threatening but unavoidable operation.'[16]

News of Germany offering an alliance to Mexico, combined with Berlin's declaration of unrestricted submarine warfare, hit Washington like a bombshell. In light of the public mood, which had swung in favour of entering the war, and given his well-known stance on submarine war in the Atlantic, Wilson was left with few alternatives but to join the fight. On 2 April 1917 Wilson announced to Congress his imminent intention to declare war on Germany. Four days later, the formal declaration of war was signed.[17] The German leaders had known that unrestricted submarine warfare would almost certainly lead to American involvement in the war but calculated that Britain and France could be defeated before the full impact of US involvement in the war would be felt. They seriously underestimated the impact that direct US involvement in the war would have. Even if it would be spring 1918 before US troops arrived in significant numbers in France, Wilson's declaration of war on Germany changed the balance in favour of the Allies.

Wilson's background and his changing attitude towards Germany and US neutrality warrant some further explanation, not least because the US entry into the war proved decisive for Germany's defeat while Wilson's Fourteen Points, and his well-publicized notion of a 'peace without victory' fundamentally shaped German expectations for the post-war order.

Wilson was not a conventional career politician and his path to the highest office in US politics was unusual. He had not entered politics—as was often the case in the United States—as a successful businessman but after an academic career at Princeton University. Born in Virginia in 1856 as the son of a Presbyterian minister, and raised according to strict Calvinist precepts, Wilson had still experienced the American Civil War (1861–5) as a child. Protestant theology and nineteenth-century liberalism were to shape his political thinking throughout his remarkable career.[18] After studying law at Princeton, he wrote a political science dissertation on 'Congressional Government' in 1885, in which he criticized the undemocratic practices of American parliamentarianism. The thesis earned him great respect in academic circles throughout the country, as did his second book, *The State* (1899), in which he drew extensively on German political science literature, which he was able to read in the original. In 1902, at the age of 46, Wilson became president of Princeton University, but his term in office ended prematurely in 1910, after a conflict with the majority of the professors, who rejected his somewhat dogmatic zeal and lack of flexibility.[19]

The abrupt end of Wilson's presidency of an elite university did no damage to his further career. That same year, 1910, he was elected Governor of New Jersey, and rapidly became one of the leaders of the 'progressive wing' of the Democratic Party, campaigning for social welfare measures and increased state regulation of economic affairs. During his time as Governor, he supported the introduction of accident insurance for workers. In the 1912 presidential election, he was nominated to lead the Democrats' campaign and won. In 1916 he was re-elected President, this time with the nationwide campaign slogan 'He kept us out of war', a promise he was about to break only a few months later.[20]

Despite the strict neutrality that Wilson had insisted on from the summer of 1914, the United States had not, in fact, been able to keep itself entirely out of the war. Numerous European immigrants in America with British, Irish, German, and Italian roots had repeatedly given public expression to their sympathies for their home countries and had argued over the merits of intervention versus non-intervention in the war.[21] In total 15 per cent of the US population had been born abroad. Neither Irish Americans (who often supported Irish independence from Britain and whose enmity towards London increased after the leaders of the failed Easter Rising of 1916 were executed) nor Eastern European Jews (who had fled tsarist Russia and anti-Semitic pogroms in the Pale of Settlement) had strong sympathies for the Allies. In addition, German-Americans constituted the largest ethnic minority in the country. In 1910, out of 92 million Americans, 2.5 million were German-born and 5.8 million US-born Americans had at least one German parent.[22] Although Wilson believed that 90 per cent of the US population favoured the Allies, he had good grounds to fear that rival ethnic allegiances would breed civil strife. Even more important for the United States were the economic consequences of the Great War. The British naval blockade of Germany and her allies severely restricted American exports. Already in 1914, partially to com-pensate for these export losses, Wilson permitted Great Britain and France to purchase goods on a credit basis—credits that grew dramat-ically over the course of the war. The longer the war lasted, the more dependent London and Paris became on American supplies and credits, while Washington relied on arms exports and other trade with Britain and France to fuel its continuing economic boom.[23]

American policy towards Germany indeed changed significantly over the course of the war. Between May 1915 and May 1916, Berlin and Washington were in confrontation over submarine warfare. If the torpedoing of the British ocean liner *Lusitania* on 7 May 1915 (leaving 128 US citizens among the 1,100 dead) and the Germans' first use of poison gas on the Western front had cost them sympathies in the United States, a majority of Americans still favoured non-intervention. Wilson was at this point confident that despite the lingering U-boat issue Germany might be willing to cooperate with his plans for a negotiated peace settlement. Even after his narrow re-election as US President in late 1916, Wilson continued to work towards a negotiated settlement and even maintained secret contacts with Germany and Austria-Hungary.[24] To that end, Wilson dispatched his trusted unofficial adviser, the Texan businessman Edward House, to Europe in order to sound out the possibility of a compromise peace without victors or vanquished. The disappointing results of these negotiations increasingly convinced Wilson that the United States would only be able to shape the nature of the future peace treaty and post-war order if it actively intervened in the war on the side of France and Great Britain, with which the United States had close economic ties and whose political systems were closer to Wilson than those of the Central Powers. Nevertheless, Wilson also remained wary of being instrumentalized by London and Paris for their own purposes and insisted on an independent US policy with its own objectives.[25]

In early 1918, Wilson shared with the public his recently developed concept for a new world order, a blueprint for a peace settlement, which he presented in a speech to both houses of Congress on 8 January 1918. His vision of a future world order—articulated that day as the famous '14 Points'—essentially rested on the concept of national self-determination, combining specific demands for the creation of an independent Poland, the evacuation of all territories occupied by the Central Powers since 1914, and the return to France of Alsace-Lorraine with much more abstract notions such as the 'freedom of the seas', and the creation of the League of Nations.

Already in his equally famous 'Peace without Victory' speech to the US Senate on 22 January 1917, a few months before the entry of the

United States into the war, Wilson had announced his intention to bring about a negotiated peace on which the future world order would rest. Justice instead of revenge, reconciliation instead of triumph, were the guiding principles: 'Victory would mean peace forced upon the loser, a victor's terms imposed upon the vanquished. It would be accepted in humiliation, under duress, at an intolerable sacrifice, and would leave a sting, a resentment, a bitter memory upon which terms of peace would rest, not permanently, but only as upon quicksand. Only a peace between equals can last. Only a peace the very principle of which is equality and a common participation in a common benefit.'[26]

Wilson also clearly viewed the war as a crusade for democracy. If anything good was to come out of this terrible war, mankind had to accept a fundamental re-structuring of the international order and the principles underpinning sovereignty. Wilson's vision for this future sovereignty drew heavily on late eighteenth- and nineteenth-century liberalism, and was based on the notion of the 'civilized' individual as rational, autonomous, and morally accountable. As the historian Leonard V. Smith has emphasized, Wilson drew heavily on Adam Smith's *Wealth of Nations* (1776) and his belief that 'free' individuals would make just and efficient decisions about resource allocations in global markets. He also subscribed to the ideas underpinning John Stuart Mill's *On Liberty* (1859), notably the belief that rational, free individuals would guarantee a just political system through responsible use of their votes in elections. Taken together and applied to the world of international politics, Wilson was convinced that properly educated individuals in a post-autocratic political system would be able to build a better world once the war had ended.[27]

Wilson's political thinking was also deeply influenced by his religious beliefs. Inspired by the Pilgrims in colonial America, perhaps even by his own Scottish Presbyterian ancestors, he believed that political individuals could and should make 'covenants', sacred and irrevocable vows to one another and to God, in order to defend their shared beliefs. While the concept of the 'covenant' has not played a prominent role in American public discourse since, it clearly featured prominently in Wilson's thinking. To him, a covenant bound the community of individuals together in a quasi-religious bond, committing its members to a better future in the interest of the collective.[28]

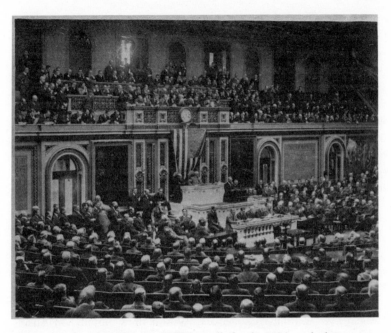

Figure 1.1 President Woodrow Wilson calls for the USA to declare war on Germany in a speech before both Houses of Congress. The relationship between the two countries had rapidly deteriorated in the preceding months, in particular on account of the German resumption of unrestricted U-Boat warfare and the Zimmermann Telegram.

In all of his political reflections on the future order of states, Wilson always had in mind the model of the United States, which was to be extended to the defeated states and their successors. In 1917–18, however, people around the world read into Wilson's words whatever they wanted to hear. While in the imperial world, some people wrongly assumed that a 'Wilsonian peace' would bring an end to colonial rule, many Germans now harboured unrealistic expectations of a 'just peace' without victors and vanquished—an illusion that was soon to be shattered.

Within seventy-two hours of Washington's declaration of war on Germany, a second fateful event occurred in neutral Switzerland, an event that was to have equally profound consequences both for the future course of the war and for popular expectations for the post-war world. On 9 April 1917 (Easter Sunday), Vladimir Ilyich Ulyanov—better known under his revolutionary nom-de-guerre, Lenin—his wife and fellow activist Nadya, and thirty of his closest associates departed from the main railway station in Zurich in a train. Their long journey back to Russia was to lead them through Germany and Sweden.[29]

The authorities in Berlin who had approved the secret journey from neutral Switzerland through German territory and provided the logistics for the onward journey to Russia placed great hopes in a man that few people outside the Socialist International had heard of at the time, a man who used the pseudonym 'Lenin' for his journalistic articles in. left-radical fringe publications with very small print-runs. Equipped with significant funds, Lenin was to take charge of the small Bolshevik movement in his home country, radicalize the February Revolution which had toppled the tsarist regime earlier that year, and end Russia's war with the Central Powers.[30]

After the fall of the tsar in February 1917, Berlin decided to revive its strategy of smuggling revolutionaries back to their home countries. The idea of inciting revolutionary upheaval in autocratic Russia dated back to the summer of 1914, when German diplomats in the neutral countries of Europe started using their informants in the growing exile communities of the radical Left to draw up lists containing the names of suitable candidates. Lenin's name first appeared on one of these lists in 1915. After the abdication of the tsar, the Foreign Office informed the German government and the OHL that they were aware of a number of radical Marxists in neutral Switzerland whose return to Petrograd would strengthen the anti-war Bolshevik faction of the Russian far Left. The political and military decision-makers in Berlin supported the plan.[31]

When Lenin embarked on his fateful train journey in April 1917, he was in his mid-forties and could already look back on several decades of revolutionary activism. Originally from Simbirsk (Ulyanovsk) on the Volga River, Vladimir and his family moved to his mother's family estate near Kazan when his father, a minor aristocrat and Director of Public Schools in the province of Simbirsk, died of a brain haemorrhage in 1886. One year later, his older brother, Alexander, was arrested and executed for participating in an assassination plot against Tsar Alexander III. Following his brother's death, Vladimir, too, became increasingly involved in Marxist circles. Expelled from Kazan State

University for participating in anti-tsarist demonstrations, he kept up
his political interest during his days as a law student in the Russian
capital and involved himself intensively in the revolutionary movement. In 1897, after returning from a trip to Europe, he was banished
to Siberia for three years as a political agitator.[32] It was during this
period that he took on the alias 'Lenin'—probably after the Siberian
river Lena.[33]

From 1900 onwards, Lenin lived in Western Europe, first in
Switzerland and then in Munich, where he edited the newspaper *Iskra*
('The Spark'), in which he published his famous programmatic essay
'What is to be done?' (1902). Although firmly based on Karl Marx's
analysis of capitalism, Lenin's ideas for the creation of a communist
society differed in at least one important way. For Marx, the final stage
of bourgeois society and the capitalist economic order would naturally
result in a spontaneous popular uprising caused by class antagonisms.
Lenin by contrast did not want to wait for this natural revolutionary
moment. It was predicated on an advanced industrial society as well as
on an equally well-developed class-consciousness among industrial
workers, neither of which existed in Russia. Instead, he planned to
seize power violently through a coup d'état, executed by a proletarian
avant-garde of professional revolutionaries.[34] Soviets (or workers' and
soldiers' councils) of the kind that had developed spontaneously in
many large cities of the Russian Empire over the course of the
Revolution of 1905 played an important role in Lenin's thinking about
the future power structures in the proletarian dictatorship in which
class-consciousness among the still largely illiterate peasants and workers of Russia was yet to be instilled.[35]

By 1917, Lenin had spent most of his life as a professional agitator—
most of it in exile. Since 1914, he had lived in Zurich, one of a handful
of places in Europe not engaged in the war, and a city with a long
history of sheltering radicals. Zurich was not only the birthplace of the
avant-garde Dadaist art movement surrounding Hugo Ball and Tristan
Tzara at the Cabaret Voltaire, but also became the temporary home of
numerous prominent figures of the European Left who were dreaming
of revolution while frequently disagreeing among themselves about
how to achieve that objective.[36]

Such disputes among the members of the socialist Left were not
new. Ever since the formation of the socialist Second International in
1889, different factions had argued endlessly about how to realize a

proletarian utopia. Divisions between those advocating reforms and those insisting on revolution deepened further at the start of the twentieth century. In the case of Russia's Social Democrats, the irreconcilable positions of the two most important factions—Lenin's radical Bolsheviks and the more moderate Mensheviks who (in line with Marx's theories) advocated a bourgeois-democratic reorganization of Russia before a proletarian revolution could take place—had led to a complete split of the party in 1903.[37]

The outbreak of war in 1914 had further deepened the rifts within the European labour movement. The majority of social democratic parties in 1914 had approved their countries' war credits, thus placing national loyalty above international class solidarity.[38] This was also the case in Germany where the outbreak of war deeply divided the Social Democratic Party, whose share of the popular vote had increased dramatically, from 1.4 million in 1890 to more than 4.2 million in 1912. Yet, the more successful the SPD became, the more acutely pressing was the question of what the parties' ultimate objective was: was it, in a conventional Marxist sense, to overthrow Imperial Germany through a revolution? Or was it the gradual reform of the existing system, a political system that did afford its citizens considerably more freedom, participatory political rights, and social security than, for example, Imperial Russia? The Russian Revolution of 1905 (and its bloody suppression by the tsarist regime) had, unsurprisingly, triggered a major debate within the socialist movement.

While radical Russian socialists like Lenin or Leon Trotsky drew the conclusion that a despotic regime like that of the tsar could never be reformed, only overthrown through a violent revolution, some leading German socialists rejected the idea that such a practice was applicable to the situation in Germany. At the SPD's 1906 Mannheim party convention the party chairman August Bebel pointed to the profound differences between Russia and Germany: 'In Russia a struggle is being waged for a new political order, but here in Germany, the conditions for which one must still fight in Russia have long been created.' After being interrupted by the audience with cries of 'Very true!', Bebel continued: 'That is why the situation in Germany cannot be compared to that in Russia. For all that we object to regarding the current state of affairs, no one here will claim that we, in our struggle, need to employ similar methods to our Russian comrades!'[39]

Even if overcoming the established class system remained the ideological goal of the SPD, the form in which the future socialist society was to be brought about remained contentious. The 'right' wing of the party and its leading theoretician, Eduard Bernstein, pushed for a break with the Marxist dogma of a violent proletarian revolution. As early as 1899, in his great polemic text 'The Conditions of Socialism and the Tasks of Social Democracy', he demanded that the SPD formally profess to being that 'which it already is in reality: a democratic-socialist reform party'.[40] This sounded very similar to the writings of the Marxist reformer Karl Kautsky in 1893: 'For the dictatorship of the proletariat I cannot think of any form other than that of a powerful parliament on the English model with a Social Democratic majority and a strong and self-aware proletariat behind it.... In Germany, a parliamentary regime means the victory of the proletariat, as does the opposite.'[41]

The party, which had been led by Friedrich Ebert and Hugo Haase since Bebel's death in 1913, was particularly deeply divided on the question of whether or not it should support the conflict that the Kaiser had declared to be a 'defensive war' through the approval of war credits. The internal dissent brought about the SPD leadership's attitude towards the war becoming more and more tense the longer the conflict lasted. If, in December 1914, only one SPD Reichstag delegate, Karl Liebknecht, refused to approve the war credits, the number of dissenters was to grow continuously as the war progressed.

This conflict was personified by the two co-chairmen of the SPD, Ebert and Haase, who were still working together harmoniously as representatives of the different wings of the party in 1913. Ebert, a long-standing Social Democratic party functionary with an immaculate worker's background, assumed the office of Reich Chancellor as the first 'man of the people' in November 1918. He would take on a central role in the November Revolution and subsequently became the first Reich President of the Weimar Republic, an office he retained until his early death in 1925.

Ebert came from a family of very modest income. A model Social Democratic career had hardly been in his stars. He was born in the university town of Heidelberg in 1871 as the seventh of nine siblings. His father was a tailor who often struggled to make ends meet. Young Ebert completed an apprenticeship as a saddlemaker before he hit the

road as a journeyman. He entered the world of politics via the still
youthful trade union movement and joined the SPD in 1889, the year
he moved to the North German city of Bremen, where he first
worked as the local editor of the Social Democratic *Bürger-Zeitung*.
But—presumably for financial reasons—he soon opened an inn, which
quickly became a meeting place for politically like-minded people.
Ebert eventually became intensely involved in local Bremen politics,
became chairman of the Bremen branch of the SPD, and was voted
into the Reichstag in 1912—the year the SPD became the strongest
political party in the German parliament. His many years of work as a
party soldier meant that he knew the SPD's party structure and its
most important functionaries very well. As a leading representative of
the centrist wing of the party he could be certain of the support of a
majority of its members.[42]

In terms of his political views, Ebert, like many other members of
the so-called 'second generation' of Social Democratic leaders in
Germany, was a pragmatist. Although he conceived of himself as a
Marxist, his primary goal in the years prior to the First World War was
the gradual improvement of living conditions for the working classes
through reforms. Following the death of long-standing party leader
August Bebel in 1913, Ebert was elected as SPD co-chairman along
with the considerably more radical Haase, a renowned lawyer, pacifist,
and socialist politician from east Prussia. At that point, the SPD counted
more than one million party members, making it the largest political
party in all of Europe.[43]

Haase was born in 1863 as the son of a Jewish shoemaker and small
business owner in the provincial east Prussian town of Allenstein near
the former German–Russian border. A gifted student, he attended the
gymnasium in Rastenburg and subsequently studied law in Königsberg.
Attuned to social injustices, he developed an interest in politics at an
early age, and joined the SPD when he was still a legal trainee. As a
young lawyer, he quickly developed a profile for defending 'political
prisoners', mainly socialists who had come into trouble with the
authorities. Frequently, he represented workers without payment if
they did not have the means to afford a solicitor.[44]

The outbreak of the Great War would lastingly alter the two men's
relationship. In 1914 the pacifist Haase begrudgingly bowed to party
discipline and voted with Ebert for the war credits, but soon after he
could no longer reconcile this position with his conscience. Two years

later, in 1916, he broke ranks with Ebert when he deviated from the party line and voted against the government's emergency budget. He and seventeen additional critics of Ebert's Burgfrieden policy were expelled from the SPD parliamentary group. The expellees then founded the 'Social Democratic Working Group', known as the SAG. The unity of the SPD was lost forever, as the following year would show. On 8 April 1917, one day before Lenin departed on his historic train journey from Zurich to Russia, a new socialist party was born in Gotha: the Independent Social Democratic Party of Germany (USPD) under the chairmanship of Hugo Haase and Georg Ledebour, a 67-year-old antimilitarist, who had been expelled from the SPD's parliamentary group alongside Haase in 1916. The new party united those within the socialist movement who were in fundamental opposition to the war but often disagreed on other matters. Its founding members included reformists such as Eduard Bernstein, an ardent critic of revolution as a means to advance socialism in Germany, 'centrists' such as Karl Kautsky, and revolutionary Marxists such as Karl Liebknecht. By the end of 1917, the USPD would count some 100,000 members— considerably fewer than the Majority Social Democrats, but by no means negligible.[45]

To a certain extent, the party schism of 1917 had been the inevitable outcome of increasingly irreconcilable ideological positions within the Left. Already in 1915, in response to public calls from the nationalist Right in Germany for a 'victor's peace' that would see, in the event of an Allied defeat, the permanent annexation of the French Channel coast and Belgium in the west and Russia's Baltic coast in the east (as well as significant reparations demands), many SPD members were increasingly alienated by their party's support for the war effort. They were outraged by the now openly articulated expansionist war aims, which they rightly considered to be at odds with the notion of a 'defensive war' that the Social Democrats had supported in 1914. On 19 June 1915, prominent SPD deputies such as Eduard Bernstein, Hugo Haase, and Karl Kautsky demanded that in light of the far Right's demands, the SPD ought to reconsider its stance on the political truce that it had entered into in 1914, namely by refusing further support for war credits.[46]

With no end in sight for the war, leftist Social Democrats in Germany and elsewhere tried to revive socialist pacifism and to restore the international cooperation that had been disrupted by the outbreak of war in 1914. The result was a conference held in the Swiss village of Zimmerwald, less than 10 kilometres outside the city of Bern, between 5 and 8 September 1915. Organized by the Swiss Social Democrat Robert Grimm, it constituted the first of three international socialist conferences during the war that served the purpose of restoring working-class solidarity and articulating resistance to the continuation of hostilities.[47]

The first document produced by the conference was a joint declaration by the French and German delegations, led by the German socialist Georg Ledebour, whose experiences as a stretcher-bearer during the Franco-Prussian War of 1870–1 had turned him into a vocal anti-militarist, and the French trade unionist Alphonse Merrheim. Their joint declaration stated that they did not support the ongoing war between their countries, a war which had been caused by the imperialist policies of governments that did not have the best interests of their people at heart. This sentiment also fed into a more general resolution, endorsed after much internal discussion, and addressed *To the Workers of Europe*. In this joint communication of the conference delegates, they demanded an end to the occupation of Belgium and a general peace without annexations that would be based on the principle of self-determination. To that end they pledged to renew the class struggle within their respective countries in order to force their governments to end the war.

Yet, the internal differences between revolutionary socialists (the so-called Zimmerwald Left) and reformist socialists that had haunted the Second International since its foundation in 1889 were difficult to bridge. Lenin and Grigory Zinoviev, who represented the Bolsheviks at the conference, called for the war between states to be transformed into international class warfare, a people's war between the oppressed and their oppressors, but such a view met with criticism from the more moderate delegates.[48]

At the end of the conference an 'International Socialist Commission' was formed with a mandate to establish a 'temporary secretariat' in Bern that would act as an intermediary between all affiliated groups. The members of the Commission were the chief organizer of the Zimmerwald conference, Robert Grimm, the Italian socialist journalist Oddino Morgari, the Swiss Social Democrat Charles Naine, and the Russian-Italian activist Angelica Balabanoff. Yet, tensions between the different socialist factions remained palpable and indeed increased during the follow-up conferences in the Swiss village of Kienthal in 1916 and in Stockholm the following year.[49]

By 1917, the divisions had become institutionalized, as new parties such as the USPD in Germany were founded and the Bolsheviks were preparing themselves to radicalize the revolution that had broken out in Russia in February 1917. The February Revolution had, in fact, taken Lenin by surprise.[50] Although aware that the war, hunger, and an inefficient and unpopular administration had increasingly undermined the legitimacy of the tsarist regime, Lenin—like most contemporary observers—did not expect the imminent fall of Nicholas II.[51] Observing developments from afar, he could only surmise that Russia's staggering military casualties in the war and the destruction of the social and economic fabrics of life in the western provinces of the Romanov Empire had fostered a situation in which revolution had indeed become the most likely outcome. Most crucial for the outbreak of revolution—in Russia but also in Central Europe the following year—were food shortages. Already in 1916 a Russian newspaper described the devastating effects of what it called a wartime 'food-supply crisis', due in large part to government mismanagement: 'A grain-rich country—the world's leading exporter of grain—had found itself facing grain shortages by the third winter of the war.'[52]

It was this protracted, war-induced food crisis that would ultimately lead to the revolution that brought down the tsarist regime in March 1917 (February in the old calendar). The revolution itself began on 8 March (23 February) 1917, when more than 7,000 female workers from the textile plants in the Vyborg district downed their tools on the occasion of International Women's Day. They protested against the continuously deteriorating food provisions. By that evening between 80,000 and 120,000 people had taken to the streets.[53] Over the next couple of days, the number of protesters continued to grow.[54] Worse still, from the regime's perspective, the demonstrations that had begun with complaints about food shortages quickly took a political turn with demands for democracy, an end to the war, and criticism of the incompetence of the tsarist regime and Nicholas II himself.[55]

After unwisely trying to stop the protests by force on 11 March, the tsarist regime was suddenly faced with increasing numbers of troops joining the protests.[56] In Petrograd, the tsar's ministers resigned and fled, while in Mogilev Nicholas II was eventually persuaded to abdicate in favour of his brother Grand Duke Mikhail Alexandrovich, who immediately rejected the poisoned chalice out of fear for his own safety.[57]

With Nicholas's abdication, the Romanov dynasty and the thousand-year-old rule of monarchy in Russia came to an end. The effects of this regime change were keenly felt in Russia and beyond. The February Revolution introduced a major new dynamic in war-torn Europe, which would, in country after country, raise profound questions about the future nature of political legitimacy. While it was as yet unclear which direction the revolution would take, the events of February 1917 marked the first successful overthrow of a major regime in Europe since 1789.

As the old order collapsed, members of the Duma formed what became known as the Provisional Government with the liberal Prince Georgy Yevgenyevich Lvov as Prime Minister.[58] At the same time, however, a rival political power was taking shape in the form of local soviets, which—following the model of the 1905 revolution—were created to express the 'unfiltered' views and voices of the crowds in the streets.[59] The creation of the soviets marked a period known as *dvoevlastie*, or 'dual power', designed as a temporary state of affairs until democratic elections to a constituent assembly could determine the country's political future.[60]

Even if the exact outcome of the revolution was still entirely open in March and April 1917, Lenin spotted his chance. Because of its 'bourgeois' composition and its decision to continue the dreaded war the Provisional Government was, in his view, no better than Nicholas II. His first 'Letter from Afar', written in March 1917, emphasized that the 'imperialist world war' had hastened the historical process, overthrowing tsarism and intensifying the bourgeois versus proletarian struggle that would transform the conflict in Russia into an international 'civil war between hostile classes'. He castigated the Provisional Government as a puppet regime allowed to exist by the British and the French only '*for the purpose of continuing the imperialist war*' and predicted the triumph of a genuine revolutionary movement 'for *bread*, for *peace*, for *real freedom*'.[61]

Unlike in 1905, when he had missed his opportunity to influence the course of the revolution, Lenin did not want to waste the opportunity to get involved this time. He needed to return to Russia as quickly as possible. Lenin was fully aware that in order to cross war-torn

Europe he needed German support. It was unthinkable that the Allies would endorse anything that might take Russia out of the war, but the Germans had long tried to weaken their opponents from within. While he was conscious that he was being instrumentalized by the Germans, Lenin felt that the end—a potentially successful Bolshevik revolution in Russia—justified the means. In negotiation with German representatives, he demanded extraterritorial status for his own train compartment and that of his fellow Russian travellers; with a piece of chalk, 'German territory' was separated from 'Russian territory'.[62]

The train soon crossed into German territory. At the train stations of Frankfurt and Berlin, the travellers from neutral Switzerland saw emaciated soldiers and exhausted civilians for the first time, raising Lenin's hopes that the war would soon also lead to revolution in Germany—a crucial step in the escalation of the proletariat's global revolution. On the German Baltic Sea island of Rügen, Lenin and his entourage were put on a ferry to Trelleborg in Sweden, before continuing their journey to Helsinki and boarding another train

Figure 1.2 Lenin is greeted by jubilant supporters on arrival in Petrograd in mid-April 1917. Only six months later the Bolsheviks would seize power in Russia by means of a putsch. Shortly after that they signed the draconian Brest-Litovsk peace treaty.

bound for the Russian capital. On 16 April 1917—after twelve years in exile—Lenin arrived back in the Russian capital, where he was welcomed by an enthusiastic crowd of Bolshevik supporters, who played the 'Marseillaise', waved red flags, and offered flowers as the train entered Petrograd's Finland station.[63]

When he returned to Russia in early April, Lenin benefited both from the regime change that had already taken place and from the fact that the Provisional Government was unable to fulfil the population's high hopes and expectations for peace and land reform. Lenin took the opportunity to push the revolutionary discourse in a more radical direction, proclaiming in the very first of his famous 'April Theses' that the Great War was an 'unconditionally predatory imperialist war' that needed to be ended.[64]

Meanwhile, in the summer of 1917, Alexander Kerensky, the Provisional Government's recently appointed Minister of War, hoped to channel the energy of the revolution into the armed forces and ordered a new offensive. Starting on 1 July 1917, Russian troops attacked the Austro-Hungarian and German forces, pushing toward the Galician capital of Lemberg. The dual objectives of capturing Lemberg and knocking Austria-Hungary out of the war were similar to those of the Brusilov Offensive of the previous year. Yet initial Russian advances in early July 1917 quickly met with stubborn resistance, notably by German forces, leading to heavy casualties amongst the attacking Russians. The soaring casualty rates undermined whatever was left of the troops' combat morale and by the second week of July, the offensive came to a grinding halt.[65]

The Russian advance collapsed altogether in mid-July when German and Austro-Hungarian troops counterattacked. Meeting with little resistance from the Russian forces, their armies quickly advanced through Galicia, Ukraine, and the Baltics. Within days, the Russians had retreated about 240 kilometres. In September, Riga, the empire's second largest port city, surrendered to German forces.[66] As the Central Powers advanced, the Russian Imperial Army disintegrated. By the end of 1917, the number of deserters amounted to as many as 370,000.[67] Even more problematic for the Provisional Government than the deserters were the over one million soldiers stationed in the hinterland and the garrisons, who increasingly turned against the Provisional Government and sided with the Bolsheviks instead.[68]

Military failure on such a scale prompted internal attempts to topple the Provisional Government. In mid-July, members of the Bolshevik Red Guards, soldiers of the Petrograd garrison, and sailors from the island naval base of Kronstadt attempted a coup in the capital. Fighting between Bolshevik supporters and troops loyal to the Provisional Government left some 400 people dead by the time government forces had stormed Tauride Palace, the meeting place of the Petrograd Soviet. Although the coup was crushed, forcing Lenin and his close associate, Grigory Zinoviev, into a temporary exile in Finland, the Bolsheviks were able to stage a second and successful coup only a few months later.[69]

This time the circumstances were more favourable. Kerensky, who became Prime Minister after the failed Bolshevik putsch in July, lost all remaining support from the military when his summer offensive ended in unmitigated disaster. Six days after German troops had conquered Riga, the army's commander-in-chief, General Lavr Kornilov, attempted a putsch against the Provisional Government. The coup quickly collapsed in the face of armed opposition from the Petrograd and Moscow Soviets and passive resistance from railway and telegraph workers. Kornilov and several other generals were arrested.[70]

The prime beneficiaries of the Kornilov Affair were the Bolsheviks. Kerensky had enlisted their help in 'saving' the revolution from Kornilov and handed out some 40,000 rifles to previously unarmed workers in Petrograd. He also freed their leaders from prison (although Lenin himself remained in Finland due to concerns about his safety). The Bolsheviks unexpectedly found their fortunes revived, while Kerensky lost any remaining support from the conservatives and liberals, the military leadership, and even much of the moderate Left.[71]

The Bolsheviks also benefited from the return of a particularly talented organizer, Leon Trotsky, from exile in America. Born as Lev Bronshteyn, the son of a modestly wealthy Jewish peasant from Yanovka, he, like Lenin, had spent several years in exile, first in Siberia, then outside Russia. A former left-wing Menshevik, Trotsky had spent the years in New York editing an émigré paper with another prominent Communist, the future General Secretary of Comintern's executive committee, Nikolai Bukharin. As Trotsky gradually moved towards Bolshevism, Lenin had come to value his intellectual abilities and organizational talent, which were coupled with ruthless ambition and a willingness to use violence to crush the enemies of Bolshevism.

It was Trotsky's theory of 'permanent revolution' which underpinned Lenin's belief that revolution could occur in a relatively backward country like Russia, before being 'exported' elsewhere. As soon as he returned to Petrograd from exile, Trotsky played a key role in building up a Bolshevik paramilitary organization: the Red Guards. Trotsky and his Red Guards were to play a decisive role in the Petrograd coup a few months later.[72]

Lenin himself was still in Finland during this time, penning his programmatic essay on *The State and Revolution* (1917), in which he attacked the compromising attitude of Social Democrats and Mensheviks at home. Calling for a more complete destruction of the state by a revolutionary 'vanguard', he invoked Marx's call for the establishment of a dictatorship of the proletariat that would ultimately lead to a classless society.[73]

The opportunity to put this theory into practice came that autumn: on 25 and 26 October (7 and 8 November in the Western Gregorian calendar), the Bolsheviks toppled the Provisional Government in a daring, small-scale coup, in which Lenin's supporters took control of the Petrograd garrison and occupied some of the capital's most strategically important points, including the electric power station, the main post office, the State Bank, and the central telegraph exchange, as well as key bridges and railway stations—a model of revolution that would soon become familiar in numerous other locations across Eastern and Central Europe. Supported by sailors from the cruiser *Aurora*, who provided covering cannon fire, pro-Bolshevik troops occupied the Winter Palace, the seat of the now completely isolated Provisional Government. Kerensky, who disguised himself as a sailor, managed to flee to the American embassy before leaving the country altogether.[74]

Compared with the violent excesses of the ensuing civil war, this was an almost peaceful revolution. The storming of the Winter Palace had left six people dead—the only fatalities of the October Revolution in the Russian capital.[75] Nevertheless, Lenin was fully aware that the Bolsheviks' grasp on power was tenuous. He had to consolidate his regime throughout the former empire, which, considering the vast lands and populations involved, was no easy task.[76]

Lenin's putsch had ramifications well beyond Russia—and it drew the immediate and undivided attention of contemporaries across Europe and further afield. In Germany, the far Left was energized by the fact that the world's first socialist state in history was being constructed. From her prison cell in Wronke near Posen, the leading socialist activist Rosa Luxemburg observed the developments in Russia with considerable enthusiasm: 'The glorious developments in Russia are like elixirs of life for me (*wirken auf mich wie Lebenselixier*). It is a message of salvation for all of us.'[77]

The Majority Social Democrats, by contrast, viewed the rise of Russian Bolshevism with considerable concern. Lenin had seized power without a mass movement behind him and had turned on the more moderate Mensheviks and Social Revolutionaries, taking the schism within the socialist camp to a new level. Lenin's ability to over-throw the Provisional Government and sideline the much stronger Socialist Revolutionaries with a handful of determined revolutionaries continued to haunt leading Majority Social Democrats in Germany, notably when Karl Liebknecht and his Spartakus Group challenged their government in January 1919. To Ebert and other MSPD politicians, it must have seemed as if Liebknecht was following Lenin's example of establishing a dictatorship of a minority.

The violence with which Lenin appeared to advance the revolution was another reason why many Social Democrats resented Bolshevism. The future Prussian Prime Minister and prominent MSPD politician, Otto Braun, left no doubt about this when he published a passionate rebuke of Bolshevism in the party paper *Vorwaerts*: 'It has to be stated unambivalently that we Social Democrats condemn the violent methods of the Bolsheviks in the strongest possible way. Socialism can-not be achieved through bayonets and machine guns. If socialism is to last, it can only be realized through democratic means...' What Russia was currently experiencing, Braun insisted, was a dictatorship 'just as brutal and ruthless as the despicable regime of the tsar'.[78]

Back in Russia, Lenin sought to increase the popularity of his regime by reiterating some of his key promises: immediate peace, democratic structures and flat hierarchies in the army, the right of self-determination for all peoples and nationalities, workers' control of the factories, and the transfer of all lands held by the nobility, the bourgeoisie, the Church, and the government into the hands of 'the people'.[79]

Lenin's regime quickly moved to implement these promises, notably with respect to land and property reform. The Decree on Land, issued on 8 November 1917, abolished private ownership of land.

The dispossessed were not to be compensated for their losses.[80] The Decree on Land did not incite the peasants to seize the land; rather, it sanctioned and encouraged what was already taking place. By February 1918, some 75 per cent of all estates in Russia had been confiscated.[81] The victims were not just aristocratic landlords and the Orthodox Church, but also 'wealthy' peasants whose property was redistributed.[82] Furthermore, between the middle of November 1917 and early March 1918, Lenin issued some thirty decrees on the nationalization of private industry, banks, and manufactures.[83] All of this was observed with great interest in Germany, sometimes to the delight and sometimes to the horror of the observer.

Lenin's second and equally popular promise was to end the war. He knew that Russia's military defeat had become unavoidable at this stage, and he indeed welcomed it. Already in 1904, at the beginning of the Russo-Japanese War, Lenin had articulated the hope that Russia would be defeated, thereby hastening the collapse of the tsarist regime. In the event, the expected collapse did not occur, but Lenin continued to adhere to this notion of 'revolutionary defeatism'. In 1917, he saw a great opportunity in defeat: not only had Russia's military misfortunes allowed the Bolsheviks to gain power in the first place, but a complete withdrawal from the conflict was now the only viable option to save the Bolshevik revolution. By taking Russia out of the war, he could concentrate on dealing with his many internal enemies. Simultaneously, he expected that war-weariness and material deprivation in Central and Western Europe would soon lead to revolution in other combatant nations, paving the way for the pan-European, if not global, triumph of Bolshevism. On 15 December 1917, Lenin's emissaries signed an armistice with the Central Powers.

With Russia de facto out of the war, the final months of the conflict were thus framed by very high but often contradictory expectations in Germany: for the far Left, Lenin's putsch raised expectations that a radical revolution was also possible in Germany, even if the MSPD did not support it. For the nationalist Right, Russia's withdrawal from the war offered a boost of optimism as it allowed Germany to go on the offensive in the West, even if a further escalation of the war, notably at sea, would bring the United States into the conflict. In any case, German politics and military decisions in 1917–18 were heavily framed by international events, namely America's entry into the war, and revolution in Russia.

2

Hoping for victory

Only days after the armistice between Russia and the Central Powers had come into force, a peace conference began in the fortress city of Brest-Litovsk, then the German military headquarters on the Eastern front. In a historical first—and in a move designed to spread Bolshevik propaganda and expose 'German imperialism'—the Bolsheviks had successfully insisted that the peace negotiations would be conducted publicly.[1]

The peace conference was also unique in its heterogeneous composition, a clash between the old forces of empire and those of a new revolutionary state. The Central Powers' fourteen representatives (five Germans, four from Austria-Hungary, three Ottomans, and two Bulgarians) represented either the splendour and glory of the *ancien régime*—as in the case of the highly strung Austro-Hungarian Foreign Minister Ottokar Count Czernin, who repeatedly complained about the Bolsheviks' table manners—or the forces of extreme nationalism, such as Talaat Pasha, one of the driving forces behind the Armenian genocide. The Bolshevik delegation at Brest-Litovsk, first led by Adolf Joffe, then by the newly appointed People's Commissar for Foreign Affairs, Leon Trotsky, made it clear that they represented the exact opposite: Trotsky's delegation, composed to reflect those who had brought the Bolsheviks to power, consisted of twenty-eight members, including casually dressed workers, soldiers, sailors, women, and a peasant. The Germans and their allies had never seen anything like it at a formal diplomatic meeting.[2]

The German delegation, headed by the state secretary in the Foreign Ministry, Richard von Kühlmann, sought the quickest possible termination of the war on the Eastern front, while simultaneously trying to establish an informal empire in East-Central Europe—an empire to be composed of newly independent nation-states on Russia's western periphery whose future could now be controlled by Germany. The German position at Brest-Litovsk gave an interesting glimpse into how the hugely controversial debate about Germany's war aims had evolved. In September 1914, the diplomat Kurt Riezler had noted down the infamous 'September Programme' for Chancellor Bethmann Hollweg, in which he reflected on Germany's territorial ambitions after victory over Russia and France had been secured. Although not altogether coherent and arguably somewhat overestimated in its importance, it nonetheless reflected the ambitions of the political leadership to turn Belgium into a permanent 'vassal state', to significantly weaken France so that it 'could never re-emerge as a great power', and to 'break' Russia's rule over its non-Russian western territories. Clearly such notions were at odds with the publicly advocated idea that Germany was fighting a 'defensive' war in order to secure parliamentary support from the parties of the centre and the Left. Since then, the debate about annexations within Germany's political and military elites had been shaped by opportunities which were more readily available in the east, while the stalemate on the Western front left no immediate prospects for annexations. In the east, however, the successful repulse of Russian advances into east Prussia and the subsequent 'Great Retreat' of the tsarist army from East-Central Europe had raised expectations for a major German land empire in *Mitteleuropa*. As Friedrich von Schwerin, a prominent member of the Pan-German League, wrote in a memorandum in March 1915 for the Chancellor's office, the war marked 'an opportunity—perhaps for the last time in world history—for Germany to re-engage its imperial mission in the East'.[3] The German Fatherland Party, which rapidly gained a million members following its foundation in 1917, also argued for expansive war aims. It viewed 'the East' as the major space for future German colonization and empire-building—an aspiration based on pre-1914 dreams of uniting ethnic German populations scattered across eastern Europe into a greater German 'Imperium', notably in the Baltic region, Ukraine, Romania, and much of Russian Poland.[4] But while the wartime dream of a German continental European empire in the East had older roots, it was actualized unexpectedly during the conflict from 1914 onwards.[5]

At Brest-Litovsk, both the German delegation and the representatives of Austria-Hungary were keen for Ukraine to gain independence, primarily in order to ensure grain and ore supplies for the Central Powers' continuing war effort on other fronts.[6] When General Max Hoffmann, the chief of the general staff on the Eastern front, revealed Berlin's support for the right to national self-determination of Poland, Lithuania, and Courland, Trotsky was outraged by what he rightly saw as ill-disguised German imperialism and threatened to break off the negotiations. The talks resumed ten days later, after the Russian delegation had an opportunity to consult with the government in Petrograd.[7]

Among the leading Bolsheviks, different opinions existed regarding the next steps to take. Realizing that the resumption of hostilities was impossible, Lenin assessed the situation pragmatically and favoured a peace agreement at any price in order to stabilize the Bolsheviks' position in their own country and secure the achievements of the revolution. Opposed to Lenin's assessment were those among the Bolshevik leadership who, like Trotsky, were convinced that an outbreak of revolution in other parts of Europe was only a matter of weeks away. Negotiations with the Central Powers should therefore be drawn out until this happened. When Trotsky returned to Brest-Litovsk, he therefore played for time. His widely reported speeches against the Central Powers' plans for annexations, coupled with appeals to the German people's desire for peace, certainly had an impact: on 14 January, the Austrian Social Democrats called for large-scale demonstrations, with strikes quickly spreading across Austria-Hungary and Germany.[8] In Berlin alone, some 400,000 workers downed their tools—by far the largest strike of the war. The USPD chairman, Hugo Haase, writing to his daughter Else, described the strike as 'the greatest event in the history of the German working class. We have not seen so much evidence of self-sacrifice and idealism for a very long time.'[9]

Haase did indeed have cause for his optimism. The January strike had been largely organized by the Revolutionary Shop Stewards— traditionally the SPD's trusted liaison people in the large factories where they fulfilled the task of rousing the workers for strikes. By early 1918, however, a large number of the Revolutionary Shop Stewards had become supporters of the Independent Socialists and had carried out their preparations largely without the knowledge of the MSPD leadership. One of the key figures in the coordination of the strike that January was the 37-year-old Richard Müller, a veteran trade unionist in the Berlin metal industry.[10] Like many other left-leaning socialists Müller had rejected the SPD's support for the war credits in 1914 and found a new political home in the USPD from 1917 onwards. Now, in January 1918, as head of the Revolutionary Shop Stewards, Müller and his men successfully mobilized hundreds of thousands of workers to demonstrate against the war and the proposed terms of the annexationist Treaty of Brest-Litovsk.[11]

Despite its major differences with the USPD, on 30 January the MSPD leadership also declared its readiness to support the strike. However, they largely did so in order to prevent a revolutionary escalation. Perhaps even more so than Ebert, the key MSPD figure during the strike was Philipp Scheidemann, co-chair of the party and one of the most prominent advocates of a 'compromise peace' with the Allies. Scheidemann was born in the city of Kassel on the Fulda River in northern Hesse in 1865 into a family of very modest means. Throughout Scheidemann's childhood, his father Friedrich, an upholsterer, had been the family's main breadwinner and his early death in 1879 left the family destitute. That same year, at the age of 14, young Philipp started an apprenticeship as a printer. By the time he had finished his apprenticeship, in 1883, Scheidemann had joined the then still illegal SPD during the time when Bismarck's Anti-Socialist Laws, designed to stop the spread of social democracy, were still in force. Until 1895, Scheidemann worked as a printer and proofreader before moving into journalism. Writing variously for a number of local socialist newspapers in the cities of Giessen, Nuremberg, Offenbach, and Kassel, Scheidemann built a reputation for tackling pressing social issues in his articles. His political engagement became more and more serious over time and he decided to fully dedicate himself to a career in politics. In the general elections of 1903, Scheidemann won a seat in the Reichstag as the Social Democratic representative of the constituency of Solingen—a seat he retained until the end of the Kaiserreich.[12]

His success as a politician was at least partly due to his approachability, jovial nature, and rhetorical talent, as the journalist and SPD politician Wilhelm Keil noted. According to Keil, Scheidemann was a 'brilliant orator with boisterous manners' whose impassioned speeches always had 'an element of the theatrical'.[13] In 1911, Scheidemann also became a member of the SPD's executive party committee; two years later—after the SPD's 1912 landslide victory and the death of their party's long-time leader, August Bebel, in 1913—Scheidemann was elected chairman of the SPD alongside Hugo Haase.

Politically, Scheidemann was a pragmatist. When war broke out in 1914, he voted for the approval of the war credits. Nonetheless, he became one of the leading proponents of a *Verständigungsfrieden* between the belligerent countries, a compromise peace without annexations or indemnities—a position that made him a target of spiteful criticism from the Right which accused Scheidemann of treason. As tensions between the different factions within the SPD grew over the question of whether or not the party should continue to support the German war effort, Scheidemann tried to mediate between the moderate and more orthodox wings of his party, but his ideas for a 'compromise peace' could not prevent the eventual split in 1917. For Scheidemann this was particularly delicate as the local social democrats in his constituency in Solingen supported the USPD and demanded (unsuccessfully) that he step down as MP.

Throughout 1917, Scheidemann had been one of the driving forces behind closer parliamentary cooperation between the Social Democrats, the left-liberal Progressive Party, and the Catholic Centre, the three parties that held the majority of seats in the Reichstag without being represented in the government. His efforts culminated in the Reichstag's 'Peace Resolution' of July 1917. Although the resolution was ignored by the Kaiser, his government, and the senior generals in the OHL, it was a powerful message that the majority of parliamentarians were backing the idea of a compromise peace.

After the MSPD and the USPD parted ways, Scheidemann became chairman of the Majority Social Democrats, alongside Friedrich Ebert. He was initially shocked by the scale of the January strikes in 1918, fearing that an uncontrolled revolution driven by the far Left might prompt a military intervention against the strikers. Indicating his support for the strike to the Revolutionary Shop Stewards, Scheidemann and the chairman of the East Prussian MSPD, Otto Braun, became members of the strike organizer's 'Executive Council', primarily to de-escalate the situation or, in Scheidemann's own words, to 'guide an unacceptable but understandable undertaking into quiet channels and also to bring it to the quickest possible end through negotiations with the government...'[14] More than a million German workers laid down their tools in armament plants, shipyards, and mines over the following days.

And yet, under pressure from the police and the military, the uprising collapsed. On 4 February the strike leaders gave up, and many of them were arrested. The strike had been unlikely to succeed at a time

Figure 2.1 At the end of January 1918 a large number of German iron and steel industry workers followed the calls of their Revolutionary Shop Stewards and went on strike as a protest against the war. It was the biggest strike to take place during the course of the First World War, and was joined by many of the women workers who had been doing the jobs of the men fighting at the front. The strike collapsed at the beginning of February in the face of state coercion, after which many strikers were arrested and their leaders conscripted into punishment battalions.

when a large portion of the German people were still looking optimistically to the future after the Russian defeat in late 1917. Hundreds of activists went to prison and thousands were drafted into penal battalions on the front lines. These included Richard Müller, the main organizer of the strike, as well as Leo Jogiches, who became the chief strategist of the small but militant and actively participating Spartacus League during the imprisonment of his partner Rosa Luxemburg, and Wilhelm Liebknecht.

Despite their ultimate failure, the massive January strikes in Germany further encouraged Lenin and Trotsky to think that the Bolshevik revolution would soon spread westwards to the industrially more advanced states of Central Europe. However, Kühlmann and the other representatives of the Central Powers in Brest-Litovsk were determined to force the Russians' hands. In order to apply pressure to Lenin and Trotsky, they signed a separate treaty with Ukraine on 9 February.

Under this so-called 'Bread Peace', Ukraine agreed to supply Germany and Austria-Hungary with a million tons of bread annually in exchange for their recognition of the independent Ukrainian People's Republic (UNR).[15]

Trotsky, on hearing about the separate peace treaty that would deprive his country of much-needed grain from Ukraine, refused further negotiations. The Central Powers responded by resuming hostilities. As of 18 February, one million German and Austro-Hungarian troops were pushing eastwards. Speeding onwards by rail, they made huge conquests, meeting almost no resistance as they conquered Dorpat (Tartu), Reval (Tallinn), and Narva. All of Latvia, Livonia, Estonia, and Belarus were overrun, as was Ukraine, whose capital, Kiev, was occupied on 1 March.[16]

The offensive led to the arrival of new, non-negotiable peace terms in Petrograd. Immediately after the fall of Kiev, the Bolsheviks signed the Treaty of Brest-Litovsk. Lenin had threatened to resign as party leader and chairman of the Council of People's Commissars if the government refused to accept peace at any price. The Treaty brought Germany closer to its initial war aim of becoming the dominant power in Europe than had been the case at any moment since 1914. For Berlin, this was a moment of extraordinary triumph. With the Treaty of Brest-Litovsk in the spring of 1918 it became clear which tendency within Germany had won out in the war aims debate: the annexationist-expansionist vision of a German Empire in the East. The Treaty of Brest-Litovsk formalized that ambition of Germany to be a major imperial player within Europe.

The annexations envisioned by Berlin at this point made those that would be included in the future Treaty of Versailles seem benign by comparison. The Germans demanded that Petrograd relinquish control over vast formerly tsarist territories with vital natural resources. Territories to become 'independent' (an independence that in many cases involved the presence of strong German forces) included Finland, Russian Poland, Estonia, Livonia, Courland, Lithuania, Ukraine, and Bessarabia. In addition, the Bolsheviks were expected to return the provinces of Ardahan, Kars, and Batumi—gained after the Russo-Ottoman War of 1877–8—to the Ottoman Empire. Soviet Russia was thus stripped of nearly all of the western non-Russian territories of the former Romanov Empire: 1.6 million square kilometres of land—twice the size of the German Empire—and a third of its pre-war population. Seventy-three per cent of Russia's iron ore output and a staggering 89 per cent of her coal, together with the major part of her industry, was lost.[17]

The mood among nationalist Germans was jubilant. Leopold von Bayern, Germany's commander-in-chief of the Eastern Armies, expressed the sentiment of many when he wrote in early March 1918: 'In our opinion, the Peace of Brest-Litovsk is to become a turning point in world history.'[18] What Leopold von Bayern could not know was that Russia's exit from the war also had unintended consequences that would hasten revolution in Central Europe. The release of hundreds of thousands of prisoners of war, particularly from the Austro-Hungarian army, was to have a deeply radicalizing effect at home in the winter of 1918–19.[19] Among those soldiers returning to their homelands there were indeed many who were to become future leaders of the central and south-east European Left, such as the Austrian socialist Otto Bauer, the Hungarian Communist Béla Kun, and the Croatian Sergeant Major Josip Broz, better known under his future nom-de-guerre, Tito.[20]

For the time being, however, there was cause for optimism that the military situation had changed in Germany's favour. Before the signing of the Treaty of Brest-Litovsk, the German army was geographically divided between east and west. Of the 6 million German soldiers in the field in early 1918, roughly 3.5 million were deployed on the Western front. The Treaty of Brest-Litovsk had left Germany with an enormous protectorate carved out of the corps of Imperial Russia and, in order to secure this empire, Ludendorff had to leave significant troops in the east: some three-quarters of a million German soldiers served in outposts that reached from the Baltic coast to Georgia.[21] Yet, he also stripped the Eastern front of its best units and transferred several divisions to the West, leaving behind smaller garrisons with primarily older soldiers, troops from Alsace-Lorraine who were deemed insufficiently reliable to serve on the Western front against French troops, and previously injured soldiers with recurrent or lasting health issues. As the Chief of Staff of the 'Supreme Commander of All German Forces in the East', General Max Hoffman, noted: 'Our troops in the East are made up of the oldest cohorts. Them and the majority of soldiers from Alsace-Lorraine. Everyone who was tolerably good has been taken from us.'[22]

Nonetheless, Russia's defeat was not the only cause for optimism among the Central Powers' military leadership in late 1917. Although the United States had extended their April 1917 declaration of war on Germany to Austria-Hungary that December, no more than 175,000 US troops, many of them inexperienced, had arrived in Europe at this point.[23] Instead, there was good reason to believe that the Central Powers now held the strategic initiative—at least until the Allies' lines on the Western front were replenished by American soldiers. Moreover, Russia's exit from the war had left another Allied power, Romania, isolated and surrounded by strong German, Austro-Hungarian, and Bulgarian forces. On 9 December 1917, Bucharest accepted the new realities and signed the draconian armistice of Focsani.[24]

On 11 November 1917, precisely one year before what proved to be the end of the war on the Western front, Germany's senior military strategist, Quartermaster General Erich Ludendorff, looked optimistically into a future that could now result in an equally matched showdown on the Western front: 'The situation in Russia and Italy will likely make it possible to strike a blow in the western theatre of war in the new year. The balance of forces will be approximately equal. Around thirty-five divisions and 1,000 heavy artillery pieces can be made available for an offensive.... Our overall situation demands that we strike as early as possible, ideally in late February or early March, before the Americans throw powerful forces into the balance.'[25]

One of his general staff officers, Colonel Albrecht von Thaer, shared his boss's optimism, as he noted in his diary on New Year's Eve 1917: 'Our position was really never so good. The military giant Russia is completely finished and pleads for peace; the same with Romania. Serbia and Montenegro have simply gone. Italy is supported only with difficulty by England and France and we stand in its best province. England and France are still ready for battle but are much exhausted (above all the French) and the English are very much under pressure from the U-boats.'[26]

Even moderate politicians joined in the chorus of those who viewed the future with optimism. In January 1918, the 42-year-old recently elected mayor of Cologne, Konrad Adenauer, wrote that 1917 'ended with the most favourable situation for us since the beginning of the war and the prospect of a good, honourable peace' along the lines of the Peace Resolution which the majority parties in the Reichstag had passed in 1917.[27]

If Adenauer and other politicians of the centre (and even of the moderate Left) hoped primarily for an 'honourable peace' that would bring the war to a swift end, the army leadership wanted more. To them, Brest-Litovsk promised land, vassal states of client states in East-Central Europe, as well as rich supplies of grain and oil to fuel the German war effort. Above all, it offered the possibility of releasing troops to launch the final offensive to win the war in the west before the Americans arrived in large numbers.

To be sure, the German High Command was well aware that victory had to be attained swiftly.[28] War-weariness and indiscipline were spreading in all combatant nations, including in Germany. In late 1917 and early 1918, there were increasing signs of exhaustion and dissent on the home front while the political 'truce' of all Reichstag parties of 1914 began to crumble when, in July 1917, the majority of parliamentarians—backed by the Majority Social Democrats, the left liberals, and the Catholic Centre Party—passed the Reichstag's 'Peace Resolution' in which they demanded a peace without indemnities or annexations.

When the Reichstag passed its Peace Resolution, it not only prompted a burst of outrage in the Army High Command about the Reichstag's 'defeatism' but also triggered the emergence of a new political party of the extreme Right, the German Fatherland Party.[29] Even if the newly appointed Chancellor, Georg Michaelis—who had been appointed at the behest of the OHL after Bethmann Hollweg's dismissal—chose to ignore the Peace Resolution, it gave a clear indication to everyone that, whatever consensus may have previously existed in German society about the purpose and aims of the war had been undermined. While the German Fatherland Party demanded a 'victory peace', the Reichstag majority's advocacy for a negotiated peace reflected the war-weariness of many Germans and the growing criticism of a 'silent' military dictatorship that was unable to deliver on its promises to bring the war to an end.[30]

It did not help the regime's legitimacy crisis that by 1917, large parts of the German civilian population were experiencing severe hunger. Already in late 1914, the Reich's population had quickly felt the economic effects of the war, notably those of the Allied economic blockade of Germany, enforced by the Royal Navy and other Allied vessels which effectively incarcerated the imperial navy and merchant fleet in German harbours.[31] Germany had never been economically self-sufficient—between 25 and 30 per cent of the food Germans consumed in 1914 was imported, as was much-needed fertilizer such as Chilean saltpetre. And over 70 per cent of those imports arrived in Germany by sea, making the country particularly vulnerable to a naval blockade.[32] Initially aimed at preventing 'absolute contraband'—arms, explosives, and other items needed for the war effort—from reaching Germany, the Allied blockade of Germany and the other Central Powers gradually expanded in scope. By early 1917, the Allies had successfully 'persuaded' neutral countries like Sweden and the Netherlands to sell their foodstuffs and raw materials to Allied states and not to Germany (which they had done, in huge quantities, in the first years of the war). The entry into the war against Germany of agrarian net exporters such as Romania came as a further blow.[33] But the Allied blockade was not the only reason why an ever-increasing number of Germans were going hungry. There were serious drops in domestic production; in addition, the number of male labourers available for work in the fields dropped sharply due to military service and large numbers of farm horses had been requisitioned by the army.[34]

These developments had a significant impact. In March 1915, bread had to be rationed, and long queues outside bakeries became a common sight in German cities, towns, and villages. Simultaneously, the cost of food went up significantly, by 50 per cent within the first year of the war, leaving working-class families in particular dangerously exposed to food shortages.[35] While the wealthy were able to procure scarce foodstuffs on the black market, farmers had direct access to whatever they needed for their diet, and soldiers were the state's top priority when it came to the distribution of food, the urban poor were the most exposed. Already in October 1915, working-class women gathered for a number of spontaneous food protests in cities across the Reich. By the winter of 1916, all main foodstuffs—including potatoes, meet, eggs, and milk—were rationed and hunger had become a widespread phenomenon, particularly (but by no means exclusively) in the larger cities.[36] The food crisis peaked during the 'turnip winter' of 1916–17 when an unusually wet autumn ruined the potato crop. Swede turnips—appalling in taste and not very nutritious—were offered as a substitute. During that winter, rations on average fell below 1,150 calories per day and person—less than half of today's recommended amount of 2,500 calories per day for adult men.[37] A postcard circulating in 1917 offered sarcastic advice to starving Germans: 'Take the meat ration card, coat it in the egg card, and fry until nicely brown with the butter card.'[38] The situation improved slightly over the following year—only to deteriorate again in the summer of 1918.[39]

By the end of the war, hundreds of thousands of German civilians had died of the direct and indirect consequences of the food supply crisis. While the claim made by the German authorities after the war that the blockade led to 763,000 civilian deaths is most likely exaggerated, it is widely accepted that the number of war-related civilian deaths in Germany was around 500,000.[40] As historian Alexander Watson and others have argued persuasively, most of these deaths were not caused by starvation but by the side-effects of malnourishment: food deprivation weakened people to the extent that diseases like tuberculosis, pneumonia, and influenza (which killed 180,000 people in Germany in 1918) were even deadlier than they would have been otherwise.[41]

The food shortages had particularly damaging effects on vulnerable groups such as children. Doctors in Munich found in 1916–17 that—compared with heights and weights of children before the war—children were now on average 2–3 centimetres shorter and 2–3.5 kilos lighter.[42] Even soldiers, the best-supplied section of the population during the war, were feeling the effects. A medical inspection of recruits in Posen in 1917 found that 15 per cent of the young soldiers had lost weight within a month of starting their military service, some of them as much as 7 kilos.[43] The food supplies offered to them were clearly not adequate for people carrying out physically demanding tasks.

As the conflict dragged on, the military censors became increasingly aware of the rapidly deteriorating morale among soldiers and civilians. The letters sent between soldiers and their relatives on the home front left little doubt that the collapse of military morale was only a matter of time. Already in the summer of 1917, the Army Command in Karlsruhe reported:

In so far as one is in a position to draw a picture of the morale of the soldiers from letters from the military post, conversations etc., one certainly would not be exaggerating if one were to prophesy a result with the next political elections that will open the eyes of certain statesmen. The men in field grey are angry and if they finally get the opportunity to express their feelings about what one justifiably can hope for from the new political orientation, the overt and covert opponents of that orientation would experience the shock of their lives.[44]

Germany was not alone in this, however. Most of the combatant nations experienced similar signs of discontent, some even more worrying for the ruling classes. In France waves of strikes occurred in the metal industry between July 1916 and May 1918, and in the spring of 1917 strikes spread through the French workforce, with calls for higher wages and an end to the war; and in May and June 1917 the French army suffered mutinies, a 'crisis of discipline' that affected perhaps as many as half of the French divisions on the Western front. Soldiers staged demonstrations and refused to go to the front.[45] In northern Italy, too, the spring and summer of 1917 saw disturbances and protests against rising prices, food shortages, and the continuation of the war, culminating in major riots in Turin in August 1917 triggered by a bread shortage.[46] In Britain the extent and frequency of strikes increased during the war, but only in Ireland with the Easter Rising in Dublin, the nationalist urban insurrection launched on 24 April 1916 by the Irish Volunteers and the 'Citizens' Army', did a revolutionary initiative really erupt in the United Kingdom during wartime.[47]

In Germany, war-weariness and political discontent culminated in the massive strikes of January 1918, but unrest was contained by a combination of police suppression and the renewed promise of an imminent victory. Military victory in the east was crucial in this context as it helped to at least temporarily alleviate the war fatigue and to mobilize public opinion for what now seemed like the final battle of the war against Britain and France, for which the OHL transferred forty-eight divisions from the Eastern front.[48] Misguided optimism and high expectations for a swift and immediate victory in the capital cities of the Central Powers represented the decisive backdrop for the events of the final year of the war. While the possibility of imminent victory boosted the morale of the troops, the raised expectations also increased the likelihood of serious disappointment and a widespread collapse of morale if no decisive victory could be achieved.[49]

The purpose of Ludendorff's spring offensive was thus to end the war swiftly before morale collapsed altogether and before US troops arrived in Europe in significant numbers. This was to be achieved by pushing the British Expeditionary Force towards the Channel, where it would be evacuated, before dealing a decisive blow against the French. The main target of the offensive, codenamed Operation Michael, was to break through the British lines in the Somme–Arras sector, where the numerical advantage for the German attackers was about 2 to 1.[50]

The surprise offensive opened in the early morning hours of 21 March with a bombardment of unprecedented intensity. For five hours, some 6,000 German guns fired well over a million shells into the British front lines. As the German infantry lieutenant Ernst Jünger noted in his diary (which would form the basis of his future international best-seller, *Storm of Steel*), the intense shelling caused a 'hurricane' of fire 'so terrible that even the biggest of the battles we had survived seemed like child's play by comparison'. After almost five hours of uninterrupted artillery fire, the infantry was ordered to advance on enemy lines. 'The great moment had come. A creeping barrage of fire rolled over the trenches. We went on the attack.'[51]

The advancing infantry of thirty-two German divisions quickly overran the southern sector of the front. On this first day alone the three attacking German armies took 21,000 men as prisoners, and inflicted more than 17,500 casualties.[52] The Allies were panic-stricken, at least temporarily. On 24 March, Field Marshal Douglas Haig indicated to the French Commander-in-Chief, Henri-Philippe Pétain, that the British front line could no longer be held and that he would have to abandon the defence of Amiens. The following day, on 25 March, Haig indeed ordered his troops to fall back to the old positions they had held in 1916.[53] Amidst a chaotic retreat, plans were made to evacuate the British Expeditionary Force from French ports along the Channel, just as Ludendorff had intended. It was the worst setback suffered by the British in the entire war and forced the Allies to overcome their internal rivalries by creating a joint Supreme Command under General Ferdinand Foch.[54]

Germany's early victories seemed to confirm the High Command's hopes and expectations. Everything seemed to be going according to plan. As early as 23 March the Kaiser, Wilhelm II, was convinced that 'the battle is won' and that 'the English have been utterly defeated'.[55] The optimistic view that victory was imminent also took hold on the German home front, representing a critical factor in how Germany later understood its defeat. On 26 March the chairman of the board of the Krupp armament company, Alfred Hugenberg, sent a congratulatory telegram to General Hindenburg: 'The peace with Russia... and the great victory of these days against the English are like two powerfully ringing hammer blows to all German hearts...Those who timidly doubted the German victory and those who never believed in it now see it as an attainable possibility before them and must bow down to the idea of victory.'[56] Even some Social Democrats such as the trade unionist Heinrich Aufderstrasse displayed genuine enthusiasm.

In a letter to a friend, he noted that 'the current flush of victory can only be compared to that of the first few months of the war'.[57]

In reality, however, the German advances during Operation Michael—impressive though they were—did not amount to anything decisive. When Operation Michael ended on 5 April, German troops of the Eighteenth Army had advanced well over 50 kilometres into enemy territory—an achievement greater than any seen in the west since 1914. The Allies suffered some 255,000 casualties, the majority of them British: close to 178,000 British soldiers were killed, wounded, or missing in action. Some 90,000 Allied troops had surrendered and 1,300 artillery pieces had been captured.[58] The strategic gains, however, were marginal. The British were bruised, but not broken. And while the territory gained by the Germans was considerable, it largely con-sisted of ravaged, worthless wasteland over which they now had to run their grossly overextended supply lines.[59] Worse still, the Germans had lost some 240,000 men in the offensive, with particularly high casualty rates among the irreplaceable elite assault units.[60] The British army, by contrast, almost immediately replaced most of its losses with new recruits shipped across the Channel—over 100,000 of them had arrived in French ports by the end of April.[61]

It was at this point that Ludendorff, under pressure to deliver success after gambling everything on the spring offensive, began to make erratic mistakes. Realizing that Operation Michael had not achieved its main purpose of breaking the British, he decided to try his luck in another sector of the front. When he devised his spring offensive in late 1917, he had initially considered a major attack in Flanders, code-named Operation George, as an alternative to Operation Michael. With Michael's failure, Operation George was back on the table, albeit on a smaller scale that was reflected in the plan's new name: Operation Georgette. Two German armies were ordered to overrun the nine Allied divisions—eight of them British and one Portuguese—that were standing between the German lines and the strategically import-ant railway junction of Hazebrouck, controlling vital Allied supply lines. Initially the offensive that began with heavy artillery fire in the early morning hours of 9 April appeared to be highly successful. German storm troops quickly overran the Portuguese defences and advanced some 10 kilometres by nightfall. The offensive continued over the following days, but ultimately came to a grinding halt, just a few kilometres short of Hazebrouck. Ludendorff's renewed failure was owed to both unexpectedly stubborn British resistance and the general exhaustion of the German soldiers, many of whom had previously participated in Operation Michael.[62]

The lack of a swift and decisive victory started to concern an increasing number of people on the home front. The well-connected German historian Friedrich Meinecke, who met frequently with high-ranking politicians, recorded his growing doubts over the success of the campaign on 1 May 1918. Meinecke, who had expressed his 'resurgent optimism' at the beginning of the spring offensive, suddenly felt a lot more pessimistic: 'I continually have to resist very dark thoughts. This war might become what the Peloponnesian War and the Thirty Years War once were: the beginning of the decline ... of European civilization ... the now released and unchained forces within frighten me. ... Equal voting rights are necessary—just as necessary as a certain amount of militarism on the other side—but the synthesis of the two may well not succeed. A heavy-handed reaction [against demands for democratization—R.G.] or revolution in response may occur. And then, as in Russia, a mushy dissolution of all things?'[63]

Ludendorff, however, was not quite ready to admit that his spring offensive had not yielded any decisive results. With the failure of Operation Georgette to break the British Expeditionary Force, his offensives became increasingly incoherent. Abandoning further action against the British, Ludendorff now lashed out against yet another sector of the front. The Aisne offensive against the French in late May, preceded by the heaviest German artillery effort of the entire war with 2 million shells fired in 4.5 hours, was a desperate final attempt to secure victory and brought the largest advance of the war in the west. After taking Château-Thierry on the Marne, German troops were once again—as in 1914—standing within reach of the French capital, where German long-range artillery fire killed nearly 900 Parisians.[64]

Yet, the military offensives of the German army in the spring and early summer of 1918 created more problems than they solved. Communication and supply lines were longer and it was difficult to bring up reserves to the front. The discovery of Allied food supplies in hastily abandoned enemy trenches—supplies of white bread, corned beef, biscuits, and wine—literally gave the deprived German soldiers a taste of their enemies' economic superiority. Moreover, the cost in men was immense, more than at any other time apart from the first two months of the war. The huge blood-letting caused by Ludendorff's gamble did not pay off. While German losses, often among the best and most experienced fighters, could not be made good, the Allies were more than replenishing their ranks with the 250,000 Americans now arriving in Europe every month.[65]

On top of the military losses, the first wave of the 'Spanish Flu', a particularly aggressive influenza virus that ultimately killed more than fifty million people worldwide, reached the German lines in the summer.[66] The German 6th Army in Alsace alone reported 10,000 new cases per day during the first half of July. In total, over one million German soldiers fell ill between May and July 1918. By contrast, the British army only suffered 50,000 cases of influenza for the entire months of June and July.[67] Other illnesses—pneumonia, dysentery, and even malaria—further undermined the strength of the army.[68]

From midsummer, the depleted German troops—weakened by the previous offensives and various illnesses—faced sustained Allied counterattacks. The French counter-offensive that began the Second Battle of the Marne in July 1918 and the successful attack launched by the British on 8 August outside Amiens confirmed that the Allies now held the initiative and that the tide had turned in their favour. Sixteen German divisions were wiped out during the Allied counterattack. Although a complete collapse was avoided, German troops were almost universally demoralized and exhausted, increasingly blaming their own leadership for the dire situation in which they found themselves.[69] The Mail Censorship Office of the Sixth Army, for example, reported that during August, more and more soldiers had openly turned against 'Prussian militarism' and the 'bloodthirsty Kaiser' himself.[70]

Without reinforcements, overextended, and weakened by illness and heavy losses from the offensive, the German troops were in no position to effectively resist Allied forces, which were now also successfully using tanks to support their offensives, making even more obvious to German troops that the Allies were gaining the upper hand in the development of new strategic weapons. Within a short time, all the territorial gains that the German army made during the spring and early summer of 1918 were lost. One week after the Allies had severely dented the lines of the German Second Army on 8 August (the 'Black Day' of the German army), Ludendorff told the Kaiser that Germany should seek a negotiated peace—a position he had continually rejected throughout the war.[71]

3

Endgame

On 14 August 1918 Reich Chancellor Georg von Hertling came together with the army leadership for an urgent meeting (chaired by the Kaiser) in order to discuss the new situation and the necessary measures. Hindenburg and Ludendorff continued to insist that the field army would succeed in securing a defensive position on French soil. They nevertheless warned Hertling that the field army could only succeed if the home front stood behind it.[1] Thus, as early as August 1918, there emerged a line of argument that would become the dominant line of the OHL in the final days of the war: military defeat could not be blamed on the failure of the supreme military leadership, but rather on the homeland, where defeatism had gained the upper hand and the army, undefeated in the field, had been betrayed.

The reality looked different. The German front was pushed further and further back. Starting on 21 August, the British regained the initiative at Arras and Péronne and made considerable territorial gains, while more and more German soldiers, tired of fighting a clearly lost war, surrendered to the Allies. The situation was considered serious enough by Hindenburg and Ludendorff to move their military headquarters back from Avesnes to the Belgian city of Spa on 5 September. It slowly dawned on them that the war was inevitably lost, possibly because they were inundated with reports about depleted morale among the troops. One of the many typical reports in this period came from the Field Mail Censorship Office of the Sixth Army reporting that 'war-weariness and dejection is universal'.[2] Ludendorff was on the verge of a nervous breakdown, as he witnessed the unravelling of his stellar military career. His meteoric rise in the German general staff after 1914 owed much to his central role in expelling the Russians from east Prussia in the Battle of Tannenberg (1914) and the Battle of the Masurian Lakes (1915), even if his direct superior, Paul von Hindenburg, a formerly retired veteran officer of the Franco-Prussian War of 1870–1, had publicly received the credit. When he was appointed Chief of the German General Staff in 1916, Hindenburg made the talented Ludendorff his First Quartermaster General. For the following two years Hindenburg was officially in charge, but it was really Ludendorff who ran the German war effort. Russia's defeat (and that of Romania) further strengthened his position, but the failure of the offensives in the west—essentially Ludendorff's brainchild—completely undermined his position.[3]

The sense of profound crisis that gripped the German High Command was heightened by the collapse of Germany's allies on other fronts in the late summer and early autumn of 1918. In the east, the Allies attacked on 14 September and routed Bulgaria's army, forcing her within a fortnight to seek an armistice. The suddenness of this collapse came as a surprise to many observers. Since Bulgaria's entry into the war in 1915, its army had fought valiantly and chalked up significant early victories in 1915 (Nish, Ovche Pole, Kosovo, Krivolak) and 1916 (Lerin, Chegan, Bitola, Strumitsa, Cherna, Tutrakan, Dobrich, Kobadin, and Bucharest). Before 1918, the Bulgarian army had not lost any major battles, repeatedly repelling Allied attacks at Doiran, a small town in Macedonia, where the Bulgarian army built a strong defence line that withstood systematic assaults by British, French, and imperial troops.[4]

Eventually, however, the Entente succeeded in breaking through at another point of the Bulgarian south-western front. During the summer of 1918 the Allies had amassed over thirty-one divisions with 650,000 men on the Macedonian front north of Salonica. The offensive launched by French and Serbian troops on 14 September 1918 completely overwhelmed the Bulgarian defenders who had been worn down by a lack of supplies and an increasingly intolerable scarcity of food for both soldiers and civilians. The French and Serbs smashed through enemy lines at Dobro Pole, while British and Greek troops pierced the Bulgarian defences at Lake Doiran. Although some units continued to resist fiercely, most of the Bulgarian army rapidly collapsed. On 25 September, the Bulgarian government sought an end of hostilities.[5]

Only four days later, Bulgaria, the last country to join the Central Powers, became the first to exit the conflict when the Bulgarian delegation signed an armistice at Salonica. In the armistice, Bulgaria agreed

to the full demobilization of its army (with the exception of a handful
of troops to guard the border with Turkey and the railway lines), the
occupation of several strategic points by Allied troops, the handover of
military equipment to Entente forces, and, most controversially for the
government in Sofia, the complete evacuation of all Greek and Serbian
territories conquered during the war, including Macedonia, a territory
that Bulgaria had laid claim to ever since national independence in
the late nineteenth century. The armistice also included secret clauses,
notably about a temporary Allied occupation as a guarantee for Bulgaria's
exiting the war. In order to ensure Sofia's 'good behaviour', a significant
number of Bulgarian troops (between 86,000 and 112,000) were to
remain interned as POWs for the foreseeable future.[6] Even worse for
the Central Powers that were still at war, Allied troops now stood on
the Danube, making it very likely that Austria-Hungary would soon
face attacks from a new front line.

Contemporaries immediately grasped the importance of these
developments: 'calamitous news about Bulgaria', Friedrich Meinecke
noted in his diary that day. 'The beginning of the end.'[7] The artist Käthe
Kollwitz, also observing from Berlin, echoed such sentiments: 'Horribly
oppressive atmosphere . . . The most contradictory of feelings. Germany
is losing the war . . . What will come now? Will patriotic feelings flare
up again in such a way that a defence to the bitter end occurs? . . . It
seems like madness to me, if the game is lost, not to end it and save
what still can be saved. Germany must keep the youth that still lives,
otherwise it will fall into absolute destitution. That is why there should
be no further day of war if one recognizes that [it] is lost.'[8]

For most politically engaged contemporaries, Bulgaria's defeat in
late September 1918 clearly reinforced the impression that the war was
lost. Not only did this defeat result in the interruption of the land
connection between the Ottoman Empire and the rest of the Central
Powers, it also effectively opened up the road into Constantinople
from the west and into Habsburg-occupied Serbia and Hungary from
the east.[9] None of the Central Powers—even Germany—had the man-
power to fight on yet another front line and Budapest was forced to
withdraw troops from the alpine front to defend Hungary against an
increasingly likely Allied attack on its borders.

Meanwhile, on the Italian front, a preliminary decision came in
mid-June in the form of the so-called Second Battle of Piave, which
had begun on 15 June with an ill-advised and poorly prepared Habsburg

offensive on an extended 80-kilometre front line.[10] The offensive quickly collapsed in the face of stubborn resistance from the Italian armed forces now coordinated by General Armando Diaz, who had been appointed the Italian supreme commander after Italy's disastrous military defeat at Caporetto the previous year.[11]

The Second Battle of Piave marked the beginning of the end for the Habsburg army, leaving over 142,000 men dead or wounded, while 25,000 of their soldiers went into Allied captivity.[12] The Dual Monarchy could no longer compensate for such losses with new recruits. Even the dismissal of the long-serving Chief of the General Staff, Konrad von Hötzendorf, in mid-July 1918, made no difference at this point.[13] On 14 September Kaiser Karl I appealed for peace. However, French and British leaders were suspicious that the Emperor's move might simply be an attempt to divide the Allies, while Washington responded that it had already communicated its peace terms. Any further discussions were thus deemed superfluous.[14]

While the Habsburg army was weakened by the ill-fated Piave offensive, Rome sought to capitalize on its strategic advantage and improve its position at the negotiation table after the war's end. On 24 October, the Italian army launched twin attacks on the Monte Grappa and across the Piave River at Vittorio Veneto. Within five days the Habsburg army was in dissolution and full retreat. At least 300,000 men and twenty-four generals were taken captive. On 30 October the Italians took Vittorio Veneto. Against this backdrop, the Hungarian government decided on 1 November to recall its own troops, a move which accelerated the collapse of the rest of the Habsburg army.[15] On 2 November, the Austrian High Command requested an armistice, prompting the Italian army's Chief of Staff, Armando Diaz, to send a jubilant 'bulletin of victory' to his troops: 'The Austro-Hungarian army is vanquished...The remnants of what was one of the world's most powerful armies are returning in hopelessness and chaos up the valleys from which they had descended with boastful confidence.'[16]

By the time the armistice with Austria-Hungary went into force on 4 November, another key player among the Central Powers, the Ottoman Empire, had already accepted defeat. The Armistice of Mudros, signed on 30 October 1918, ended the Ottomans' long and bitter war, which had effectively started in September 1911 when Italian troops invaded and captured the Ottoman province of Tripolitania (today's Libya), marking the beginning of seven years of almost uninterrupted conflicts which included the Balkan Wars (1912–13) and the First World War. Following the British breakthrough in Palestine (20 September 1918), and the British–Arab advance into Damascus (1 October 1918), Constantinople's capitulation had only been a matter of time and the Germans knew that.[17]

By the beginning of November, the last of the Central Powers to be at war was Germany. Remarkably enough, despite the increasingly desperate military situation, the German forces on the Western front continued to hold the front along a 400-kilometre line for almost another month and a half after the collapse of Berlin's Bulgarian allies. Nonetheless, very few people doubted the outcome of the war at this stage. For the soldiers themselves, caught up in the retreat on the Western front, the last weeks of the war primarily revolved around trying to survive, as the German Jewish lieutenant Otto Meyer noted in a letter to his wife Gertrud: 'Now I know what war is really like.... We crawled on the ground and ran and jumped into bomb-craters or remnants of trenches, surrounded by barbed wire. All around us, there was the impact of artillery fire of all calibres, the smell of sulphur and all kinds of poison gas. Even at the break of day, it was impossible to see further than two metres through the fog and the smoke.'[18]

While the soldiers on the front suffered the fatal consequences of decisions made elsewhere, Bulgaria's exit from the war offered Ludendorff a convenient excuse to end the war without assuming responsibility for the consequences. On 29 September, the day of the armistice in Bulgaria, Ludendorff and Hindenburg gave the Kaiser their assessment of the military situation and its political consequences: 'I have asked His Majesty to bring into government those circles whom we mostly have to thank for getting us into the present situation', Ludendorff informed high-ranking officers at the OHL on 1 October. He frankly admitted that the haste to close down hostilities was a response to an expected imminent Allied victory and to the poor morale of German soldiers (Figure 3.1). 'No more reliance could be placed on the troops', he insisted.[19] Yet Ludendorff was equally sure that it was the representatives of the political Left in the Reichstag, not the army leadership, that were to be blamed for Germany's 'unavoidably imminent' defeat: 'I have advised his Majesty to bring those groups into government whom we have to thank for the fact that matters have reached this pass. We shall now see these gentlemen moving into the country's ministries. Let them conclude the peace that must now

Figure 3.1 The Allies mounted a successful counter-offensive after the collapse of the German Spring Offensive in 1918. Over 386,000 German soldiers were taken into Allied captivity in the last months of the war, from August to November 1918.

be made. Let them eat the broth they have cooked for us.'[20] Apart from allowing the OHL to shift responsibility for the now inevitable defeat, the proposed 'revolution from above' had an additional advantage: President Wilson, the Allied leader most likely to offer lenient terms, would be more inclined to conclude a peace based on his 'Fourteen Points' address to Congress on 8 January 1918 if he was to negotiate with a democratically sanctioned government in Berlin.[21] Both in that speech, and again in February, Wilson had emphasized 'self-determination' and a just peace as key principles of the future international order. As he pointed out in his speech to Congress on 11 February:

There shall be no annexations, no contributions, no punitive damages . . . National aspirations must be respected; peoples may now be dominated and governed only by their own consent. 'Self-determination' is . . . an imperative principle of action, which statesmen will henceforth ignore at their peril.[22]

Wilson's ideas for a 'just peace' had been of no importance for the strategic considerations of Hindenburg and Ludendorff between

January and September 1918. Now, however, a moderate 'Wilsonian peace' without victors or vanquished was the best Germany could hope for. After Germany's blatant disregard of Belgian neutrality, the serious destruction caused on French, Belgian, and Russian territory, and the sinking of countless British merchant ships and millions of dead Allied soldiers, Ludendorff and Hindenburg knew that neither London nor Paris was likely to make a generous peace offer, particularly now that their troops were advancing again. They understood that the Americans would need some sign of domestic reform before they would negotiate seriously with Germany. It is only against this backdrop that the OHL's sudden 'change of mind' about the parliamentarization of the German political system becomes understandable.

Following the advice of the OHL, Wilhelm II publicly announced on 30 September that 'men who have the confidence of the people should have a broad share in the rights and duties of government'.[23] With this decree, the Kaiser initiated a cynical process of 'democratization', which also aimed at defusing a potentially revolutionary situation in Germany similar to the one that had brought down the tsarist regime in Russia.

One of the immediate consequences of this abrupt reform was the replacement of Chancellor von Hertling—a strong opponent of reforms and essentially a willing tool of the OHL—with the 51-year-old Prince Max von Baden. Prince Max, an intellectual liberal from southern Germany, differed significantly from his predecessors, as did his government, which was backed by a wide range of political parties.[24] Prince Max could count on the support of the Progressive People's Party, the National Liberals, the Catholic Centre Party, and the Social Democrats—representing an overwhelming majority within parliament. Friedrich Ebert, although himself not a member of the von Baden government, had strongly advocated his party's involvement, notably to prevent a Russian-style revolution: 'No one who has experienced the revolution in Russia can, in the interest of the proletariat, wish for a similar development to occur here. On the contrary, we must throw ourselves into the breach, we must see whether we can gain enough influence to assert our demands and, if possible, link them to the rescue of our country, for we are duty-bound to do so.'[25]

Instead of Ebert, Philipp Scheidemann joined the von Baden government as a state secretary without portfolio. As chairman of the 'inter-factional committee', composed of leading representative of the

Figure 3.2 The Kaiser appointed the liberal aristocrat Prince Max von Baden as Reich Chancellor on 3 October 1918. The appointment of a Chancellor backed by the Social Democrats, the Centre Party, and the Progressive People's Party, was part of the 'October reforms' designed to make Germany appear more democratic in the eyes of US President Woodrow Wilson.

three parties that had instigated the Reichstag's 'Peace Resolution'—the MSPD, the Progressive Party, and the Centre—Scheidemann had been a leading advocate of peace negotiations for some time. Although he initially had reservations about supporting a government headed by an aristocrat and worried about the MSPD joining the government when military defeat was clearly in sight, he eventually agreed with Ebert, hoping to implement meaningful reforms that would make a Bolshevik-style revolution in Germany unnecessary. Throughout October, Scheidemann devoted his energies to a range of policy issues, notably the implementation of the far-reaching October reforms that led to a parliamentarization of Germany, the exchange of diplomatic notes with the US government about armistice conditions, and an amnesty for political prisoners, including, controversially, the leader of the revolutionary Marxists in Germany, Karl Liebknecht.

What Ebert, Scheidemann, and other MSPD politicians wished to achieve via their participation in the new Baden government was revolutionary enough without requiring their supporters to take to the streets: the dictated peace with Romania and Russia was to be annulled while Belgium, Montenegro, and Serbia were to be evacuated. On the domestic front, the Social Democrats demanded free, general, and equal elections, including in Prussia, where a three-tier voting system prevailed. They also sought the appointment of government members who represented the Reichstag majority, that is to say from the ranks of the MSPD, the Liberals, and the Catholic Centre Party. Taken together, these demands amounted to more than the SPD had achieved in decades, namely the complete parliamentarization and democratization of the German political system. It was the reversal of military fortunes in 1918 that finally brought these objectives within reach even if it left the new government in the unfortunate position of having to bring to an end a war that was already lost.[26]

On 3 October, the very day of his appointment, and urged on by Ludendorff, who insisted on the 'speediest possible' conclusion of hostilities, Chancellor von Baden initiated contact with Wilson's government (but none of the other governments of Allied countries), requesting an immediate end to hostilities.[27] In its note to the American President, the German government referred to the Fourteen Points he had presented in January 1918 and his recent 'Mount Vernon Speech' of 27 September as a basis for future negotiations.[28]

Back in Berlin, political insiders like Friedrich Meinecke worried about the immediate consequences. On 3 October, he wrote in his diary: 'What prospect if the front troops, shattered and stunned, flow homeward and its masses come gushing upon us.... Most people do not yet know how serious matters are.'[29] Some field commanders also remained sceptical about the outcome of the approach to Wilson. On 7 October 1918, Major General Max Hoffmann, for example, noted in his diary: 'I am waiting to hear how Wilson will respond to our request—I assume he will set such conditions that it will amount to a "no".... The times are not pretty.'[30]

The exchange of notes was less straightforward than either von Baden or Hoffmann had assumed. Initially, Wilson's reply of 8 October gave reason for cautious optimism, as it sought further clarification on whether the German government was now representative of the people's will and whether it accepted the Fourteen Points as the basis for peace.[31]

On the German side, deliberations regarding a response to the American note began on 11 October. There was uncertainty within the cabinet as to what exactly a German commitment to Wilson's

Fourteen Points might mean in practical terms. Should they be accepted, without reservation, as the basis for a future peace treaty? Or should they merely be the starting point for negotiations? State Secretary Wilhelm Solf from the German Foreign Office pointed out that an unreserved acceptance of the Fourteen Points would immediately make both Alsace-Lorraine and the eastern German provinces the subject of the future peace conference. His cabinet colleague, State Secretary Matthias Erzberger from the Catholic Centre Party, by contrast, argued that the Reich should accept the Fourteen Points as the basis of the future peace treaty. He believed them to be vague enough to leave space for negotiations. If, during those more detailed negotiations, the Fourteen Points were continuously interpreted to the detriment of the Reich, the German government would then simply have to let the negotiations fail. Like the OHL, the cabinet thus still assumed that a 'peace without victors' was possible.[32]

Even the OHL could agree to the military evacuation of France and Belgium, but the precondition for this evacuation would have to be the signing of an armistice. Hindenburg and Ludendorff wanted the troops then returned to the Reich in order to re-establish the military status quo of 1914 for the duration of the peace negotiations. The question of the military evacuation of the occupied areas in Eastern Europe proved more controversial. Both the OHL and the Foreign Office were still hoping that German troops could remain there for the duration of the peace talks. Regarding a halt to submarine warfare, no statement could be made due to the lack of a response from naval command. However, it was made clear to the US government through diplomatic side channels that submarine warfare along the American coast would end. Regarding Wilson's query, in whose name the first German note had been sent, the cabinet agreed on an evasive response: both the past and current political leadership (backed by a parliamentary majority) were behind the request for an armistice.[33] The German note also contained a passage intended to commit Washington's allies to the Fourteen Points as a basis for further negotiations. On 12 October, the discussions between the cabinet and the OHL were completed and the German response was dispatched.[34]

Wilson's response of 14 October proved to be a heavy blow to German hopes for a negotiated peace without victors. Written in a much sharper tone than the first note, it made it clear that the conditions for an armistice would be defined by the Allies, not the Germans.

Wilson's second note also strongly criticized Berlin for the continuation of 'illegal and inhumane practices' of warfare. Under pressure both domestically from Republicans in both houses and from his allies in Paris and London, Wilson further noted that in his view, Germany was still controlled by an 'arbitrary power'—presumably the Kaiser and the army leadership around Hindenburg and Ludendorff, whose abdication and resignation were implicitly recommended.[35]

There were a number of reasons for Wilson's change of tone. First, there was the important factor of domestic politics in the run-up to the congressional mid-term elections. Wilson's republican critics did not fail to remind him of his speech of 27 September 1918 about the 'outlaw' German government—a government he now wished to make peace with. Domestic pressure made it imperative to Wilson to demand an irreversible regime change in Germany as a precondition for armistice negotiations. A second reason for the hardening of Wilson's position lay in Germany's seemingly schizophrenic approach to submarine warfare. On 11 October, the day before the German government dispatched its second note to Wilson, the German *U-123* had sunk a British passenger ship, the *Leinster*, outside Dublin Bay, claiming the lives of some 500 passengers. Wilson's government was appalled and emphasized this in its second note: 'While the German government is approaching the government of the United States with peace proposals, its submarines are busy sinking passenger ships on the seas, and not only the ships, but also the boats in which their passengers and crews attempt to bring themselves to safety. The German armies, during their now forced withdrawal from Flanders and France, are blazing a trail of wanton destruction, which has always been regarded as a direct violation of the rules and customs of civilized warfare.'[36]

The third, and arguably most important, factor for the hardening of Wilson's position was the growing involvement of Washington's allies in Europe. The French secret service had intercepted the first German note to Wilson and immediately shared the information with the prime ministers of the other Entente states. London and Paris were suspicious as to why the Germans were only making contact with Wilson (a concern shared by the Allied Supreme Command under Marshal Foch) and immediately began to work on a catalogue of conditions for an armistice. These included the immediate German withdrawal from France and Belgium and the evacuation of German troops beyond the Rhine River, the Allied occupation of the evacuated non-German areas, the internment of the German navy, and the surrender of sixty submarines.[37]

When Wilson's first response to the German government of 9 October became known in Paris, the officials gathering in Paris were horrified by the moderate tone of his note. They demanded categorically that the conditions for an armistice had to be defined solely by the Supreme War Council. In order to ensure a unified approach between the Allies, Wilson was requested to send his adviser, Edward M. House, to Paris where he would liaise with the British Prime Minister, Lloyd George, the French President Clemenceau, and the Italian Prime Minister, Orlando.[38] Wilson was therefore not only trying to appease his critics at home when he formulated his second note to the German government on 14 October, but also to reassure his allies in Europe that he would not act against their interests.

The tone of Wilson's second note demoralized the Reich government and the OHL. The strategy to communicate solely with Wilson, thereby bypassing the more hostile governments in London and Paris, did not seem to have paid off. For Ludendorff, Hindenburg, and von Baden, the only consoling aspect of Wilson's second note was that the abdication of Kaiser Wilhelm II had not, as yet, been made a condition for an armistice.[39] The German public also perceived Wilson's second note as a severe setback. Käthe Kollwitz, for example, noted in her diary on 15 October 1918: 'Wilson's response. A terrible disappointment. The mood for a defensive war to the end is growing. I am writing against it.'[40]

The German response to Wilson's second note was an exercise in damage control. Dated 20 October but only dispatched the following morning, the note emphasized the far-reaching political reforms that had been enacted within Germany: the decision-making power to end the war had been transferred to the Reichstag. The note further stated that Germany would end the sinking of passenger ships. At the same time, however, it pointed out that there had been no state-sanctioned violations of international law on the Western front. 'The German troops have strict instructions to spare private property and to provide for the population to the extent of their ability. If, nevertheless, excesses occur, the guilty parties will be punished.' In addition, the note emphasized that Germany was not prepared to accept a peace that was 'not reconcilable with both the honour of the German people and the ambition to conclude a just peace'.[41]

The American government responded quickly. On 23 October, Wilson's third and final note arrived in Berlin. Wilson had been rather pleased by the German response to his second note and was further strengthened in his position when a Republican motion to stop Wilson from negotiating with the Germans before their surrender had been defeated in the Senate on 21 October.[42] In its previous exchange of notes the German government had accepted the Fourteen Points as the basis for an armistice. In Wilson's view it was now time to demand the same commitment from the Allies so that 'they [do not] reach out for more than that to which they are legally entitled'.[43] Wilson wanted to ensure that the armistice would come about quickly, being convinced that otherwise London and Paris would dictate the peace terms and ignore Wilson's ideas for a just peace treaty.[44]

Wilson had also become increasingly concerned about Germany's political destabilization, which he believed could end in a Bolshevik-style revolution. In the middle of October, the American government had for the first time received information from the US embassy in Switzerland regarding the Spartacus Group to the left of the USPD. In Washington, fears spread that Germany might become a 'second Russia'. This possibility also softened Wilson's attitude toward the abdication of Wilhelm II. Up to that point, the US notes to Germany had suggested—implicitly rather than explicitly—that an abdication could be a favourable precondition for the armistice negotiations. Now Wilson saw the Kaiser as a potential aid in the prevention of a further spread of Bolshevism. As noted by his Interior Secretary, Franklin Knight Lane, he stated on 23 October that 'he was afraid of Bolshevism in Europe, and [that] the Kaiser was needed to keep it down—to keep some order'.[45] It was less the Kaiser that Wilson wanted to bring under democratic control than the German military which, he argued, ought to submit to the will of the people.[46] Wilson insisted that 'the United States cannot deal with any but veritable representatives of the German people . . . If it must deal with the military masters and the monarchical autocrats of Germany . . . it must demand, not peace negotiations, but surrender.'[47]

The German High Command rejected Wilson's note of 23 October outright and ordered its troops to prepare for a 'fight to the bloody end' to avoid a shameful peace. In its view, Wilson demanded capitulation without offering the option of an 'honourable' peace through

negotiations.[48] Some high-ranking officers agreed. As Major General
Max Hoffmann noted privately in October: 'The terrible thing about
the general collapse is that it is occurring for no good reason. Our
troops remain in good shape. We can hold the West, it must only be
demanded, and I can hold the East, if necessary, without troops. Instead,
everyone is losing their nerves.'[49]

With Germany's diplomatic options dwindling, the different positions
of the OHL and Baden's government were now increasingly irreconcilable. Against Baden's instructions for them to remain in Spa,
Ludendorff and Hindenburg came to Berlin on the morning of
26 October and demanded the German government break off negotiations with the Americans immediately. Thus challenged, von Baden
gave Wilhelm II a choice: he could either order a change of personnel
at the head of the OHL or accept his resignation as Chancellor.[50]
When given the ultimatum, Wilhelm was prepared to support his
new Chancellor against the High Command.[51] On the morning of
26 October, Ludendorff and Hindenburg were summoned for an
audience with the Kaiser, and Ludendorff was dismissed.[52]

As Major General Hoffmann noted the following day: 'Yesterday
evening we received a telephone message that Ludendorff had resigned
and was taking his leave. . . . Although Ludendorff undoubtedly bears
guilt for the present collapse—he should not have undertaken the
offensive—it will nevertheless be difficult, nearly impossible, to replace
him. . . . Whether Hindenburg will remain, I do not know, I hope so,
because it would have a bad effect on morale among the people and
the army if he went.'[53]

Precisely for that reason—fears that Hindenburg's departure might
lead to further demoralization—the Field Marshal was ordered to
remain in his post by the Kaiser. That same day, on 26 October, the
Chief of Staff of Army Group Kiev in the Ukraine, General Wilhelm
Groener, received a telegram from Hindenburg, ordering him to
report to the Field Army Headquarters in Spa, where he was appointed
First Quartermaster General of the German Army. As Ludendorff's
replacement, Groener was now charged with salvaging what could be
rescued from a lost war.

On 27 October, one day after Ludendorff's dismissal, the German
government accepted Wilson's conditions while also emphasizing that
Germany was undergoing a profound reform process: 'The peace

negotiations are being conducted by a popular government in whose hands decisive political authority has been placed by the constitution. The military powers have also been subordinated to it.'[54]

Germany's transformation into a constitutional monarchy with a government that depended on a parliamentary majority was indeed finalized on 28 October 1918 when the constitution of 1871 was altered accordingly.[55] Democrats such as the leading Bavarian MSPD politician Erhard Auer were ecstatic: 'We are living through the greatest revolution that has ever occurred! Only the form is different today because it is possible to achieve through legal means what we have been fighting for for centuries.'[56]

Yet Germany's constitutional reforms came too late to prevent a revolution. As in Russia the previous year, military setbacks and general war-weariness created the conditions for popular dissent. It was not—as nationalist circles were to claim in the following years—revolution that caused defeat. Just as in Russia, revolutionary events in Germany were sparked by material deprivation, strikes among industrial workers, and discontent among the soldiers. The strains of war undermined the legitimacy of the imperial regime and the 'silent' military dictatorship into which it had degenerated during the last two years of the war—a regime that was able neither to mitigate the hardships of the civilian population nor to bring the war to the promised victorious conclusion.[57] With the military collapse in the autumn of 1918, any remaining support for the imperial state evaporated. The deterioration of military discipline, the crumbling of the authoritarian governing system, the mounting military and political pressures from the Allies—alongside extreme war-weariness at home and the example of Russia—combined to create an overwhelming crisis of legitimacy.

4

The sailors' mutiny

The German Revolution itself began with a fundamental miscalculation by the Imperial Naval High Command under Admiral Reinhard Scheer, prompting a revolt by sailors and soldiers stationed in Germany's ports and naval garrisons. Its main trigger was the Naval High Command's order of 28 October 1918 to send out the German High Seas fleet to confront the Royal Navy in a final, major battle. 'Even if it is not to be expected that this will bring a decisive turn,' a naval strategy document of 16 October observed, 'it is nonetheless a question of the Navy's honour and existence that it does its utmost in the final battle.'[1]

Restoring 'honour' seemed particularly important to the Naval High Command because the German fleet, whose massive expansion had contributed significantly to rising tensions between Germany and Great Britain in the early twentieth century, had been fairly useless during the war. In contrast to the German land forces, which had been involved in heavy fighting on all fronts since August 1914, the German High Seas Fleet, which had been developed at considerable expense from 1898 onwards, had remained largely inactive. It had also been unable to prevent the Royal Navy's naval blockade designed to starve Germany into submission. Ever since the inconclusive and strategically unimportant Battle of Jutland in late May 1916, the navy's activities had been confined to submarine warfare.[2] This did not remain unnoticed by the German public, and was reflected in the mocking lyrics: 'Dear Fatherland, no fear be thine, the fleet is sound asleep in the harbour.'[3]

Frustration and boredom, coupled with highly unequal food supplies for officers and ordinary sailors, as well as an extremely regimented disciplinary system onboard ship, significantly increased dissatisfaction throughout the fleet. Already in early August 1917, there had been several cases of insubordination and refusal to obey orders. The naval command responded with draconian punishments. The two 'ringleaders', Albin Köbis and Max Reichpietsch, were executed on 5 September 1917, while seventy-six stokers and sailors were sentenced to long prison sentences.[4] For plotting a fleet strike to bring about peace negotiations, Max Güth and Arthur Sens, the two chairmen of the Kiel Independent Socialists (USPD), were also sentenced to long prison sentences that month.[5]

Although discipline in the navy was temporarily restored through these draconian measures in September 1917, tensions persisted and even increased over the rest of the year. With Germany's intensification of unrestricted submarine warfare, the best and most experienced naval officers were put on the U-boats while the larger surface ships were increasingly staffed with junior officers and even officer cadets untrained in leading ordinary sailors.[6]

But of particular importance for the perilous development within the navy were faulty perceptions of the navy's effectiveness during the final phase of the war. While the army Supreme Command gradually realized after the unsuccessful spring and summer offensives of 1918 that a military victory could no longer be achieved and began to favour armistice negotiations, this view did not prevail in the Naval Supreme Command (SKL) under Admiral Reinhard Scheer.[7]

The Naval Supreme Command was not prepared to accept the potential surrender of the fleet to Great Britain, which Scheer and other senior naval officers quite rightly assumed would be one of the key British demands for an armistice. When the naval liaison officer at the Army High Command's field headquarters in Spa, Lieutenant Commander von York, reported back to Scheer on 4 October 1918 Ludendorff's opinion 'that a possible demand from England to surrender the German fleet would likely have to be obeyed, that overall it would be the navy that would largely have to pay the price',[8] the High Seas Fleet Chief of Staff, Rear Admiral Adolf von Trotha, first suggested the idea of a final comprehensive assault against the Royal Navy. As von Trotha explained to Admiral Magnus von Levetzow, this option would have to be chosen or 'our fleet would otherwise face a shameful end'. The 'fleet regards such a final battle as its highest goal so as not to end this war without displaying the national strength that rests within it with decisive effect'. An 'honourable battle of the fleet, even if it becomes a fight to the death in this war, will—as long as our people does not fail as a nation—give birth to a new future German fleet; a fleet shackled by a shameful peace will have no future'.[9]

Trotha's covering letter for Levetzow emphasized the notion of an 'honourable downfall' of the German fleet even more strongly: 'It goes without saying that the sheer thought of the fleet's destruction, without ever having gone into battle, fills us with the shock of shame. The mission of going down with honour is still worthwhile, for we would certainly inflict some serious wounds on England.'[10] Now that the war was drawing to a close and defeat seemed inevitable, the admirals felt that dramatic action—a full-blown naval attack on their British opponent—was needed, even if it meant the complete destruction of the German High Seas Fleet. The discussion of these plans also showed the degree of contempt the leaders of the navy had for the 'democratization' of Germany—the plans were kept secret from the Baden government and the civilan politicans that were nominally in charge of overseeing the navy.[11]

The operational plan that Trotha prepared by 24 October and Scheer approved three days later called for the night-time deployment of the entire Imperial High Seas Fleet into the Hoofden, the section of the North Sea located between the English Channel, the east coast of England, and the Dutch coast.[12] From there, small units would paralyse the naval traffic along the Dutch coast and launch initial attacks in the direction of the mouth of the Thames. It was anticipated that the Grand Fleet would react by attempting to cut off the German High Seas Fleet's retreat route north of the Hoofden. Along the way, numerous British ships would be sunk by U-boats and minefields, thus providing the Germans with a strategic advantage in the main naval battle that Trotha envisaged to take place near the Dutch island of Terschelling.[13]

The fleet's operational plan was only to be revealed to the crews at sea when all connections with the mainland had been cut off. But the plan was never to be realized. Despite all attempts at secrecy, rumours of an impending combat mission had quickly spread among the crews. As the sailors were also aware of the ongoing peace negotiations between Germany and the United States, many of them objected to the idea of being sacrificed in a now pointless war. According to one contemporary account, farewell letters being written by officers aboard the battleship SMS *Markgraf* reinforced the impression among the crew that the fleet was about to go on a suicide mission.[14]

On the eve of the launch, when the commanders aboard the flag-ship were about to receive their orders, reports of serious cases of insubordination were reported on the massive battleships *Helgoland* and *Thüringen*, which had sunk the HMS *Black Prince* during the Battle of Jutland. Now, the sailors simply refused to weigh anchor, leading to open confrontations between officers and crew.[15]

The senior commanders of the High Seas Fleet were clearly sur-prised by the extent of sailors' refusals to obey orders, but decided on a heavy-handed response, ordering the arrest of all mutineers.[16] When the officers onboard the two dreadnoughts were unable to re-establish order this way, the Naval High Command brought two torpedo boats, *B 97* and *B 112*, into position against the *Helgoland* and the *Thüringen*, two dreadnoughts with more than 1,000 crew members and twelve main guns each. While the smaller boats were getting ready to dispatch their deadly torpedoes, the mutineers on the much larger *Helgoland* began lowering their guns onto the torpedo boats. An escalation was only narrowly avoided as both sides shied away from firing the first shot. By the end of the day, some 600 mutinying sailors—more than a quarter of both crews—had been arrested and taken on land.[17] Following these dramatic events, the commander of the Third Squadron, Vice-Admiral Hugo Kraft, and his superior Admiral Franz Ritter von Hipper, decided to move his five largest vessels with more than 5,000 crew members from Wilhelmshaven to the naval port of Kiel in the hope that some shore leave for the crews might appease them and prevent the further spread of the mutinies.[18]

This decision was to have far-reaching consequences (Figure 4.1). As the five giant vessels—*Koenig*, *Bayern*, *Grosser Kurfürst*, *Kronprinz*, and *Markgraf*—passed through the Kaiser-Wilhelm-Canal towards Kiel, further incidents of insubordination occurred. The squadron commander, Vice Admiral Hugo Kraft, responded by having forty-seven seamen—the alleged ringleaders of the Wilhelmshaven uprising—placed under arrest. They were to be brought to detention centres as soon as the battleships arrived in Kiel in the early hours of 1 November.[19]

More than any other city in Germany, Kiel had been dominated and shaped by the imperial navy for the previous twenty years. Many of the fleets' dreadnoughts lay at anchor here, along with smaller ships and

Figure 4.1 The broad public support for the rebellious sailors of the High Seas Fleet was decisive for the success of the revolution. Within days of the Kiel mutiny, large-scale demonstrations occurred in many German towns and cities, like this one on 6 November 1918 in Wilhelmshaven.

other naval units. It was also a city of soldiers—some 50,000 were stationed in its barracks—and of industrial workers in armaments factories and shipyards who, when taken together, represented two-thirds of the city's workforce. Against this background, it was hardly surprising that the Social Democrats considered Kiel one of their strongholds. In 1910 the SPD had won more than half of the votes in the city council elections and continued to exert considerable influence on the city's workers through their unions well into the war.

The naval leaderships' strategy to bring the rebellious sailors of the Third Squadron from Wilhelmshaven into this deeply working-class city to 'let off some steam' in sailors' pubs was thus not without risk. The Third Squadron's commander, Kraft, and the newly installed Governor of Kiel, Wilhelm Souchon, had agreed on a bifurcated approach that would see the ringleaders of the mutiny put on trial while the majority of sailors would be granted generous shore leave. Both believed that the sailors' long absence from their main base in Kiel was the primary reason for their discontent. Kraft and Souchon hereby disregarded the warnings from other senior officers who—quite rightly—feared that 'the presence of the Third Squadron with its unreliable elements among the crews [represents] a high risk in view of the high concentration in Kiel of troops and munitions workers'.[20]

Those urging caution were soon proved right. Some 250 sailors from the *Markgraf, König*, and *Bayern* took advantage of their promptly granted shore leave on the evening of 1 November to organize a meeting with MSPD and USPD representatives in the Kiel trade union headquarters. Their discussion revolved around how to prevent a repeated order of the naval leadership to fight the Royal Navy and the demand for an immediate release of their imprisoned comrades who were likely to be charged with inciting a mutiny.[21]

A further meeting was planned for the following day in order to discuss further steps. Twice as many people showed up for the meeting of 2 November and the event had to be moved to a large parade ground in the city.[22] One of the speakers was Karl Artelt, who soon emerged as a leading figure in the Kiel revolt. Artelt, a 27-year-old sailor of sturdy build, had already spent time in prison in 1917 for participating in a strike, and subsequently had to serve in a penal battalion in Flanders. From early January 1918 he was back in Kiel, now working in the 'Germania' shipyard while simultaneously intensifying his political engagement on the far Left as a member of the Independent Social Democrats.[23] In his speech to the sailors on 2 November 1918, Artelt quickly moved beyond the initial demand to release the prisoners and began formulating political objectives, including the abolition of 'militarism' and the disempowerment of the ruling classes. According to a police report, he did not rule out the use of violence to achieve these objectives.[24] Artelt also called for a large public gathering on the parade grounds to take place on 3 November and a subsequent demonstration march designed to lend weight to their demands. With the help of other members of the Kiel Independent Socialists, leaflets were printed that same evening, calling on other soldiers and workers to show solidarity: 'Comrades, don't shoot at your brothers! Workers, demonstrate in masses, don't abandon the soldiers.'[25]

The revolt against a 'suicide mission' now took a more overtly political turn, as the revolutionaries began to demand peace at any price and the immediate abdication of the Kaiser—demands that sounded uncomfortably similar to those articulated by Russian protesters in Petrograd in early 1917 in the lead-up to the first Russian Revolution that year.[26]

The local civilian and military authorities were unsure how to respond. A small reaction force had been set up to quell strikes and unrest in the city, mainly to prevent plundering. But it had no experience in dealing with an outright mutiny. The commanding officers of the Kiel naval station met on the evening of 2 November to discuss their options for ending the rebellion, but failed to agree on a strategy.[27] It was only on the following day that an agreement was reached: in order to prevent the sailors from carrying the rebellion into the city, it was decided that a citywide alarm should be sounded one hour before the next scheduled soldiers' assembly, thus requiring all sailors and soldiers to return to their units. Back in their quarters, the units' officers should then attempt to calm the assembled men and convince them of the futility of their mutiny.[28] In addition, on the morning of 3 November, Kraft ordered the arrest of a further fifty-seven sailors and stokers on the SMS *Markgraf*.[29]

After the meeting on 3 November, Governor Souchon turned to Berlin for the first time and reported the occurrence of 'extremely dangerous events' in Kiel. All 'possible security measures' would be applied to safeguard discipline among the sailors. At the same time, however, Souchon did not seem to believe in the success of such 'measures'. He demanded that the Reich government should send 'outstanding Social Democratic deputies' to the city in order to convince the sailors to 'avoid revolution and revolt'.[30]

In Berlin, panic ensued among the government's ministers. A sailors' mutiny at a time when negotiations with the Allies about an armistice were still ongoing could only weaken Berlin's hand. Even senior Majority Social Democrats like Philipp Scheidemann, who had joined the cabinet of Max von Baden in October, felt anxious that an unchecked rebellion in Kiel was likely to start an uncontrolled revolution and a violent response from anti-democratic forces of the old order.[31] Responding to Souchon's request, the government immediately dispatched the MSPD's military expert in the Reichstag, Gustav Noske, and State Secretary Conrad Haussmann from the liberal Progressive Party to Kiel. Both hoped that their presence might contain the rebellion by assuring the mutineers that the government was working towards an immediate peace and further political reforms.[32]

Yet before Noske and Haussmann had even left Berlin, events in Kiel started to get out of hand. When, in the afternoon of 2 November, the citywide alarm was sounded to recall all sailors back to their ships, few sailors answered the call. By 7.30 p.m. only half of the sailors on shore had returned to their units. Failing to achieve its main objective, the alarm instead alerted the city's civilian population to the fact that something unusual was going on in Kiel. Over the following hour, more and more civilian onlookers joined up with the large number of rebellious sailors who ignored the alarm and instead headed for the scheduled meeting on the nearby parade ground.[33]

The public meeting on the parade ground 'Viehhofer Gehoelz' was opened at 5.30 p.m. Between 5,000 and 6,000 people gathered, mainly sailors. Several speakers closed their addresses with a demand for an end to the war and for peace, freedom, and bread.[34] Appeasing words from Kiel's trade union chairman, Gustav Garbe, fell on deaf ears. Instead, some speakers called for an assault on the city's main detention centre in Feldstrasse where a large number of the arrested sailors were being held, and a march on a nearby officers' mess. Shortly afterwards, a sizeable column of demonstrators set out towards Kiel's main detention centre.[35]

Along the way, the protesters passed the 'Waldwiese', a pub temporarily serving as an improvised prison, and demanded the immediate release of those sailors who were being detained there for not observing the citywide alarm. Initially, the commanding officer in charge refused, but he yielded when the demonstrators began smashing the pub's windows and forced their way in, seizing a number of weapons along the way. To avoid bloodshed, he released the prisoners who subsequently joined the protest march into the city centre. Thus armed and reinforced, the crowd marched on towards the train station. There, demonstrators managed to seize further guns during a scuffle with a patrol that led to the first, albeit accidental, death of the November Revolution when a female bystander was accidentally pushed under a moving streetcar.[36] Despite this tragic loss of life, the procession continued through the city centre. Customers in the bars and cafés along the way shouted their support to the demonstrators. Thus fired up, they encountered some thirty to forty younger soldiers, mainly officer cadets, under the command of Reserve Lieutenant Oskar Steinhäuser. Together with his men, Steinhäuser had set up a road block in the city centre's Karlstrasse to prevent the crowd of unruly sailors from reaching their destination and freeing their detained comrades.

Earlier that day, the station commanders had been informed of the unfolding events in the city. Responding to the growing unrest,

Souchon ordered the last loyal units, mainly composed of officer cadets and recruits, to stop the procession of demonstrators with all means necessary and to make ruthless use of their weapons if required.[37] As the large crowd of protesters approached, the front being pushed forward by people in the back, Steinhäuser and his men nervously clutched their guns. Steinhäuser shouted at the demonstrating sailors, warning them that he had orders to shoot if the crowd used force against his men.[38]

What contributed to the further violent escalation of the situation cannot be reconstructed with absolute certainty. Presumably the marchers in the rear pushed those up front further towards Steinhäuser's road block, prompting him to order his men to open fire.[39] As the first rounds were fired into the crowd, some protesters returned fire. Steinhäuser himself was hit by several bullets, but was rescued from the angry sailors by local policemen who had come racing onto the scene and the Kiel fire brigade, which dispersed the crowd with water cannons. The incident left seven dead and twenty-nine wounded—two of whom would subsequently succumb to their injuries.[40]

The escalation of violence came as a shock to both sides involved. Yet Governor Souchon and the senior officers in Kiel continued to underestimate the extent of the problem confronting them.[41] They still assumed that they were primarily facing a revolt of those units that had been brought in from Wilhelmshaven while the majority of soldiers and sailors stationed in Kiel remained loyal. What drastically changed that mistaken perception was the sudden announcement on 4 November that the Kiel-based First Torpedo Division had joined the open rebellion. Up to this point, the mutiny had largely been carried out by the sailors from Wilhelmshaven and by the local, politically non-dominant Independent Socialists and the Revolutionary Shop Stewards sympathizing with the radical Left. Now, the revolution's base was broadening and it was only a matter of time before the rebellion would spread to other Kiel-based units and the dockyard workers (Figure 4.2). Worse still, the First Torpedo Division issued demands that went well beyond the release of detained sailors and an end to the war. Instead, their demands now included the abdication of the Hohenzollern dynasty and the introduction of universal suffrage for both men and women.[42] A further politicization of the demonstrations and a broadening of the protests to the shipyard workers and the U-boat divisions stationed in the same barracks would only be a matter of time.[43]

Figure 4.2 Kiel was both the birthplace and the heart of the revolution in early November 1918. This rebellious brigade of naval stokers displays its sympathies for the Bolshevik ideology so feared by the elites. In reality, most of the leaders of the revolution—including the Independent Social Democrats— were not uncritical of Lenin's revolution in Russia.

Shortly after midday, several senior officers in Kiel reported to Governor Souchon that they and the military police could no longer guarantee the maintenance of public order, thus forcing Souchon to meet with a delegation of mutineers already calling itself a 'soldiers' council'.[44] The councils were to become key institutions in the revolutionary process in November 1918, but their emergence and subsequent role deeply divided the German Left. Typically, councils were elected at mass gatherings of workers on strike or of sailors and soldiers defying orders. Originally invented in the Russian revolution of 1905, they had re-emerged in 1917 when the tsar was toppled, and their 'Russian origins' were part of how they were perceived. To their supporters, notably the Independent Social Democrats and the Spartacists, the councils were an undiluted form of grassroots political representation. By contrast, their opponents, including some leading figures within the MSPD, viewed the councils as agents of 'Bolshevism' that would spread chaos and economic upheaval in Germany. For those moderate Social Democrats who initially supported the councils, they were at best a temporary stop-gap on the way to a parliamentary democracy.

In early November 1918, the Kiel soldiers' council under the leadership of Karl Artelt primarily saw its role as conveying the key demands of the sailors to Governor Souchon, who had reluctantly agreed to meet with the sailors' delegates in an attempt to calm them down.[45] Yet despite offering some concessions, he failed in that endeavour and the city's workers' representatives—the so-called Revolutionary Shop Stewards—announced that a general strike in all Kiel factories would be held on 5 November.[46]

To avert a general strike, Souchon had no choice but to continue the negotiations with both sailors' and workers' representatives who repeated with greater urgency their demands for peace and democracy, as articulated by the First Torpedo Division two days earlier. When Souchon unwisely mentioned that he could always bring in troops from outside the city, he received an ultimatum: if external troops were brought into the city to quell the rebellion, the battleships in the harbour would start shelling the city's strategic points from the sea.[47]

This was undoubtedly a strong argument. As the journalist Bernhard Rausch observed on 5 November, the rebellious sailors in Kiel held all the cards. They now had some 40,000 heavily armed men with whom to defend the city, along with naval artillery as their strongest weapon. As Rausch noted, the city had suddenly entered 'an entirely transformed world. Above the German fleet, on top of the Kiel town hall, and on the castle tower flew the red flag of the revolution.'[48]

If nothing else, Souchon at least managed to win some time through his negotiations with the sailors' and shop stewards' delegations. His main objective at this point was to 'keep the excited masses at bay with negotiations until the arrival of Deputy Noske and State Secretary Haussmann'.[49] He could only achieve this by yielding to their earlier demands for the immediate release of those arrested stokers and sailors—sixteen in total—who had not committed any criminal acts. On their release from the detention facility in Feldstrasse later that day, they were enthusiastically greeted by several thousand sailors.[50]

With his options dwindling quickly, Souchon focused his hopes on the arrival of Haussmann and Noske on the evening of 4 November. Ironically, the sailors and striking workers, too, pinned their hopes on their arrival—after all, Haussmann was a leading liberal MP who had been one of the key drivers behind the Reichstag's 'Peace Revolution' of 1917 while Noske was the MSPD's spokesperson on military matters. They naturally assumed that Noske and his party would join in their efforts to revolutionize Germany. When the train from Berlin finally arrived in Kiel's main station, Noske in particular was 'welcomed with cheers by hundreds of rebellious sailors'.[51] A car brought Noske and Haussmann to the city's central Wilhelmplatz, where thousands of protesters were already awaiting them. The two deputies quickly realized that this was no simple mutiny. Noske gave a speech promising an amnesty for those involved in the mutiny. He also announced that an armistice would be signed within the next few days.[52]

Haussmann and Noske were subsequently driven to the Kiel trade union house, where some forty sailors' and workers' representatives were already discussing what would soon become known in all of Germany as the 'Kiel Points'. Among other things, their demands included the release of *all* detained sailors and political prisoners, complete freedom of speech and press and the end of censorship, the appropriate treatment of soldiers by their superiors, unrestricted personal freedom for every man from the end of one duty period to the beginning of the next, and the involvement of the soldiers' councils in all future decision-making processes.[53]

Essentially, the 'Kiel Points' followed the suggestions made by Lothar Popp, the USPD chairman in Kiel. Originally from a humble background in north-eastern Bavaria, Popp had earned himself a decent living before the war by opening and successfully running a number of sweetshops. A long-time member of the SPD and a pacifist, Popp had radicalized after the SPD's approval of the war credits in 1914 and became the leading USPD figure in Kiel during the January strikes of 1918. Now, in November 1918, it was Popp who played a key role in articulating the 'Kiel Points' that would become a model for many other revolutionary soldiers' and workers' councils in the following days.[54]

No decision on these demands was made in Kiel. Haussmann and Noske had travelled to Kiel without a clear political mandate by the Chancellor. Neither of them felt that they had any authority to make decisions regarding Germany's political future. And yet, Noske signalled his support for their demands.[55] In a high-level meeting with Governor Souchon and some sailors' representatives later that night, Noske also impressed on Souchon that no external troops should be brought into the city. He realized that the rebellion could by now count on the support of thousands of heavily armed sailors and soldiers, with the naval artillery on the dreadnoughts in Kiel harbour as their strongest weapon. He therefore pointed out that further bloodshed in Kiel was likely to lead to a nationwide strike, which should be prevented at all costs while armistice negotiations with the Allies were still ongoing.[56]

When Noske eventually managed to telephone the Reich Cabinet in Berlin, he reported that all naval discipline had broken down, that the mutineers were demanding an immediate armistice and the abdication of the Kaiser—and that they had elected him, Noske, as chairman of the city's workers' and soldiers' council. None of the Kiel revolutionaries imagined that, by electing Noske, who also assumed Souchon's office as Governor of Kiel the next day, they had chosen a leader who, in reality, intended 'to put an end to the mutiny, which I personally condemn in the extreme'. Instead, they regarded the man from Berlin as a powerful ally.[57]

For many contemporaries it seemed perfectly clear though that the hour of the revolution had struck. On the same evening, Prince Heinrich, Wilhelm II's brother and Inspector General of the Imperial Navy, fled from Kiel Castle. Well-informed observers could not help but grasp the significance of the events in Kiel for Germany as a whole. In Berlin, the historian Friedrich Meinecke noted in his diary: 'The dam has broken.'[58]

5

The revolution spreads

Any hopes that the mutiny at Kiel could be contained were quickly dashed. Within a few days, it became a full-blown revolution as it spread without serious resistance and reached other port cities along the German coast, from Bremen in the west, to the naval garrison of Tilsit on the Memel River in east Prussia. In the country's largest port, Hamburg, workers and sailors ceased work on 5 November. On the warships in Hamburg habour, the crews hoisted red flags—symbols of solidarity with the comrades in Kiel. Sailors and soldiers with red armbands patrolled the streets of Altona and St Pauli bearing guns.[1]

On 6 November, the future Chancellor of the Weimar Republic, Hermann Müller (MSPD), travelled by express train from Berlin to Kiel. The train was brought to a halt in the Hamburg workers' district of Rotenburgsort. The platform was full of armed sailors who were busy tearing off the officers' epaulets. Müller, who spent the night in Hamburg, heard heavy footsteps in the hotel corridor that evening, then loud knocking on all the doors. Sailors with red armbands inspected the guests' identification papers. Tired, Müller opened the door and handed his passport to one of the men, who studied the document closely before pointing out to him that it had already expired on 17 March 1918. Then, saluting with a smile on his face, he departed. Müller was astonished: 'Is it even imaginable that in another country, the night after the start of a revolution, a revolutionary would be concerned about a passport renewal?'[2]

Revolutionary unrest even reached Heligoland, a small fortified archipelago with imposing cliffs some 50 kilometres off the German north-western coast—an island that had once been a British colony before being handed over to Germany in 1890. On 6 November, soldiers and naval crews stationed here refused to obey orders from their officers. Marching through the streets, they eventually established a council which then took matters into its own hands while the red flag was raised over the island.[3]

The fact that the German Revolution originated in the peripheries—in naval bases and coastal towns—is one of the peculiarities that sets it apart from other major revolutions of the modern age, be it in France in 1789 or in Russia in 1917, where unrest started in the capital, the centre of power. In Germany in November 1918, by contrast, Berlin was the last major city to fall into the hands of the revolutionaries. Before the abdication of Kaiser Wilhelm II and the official proclamation of the republic on 9 November, the revolution unfolded in a highly regionalized way. This was partly due to the federal structure of Imperial Germany with its twenty-six constituent territories, most of them ruled by their own princes, kings, or dukes. In the first week of November, the revolutionary events in all these territories tended to follow the same pattern: they began with soldiers' and workers' protests which often self-radicalized within hours in response to poor crisis management by the authorities. The marines, military police, replacement units, and other local garrison forces placed in the path of the revolutionary tide by the imperial authorities proved unable or unwilling to stop the revolution. Instead of fighting, the soldiers of the Home Army hailed the mutineers as comrades and joined the revolution, as did large numbers of industrial workers.[4] Yet, the revolution in Germany was not a planned event—as had been the case in Russia when the Bolsheviks took power—but primarily a spontaneous anti-war movement that involved disparate actors, sentiments, and sites of action. Its hunger protesters, munitions strikers, and deserting soldiers never formed a singular force.[5]

Harry Graf Kessler, who was residing in Berlin at the time, ascertained the pattern of this highly regionalized revolution as early as 7 November when he noted in his diary: 'The physiognomy of the Revolution is becoming clearer: gradual appropriation [of power], [it spreads like] an oil stain through the mutinying sailors from the coast. They isolate Berlin which soon will remain an island [in the sea of revolution]. In contrast to France [in 1789] the provinces revolutionize the capital, the sea revolutionizes the land: Viking strategy.'[6]

On 7 November, the day that Kessler penned this prediction, the revolution indeed moved inland, and quickly reached the southern kingdom of Bavaria. As elsewhere war-weariness and a burning desire for peace had become widespread in this traditionally conservative and rural kingdom. And like the populations in other German states, Bavarians had suffered profoundly from the war and the loss of sons, brothers, and fathers. About 13,000 young men from Munich alone had died in the Great War. Across Bavaria, more than 170,000 had been killed, about 65 per cent of whom were between 20 and 29 years old.[7]

In late October, the already tense situation became even worse. The military collapse of Austria-Hungary made it necessary to dispatch Bavarian troops to Salzburg and the Tyrol in order to secure Bavaria's southern border.[8] This further agitated the already war-weary population. Protests and demonstrations for peace and democratic reforms became a daily occurrence. On 2 November 1918, the ageing Bavarian king, Ludwig III, approved a series of reforms that essentially mirrored the Reich's October reforms: the Bavarian government would now be dependent on a parliamentary majority, not on royal consent.[9] But here as elsewhere, it was too late for a 'revolution from above'. The following morning some 1,000 German sailors from the Austro-Hungarian port of Pola in Istria passed through Munich on their way to Kiel and Wilhelmshaven. The Bavarian authorities stopped the train, but that only made the situation worse. The disembarking sailors poured into the Bavarian capital and added further potential for unrest in Munich.[10]

It was in this situation that the Independent Social Democrats—with far fewer supporters than their more moderate cousins from the MSPD—landed a major coup. Together with the MSPD, the Independent Socialists called for a major peace demonstration on the Theresienwiese, a large open space in the city where the annual Oktoberfest had been held since the nineteenth century.[11] The events of 7 November were to become a turning point for future developments in Bavaria. An estimated 60,000 people attended the demonstration.[12] Several speakers, among them the head of the Bavarian MSPD, Erhard Auer, demanded peace and democracy, although Auer tellingly did not call for the introduction of workers' and soldiers' councils. Soon after his speech, Auer and most of the MSPD supporters departed, led by a musical corps. The Independent Socialists and their supporters stayed behind, and now listened to somewhat less moderate speakers demanding the immediate creation of a workers' and soldiers' council. The protesters also passed a radical resolution that demanded the immediate abdication of the Kaiser, the introduction of democracy and the dismissal of all 'reactionary elements' from the state bureaucracy, peace at any price, and an eight-hour working day.[13]

The key figure to capitalize on this situation and lead the revolution was the Independent Social Democrat Kurt Eisner. Despite being the leader of a relatively small political party, it was Eisner who would set the tone of the revolution in Bavaria over the coming weeks. A drama critic of the *Münchener Post*, Eisner seemed to fit the stereotype of a typical leftist intellectual who frequented the coffee houses in the Bohemian suburb of Schwabing. Yet he was not actually Bavarian. Eisner came from Berlin, where he was born into a middle-class Jewish family in 1867. After studying philosophy and German at university, he started to write for several newspapers, among them the liberal *Frankfurter Zeitung*, before joining the Social Democratic flagship publication *Vorwärts* in 1898. He was originally identified with the 'right-wing' fringe of the Social Democratic Party, losing his job with its local newspaper in the early 1900s because of his support for the 'revisionists' who wanted the Social Democrats to abandon their revolutionary, orthodox Marxism.[14]

Eisner had been a protégé of Karl Liebknecht's father Wilhelm, who had made him his successor as editor of *Vorwärts* in 1899. Yet he was dismissed in 1905, after falling out with his colleagues on the paper over his 'revisionist' take on Social Democracy, and moved to Bavaria, where he worked as a journalist, first in Nuremberg and then in Munich. The outbreak of the First World War prompted Eisner to reconsider his own political views, which became more radical as the war progressed. Although he initially supported the SPD's approval of the war credits in 1914—primarily because he hoped that the war would hasten the collapse of Russian despotism—his position changed in 1915 when he began to articulate strongly pacifist views. His deviation from the official party line led to clashes with the Social Democratic editor of the *Münchener Post*, as well as with the military censor's office. When he openly criticized Germany's 'offensive spirit' and annexationist ambitions, he was sacked from his job as a political journalist and only allowed to occasionally publish literature reviews.[15]

By the spring of 1917, Eisner had officially parted company with the Majority Social Democrats. In April that year, in the city of Gotha, Eisner participated in the founding conference of the Independent Social Democratic Party and subsequently became one of the key figures in the Munich branch of the party.[16] Together with other Independent

Socialists in the rest of Germany, he led calls for a general strike in the armament industry in January 1918.[17] His involvement in the January strikes led to his arrest and he spent the next eight and a half months in Stadelheim prison.[18] On 15 October he was suddenly released as part of a general amnesty for political prisoners and immediately threw himself into revolutionary activity again.[19]

On 3 November 1918, Eisner announced to some roughly 2,000 listeners that the constitutional reforms introduced in Bavaria the previous day were absolutely insufficient. Instead he demanded immediate peace—a Bavarian separate peace if necessary—and a people's government that would work closely with the democratic government that had just been established in neighbouring Austria: 'We greet, across the frontier, the new Austrian Republic. In the event that there is not sufficient political will or power in Berlin to bring about peace immediately, we demand that a Bavarian people's government must, together with the German republicans of Austria, declare peace in the name of Germany.'[20]

The large peace demonstration on 7 November only very superficially bridged the divide between the two Bavarian social democratic parties. Although united in their demand for immediate peace and political change, there remained significant differences as to what exactly the political future of Germany should look like. While the demonstration on Theresienwiese was still ongoing, Eisner, accompanied by a group of followers, proceeded to 'liberate' the military garrisons in the city, meeting with no resistance from the soldiers.

One of those supporting Eisner was the young socialist Hilde Kramer who had attended the large-scale peace demonstration on 7 November and felt energized by seeing red flags everywhere and people shouting 'Down with the war!', 'Long live peace!' and 'Long live the Republic!' 'I thought that's what a revolution looks like: masses of soldiers with partly unbuttoned uniform jackets and without their caps streaming through Dachauer Strasse. Them and countless civilians—men, women, and children…I became part of a swirling mass movement without knowing where the path would lead us.'[21]

By 9 p.m. that evening, all garrisons had signalled their support for the revolution and there were no troops left in the Bavarian capital that could be mobilized against the revolutionaries as they occupied the city's main train station, the central telegraph office, and the Bavarian parliament.[22] That same night, a workers' and soldiers' council elected

Figure 5.1 Soldiers celebrate on 8 November in front of the Mathäser brewery in Munich—the seat of the newly constituted Council of Workers and Soldiers, where, during the previous night, Kurt Eisner had proclaimed the republican Free State of Bavaria.

Eisner as its chairman. One of the revolutionaries in Munich, Felix Fechenbach, recalled the breathless speed of this political transformation: 'Lorries with guns and ammunition arrived. Soldiers and workers came, they were armed, assembled into small units, and sent off to occupy public buildings... At ten in the evening, all ministries, the general command, the railway station, as well as the post and telegraph office were in the hands of the revolutionaries. Then the workers' and soldiers' council, accompanied by sixty armed men, marched to the state parliament building, which was handed over without resistance.... All entrances were occupied by machine gunners, and the access road was also secured. At half past ten in the evening, Kurt Eisner opened the provisional constituent assembly of workers', soldiers' and peasants' councils.'[23] Eisner himself proclaimed Bavaria a republic, thus ending the 1,000-year rule of the House of Wittelbach, and established a provisional government, sanctioned by the councils and composed of both Majority and Independent Social Democrats, with Eisner at its head. Eisner had cleverly outmanoeuvred the much

Figure 5.2 Kurt Eisner on the way to a meeting with Friedrich Ebert. Eisner was the key figure in Bavaria's November Revolution. In spite of the relatively weak position of his Independent Social Democratic Party, he managed to prevail against Erhard Auer, the chairman of Bavaria's Majority Social Democrats, to become the leader of the Bavarian revolutionary movement.

larger Bavarian Majority Social Democrats whose chairman, Auer, came to serve as Interior Minister in Eisner's government.[24]

Contemporary responses to Eisner's coup varied, of course, depending on political affiliation. For many people on the political Left, participating in the revolution gave them a sense of being able to shape their own political future for the first time. The well-travelled and highly regarded poet Rainer Maria Rilke noted as much after attending a mass meeting of soldiers, workers, and intellectuals in a hotel ballroom in Munich on 7 November 1918. According to a letter to his wife Clara, he listened to speeches by the famous sociologist Max Weber, the anarchist Erich Mühsam, and a number of lesser-known activists for peace and revolution. At some stage, a young worker stood up and asked the speakers: 'Have you made the armistice offer yet?' He continued: 'We must do it, not the gentlemen at the top; let us occupy a telegraph station and there we will talk, our common people to the common people over there, and there will be peace immediately...'[25]

Rilke was clearly sympathetic to the enthusiasm of those who had gathered in the hotel that day, but not everyone shared that view. The conservative philosopher Oswald Spengler, best known later for his two-volume book *The Decline of the West* (1918 and 1922), seemed significantly less impressed by what he saw in Munich on 7 November 1918:

I experienced the disgusting scenes of 7 November first hand. . . . and almost choked with disgust. . . . I now see clearly that the German revolution has taken a typical course: a gradual destruction of the existing order, collapse, wild radicalism . . . We need punishment . . . until the time has come, as in 1813 and 1870, for that small group of people to act as leaders: Prussian noblemen and Prussian officials, the thousands of our technicians, academics, artisans, workers with Prussian instincts. . . . And then blood has to flow, the more the better.[26]

For now, however, Spengler's hour of reckoning had not come. The old order in Germany collapsed almost without resistance. Germany's twenty-two lesser kings, princes, and dukes were all deposed—it was an 'almost silent implosion' of the monarchical regime.[27] In Dresden, the capital of the kingdom of Saxony, soldiers demanding immediate peace led huge street demonstrations and took control of the city. The last Saxon king, Friedrich August III, ordered his troops not to fire on the protesters and voluntarily abdicated the throne which his family, the House of Wettin, had occupied since the fifteenth century.[28]

In Leipzig, events followed a similar pattern according to the first-hand account of the Australian music student Ethel Cooper, who had spent the war years in the city, unable to return home while the war was raging. In a letter to her sister, she wrote: 'On Tuesday and Wednesday, the other large port cities of Lübeck, Bremen and Hamburg followed this example—on Thursday, it reached Munich and, with it, all of Bavaria. On Friday, when I was on my way to lunch, I saw a dense, grey crowd of people with a red flag at their front heading towards me. I must say that I stood there as if rooted to the ground, my heart was beating in my throat. As you know, I have been expecting this for weeks, but when one sees it for the first time it takes one's breath away. . . . In the evening, the entire town was filled with posters and announcements that the "workers' and soldiers' council" had taken over the city government and that the military and civil authorities had submitted themselves to it. On Saturday morning (I have been living on the street recently) I saw the mayor raise a red flag above the city hall . . .'[29]

In Magdeburg, the situation was similar. A report by the local police president illustrated the swiftness of the revolutionary transformation and the utter powerlessness of the old authorities to control the situation:'This morning at 7.30, I was informed about the approach of a large number of artillerymen.... Their number—roughly 200—was too large for the police to stop them.... The local Social Democratic party leadership attempted to appease the people. They called for a public assembly on the Domplatz at 3 a.m. which was attended by 15,000 people.... The speakers reminded everyone to remain level-headed before a Workers and Soldiers Council was elected.'[30]

The medical doctor and writer Alfred Döblin, who would become world famous on the publication of his 1929 novel *Berlin Alexanderplatz*, witnessed the arrival of revolution in early November in a soldiers' hospital in the then German city of Strassburg, where he had been stationed since early 1917:[31]

Towards four o'clock in the afternoon, after rumours had already been circulating, one suddenly hears music coming from the enormous barracks and a gigantic horde of soldiers, a sergeant at their head, moves up the street. The men are smoking and moving in dissolved formations, their hands in their pockets, without weapons, following a wildly swung red flag. They congregate tumultuously around the barracks gates, the guards grin and let them through; they march from barracks to barracks, the procession becomes longer and longer, jeering, yelling, soon joined by civilians and prisoners freed from the arrest cells.... A peculiar restlessness and tension fills the town. People surge into the streets, everything is packed with soldiers wearing red ribbons... The barracks yards have released their human masses, raw young badgers, cripples from the convalescent companies, old home guardsmen.[32]

Unlike many other soldiers, who deserted in the first week of November, Döblin remained in post and, within the confined world of his hospital, witnessed the inversion of military hierarchies that was to become one of the hallmarks of the revolution: 'Here, in this now empty house, the bigwigs—the inspector general or the surgeon general—had ruled until recently, decorated with titles and medals; everyone shivered in their presence as they inspected every inch, the sergeant running behind them with a book, in which every detail was noted—every carelessness in dress, in the making of the beds, in the painting of the slateboards.' Now the situation was very different indeed: on a nearby square—'that beautiful, broad, old square with shingle-roofed houses'—Döblin encountered 'excited civilians' and 'masses of unorganized soldiers with red cockades. The light flashes; a babble of voices.... officers—the dethroned—are standing in the midst of it all, without epaulets, in wary groups like lambs in the wolf pack; they have been made to wear red cockades, the designated victims.'[33]

As the revolution unfolded in Alsace, rumours about its national and international impact dominated the conversations of soldiers, officers, and civilians alike. Some suggested that the Kaiser had already abdicated, that Belgian and French troops at the front had fraternized with the German 'red soldiers', and that the British fleet was also sailing under the red flag. More sober minds did not engage in this kind of fanciful thinking, Döblin noted: 'Only Professor E., whom I met on the way to the train, . . . smiles and holds up his hand defensively: "A victorious army doesn't engage in revolution." '[34]

The situation was not fundamentally different in the eastern territories controlled by Germany, which had expanded significantly after the Treaty of Brest-Litovsk. Here, too, Germans serving in the armed forces reacted to the 1918 revolution in a wide variety of ways. Perhaps the most detailed account we have of an individual's response to the events there is from the diaries of Victor Klemperer. Later of international repute when the diaries of his life as a Jew in Nazi Germany were published, Klemperer worked at the time of the November Revolution as a censor of books and newspapers on the Eastern front, after serving in the artillery on the Western front and being transferred to the East in 1916 because of persistent dermatological problems.[35]

Before the war, Klemperer had worked as a freelance journalist until he decided to return to academia and the world of German and French literature. Klemperer started his academic career at the University of Naples, from where he observed the deterioration of the international situation before 1914 with concern. He supported the German declaration of war in 1914 and considered the German cause a just one. He returned to Germany and joined up, first serving on the Western front until his 1916 transfer to the press and censorship office of the Supreme Commander of the German Forces in the East (OberOst), Prince Leopold von Bayern. Based in the formerly Russian fortress city of Kaunas (Kowno) in today's Lithuania, Klemperer remained there until the end of the war. The city had fallen into German hands in 1915 during the retreat of Russian forces that year and remained so until the end of the war, when it became part of the newly independent Lithuania. From 1917 onwards, Klemperer worked in the same office as Maximilian Müller-Jabusch, who was to become one of the leading liberal journalists of the Weimar Republic, and Arnold Zweig, whose pacifist novels about the Great War, *Der Streit um den Sergeanten Grischa* (1927) and *Erziehung vor Verdun* (1935), were to make him famous in Germany.

On Friday, 8 November 1918, the revolution suddenly entered Klemperer's otherwise uneventful routine. When he came to work that morning, there were office rumours—'true? exaggerated? altogether imagined?'—about 'bloody upheavals in Germany. The fleet is flying the red flag, Wilhelmshaven, Kiel and the entire coast is in the hands of mutinous sailors. . . . Everyone has a home town, a relative, to worry about', Klemperer added. 'I do not need to emphasize how worried I was myself: Leipzig was a hotbed of radicals, who knew how much shooting was going on there? We also discussed what might happen when the revolution reached Wilna. "First they will come after the officers", [Arnold] Zweig believed. "No, after the female support staff" said Müller-Jabusch, "they are even more hated." And he added in all seriousness: "They will all be raped." '[36]

Klemperer's first real contact with the revolution came in the unlikely form of a German military plane that crashed near his office. Rushing to the crash site, he saw 'the aeroplane, with a crumpled fuselage and broken wings. . . . From many metres away one could see the gleaming red of a long and wide flag that had been wrapped around the gondola, the way one drapes a wreath ribbon around a coffin . . . Before the aeroplane stood a man with mounted bayonet, a very dapperly dressed young man in a fur coat . . . The image stayed with me: the shattered aeroplane, the red ribbon, the young, excitedly talking soldier, his flashing bayonet, his fur coat. So that was the revolution . . .'[37]

As elsewhere, the revolution in Kaunas was mainly peaceful. Even the Chief of Staff of the German troops in the East, Max Hoffmann, admitted as much: 'The revolution has generally happened very quietly here. Soldiers' councils are being founded everywhere, and they strangely have one fear only: that we, the senior officers want to depart. How they came up with this idea is a riddle to me, I myself have never even dreamt of it. On the contrary, we must use all our strength to bring the Eastern armies home in an orderly manner. We are now beginning with the evacuation. I feel sorry for those people whose territory we are thereby handing to the Bolsheviks, but I cannot hold back our men—they want to go home.'[38]

Yet, fears of 'the Russians' or 'Russian conditions' quickly gave way to fears of Polish insurgents trying to attack the defeated Germans in an attempt to secure the city for themselves. 'A home guardsman, seemingly an older worker, told me that the Poles might attack us, but only out of fear of the revolution. They could only imagine a revolution to be Russian-style, with murder and robbery. Once they have grasped that our German revolution is occurring without bloodshed and without plunder, they would certainly keep the peace.'[39]

On 8 November, the day Klemperer witnessed the plane crash in Kaunas, the 'oil patch' of revolution spread further. That very day, a military situation report prepared for Chancellor Max von Baden described the revolution's gradual expansion: '5pm: Halle and Leipzig red. Evening: Düsseldorf, Haltern, Osnabrück, Lüneburg red; Magdeburg, Stuttgart, Oldenburg, Braunschweig, Cologne red.'[40]

By the morning of 9 November, the King of Prussia and Emperor of Germany, Wilhelm II, was one of the last crowned heads to remain on his throne (the other being Wilhelm of Wurttemberg).[41] Berlin, the political centre, was the last major city to resist the revolution. A strange sense of calm appeared to dominate the German capital. As Käthe Kollwitz noted in her diary on that day: 'Was on Unter den Linden this morning. No special occurrences.'[42] Friedrich Meinecke and his wife Antonie attended a Beethoven concert that evening and also felt the eerie, prescient feeling of the calm before the storm: 'It was curiously quiet on the squares and streets as we walked home. My feeling was: we have just listened to the final tunes of a better, now collapsing world.'[43]

The only person who appeared to be oblivious to the approaching end of the monarchy in Germany was the Kaiser himself. Against Chancellor von Baden's expressed wishes, Wilhelm had left Berlin and removed himself and his main entourage to the OHL's military field headquarters in the Belgian town of Spa on 29 October, shortly after the constitutional reforms—'the revolution from above'—had stripped him of much of his power.[44] The Kaiser flatly refused even to contemplate abdication, despite much discussion in Berlin about Woodrow Wilson's third note of 23 October which at least implicitly demanded Wilhelm's abdication as a precondition of peace.[45] In the presence of his generals and well away from the revolutionary turmoil, Wilhelm hoped to be better able to resist the mounting pressures.[46]

While he temporarily avoided a direct confrontation with the government, Wilhelm simultaneously restricted his own freedom of action. In Spa, the Kaiser had only three options left for responding to the imminent end of the war and the resulting consequences: the staging of a 'heroic' death in a daring front-line operation (which might have saved his reputation, or at least that of the Hohenzollern dynasty in the eyes of German monarchists); a march on Berlin at the helm of loyal troops in an attempt to put down the revolution; or a complete withdrawal from all responsibilities by escaping to a neutral country.[47]

In the meantime, the Reich Chancellor had already attempted to contact the Kaiser by telephone and telegram in order to persuade him to return to Berlin. In view of the impending negotations for an armistice, he felt that the Kaiser's absence from Berlin was unhelpful.[48] Like a large portion of the German population, von Baden was now convinced that Wilhelm's abdication had become inevitable in the context of the armistice negotiations with the Entente.[49] Yet as a fellow aristocrat, he still entertained considerable scruples about demanding an abdication from his Kaiser. So instead he ordered the Prussian Interior Minister, Bill Drews, to confront Wilhelm with the unavoidable. On 1 November, Drews dutifully travelled to Spa. Wilhelm, however, rejected any notion of renouncing his throne, and was backed in this stance by some of his senior generals. Instead, he told Drews to convey the following message to the Reich Chancellor: 'I will not abdicate. It would be irreconcilable with the duties that I have as Prussian king and successor to Frederick the Great before God, the people and my conscience. I cannot and may not leave my post at the most dangerous moment. My abdication would be the beginning of the end of all German monarchies.... But above all, my duty as supreme commander demands that I do not now abandon the army. The army is engaged in a heroic struggle against the enemy. Its inner cohesion depends on its supreme commander. If he should leave, the army would collapse and the enemy would break through into the homeland unhindered.'[50]

Instead of giving in to demands for his abdication, Wilhelm, surrounded by his generals, sought to re-establish a semblance of normality. On 3 November 1918, the first day of the High Seas Fleet mutiny, Wilhelm II left the Field Army Headquarters on a previously planned visit to the front. The events in Kiel did not seem to overly concern him. Instead, he openly threatened the revolutionaries with a violent response by 'writing my answer [to them] on the pavement with machine guns. Even if I need to shoot my own castle into pieces, there must be order...I have no intention to leave my throne just because of a few hundred Jews and a thousand workers.'[51]

The trip west toward the front line offered him some form of relief from the stress of previous days. As Colonel Alfred Niemann, the OHL liaison officer to the Kaiser's court, noted, Wilhelm wanted to escape the 'poisonous atmosphere that threatens to kill every healthy feeling in the homeland. Out at the front, the breeze of noble patriotism will free the soul.'[52] The Kaiser and his entourage travelled west, first by Wilhelm's personal train, and then by automobile convoy. In the course of a busy day, Wilhelm visited front-line troops in the rest areas of fourteen different divisions. At every location, the Kaiser spoke with the soldiers and officers and took pleasure in handing out large numbers of Iron Crosses. At one point, the ceremonies were interrupted by approaching enemy aircraft and the loud roar of anti-aircraft weapons. The monarch made a show of indifference, continuing to talk to soldiers about home and relatives. When the attack passed, Wilhelm turned to the men and said: 'May you feel how gladly I share every privation and danger with you!' Clearly the field visit had a rejuvenating effect on him, and when he returned to Spa, the Kaiser reported to those that had stayed behind that his reception at the front had been enthusiastic.[53]

On the afternoon of 6 November, Max von Baden decided to travel to Spa himself and to convince the Kaiser of the inevitability of his 'voluntary' abdication.[54] However, the Chancellor was forced to cancel his travel plans as the political situation in Germany was growing increasingly tense on 7 November. That morning, the Social Democratic government members under Scheidemann's leadership informed the Chancellor that they would leave the government and lead the revolution if Wilhelm had not abdicated by noon of the following day. This ultimatum was reiterated in writing that afternoon. Yet Wilhelm remained stubbornly committed to staying put. Even when the Bavarian monarchy ceased to exist after the revolution reached Munich on 7 November, and the MSPD leadership threatened to withdraw from the government, the Kaiser did not relent. He still relied on his support among the troops. As late as 8 November, Wilhelm announced his determination to march on Berlin with reliable front-line troops to put down the revolution.[55]

The problem with the Kaiser's plan was that it was built on sand. This became apparent to General Groener when he returned to Spa on 7 November, after a brief two-day trip to Berlin. Observing the situation in all parts of Germany, Groener began to doubt that the revolutionary tide could be stopped. As for putting loyal troops in the path of the revolutionaries, the elite combat formations needed for such an operation were currently committed to the bitter defensive fighting at the front.[56] Besides, any troops dispatched to Berlin potentially had to march across 600 kilometres of territory between the German border and the capital, territory that was now firmly in the hands of revolutionaries.

In order to avoid the unpleasant task of breaking the news to the Kaiser himself, Groener came up with an unconventional idea: the field commanders were to convince Wilhelm that he could no longer rely on the army's loyalty. On 8 November, some fifty mid-level front-line commanders of the ten German armies closest to Spa were summoned to the field headquarters for a meeting the following morning. Thirty-nine of them arrived on the morning of 9 November. One of them, a regimental commander named Major Hünicken, recalled in detail how he travelled to Spa in terrible weather conditions, unsure what the purpose of the meeting might be.[57]

According to Hünicken, he and his fellow front-line officers were welcomed by Colonel Heye of the OHL's operations staff: 'On behalf of the Field Marshal [Hindenburg] allow me to welcome you here. The Field Marshal wanted to greet you himself, but is momentarily unavailable since he is with His Majesty in an extremely important, urgent meeting.' Heye went on to emphasize the gravity of the situation to the officers present. Unrest had broken out in the homeland. There were urgent demands for peace at any price. Deserters in the army's rear areas had seized several key rail junctions, threatening to cut off the army's supply lines. Heye went on to tell them they would each, in turn, be asked two questions regarding the mood of their troops. First: 'How do the troops feel toward the Kaiser? Will it be possible for the Kaiser to lead the troops in battle to recapture the homeland?' And second: 'How do the troops stand on Bolshevism? Will they take up arms to combat Bolshevism in their homeland?'[58]

Before the assembled officers could answer the questions, Hindenburg entered the room, greeted the assembled officers, and offered a bleak assessment of the military situation at the front and the escalating revolution at home. The Kaiser, he said, wanted to turn the army around and march on Berlin.[59] The officers in the room were stunned. They had not received word about the revolution back in Germany and responded with a mixture of anger and despair.[60]

THE REVOLUTION SPREADS 105

With little time to digest the news, the officers were now asked one by one to answer Heye's two questions. To question one, on attitudes toward the Kaiser, only one officer believed that his men would follow their Supreme Warlord against the revolutionaries. Fifteen recorded that their loyalty was doubtful; twenty-one rejected the idea outright. To question two, on the troops' attitude towards Bolshevism, eight ruled out the possibility of employing their men against the Bolsheviks. Twelve believed that such an operation was only possible after an extensive period of rest and training for civil war. Nineteen doubted that their soldiers would be willing to fight against the Bolsheviks under any circumstances.[61]

Colonel Heye summarized the officers' positions as follows:

In general, the participants stated that the troops had nothing against their Kaiser, that they were actually indifferent toward him, that they had only one desire, namely to go home as soon as possible, to peace and order.... The troops are totally exhausted and fought out, they want to return to their homeland and want nothing but peace there; only if their own hearth and home, wives and children were threatened by the Bolsheviks would the men at the front take up arms against their compatriots at home.[62]

Together with Hindenburg, Groener confronted Wilhelm with the results of this 'survey' in the garden hall of his quarters. Groener broke the news that a counter-revolutionary operation was out of the question as the front-line troops could not be relied on. 'Events have overcome us', he told the Kaiser and his stunned entourage. The Kaiser questioned the basis of this assessment and insisted that after four years of fighting, he would lead the army in good order back into the homeland. Groener replied: 'The army will march home in good order under its generals, but not under the leadership of Your Majesty.' In his memoirs, Groener vividly recalled that moment—not least because as First Quartermaster General he had uttered a 'monstrosity' to his supreme commander. Even years later he was stunned that he had not been shot on the spot by someone in the Kaiser's entourage in response to his statement.[63] Fortunately for Groener, Hindenburg seconded him by arguing that neither he nor Groener could be held responsible for the army's lack of reliability. While Wilhelm was still digesting the devastating result of the officers' poll, further bad news for him arrived from the German capital.

6

Showdown in Berlin

In the lead-up to 9 November 1918, far-reaching measures had been taken in Berlin to prevent unrest from spilling over into the Reich capital. The Military Governor of Berlin, General Alexander von Linsingen, had ordered the arrest of some 300 sailors who had congregated at Lehrter Train Station in Berlin on 7 November.[1] Moreover, all railway connections between Berlin and the major junctions in Hanover and Hamburg had been cancelled to prevent an influx of revolutionary troops. Von Linsingen also reinforced the police presence on Berlin's streets and secured all roads leading to the city centre and the royal palace with military posts. In order to suppress any potential revolutionary activity in the capital, an additional three fusilier battalions regarded as particularly loyal to the Kaiser were deployed to Berlin, notably the Lübbener and Naumburger Riflemen. General von Linsingen and senior figures in the German War Ministry were also confident to the point of self-delusion that other units already stationed in Berlin would gladly support the Kaiser against any revolutionary onslaught. As late as 7 November, the deputy Minister of War assured the capital's mayor: 'Berlin will hold, you can rely on that. The troops stationed here are loyal, and additional unconditionally reliable men are arriving from the outside every hour.'[2]

Whatever the merits of such an assessment, the arrival of large numbers of combat troops on the streets of Berlin certainly did not fail to make an impression on the key organizers of the planned strikes and demonstrations in Berlin. As Richard Müller, the chairman of the Berlin Revolutionary Shop Stewards, noted nervously: 'On the evening of 8 November I was standing at Hallesches Tor. Heavily armed infantry columns, machine gun companies and light artillery passed by me in an endless procession.... The human material looked quite audacious.

They had been deployed in the East to crush the Russian workers and peasants, and in Finland, with success. There was no doubt about the intention to drown the revolution in the blood of the people.... Now, that the decisive hour was fast approaching, a nightmarish feeling gripped me, a great fear for my comrades...'[3]

Yet von Linsingen's preparations for preventing any revolutionary activities in Berlin were not as seamless as he himself assumed or the arrival of combat troops in the capital suggested. The interruption of rail traffic between Berlin and other cities in the Reich did not only prevent revolutionary soldiers from reaching Berlin. It also hindered hundreds of soldiers on leave from departing from Berlin. Already impatient, these men were further aggravated by not being provided with either pay, food, or accommodation.[4] In an already tense situation for the central government, General von Linsingen also added fuel to the kindling flames by preventing any meetings of potentially revolutionary groups. On 7 November, von Linsingen had ordered the Berlin police president to ban five USPD assemblies from commemorating the anniversary of the Russian Revolution. He also prohibited the formation of any workers' and soldiers' councils in the capital: 'In certain circles, there is an intention to form workers' and soldiers' councils on the basis of the Russian model, in violation of legal regulations. Such institutions are inconsistent with the current system of government and threaten public safety. On the basis of Section 9b of the law on the state of siege, I prohibit the formation of any such associations and any participation therein.'[5]

Meanwhile, the MSPD leadership under Ebert and Scheidemann was increasingly under pressure to act. Their members demanded decisive action on the abdication question so as to avoid a situation in which only the more radical USPD and the Spartacus League were seen to be agitating for an end to the Kaiser's rule. The MSPD party executive and its Reichstag parliamentary group thus responded to the state's clampdown with an ultimatum to the Chancellor. As Scheidemann told the war cabinet on the evening of 7 November, the MSPD would withdraw its support for the government unless the Kaiser and the Crown Prince had abdicated by noon the following day. Furthermore, both military and police were to be instructed to act with particular restraint so as not to further escalate the already tense situation in the capital. Finally, Scheidemann demanded more influence in the Reich government for his party.[6]

Max von Baden, who was not present at the cabinet meeting but was informed immediately, appears to have been surprised by these demands. After all, he and Ebert had agreed only a few hours earlier that they both wished to avoid anything that resembled a 'social revolution'. What is most likely to have changed Ebert's mind was the mounting pressure from the streets, the far Left, and his own party to act decisively.[7] In any case, the Chancellor responded by holding out the prospect of his own immediate resignation—a move that did not fail to make an impact. Scheidemann withdrew the tight deadline for his central demand—the abdication of the Kaiser. Instead, he proposed that Wilhelm be informed about the ultimatum as soon as possible but that neither the MSPD nor the Chancellor was to make any rash decisions until the armistice was concluded.[8] Scheidemann further passed on a message from Ebert to the central government's cabinet members, a message which made clear how torn the MSPD leadership was between its contradictory objectives of preventing an open social revolution and keeping the support of its party members. According to Ebert 'our demands have had an extraordinarily calming effect on the workers. They have promised not to undertake anything until a decision has been made. You, gentlemen, and the Reich Chancellor, must appreciate that we have done what we could to keep the masses in line.'[9]

That this assessment was strangely out of touch with the reality on the ground became clear that evening. The pressure on the MSPD leadership kept mounting because Wilhelm had still not abdicated by the evening of 8 November and the armistice negotiations were still ongoing and unresolved. Although Ebert and Scheidemann could point to a number of concessions they had extracted from the Baden government—notably the imminent introduction of equal, general voting rights in Prussia, a greater influence of the MSPD in the Prussian and Reich governments, and an immediate end to conscription to the military—these remarkable reforms were overshadowed in the public perception by the urgent demands for peace and an end of the monarchy. While the MSPD leadership once more asked party members for their patience—'only for a few hours' as the *Vorwärts* put it on the morning of 9 November—that patience was wearing thin.[10]

At this point, the MSPD leadership was no longer in control of the situation on the streets where mass demonstrations were pushing for fundamental political changes. While the MSPD was still hoping to 'manage' the revolution, the USPD and the Revolutionary Shop

Stewards, who had played a central role in the January strikes of 1918, were pushing for more decisive action. They had been discussing a suitable date for mass demonstrations on the streets of Berlin for some time when, on 8 November, news broke about the arrest of Ernst Däumig, the co-chairman of the USPD. There were also rumours circulating about the imminent arrest of Karl Liebknecht. Däumig had been on his way to a meeting with senior figures of the Revolutionary Shop Stewards when the police arrested him. As he was carrying detailed material on the planned demonstrations and strikes, the far Left felt that they had to act immediately if there was to be any prospect of success.[11]

Only a few hours later, their supporters started printing hand-outs to be distributed in factories and barracks the following morning (Figure 6.1).[12] 'Workers, soldiers, comrades! The hour of decision has arrived! Now we must live up to the historic task ahead of us. While all along the German coast, the workers' and soldiers' councils have taken over power, ruthless arrests are occurring in the capital. Däumig and

Figure 6.1 Political leaflets proved the most effective way of disseminating the latest political news, alongside the daily newspapers, which sometimes went through several editions in a day. It was a great spectacle for the children of Berlin to see the revolutionary soldiers distribute these leaflets to the population.

Liebknecht have been arrested. That is the start of a military dictatorship, that is the beginning of useless slaughter. We do not demand the abdication of one person, we demand a republic! The Socialist Republic with all its consequences. Let us fight for peace, freedom and bread! <u>Come out of the factories! Come out of the barracks! Take each other by the hand! Long live the Socialist Republic!</u>'[13]

A second leaflet, signed by (the clearly not arrested) Liebknecht and the 'Group »International« (Spartakus League)', was distributed at the same time:

Now that the hour for action has arrived, there can be no going back. The same 'socialists' who for four years have performed pimping services for the government, and who in the past few weeks have been putting you off... with parliamentarization and other rubbish, are now trying everything to weaken the revolution by appeasing the movement. Workers and soldiers: what your comrades in Kiel, Hamburg, Bremen, Lübeck, Rostock, Flensburg, Hanover, Magdeburg, Brunswick, Munich, and Stuttgart have achieved, you must achieve as well. Because from what you are struggling for, from the toughness and the success of your struggle, depends also the success of the proletariat in all the world.

Liebknecht also explicitly called for 'a takeover of government by the representatives of the workers' and the establishment of 'immediate connections with the international proletariat, notably with the Russian republic of workers'.[14]

During the night, the conspirators made organizational preparations for the printing and distribution of leaflets outside the plant gates. At the same time, hoarded weapons were brought to a number of distribution points. The strike the following morning was to be as comprehensive as possible. During their breakfast break, the strikers were to leave their plants and factories, and, together with armed workers' units, march into the government district in the city centre from all directions.[15] Cläre Derfert-Casper, the only woman in the leading circle of the Revolutionary Shop Stewards, experienced the morning of 9 November as a well-planned and comradely event:

When, in the early hours of 9 November, I visited our friend Arthur Schöttler, I woke him with the words: 'Get up, Arthur, today's the day of the Revolution!' He thought he was dreaming. Only when I shook him again, he tore his eyes open and said: 'Blimey, Cläre, is it you?' He quickly jumped into his trousers and after ten minutes we left the house. In time for the morning shift, we were both standing in front of the weapons plant [in Berlin-Charlottenburg] and distributing our leaflets, in which the workers were called upon to walk out of the plants at 9 am. Once we had completed our task around 7 am, we went into a pub in Erasmusstrasse. We were happy to warm ourselves up a little. There we helped our comrades unpacking the revolvers and inserting the cartridges into the magazines.... Finally, all the guns had been distributed, and the protest march began. In front were the armed men, then the unarmed ones, and then the women.[16]

Derfert-Casper's recollection is borne out by other contemporary accounts: in the morning hours of 9 November the workers of all major factories in Berlin embarked on a general strike, although the weapons factories had been the primary focus of the mobilization efforts of the Revolutionary Shop Stewards.[17] Like other observers, Richard Müller recalled how, at first, a deceptive calm and semblance of normality prevailed, before the strike and demonstrations were unleashed:

When the gloomy November day broke, there was nothing to distinguish it from other days. The means of transport were entirely in operation, and the masses of workers flowed into the factories, offices and business premises as usual. The philistine could quietly enjoy his regular morning coffee. A revolutionary atmosphere was nowhere visible. But things became lively after the breakfast break. The factories emptied at an unbelievably fast pace. The streets filled with huge masses of people. On the city's periphery, where the largest factories are located, great protest marches assembled, flowing into the centre of the city. That this was not a peaceful demonstration became evident from the numerous pistols, guns and hand grenades that were visible everywhere.[18]

From the outer districts, long protest columns moved towards the government quarter around Wilhelmstrasse, as the factory owner Oskar Münsterberg described in his diary: 'As I ... walk down Wilhelmstrasse, I see black rows of people ... An animated mass scene. Cars sporting red flags are racing by. Soldiers and civilians with and without guns are sticking to the insides and outsides of the automobiles like bees, and shout: "Long live the republic".'[19]

At long last, the MSPD leadership was forced to abandon its moderate stance. If Ebert and Scheidemann did not want to lose all remaining influence over their supporters with the USPD and the Revolutionary Shop Stewards, they had to send out more decisive signals to their followers. In a meeting with the MSPD's factory liaisons that morning, the Berlin party leader Otto Wels announced that the MSPD would back a general strike, thus trying to regain at least some of the political initiative. Wels called upon all workers to engage in the 'decisive battle under the old common banner' of Social Democracy.[20] Shortly thereafter, Scheidemann declared his resignation from the Baden government. Abandoning the compromise it had struck with the Chancellor only the previous day, the MSPD leadership now firmly placed itself at the head of the revolutionary movement. Contact was established with senior USPD politicians to discuss the possibility of forming a joint government as soon as the Kaiser had abdicated and von Baden had resigned. As Ebert, Scheidemann, and Otto Braun told Georg Ledebour and Wilhelm Dittmann (USPD/Revolutionary Stewards) in separate meetings in the Reichstag building that morning, the MSPD was backing the strike and would call on its members to stage an uprising if Wilhelm had not abdicated by noon that day. Ledebour stated that he would first have to confer with his party colleagues while Dittmann immediately agreed to a common government.[21]

A significant prerequisite for the success of the uprising in Berlin was the ability of the revolutionaries to bring the troops stationed in the capital on their side. A key role in this was played by the Naumburg Rifle Battalion, which all contemporary reports had described as 'absolutely' loyal to the Kaiser. As the philosophy professor Ernst Troeltsch noted only two days before the revolution arrived in Berlin: '. . . all houses on Unter den Linden are occupied by the military, including the Naumburg Riflemen, whom their officers judge to be particularly loyal to the king . . . Matters look serious enough now, but we have no doubt about the success of the Riflemen.'[22]

Now, only two days later, the MSPD party executive was stunned when a delegation from the Naumburg Riflemen arrived in the Reichstag to request that a member of the executive should come to their barracks to explain the political situation.[23] The battalion had experienced acts of insubordination the previous night when the soldiers had been put on high alert and given large quantities of ammunition and hand grenades. Otto Wels immediately followed up on the request and raced to the Alexander Barracks near the Kupfergraben, where the Naumburger were quartered. Unhindered by their officers, he managed to appeal to the assembled soldiers to side with the revolution:[24] 'Now it is up to you to put an end to the bloodletting out there. But you must also decide whether you wish to raise your weapons against your fellow countrymen [*Volksgenossen*]. I do not ask to which party you belong. If you want the German people to decide its own fate in the future, then place yourself at the disposal of the Social

Democratic Party today. Affirm this by shouting: Long live peace! Long live the free German People's State!'[25]

Elsewhere, too, the revolutionaries quickly convinced soldiers in their barracks to join the revolution. As the worker Paul Mau recalled: 'When the demonstrators passed by the barracks, the guards peacefully let us go in. They knew what was at stake. Our destination was the police headquarters, which we were to occupy. Some of the blues [policemen] we encountered on our way probably did not agree with what was happening, but the majority of them had grasped the situation quickly. They undid their police belts, threw their sabres and revolvers onto a heap and declared that for them, this business is finished.'[26]

To be sure, the events of 9 November were not everywhere peaceful and occasional resistance was encountered. Shortly before noon, an officer shot three 'agitating' workers in front of the barracks in Chauseestrasse.[27] There was also an exchange of fire when the revolutionaries stormed the city's main police station on Alexanderplatz.[28] Generally speaking, however, the revolution in Berlin was remarkably peaceful and successful, as Cläre Casper-Derfert observed:

Without encountering any resistance, our group marched along Kaiserin-Augusta-Allee to the Palace Bridge. The guards in the police station were disarmed, the gasworks, the factories, the military hospital and the palace guardhouse, the Charlottenburg town hall and the Technical University were occupied without firing a shot. Our column of protesters had long since counted thousands of people and ended at the Reichstag toward noon, where we came together with other groups of protesters...comrades and friends. There were joyful embraces and jubilation among those who saw each other again for the first time after months of anxiety, fear and labour.[29]

Just before 11 a.m. on 9 November, Chancellor von Baden telephoned the military field headquarters in Spa to inform the Kaiser that the revolution might triumph in a matter of minutes not hours, as police battalions in the capital were defecting to the revolutionaries. The Kaiser mentioned the possibility of abdicating as Kaiser (though not as King of Prussia) for the first time.[30] A few minutes later, a second telephone call connected to Berlin. Baden was informed that 'the Kaiser has resolved on abdication; you will receive the declaration which is being formulated within half-an-hour's time'. Von Baden dutifully waited out the thirty minutes but no further phone call came in. He repeatedly but unsuccessfully tried to contact Spa again.[31]

Around noon, with tens of thousands of people out on the streets of Berlin demonstrating for the establishment of a republic, Baden decided to act unilaterally. Without Wilhelm's consent or knowledge, he released a short communiqué through Germany's semi-official news agency, Wolff's Telegraphisches Bureau (WTB), announcing the end of the Kaiser's reign: 'The Kaiser and King has decided to renounce the throne. The Reich Chancellor will remain in office until the issues connected with the Kaiser's abdication, the renunciation of the throne by the Crown Prince of the German Empire and of Prussia, and the installation of the Regency have been settled. He intends to propose to the Regent that Mr Ebert be appointed Reich Chancellor and a bill be drafted for the holding of immediate general elections for a German National Constituent Assembly which would have the task of giving final form to the future constitution of the German people...'[32]

News of the abdication spread fast, both in Germany and abroad. From Leipzig, the music student Ethel Cooper wrote to her sister Emmie in Australia: 'the Kaiser had abdicated. It was as if a great weight had been lifted from everyone's shoulders. One could only hear one commentary: "Thank God—finally!"...One can only admire the perfect order and discipline with which these enormous revolutionary changes have been carried out so far.'[33]

Of course, not everyone was filled with undivided joy. Shortly after the abdication, Harry Graf Kessler noted thoughtfully: 'At the corner of Königgrätzer and Schöneberger Strasse they were selling special editions: "Abdication of the Kaiser". It gripped my throat, this way the House of Hohenzollern ended; so pitiful, so incidental, not even the centre of events.'[34]

Only thirty-five minutes after the abdication notice had been published, von Baden received a visit from Friedrich Ebert and an MSPD-delegation in the Chancellery buildings. Ebert demanded Baden hand over government responsibility immediately and insisted that this was the only way unnecessary bloodshed could be avoided. Ebert also told von Baden that discussions were already being conducted with the USPD regarding their possible participation in government. Ebert did not reject the participation of bourgeois politicians in government provided that the MSPD supplied the majority of ministers. Responding to von Baden's question as to whether the MSPD and the USPD were in a position to prevent violence, Scheidemann responded that all troops within Berlin had already gone over to the SPD.[35]

Figure 6.2 The sailors of the German High Seas Fleet in Wilhelmshaven celebrated the Kaiser's abdication with a giant fireworks display using their stored munitions.

At around 12.30 p.m., the Military Governor of Berlin, Alexander von Linsingen, had informed the Prussian Minister of War, Heinrich Schëuch, that soldiers' councils were being formed in most of the units under his command. It could no longer be assumed that they would follow orders to shoot at demonstrators, if required.[36] Schëuch was himself present during the discussion with Ebert. The Reich Chancellor still tried to make a case for a possible regency once Wilhelm had abdicated, but Ebert categorically ruled this out, saying that it was now too late for that.[37] Confronted with a revolutionary situation on the streets of the capital and accepting the fact that he no longer had any loyal troops at his disposal, Max von Baden offered Ebert the office of Reich Chancellor.[38]

Ebert firmly believed that this was the only possible course of action that would prevent a descent into chaos and 'Russian conditions'. He fundamentally rejected a Bolshevik-style revolution and hoped for a peaceful transformation of Germany's political system into a parliamentary democracy. In his final conversation with von Baden, he insisted that a communist revolution was the last thing he wanted: 'I don't want it, yes, I hate it like sin.'[39]

Ebert's words demonstrated just how far the MSPD had moved away from revolutionary, orthodox Marxist roots. By 1918, its political objectives had long moved to the evolutionary creation of a parliamentary democracy, the introduction of full equal voting rights for all adult Germans, the improvement of working conditions in the factories, and the expansion of the welfare state. All of these aims were to be achieved through reforms. Ebert knew too well that Imperial Germany—unlike tsarist Russia—was not an autocratic state. Despite its semi-authoritarian constitution that limited parliamentary control of the government, the German working classes had long enjoyed rights—from the right to unionize to universal male suffrage, to social benefits—that ordinary workers in Russia could only dream of. Even if social and economic injustices persisted, most German workers in 1914 would have agreed that they would benefit more from reforms than from revolution.[40]

In order to appreciate Ebert's strong views on Bolshevism, it is worth bearing in mind how quickly the Bolshevik Revolution and the subsequent civil war had interacted with revolutionary movements further afield, notably as a beacon of hope for those longing for violent socio-economic and political change.[41] For those who objected to Bolshevism, the 'spectre of Communism', which Marx and Engels had identified in Europe in the spring of 1848 in their Communist Manifesto, was, in reality, something that was felt much more keenly by everyone in Europe after 1917. Prior to 1914, Marxist-inspired revolutionary violence had been confined to underground movements of the extreme Left which carried out individual assassinations against crowned heads. The Bolshevik Revolution changed everything.

Conservative and liberal politicians in Germany, even Social Democrats like Ebert, reacted with horror to events in Russia, and feared that something akin to the Russian Revolution might be repeated in their own country.[42] A Social Democratic German newspaper published a lengthy article on the Bolsheviks' 'unlimited terrorism', and reports became even more critical of the situation in Russia after the German Ambassador, Count Mirbach, was shot dead by socialist revolutionaries in his Moscow residence in July 1918.[43] Fears of contagion were fuelled further by Lenin's and Trotsky's exhortations about world revolution, the founding of communist parties across Europe, and Bolshevik-inspired putsches.[44]

The first and most immediate case of 'contagion' and its consequences—or so it was perceived in Germany and elsewhere—was
Finland in 1918. Due to its status as an autonomous duchy within the
Russian Empire, Finland had been a non-combatant in the Great War,
even if some 1,500 Finns volunteered to fight on either the Russian or
the German side between 1914 and 1918.[45] Despite the lack of 'brutalization' through war, Finland experienced one of the proportionally
bloodiest civil wars of the twentieth century: over 36,000 people (1 per
cent of the overall population) died within the little more than three
months of the conflict and its immediate aftermath.[46] The prelude to
the civil war came in mid-November 1917 when, in the shadow of
revolutionary events in Russia, the Finnish trade unions joined forces
with the Social Democrats and Otto Kuusinen's Finnish Bolsheviks in
calling for a general strike, in which armed Red Guards were pitted
against supporters of Finland's independence.

Just over a month after the centre-right government of Pehr Evind
Svinhufvud had declared his country's breakaway from revolutionary
Russia in early December, Red Guards, with the support of Petrograd,
toppled the government in Helsinki. While Svinhufvud fled on an
ice-breaker across the Baltic Sea, a new government—the Council of
People's Representatives—was set up. The script of the putsch seemed
to follow the familiar trajectory of the Bolshevik Revolution in
Petrograd a few months earlier even if—in reality—the alleged 'Russian
involvement' in the Finnish revolution was actually rather marginal.[47]

Despite the fact that the Finnish civil war ended with a White victory, observers in the West remained concerned. 'Bolshevism', or so it
seemed, was not peculiar to Russia; it was clearly spreading west—an
impression reinforced by the Central European revolutions of 1918–19.
Contemporaries, mindful perhaps of the global pandemic of influenza
that began in the summer of 1918, spoke of Bolshevism as a virus or a
plague which had to be contained. This was the background against
which Ebert decided to assume the office of Reich Chancellor and to
do his best to prevent a descent into chaos. Shortly after the release of
Baden's abdication statement, published in a second special edition of
Vorwärts that day, Ebert addressed the German people via mass-circulated
leaflets to emphasize precisely that point:[48] 'The previous Reich
Chancellor, Prince Max von Baden, has . . . transferred to me the office
of Reich Chancellor. . . . The new government will be a people's
government. Its endeavour must be to bring the German people

peace as quickly as possible and to secure the freedom it has achieved. Fellow citizens! I ask you all for your support in the difficult work that awaits us.'[49]

Yet Ebert's conciliatory words, coupled with a government request for the protesters to leave the streets so that law and order could be restored, initially seemed to fall on deaf ears. By 2 p.m., the bulk of protesters on the streets of Berlin had reached their destination: the Reichstag building in the centre of the German capital. It was clear that they wanted more than just a few de-escalating words from the politicians who had now taken control of the government. What was demanded was a rousing public statement, providing assurance that the voice of the people had been heard. But that was not Ebert's intention. Instead, State Secretary Philipp Scheidemann (MSPD) turned to those waiting before the Reichstag. By his own account, he did so on the urging of a group of workers and soldiers who had entered the Reichstag's dining room, and because he wanted to pre-empt the proclamation of a Councils' Republic by Karl Liebknecht.[50] From a window of the Reichstag he exclaimed:

The German people have been victorious all along the line. The old and rotten has collapsed; militarism is finished! The Hohenzollerns have abdicated! Long live the German Republic! Deputy Ebert has been proclaimed Reich Chancellor. Ebert has been authorized to assemble a new government. All the socialist parties will belong to this government. Our task now lies in not allowing this radiant victory, this complete victory of the German people, to become soiled, and that is why I ask you to ensure that public safety is not disturbed! We must be able to feel proud of this day for all the future! Nothing must exist that one could later blame us for! Calm, order, and safety are what we need now! . . . Ensure that the new German Republic that we will erect is not endangered by anything. Long live the German Republic![51]

One of the observers in front of the Reichstag was the artist Käthe Kollwitz, who recorded her impressions in her diary: 'Today it is true. This afternoon, after one o'clock, I came through the Tiergarten to the Brandenburg Gate, where handbills were being circulated confirming the abdication. A column of demonstrators was marching out of the gate. I joined it . . . Down from a window, Scheidemann proclaimed the republic. . . . Then, I joined the swarm onwards down Wilhelmstraße [the government district—R.G.] for a bit . . . I saw soldiers who tore off their cockades and tossed them on the ground, laughing. . . . This is

Figure 6.3 On 9 November 1918, at the highpoint of the mass demonstrations in Berlin, tens of thousands of people gathered on the Königsplatz in front of the Reichstag to witness Philipp Scheidemann proclaim the German Republic from a balcony of the building.

how things are now. One experiences it first hand, but cannot quite grasp it...'[52]

While Scheidemann's speech had been greeted with immense enthusiasm by the crowd outside the Reichstag building (Figure 6.3), Ebert was anything but pleased about Scheidemann's proclamation. When Scheidemann returned to the dining room, an outraged Reich Chancellor slammed his fist on the table and said that it was not up to him to decide Germany's future form of government. This would be decided by an as yet to be elected National Assembly.

While Scheidemann's proclamation went too far for Ebert, the more radical socialists thought it did not go far enough. Just two hours after Scheidemann's proclamation of the German Republic, the red flag was raised over the roof of the Berlin City Palace, the royal residence of the Hohenzollern family. On a balcony with golden railings covered by a red blanket appeared the leader of the far Left, Karl Liebknecht.[53] Liebknecht proclaimed the 'Free Socialist Republic of Germany': 'The rule of capitalism, which has transformed Europe into a morgue, is broken', he shouted with excitement. But then Liebknecht made it clear that the actual work of the Revolution still lay ahead: the goal had to be the creation of a 'government of workers and soldiers, a new state order of the proletariat, of peace, of happiness and the freedom of our German brothers and our brothers in the entire world. We extend to you our hands and call upon you to complete the World Revolution.'[54]

Liebknecht's speech had enormous explosive potential for the already tense relationship between the different wings of the German workers' movement. So as not to allow these tensions to escalate into a violent internecine struggle, and in order to prevent at all costs conditions developing in Germany that might resemble those of Russia after the Bolshevik Revolution in November 1917, Ebert was determined to form a government together with the USPD. Carrying the revolutionary title of the Council of People's Deputies (or *Rat der Volksbeauftragten*), it had six members with equal representation from the MSPD and the USPD, thus bringing together in government the two parties that had split in 1917 over their divergent attitudes towards the war: three Majority Social Democrats (Ebert, Scheidemann, and Otto Landsberg, a lawyer from Upper Silesia who represented the 'right' wing of the MSPD), and three Independent Socialists (Haase, Wilhelm Dittmann, and Emil Barth). Ebert would lead the government.[55]

What this meant in practice was that the Council represented the full breadth of the Social Democratic movement. Ebert and Scheidemann were not the only politicians on it that were well known to a majority of Germans. Wilhelm Dittmann, for example, had been a hero of the Left for years. Born in 1874 in Eutin, Dittmann had trained as a joiner but also joined the SPD and the union of metal workers at a young age. He had been an SPD Reichstag deputy since 1912 and became one of the most outspoken critics of the SPD's *Burgfrieden* policy after the outbreak of war in 1914. He was ousted from the parliamentary party in 1915 after refusing to approve further war credits, thus violating party discipline, and had been sentenced to five years' imprisonment because of his prominent role in the January strikes of 1918.

His fellow USPD and Council member Emil Barth was a plumber by trade and hailed from Heidelberg, where he was born in 1879. He had joined the USPD during the war, whilst on active military service, and rose to prominence in February 1918. After the arrest of Richard Müller, he became the leader of the influential Revolutionary Shop Stewards. Ever since, Barth had secretly been busy stockpiling arms and ammunition for the next attempt at revolution, playing a central role in the November demonstrations in Berlin that eventually led to Max von Baden's abdication.

None of the members of the Council of People's Deputies was thus a stranger to the German public. Yet, nobody knew for sure what the uneasy coalition between MSPD and USPD would stand for politically. Some people, such as the prominent historian Friedrich Meinecke, speculated as to whether or not Social Democracy would rise to the challenge of ruling Germany at the time of national peril: 'That is the burning question now: to what extent was their previous patriotic, moderate stance during the war a tactic, a mere calculating move, and to what extent was it the result of an inner transformation? Will they be serious about respecting the democratic majority will, or will they instead be tempted by the prospect of a dictatorship of the proletariat?'[56]

While there was considerable disagreement between the MSPD and the USPD about the future form of government—parliamentary democracy or a councils' republic—there was consensus on at least one matter: the war had to be terminated as soon as possible. Like von Baden and his government, Ebert and the Council placed their hopes in US President Wilson, but no one could be sure what exactly the armistice would look like. For although the German delegation had arrived in the forest of Compiègne on 9 November, the day the revolution successfully ended the Hohenzollern regime in Berlin, nothing was known as yet about the Allies' specific conditions.

7

Making peace in the West

On 6 November 1918—the very day that the von Baden government received word of the spread of the revolution from Kiel to Hamburg and elsewhere, and General Groener reported that military resistance could only be of short duration—Matthias Erzberger was selected as the chief German negotiator for the forthcoming armistice talks.[1] Erzberger left Berlin that day, with a copy of Wilson's note of the previous day and an authorization letter from the Chancellor in his briefcase.[2] He first headed towards OHL headquarters in the Belgian city of Spa, where he had a brief meeting with senior generals, including Hindenburg, who noted the uniqueness of armistice negotiations being led by a politician rather than a military man, but expressed his support for Erzberger's mission.[3]

Following a late breakfast, Erzberger and the other members of the German delegation left Spa toward noon on 7 November in a convoy of five cars, approaching the front line near Chimay. Several problems slowed them down. The roads were blocked by retreating German troops and a car accident occurred, in which Erzberger's vehicle and another car were damaged, but no injuries were inflicted. The trip through Belgium continued in the remaining undamaged cars, reaching Chimay at dusk. From Chimay, the convoy continued through blocked and muddy roads arriving at Trelon by 7.30 p.m., where Erzberger had to wait again for a squad of sappers to remove mines that had been laid to secure the withdrawal from the rear. The delegation crossed the outer German front line at 9.20 p.m., after a trumpeter assigned to the delegation signalled the approach of the German delegates to the enemy. As they drove through no man's land, flying a white flag, they spotted the first French soldiers only 150 metres after crossing the German front line.

General Maxime Weygand, Marshal Foch's Chief of Staff, recalled the arrival of the Germans that evening:

Night falls; the weather is appalling; drizzle is falling without the rather dense fog dissipating. At 8 p.m. the guards finally perceive a glow of light; they hear a few notes from a trumpet, proclaiming 'hold your fire'; a few seconds later, a column of vehicles roars up the road with their headlights switched on; way at the front, on the first car, an enormous white flag gleams out of the dark night; standing upright on the running board, a trumpeter blows constantly. A hand motion stops the car. A young 25-year-old captain steps forward. He is Captain Lhuillier, battalion commander of the 171st Infantry Regiment, who recognizes the parliamentarians and climbs into the first of the five cars.... the journey continues to La Capelle. The trumpeter blows 'garde-à-vous' [attention], while our troops now have this concluding image of four years of struggle and suffering before their eyes.[4]

From La Capelle, the trip continued in French vehicles. The convoy moved very slowly over the deeply rutted road eventually reaching the headquarters of the First French Army in Homblières near Saint-Quentin around 1.00 a.m., where, in a parsonage serving as an army headquarters, dinner was served in the presence of General Debeney, the supreme commander of the First French Army. An hour later, the journey was continued toward Chauny.[5]

After a dinner with General Marie-Eugène whose First Army had played a decisive role in the Allied counter-offensives that eventually broke the Hindenburg Line, the German delegation was sent to the train station of the entirely destroyed town of Tergnier, where a special train with Napoleon III's saloon car had been readied.[6] Cognac was served, and the train left the station for an unknown destination. The window curtains had been drawn and were not to be opened during the journey. Towards 7.00 a.m. on 8 November—the day for which the meeting had been scheduled—the train stopped in a forest, and Erzberger noticed that a second train had stopped on a neighbouring track some 100 metres away. The train personnel were not able, or permitted, to answer any questions regarding their location. Up to 10 November, the German delegation appears to have had no precise knowledge where they were. It was only when Erzberger, a devout Catholic, expressed his desire to attend mass on Sunday morning and was informed that this would not be possible because Marshal Foch was attending mass in the closest church at Rethonde, that he figured out that the trains must have stopped in the forest of Compiègne.

Two hours after their train's arrival, the German delegation was told that Foch would receive them at 10 a.m. Erzberger, wearing an ordinary travel suit, led the German delegation across the train tracks.[7] In Foch's saloon car, the German delegation was assigned seats at the negotiating table. Foch, who entered the compartment in the company of the British First Lord of the Admiralty, Sir Rosslyn Wemyss, his deputy, Rear Admiral George Hope, and Foch's Chief of Staff, Weygand, gave a brief military salute. As Erzberger noted with horror, no Americans had been included in the armistice negotiations.[8]

Foch's reception was predictably cool. He was deeply suspicious of his German opponents, who in turn saw him as the embodiment of French vengefulness.[9] In Erzberger's memoirs, Foch is described as 'a small man with hard, energetic features, which immediately betrayed a habit of commanding others...'[10] Foch examined Erzberger's authorization letter from von Baden before somewhat sanctimoniously asking him about the concerns that had led the German delegation to him. Erzberger responded that he had come to receive suggestions pursuant to the effecting of an armistice. Foch countered by saying he had no such 'suggestions' to make. Only when Erzberger added that they had come on the basis of President Wilson's last note of 5 November, and had it read aloud in the original, did Foch ask Weygand to read the conditions for an armistice in French.

The conditions put forward by the Allies were very hard to accept for a German population who, only a few months earlier, had assumed that victory would soon vindicate the sacrifices of four long years of deprivation. The German army was obliged to immediately evacuate all troops—some 190 divisions—from the invaded territories of France, Belgium, and Luxembourg, as well as from Alsace-Lorraine, annexed by Germany in 1871. German territory on the left bank of the Rhine would be occupied by French troops. The Brest-Litovsk Treaty, which had given Berlin control over vast territories in Eastern Europe, was to be immediately revoked, while Germany would also be required to surrender large amounts of weaponry and its High Seas Fleet to the Allies. To ensure compliance with these demands and good behaviour until a formal peace treaty was signed, the British naval blockade of Germany would continue, thereby threatening large parts of the German civilian population with starvation.

A stunned Erzberger asked for permission to telegraph the conditions to Berlin and to the German military headquarters in Spa, which

Foch refused, stating that the text could only be sent in encrypted form or through couriers, and that any premature publication was to be prevented. As Erzberger saw no possibility of encrypting it, he asked Foch to extend the deadline for responding to the conditions from seventy-two to ninety-six hours, since a courier would require at least twelve hours to reach Spa. Foch was suspicious that the Germans would simply use the time to regroup and further reinforce their defences. He thus rejected an extension of the deadline as well as Erzberger's further request to declare a provisional truce during the negotiations. He also declared that negotiations over the armistice conditions would not be permitted under any circumstances. The conditions could only be accepted or refused.[11]

This first meeting of the German and Allied delegations lasted only forty-five minutes and revealed that there would be no 'negotiations' in the normal sense of the word. Even so, Erzberger did succeed in getting Foch to agree to 'explanatory discussions' between the German delegation and Foch's companions later that afternoon. Simultaneously Erzberger sent one of the officers in his company, the future SS general and Nazi police president of Berlin, Wolf-Heinrich Count von Helldorff, to Spa. Helldorff was instructed to deliver the armistice conditions to the OHL and to report that no concessions were to be expected regarding the key Allied demands for an armistice. All that the delegation could hope for were for minor accommodations regarding the implementation of Foch's demands.[12]

Erzberger himself contacted Spa by radio on 8 November to report on the difficult start to the armistice talks and to ask whether he should still sign the armistice, even if he was unable to get any improvements. If he was instructed to accept the Allied conditions by the government, Erzberger wished to do so only under protest: 'However, in the interests of the sincerity of the relations between Germany and its enemies, the undersigned regard it as a duty of conscience to point out that the execution of these conditions must plunge the German people into anarchy and famine, and that, without any blame on the part of the German government and the German people, a situation can emerge that will render the further maintenance of all obligations impossible.'[13]

While Erzberger waited for instructions from Berlin and Spa, some of the senior officers in his entourage met with Admiral Hope and General Weygand, and attempted to communicate this specific point to the Allied side. If Germany accepted the conditions placed upon it,

Germany would fall to Bolshevism, and a phase of anarchy and famine was to be expected. For their part, the Allies expressed their suspicion that Germany could feel tempted to reorganize the troops it was withdrawing from Belgium and France in order to recommence the conflict.[14]

On the following day, 9 November, Erzberger presented the written German objections to the schedule for withdrawing German troops, for establishing bridgeheads on German territory, and above all regarding the quantity of war materiel and locomotives to be delivered up. General Weygand, who received the objections, noted that these were arguments that had already been rejected the previous day and that they were thus unworthy of being noted.[15]

Foch met with French Prime Minister Georges Clemenceau in the nearby historic town of Senlis that same day in order to discuss the progress of the armistice negotiations. When Clemenceau asked whether Foch still had reservations about an armistice, Foch responded that he only saw advantages at this point. In his view, a continuation of the war and a potential occupation of Germany would cost the lives of an additional 50,000 to 100,000 Frenchmen. Foch also seemed genuinely surprised by the degree to which the Germans were 'broken'; he had expected much fiercer resistance to the proposed armistice terms.[16]

As Saturday night faded into Sunday morning, the High Command informed Erzberger that a new government had been formed in Germany. Erzberger and his delegation at this point had no idea that the Kaiser had abdicated, only that Ebert was the new Reich Chancellor.[17] While uncertainty about the future political course of the new government prevailed, the delegation continued to do its best to seek improvements of the proposed armistice terms. That Sunday morning was filled with discussions between the two sets of delegates— discussions that concluded without the Germans achieving any success in easing the armistice conditions or the Allies paying any heed to the suggested danger of a Bolshevik radicalization in Germany. Wemyss instead expressed internal concerns that, due to the change in government, the German delegation might no longer possess the legitimacy to continue negotiations. On higher levels as well, the events in Germany provoked uncertainty. Clemenceau asked whether Lloyd George could come to Paris in case fast decisions became necessary, yet the British Prime Minister was unable to come to Paris before the 13th. In the meantime, Foreign Secretary Lord Curzon was authorized to make decisions on behalf of the British government, since he was already in Paris.[18]

Before Erzberger received an official authorization from the new government, the OHL informed him by radio at 8.00 p.m. on 10 November of the terms requiring continued negotiation. Hindenburg's main concerns lay in extending the evacuation deadline, requesting the honourable surrender of East Africa, reducing the volume of war materiel to be relinquished, and an end to the British naval blockade. 'If it is not possible to assert these points,' Hindenburg added, 'you should conclude the armistice anyway.' Should such a situation arise, Erzberger was to sign under 'flaming protest with reference to Wilson'.[19]

In the meantime, Clemenceau had instructed the German delegates to issue two declarations: first, a confirmation that they represented the new German government, and second, that the new government was committed to implementing the armistice conditions.[20] At least on the first point, Erzberger was able to deliver an affirmative reply on the evening of 10 November. Two and a half hours after receiving the radio message from the headquarters in Spa, a message from the Ebert government arrived in Compiègne stating that Erzberger was 'authorized' to sign the armistice. At the same time, the new message contained a declaration of reservations regarding individual conditions. Ebert declared that the new Reich government would fulfil the conditions of the armistice, but asked the Allies for concessions regarding the relinquishment of 'supplies in the areas to be evacuated that are intended for the provisioning of the troops' and a rapid end to the blockade in order to guarantee the nutrition of the population. In addition, Ebert also requested an honourable capitulation of the undefeated German *Schutztruppe* in East Africa under the command of General Paul von Lettow-Vorbeck.[21]

Erzberger, who that evening had been reminded by Weygand in a 'formal notice' that the deadline for Germany's acceptance of the terms of the armistice was the next day at 11.00 a.m., informed Foch that the negotiations could continue through the night. After the German delegation had prepared a statement of protest, the final round of talks began at 2.15 a.m. on 11 November. Despite instructions to the contrary, Foch accommodated the German delegation on a number of smaller points: Germany would 'only' hand over 25,000 machine guns instead of 30,000, and the number of aeroplanes to be surrendered was lowered from 2,000 to 1,700. Instead of the originally demanded

10,000 trucks, the Germans only had to give up half that number. More important were the changes to the delineation of the neutral zone alone the right bank of the Rhine. Its depth was set at 10 kilometres, and Germany would receive six more days in which to evacuate it. The 'honourable evacuation' of the troops in East Africa demanded by the Reich government was also accepted. Decisions regarding the approach to Germany's Eastern front were more significant. Erzberger managed to persuade Foch that an immediate German withdrawal would expose the local population to the influence of Bolshevism. As a result, the deadline for an evacuation was not clearly set. On the question of continuing the economic blockade of Germany, however, Foch remained unyielding. He merely stated that the Allies would examine supply deliveries but did not set a date for their approval.[22]

A formal protest read out by Erzberger warned that the terms would drive Germany into anarchy and famine. But despite his protest, Erzberger signed the armistice document at 5.20 in the morning on 11 November. Less than six hours later, at 11 a.m. French time, the guns fell silent along the Western front. The Great War had come to an end—at least in the West.[23]

Reactions in Germany to the armistice conditions were more mixed than one might have expected. To be sure, the vast majority of Germans felt deep resentment for what was perceived—rightly or wrongly—as Allied vengefulness. One did not have to be an arch-nationalist to criticize the terms of the armistice. On Monday, 11 November 1918, Käthe Kollwitz bemoaned the 'terrible terms of the armistice. We can only hope that the peace treaty will bring improved conditions.'[24] And Alfred Döblin, still in Alsace at the time, felt the same: 'How low we have fallen. And everyone rejoices, drags away, robs, thinks of his possessions. We have been beaten to the ground overnight in a most epic fashion...'[25] Yet, at the same time, there was also considerable relief that the war was finally over and that the revolution had thus far been considerably less violent than was expected, notably against the backdrop of events in Russia and Finland. As Döblin observed: 'An officer's wife, whose child was ill, had told me a few days previously during my visit: "If they depose our Kaiser, then I no longer want to live." She did not say that in a state of passion; it was entirely genuine; but now I met her again, she is alive, and fears only for what will become of her furniture.'[26]

Just like the officer's wife in Döblin's report from Alsace, other members of the old imperial elite also noted with relief that the orgies of violence they had expected had not occurred in Germany. In early November, many members of the German aristocracy as key beneficiaries of the imperial regime had convinced themselves that they would soon share the fate of Louis XVI in 1793 or that of the tsar, who had been brutally murdered with his family and servants in July 1918. Much to their surprise and relief, hardly any violent excesses against their property or lives occurred during the revolution. Karl Anton Prince Rohan, for example, recorded his fears about returning from the Eastern front to a home burnt down and murdered relatives. Much to his surprise, on the night of his return his parents' castle was still standing and his relatives and their friends were happily listening to a string quartet in their large living room: 'An immense surprise erupted within us. So, the world had not collapsed after all?'[27]

Most importantly, those who had survived the war were relieved that the fighting was finally over. Victor Klemperer, who strongly criticized the 'cruelty of the French' in relation to the armistice, was nonetheless relieved that peace was now a reality:[28]

On 10 November, at half past four in the afternoon, when the message on the imminent armistice came by telephone from Kowno, my very first thought was: The war is over! From that point on I had no patience. I now wanted to escape from this meaninglessness, from this chaos, I now no longer wanted to content myself with the couple of hours that, by squandering my life here and there, I stole for my true existence; I had been a soldier long enough, I had been a marionette whose strings had been pulled by other people, I wanted to be free, I wanted to be an individual, I wanted to be a scholar, I wanted to be myself. Was I behaving unpatriotically? Maybe, but the broken fatherland would now need trained workers in all areas, and among all workers, perhaps, it would need teachers most urgently. My place was at a lectern.[29]

At the same time, Klemperer, like other middle-class Germans, felt deeply distraught by Germany's defeat. In a letter to his wife Eva back in Leipzig, Klemperer wrote: 'These are mad, wild hours, more surreal than in August 1914 and more uncanny; back then it was an enthusiastic upsurge, today it is the day of judgement. Impossible to focus on any reading, any occupation.'[30]

Soon after writing this letter, Klemperer managed to get on one of the overcrowded trains bound for Germany. 'I stretched myself out, wrapped in an illegally obtained woollen blanket, my boots on the cushions, a victorious revolutionary. The train began to move. My last thought before falling asleep was: Now the war is truly over.'[31]

8

Challenges for the young Republic

While the Great War was drawing to a close, Friedrich Ebert and the newly instituted Council of People's Deputies expended much energy on pressing day-to-day issues. And there were many. Taking over the reins of government in Germany's greatest moment of crisis was not a promising proposition: it would fall on the Ebert government to sign a peace treaty whose conditions were as yet unknown but unlikely to be favourable, to ensure adequate food supplies for a starving population, and more generally to stabilize a dislocated economy, which would have to re-absorb millions of returning veterans, and to avert the very real risk of civil war (Figure 8.1).[1] Each of these problems represented an enormous challenge for an inexperienced government. Germany had just lost a war of unprecedented scale and destructiveness—a war in which more than thirteen million Germans (nearly 20 per cent of the country's population in 1914) had served and two million had died. In addition, some 2.7 million German soldiers had been physically or psychologically damaged during the war.[2] Unlike in the victor states of the Great War, the dilemma of how to vindicate the sacrifices of sons, brothers, and fathers after a lost war preoccupied (and divided) Germany's public for years to come.[3]

Furthermore, some six million German soldiers were still in arms on 11 November 1918, when the armistice was signed. They were scattered around Western Europe (north-western France and Belgium), and across East-Central Europe and the Middle East. Hundreds of thousands of men now made their way back from France, from Russia, from Turkey.[4] Many of them, consumed by the desire to get home, had simply started off on their own, while others—such as

Alfred Döblin—waited for a more orderly demobilization and return to Germany, in his case from Alsace in early December 1918:

We travel for days. One freezes to death. . . . One day, from the Würzburg freight station, I take a walk through the town. Atop the castle a red flag flies, visible to the eyes, a red flag! One sees posters on the columns signed by 'The republican City Commander'. Into what kind of world are we travelling? No newspapers for days, only the Würzburg local paper can be bought, with the headline: 'Free from Berlin'. It is the same old song again and again: clerics are speculating on Bavarian pride, and work with the image of the 'Berlin terror'. On Wednesday, in Berlin . . . one sees rows upon rows of people, from Potsdamer Platz across the entire city to Friedrichshain. In the endless procession, one spots wreaths with red bows, red flags, proletarian exhortations—otherwise, nothing that could remind me of a revolution. More like a well-ordered petit bourgeois event on a vast scale. I must first get my bearings.[5]

Figure 8.1 One major achievement of the Ebert government was the peaceful and orderly return to Germany of millions of German soldiers. This would have been virtually impossible without the alliance with General Groener and the Army High Command. It proved difficult enough even with the benefit of this alliance, as is suggested by this photo of German troops from Alsace crossing the Rhine on their return from the front in late 1918, the military flag of Imperial Germany held aloft in a spirit of defiance of the new Republic.

This sense of disorientation was quite common for the returning soldiers arriving on foot or by train in their home towns, where they were welcomed by equally perplexed representatives of the new order who were unsure what to expect from the often heavily armed men who returned after four years of fighting.[6] The return of the troops was a major challenge for the republic, and one that featured very prominently in the literature of the time. In Alfred Döblin's four-volume novel about the revolution, *November 1918*, the severely wounded Lieutenant Friedrich Becker returns to Berlin, where he attends countless political rallies without finding satisfactory answers. Becker, a former classics teacher, returns to his old school, but the director tells him that there is no work for him. With no prospect of finding work, Becker suffers a severe mental breakdown.

Becker was not the only literary figure to return from the war and feel despair. Paul Bäumer, the lead character in Erich Maria Remarque's best-selling war novel *All Quiet on the Western Front* (1929), makes this point very strongly when he says: 'Had we returned home in 1916, out of the suffering and the strength of our experience we might have unleashed a storm. Now if we go back we will be weary, broken, burnt out, rootless, and without hope. We will not be able to find our way anymore. And men will not understand us—for the generation that grew up before us, though it has passed these years with us, already had a home and a calling; now it will return to its old occupations, and the war will be forgotten—and the generation that has grown up after us will be strange to us and push us aside. We will be superfluous even to ourselves...and in the end we shall fall into ruin.'[7]

The war remained visible on German streets where penniless, maimed veterans begged for money, but also in the upper echelons of society, where the absence of young men was keenly felt. The German aristocracy, for example, suffered a particularly high percentage of casualties during the war: roughly 4,500 aristocratic officers—a full quarter of German aristocratic men over the age of 18—died on the battlefields of the Great War.[8] Where former officers and ordinary soldiers had survived the war, they often bore invisible or visible scars—from missing limbs to 'shell shock'.[9] In Vicki Baum's best-selling novel *Menschen im Hotel* (1929), set in the luxurious *Adlon Hotel* in Berlin, the scars of war are personified by a man called Dr Otternschlag, who only has half of his face left due to a war injury: 'The other half of his face was non-existent. There was only a crooked, sewn and folded up

Figure 8.2 Returning German soldiers parade through Berlin on 10 December 1918. Contrary to what is often maintained, the returning soldiers were generally warmly received, both by the general public, who gathered in large numbers at the Brandenburg Gate to welcome them, and by senior representatives of the new Republic.

muddle, where, between seams and scars, a glass eye peaked out.'[10] Otternschlag calls this artificial eye his 'souvenir from Flanders' and it embodies the striking contrast between the glamorous façade of the hotel and the grim reality of a broken existence: 'It is horrific', he says. 'The world is a dead star, it no longer warms us.'[11]

It was against the background of these seemingly or actually devalued existences, and the dilemma of how to reintegrate the veterans into the new republic, that Ebert greeted returning front troops at the Brandenburg Gate in Berlin on 10 December 1918 (Figure 8.2) with the words: 'No enemy has defeated you.' As one woman among the observers that day noted in her diary: 'Artillerymen. Cannons, horses, helmets, all wreathed in colourful paper, fir branches and ribbons. It looked so beautiful, but it was also so sad to see. In the past, I have always been afraid of seeing a retreat. On Alexanderplatz, the hustle and bustle.... Children sat on the cannons and the soldiers with their girls on the horse. Everyone marched together. A jubilation, as if a victorious army were returning. At the Brandenburg Gate, they were welcomed by Ebert as the representative of the Republic.'[12]

Ebert's words were born out of a desire to co-opt the army into supporting the new regime in the face of a potential challenge by either right-wing opposition or those advocating a more radical revolution in Germany. Although sailors and soldiers stationed in the rear had started the November Revolution, Ebert was well aware that the regime change was not universally popular among the troops. Instead, there was a deep rift between some of the front-line troops, notably in the West, and those stationed in the rear and in the home garrisons within Germany. The vast majority of German occupation units in the east and in the garrisons of the Home Army deposed their officers, established soldiers' councils, and declared their emphatic support for the revolution and for the sailors who had started it. The combat troops (numerically much smaller than the support divisions and homeland garrisons), by contrast, remained under the command of the old officer corps, marching across the Rhine after 11 November under the black, white, and red flag of the bygone imperial regime. Long-standing resentments for the allegedly lazy, untested, and bored 'rear-area pigs' (*Etappenschweine*) were reinforced at the time of defeat when the fighting troops accused the rear of betraying their sacrifices. The potential for at least some of these heavily armed, battle-hardened, and deeply resentful front soldiers to violently oppose the regime change was considerable, and not just in Ebert's estimation.[13]

For that very reason, and in order to tackle the extraordinarily difficult task of demobilizing some six million men within a few months, Ebert had come to a pragmatic agreement with Ludendorff's much less dogmatic successor in the Army High Command, General Wilhelm Groener, an agreement that has often wrongly been derided as a Faustian pact with the old imperial army. On 10 November, Groener assured Ebert of the loyalty of the armed forces and accepted the new political realities. In return, Ebert promised that the government would take prompt action against potential far Left uprisings, that he would call elections for a National Assembly, and that the professional officers' corps would remain in control of military command.[14] From Groener's point of view—and that of Hindenburg—this was an exercise in damage control as it secured some kind of influence for the soon-to-be much reduced old officer corps in the much changed circumstances of post-revolutionary Germany.

Hindenburg and Groener 'hold the view that one can only compare our people with a severe fever victim, and that, with time, even this fever will calm itself', wrote Major General Albrecht von Thaer to his wife in a letter on 20 November 1918. He added how much he admired the calm that Hindenburg and Groener radiated.[15] In his memoirs published in 1939, Groener reported in detail on the 'alliance that the OHL concluded with Ebert'. On 10 November, he placed the army at the disposal of the new government in Hindenburg's name, and declared that, in return, he expected Ebert's support both in 'combating Bolshevism' and 'in maintaining order and discipline within the army'.[16] Seven days later, Groener wrote to his wife that he, along with Hindenburg, wished to support Ebert, whom he personally appreciated 'as an upright, honest and decent character, as long as possible, so that the wagon does not skid further to the left'.[17]

There was widespread support from senior military figures for this arrangement, partly because it meant that the army still had a role to play in the post-war world and partly because there were genuine concerns that Germany might descend into chaos and Bolshevism: 'If the Spartacus Group gets into power, this must irretrievably lead to a civil war, just like in Russia. In addition, the Entente would send troops to establish order. We would then be forced to endure the last thing which, despite all calamities to date, we have been spared: war in our own country. That is why one must vote for one of Ebert's followers or for a bourgeois democrat!'[18]

Despite the agreement between Groener and Ebert, the demobilization process proved to be complex, not least because it involved much more than turning soldiers into civilians. The war economy had to be transformed into a post-war economy and countless armaments factories were shut down. This process particularly affected women who had been recruited into the factories during the war.[19] Between 1914 and 1918, women working in war-related industries experienced significant wage increases to meet the pressing demands for munition workers.[20] In other areas of public and professional life, too, the presence of women became much more visible. Women's matriculation in German universities, for example, increased some 77 per cent from 1914 to 1918.[21]

The women's rights activist Henriette Fürth captured these changes and the rising expectations for change in her book *Die deutschen Frauen im Kriege*, published in 1917: 'This war's unbelievable transformations

Figure 8.3 During the First World War women increasingly stepped in to do jobs that had previously been reserved for men. This development was most marked in the munitions industry, but women did a whole range of artisanal jobs at this time, as for instance in this photo of two women in 1916 earning their money by window cleaning.

have revolutionized the daily experiences of women to an extent that we would have considered unthinkable in its first months.'[22] Female employment rates continued to rise after 1918, notably in the rapidly expanding service industry, but also increasingly in the medical and teaching profession, and women made up a third of the overall German workforce in the interwar period.[23]

Nonetheless, the economic outlook in 1918 was bleak and Ebert's government was facing debt levels and inflation rates unprecedented in German history. The main reason for this, of course, was the First World War and the way Germany financed its war effort. Prior to 1914, Germany had been the most economically powerful country in Europe, but its specialization in high-end technology products, many of which were exported, left the country vulnerable to any disruption of global supply chains and trade. Between 1914 and 1918, the Kaiser and his governments had borrowed and printed increasing amounts of money to cover the spiralling cost of war. None of this would have mattered in the event of a German victory which would have opened up new economic opportunities in Eastern Europe and the possibility of imposing high reparations payments on the losers (as was done at Brest-Litovsk). Now, however, Ebert's government was not only left with Germany's own debts but also with a not yet specified reparations bill from the Allies and the very high social costs of war. Payments had to be made to soldiers who had lost their limbs, widows, and orphans, food supplies were subsidized, as were certain industries to achieve full employment and maintain the social peace. Meanwhile, inflation rates continued to be high, making the purchase of basic commodities and imports more and more expensive. If, in 1918, a US dollar could still be purchased for eight marks at the Berlin exchange, that rate rose to nearly fifty marks for one dollar by the end of 1919.[24]

Yet, during the first years of the Weimar Republic, until the summer of 1922, significant foreign investment in German securities of up to fifteen billion gold Marks (driven by the belief that the Mark would soon fully recover) helped to keep the currency rate more stable than it could have been otherwise.[25] Although long term the inflation (which culminated in the worst hyperinflation in history in 1923) wiped out Germans' savings there were some positive short-term effects: the inflation helped to stabilize employment and facilitated the German economic recovery after 1918. Between the end of the war and the summer of 1922, economic growth rates in Germany were actually higher (and unemployment rates lower) than those in most other European countries. Some historians have even suggested that the early Weimar governments bought much needed social peace and precarious stability by excessive use of the printing press.[26]

Another reason for the initially relatively smooth transition from war to peacetime economy was that Ebert and the Free Trade Unions advocated gradual change during the initial phase of the German Revolution of November 1918. This applied both to the world of politics and to the social arena: on 15 November, business leaders and trade unions forged an agreement on wage arbitration, the introduction of the eight-hour day, and workers' representation in companies with more than fifty employees. All of these issues had been key demands of the organized labour movement for decades. Now they became a reality. Known as the Stinnes–Legien Agreement after its two main signatories—the leading heavy industrialist, Hugo Stinnes, and the chairman of the Free Trade Unions, Carl Legien—the deal pre-empted a potential nationalization from below and a radical redistribution of property that would have been in the interest of neither the employers nor the SPD-dominated Free Trade Unions.[27]

While the Council of People's Representatives made pragmatic decisions to keep the country running, including guaranteeing 'the wage, pension and other legal claims of officials and employees in the public services',[28] there remained considerable dissent on the future course of the revolution. The long-term question of Germany's political future was to be decided by a democratically elected constitutive National Assembly—at least, that is what Ebert, the MSPD, and parts of the Independent Socialists intended. From their perspective, a revolutionary fait accompli—in the form of a Council Republic—would have had no democratic legitimization, thus threatening the political integration of large segments of the population into the new republican state. Many middle- and upper-class Germans would have perceived the nationalization of key industries as a severe violation of the law, thereby mobilizing even more counter-revolutionary forces than was already the case.

However, significant segments of the workers' movement, notably on its left-wing fringe, did not accept the MSPD's rejection of a Council Republic. The anarchist Gustav Landauer, for example, wrote to his friend the essayist and poet Margarete Susman on 14 November 1918: 'If a national assembly comes now, if all important decisions are put in its hands, then everything will be lost... "National assembly" means that the revolution unhitches the horses and puts them in the stable. This is not at all what we need!'[29]

Although the extreme Left had never had any chance of gaining a majority, once the revolution had begun, it encouraged certain expectations among many workers and agitators for more radical political and socio-economic change. The tensions between the different camps, and between different expectations for the future, would explode into violence in late 1918.[30]

9

Fighting radicalization

In the winter of 1918–19, these unresolved tensions between moderate and radical revolutionaries erupted violently. Ebert and the Majority Social Democrats were adamant that only a democratically elected National Assembly could decide on the future constitution of the country. Not everyone was willing to accept this position. The representatives of the left wing of the USPD, the so-called 'Spartacus League', rejected the idea of a National Assembly and preferred a political system in which all power was in the hands of the soldiers' and workers' councils. At the very end of 1918, they united with other left-wing groups to form the German Communist Party (KPD).[1]

The two dominant figures of the communist left in Germany at this point were Rosa Luxemburg and Karl Liebknecht. Liebknecht, arguably the most prominent proponent of radical revolutionary change outside Russia, was descended from socialist royalty. Born in Leipzig in 1871, he was the son of Wilhelm Liebknecht, a close friend and collaborator of Karl Marx and, alongside the SPD's long-serving chairman August Bebel, one of the founding fathers of Social Democracy. Karl was significantly more radical than his father. Having studied law and political economy at the universities of Leipzig and Berlin, he opened a law practice in Berlin in 1899, and specialized in defending fellow socialists in the German courts.[2]

In 1907, Liebknecht's anti-militarist writings got him into trouble with the courts, which sentenced him to eighteen months in prison. His imprisonment only helped to improve his standing among his followers. Liebknecht was elected to the Reichstag as a Social Democrat in 1912. In 1914 he was the only Member of Parliament to vote against the war credits. Liebknecht and other prominent left-wing critics of the war—including Rosa Luxemburg and Clara Zetkin, a pioneer of

Figure 9.1 This contemporary poster nicely summarizes what were probably the biggest challenges facing the Ebert government in the early months of the Weimar Republic: 'smooth demobilization', 'building the Republic', and 'Peace'.

the socialist women's movement—soon formed their own organization within the SPD: the 'Group of the International', which renamed itself as the Spartacus League in 1916. In their periodic pamphlets *Spartakusbriefe* ('Spartacus Letters'), Liebknecht and his followers called for a workers' revolution and an immediate end to the war. Unsurprisingly, the 'Spartacus Letters' were soon banned, and Liebknecht was arrested and sent to a penal battalion on the Eastern front. Back in Berlin the following year, Liebknecht led an illegal war-demonstration on May Day 1916 and was arrested again. This time he was sentenced to four years' imprisonment for high treason. He was released in late October 1918, under Prince Max von Baden's declaration of amnesty for political prisoners, and immediately returned to Berlin. Here he led another anti-war demonstration that culminated in a symbolically charged march to the Russian Embassy, where Bolshevik emissaries hosted a reception for him.[3]

The 'Russian connection' made officials in Berlin increasingly nervous. On 6 November, three days before the revolution reached Berlin, the Soviet delegation in the German capital, headed by Adolf Joffe, was expelled from the country on charges of preparing a communist uprising in Germany. Such accusations were not altogether unfounded, even if the imagined impact of Russian propaganda on the German far Left was certainly exaggerated. Yet Lenin, and by extension Joffe, were clearly hoping for a westward expansion of the global proletarian revolution in which Germany, now on its knees with military defeat all but certain, was of particular importance.

Lenin was encouraged in his hopes by his adviser on German matters, Karl Radek (his real name at birth was Karol Sobelsohn). Born to Jewish parents in 1885 in Lemberg, the capital city of the Austro-Hungarian crownland of Galicia, Radek had joined the Social Democratic Party of the Kingdom of Poland and Lithuania in 1904. The following year, he participated in the 1905 revolution before fleeing to Germany to avoid arrest by the tsarist police. After years of working for socialist newspapers and engaging in the increasingly vicious debates between orthodox Marxists and 'revisionists', Radek found himself on the wrong side of the argument and was expelled from the SPD (which he had joined after moving to Germany) in 1913 for views that were deemed damaging to the party. His expulsion had been opposed by Karl Liebknecht and was criticized by international representatives of the far Left such as Lenin and Trotsky. The following year, after the outbreak of the Great War, Radek moved to Switzerland, working closely with Lenin and the Zimmerwald Left. Radek in fact joined Lenin on his train journey from Zurich in 1917, and supported his efforts at radicalizing the revolution once they were back in Russia. After the Bolshevik revolution, Radek became a member of the Russian delegation at Brest-Litovsk. As an expert on Germany, Radek served as deputy of the People's Commissar for Foreign Affairs, Georgy Chicherin, from March 1918. When, in April 1918, diplomatic relations resumed between Germany and Russia, Joffe was accepted as the Russian envoy in Berlin while Radek, who had hoped to join Joffe in Berlin, was denied a visa after the Foreign Office, in a secret report, had classified him as a 'dangerous revolutionary'.[4]

When the revolution broke out in Germany in November 1918, Radek and others in Moscow were taken by surprise. With 'very unclear knowledge about the events on the ground', in Radek's own words, he decided to travel to Germany to try and influence the course of the revolution.[5] In December 1918, Radek crossed the German border illegally and installed himself in Berlin, where he participated in the discussions and conferences leading to the foundation of the German Communist Party (KPD) in late December 1918.

However, Liebknecht's most important ally in the weeks and months after the war was certainly not Radek, but the Polish-born Marxist activist and intellectual Rosa Luxemburg, with whom he shared the editorship of the Communist flagship publication, *Die Rote Fahne* ('The Red Flag'). Born as Rozalia Luksenburg in the then Russian city of Zamość in the same year as Liebknecht, she was the youngest child of a secular Jewish wood merchant. Luxemburg became involved in revolutionary anti-tsarist activities as a schoolgirl in Warsaw and had to flee the city to escape persecution by the tsarist police. From 1889, she lived in Zurich, one of the centres for socialist refugees from all over Europe, where her lover, Leo Jogiches, a socialist from Vilnius, financed her studies in philosophy, history, economics, politics, and mathematics at Zurich University, and also backed her in founding the Social Democratic Party of Poland and Lithuania.[6]

In 1898, Luxemburg obtained German citizenship through marriage to the only son of her Zurich host family, Gustav Lübeck, while continuing her relationship with Jogiches. Moving to Berlin that same year, she immediately joined the SPD and actively engaged in the ongoing controversy between reformist and revolutionary Social Democrats. As a radical proponent of revolution, she was imprisoned three times between 1904 and 1906, and again during the Great War, during which time she still managed to write a series of anti-war pamphlets that were smuggled out of her prison cell in Breslau and printed and distributed among workers and soldiers by Jogiches.

It was during her time in prison that her thoughts began to revolve around the recent Bolshevik revolution and what it meant for the future of proletarian revolutions elsewhere. Although broadly supportive of the Bolshevik coup, Luxemburg also remained critical of Lenin's 'vanguard revolution' theories and felt that his dictatorial leadership was suffocating a genuine revolution carried by the masses. She felt that Lenin's view of the party's role as a dictatorial watchman directing the proletariat in their struggle against the bourgeoisie, while eliminating all internal opposition within the socialist movement, would indeed be outright dangerous:

When all this is eliminated, what really remains? In place of the representative bodies created by general, popular elections, Lenin and Trotsky have laid down the soviets as the only true representation of political life in the land as a whole, life in the soviets must also become more and more crippled. Without general elections, without unrestricted freedom of press and assembly, without a free struggle of opinion, life dies out in every public institution, becomes a mere semblance of life, in which only the bureaucracy remains as the active element. Public life gradually falls asleep, a few dozen party leaders of inexhaustible energy and boundless experience direct and rule. Among them, in reality only a dozen outstanding heads do the leading and an elite of the working class is invited from time to time to meetings where they are to applaud the speeches of the leaders, and to approve proposed resolutions unanimously—at bottom, then, a clique affair—a dictatorship, to be sure, not the dictatorship of the proletariat but only the dictatorship of a handful of politicians, that is a dictatorship in the bourgeois sense, in the sense of the rule of the Jacobins (the postponement of the Soviet Congress from three-month periods to six-month periods!). Yes, we can go even further: such conditions must inevitably cause a brutalization of public life: attempted assassinations, shooting of hostages, etc.[7]

Luxemburg felt that if Lenin's model was adopted elsewhere, it would create a small revolutionary elite out of touch with ordinary workers in whose organizational capacities and revolutionary ambitions she firmly believed. Most importantly, communist parties across Europe ought to allow for opinions at odds with party doctrine: 'Freedom only for supporters of the government, only for members of a single party, however numerous, this is not freedom. Freedom must always be for those who think differently.'[8] To be sure, what Luxemburg had in mind was not lenience towards, or tolerance of, the 'class enemies' of revolution, but socialist pluralism within the future dictatorship of the proletariat.

After nearly three years of imprisonment, Luxemburg was released in early November 1918. From Breslau, she immediately returned to Berlin, where she rejoined her friends pushing for a 'proper' revolution.[9] Ten days after her release, Luxemburg wrote to her old friend Clara Zetkin: 'Dearest, in all haste, just a few lines. Since I got off the train I have not yet set foot at home. Up until yesterday the entire time has been taken up in pursuit of the *Rote Fahne*. Would it appear or wouldn't it? The struggle turned on this question from early in the morning till late at night.'[10]

Luxemburg and Liebknecht frantically demanded 'a second revolution', notably in their articles in *Die Rote Fahne*. On 18 November, ten days after her release from Breslau prison and return to Berlin, Luxemburg published an essay that insisted on the continuation of the revolution beyond the overthrow of the imperial state: 'Scheidemann-Ebert are the appointed leaders of the German Revolution in its current stage. But the Revolution is not standing still. Its law of life is rapid advancement...'[11]

It was not only bourgeois contemporaries who failed to relish such a prospect. In a letter of 13 December 1918 to the left-wing essayist Margarete Susman, Gustav Landauer described Liebknecht and his 'Bolshevist' followers as 'pure centralists like Robespierre and his crew, whose ambition has no content but is solely concerned with power. They are working towards a military regiment that would be much more hideous than anything the world has seen before. Dictatorship of the armed proletariat—in that case, I'd really prefer another Napoleon!'[12]

Moderate Social Democrats found Liebknecht's and Luxemburg's rhetoric even more threatening, albeit for different reasons. Even if the actual power base of the 'Spartacus Group' was small, the example of the Russian Revolution nevertheless vividly demonstrated that all that was needed for a takeover of power was a small group of determined professional revolutionaries. Ebert had seen how, in autumn 1917, the minority of the Bolsheviks in Russia had chased off the parliament and plunged the country into a devastating civil war. As a result, he wanted to keep the radicals around Luxemburg and Liebknecht away from power at any price.

The deep rifts between the different factions of the Left became even more apparent in mid-December 1918 when the General Congress of the Workers' and Soldiers' Councils met in Berlin, with delegates elected from all over Germany in attendance. The various speakers presented their often fundamentally opposed ideas for the future direction of the German revolution. The Majority Social Democrat Max Cohen presented the government's views, to huge applause and loud shouts of disagreement all at the same time.[13] For Cohen democracy and socialism were entirely compatible. The imperial regime had collapsed, democracy had prevailed. Now it was time for serious reforms. In order to achieve that objective, and to prevent Germany from descending into chaos, 'order' and 'discipline' were required. He emphasized the very real dangers that Germany was facing, the threat of being split up once more into small states as a result of Allied decisions or separatist movements within Germany, be it in Bavaria or the Rhineland. A socialist democracy would only be feasible with a functioning economy. The alternative was 'Russian conditions'—a state of violence, chaos, and starvation. 'When production is halted, as it is with us, when neither raw materials nor factories are available: what is there actually to socialize? In these circumstances *immediate socialization is complete madness*. There is nothing whatsoever to socialize!' Germany's future depended on the German people's ability to work across class boundaries. Only a National Assembly, elected by all adult Germans, had a proper mandate to make decisions about the country's future constitution. Germany also needed a legitimate government to negotiate a peace treaty with the Allies.[14]

Cohen's position was endorsed by the majority of the delegates at the congress, but it also provoked strong objections from the far Left. They demanded a radical break with the past: the immediate nationalization of key industries, direct democracy through a system of workers' and soldiers' councils, and the purging of the civil service and judiciary of those loyal to the old imperial regime. Furthermore, the German left should build a global proletarian alliance across borders and reach out its hand in friendship to the revolutionary regime in Russia. Cohen's main antagonist at the congress, the Independent Socialist Ernst Däumig, proclaimed: 'Seventy years ago the poet of the [1848] revolution [Ferdinand Freiligrath] said *that the proletariat is called to destroy the old world and build the new one*. That task was not fulfilled in his day. But that is our task; that is the demand of this hour and this day.' For Däumig, a great admirer of the Bolshevik revolution in Russia, immediate action was required if the German proletariat wanted to destroy the 'rotten' imperial state once and for all. This could not be achieved through parliamentary debates and negotiations with employers. Deeds, not words, were needed. Däumig therefore rejected the idea of general elections for a National Assembly.[15]

Despite Däumig's passionate speech, the Majority Social Democrats triumphed at the congress. The majority of delegates rejected the idea of a councils' republic and instead voted in favour of the quick convening of a National Assembly after free and universal elections, to be held in January 1919. Yet the decision to call general elections failed to resolve the tensions within the Left. Just how tense the relationship between the different factions within Germany's labour movement had grown became evident by Christmas 1918, when a long-smouldering conflict between the left-leaning People's Navy Division (*Volksmarinedivision*) and Berlin's military commander, Otto Wels (MSPD), finally escalated. Wels perceived the People's Navy Division as a threat, an armed unit in the capital that appeared to sympathize with Bolshevism. He insisted on a significant reduction of the Division and withheld the soldiers' wages as leverage. In response, on 23 December, the mutinous sailors took Wels prisoner. Ebert reacted quickly: without conferring with his coalition partner, the USPD, he asked the army for immediate military assistance. The ensuing bloody fighting in the city centre, around the Hohenzollerns' Imperial Castle, ended with an embarrassing military defeat of the government troops.[16]

Many contemporaries observing the events in Berlin regretted the escalation of violence on the streets of the capital: 'Christmas! And in the city they are shooting cannons...From 8 to 11 o'clock they are shot at the Castle and Marstall with gas shells and machine guns. Dead and wounded. At noon it is said that the sailors have surrendered. But the outcome is more a victory for the soldiers than for the Ebert government.'[17]

The 'Battle of Christmas Eve' was indeed very violent (Figure 9.2), even though the use of poison gas was just a rumour. As well as emphasizing the relative weakness of Ebert's government, it had two immediate consequences: the first was the end of the short-lived pragmatic alliance between the USPD and the MSPD. On 29 December, the three USPD representatives left the Council of People's Deputies, strongly protesting against Ebert's unilateral decision to dispatch troops against the sailors. Second, the Prussian Prime Minister, Paul Hirsch (MSPD), decided to dismiss the chief of the Berlin police, Emil Eichhorn (USPD), who had come to the aid of the People's Navy Division by sending out the Berlin Security Guard (*Sicherheitswehr*).[18] Eichhorn had also told his direct superior, the Prussian Minister of the Interior, Paul Hirsch (MSPD), that he did not accept his authority.[19] The USPD and the more radical Left, including the newly founded Communist Party (KPD), reacted to what they regarded as a deliberate provocation by calling for a mass demonstration against the Ebert government on 5 January. The situation quickly escalated, not least—as the historian Mark Jones has shown—because each side believed the rumours that their opponents were about to attack with force.[20] One

Figure 9.2 Intensive fighting over Christmas 1918 between government soldiers and revolutionary troops from the People's Navy Division ended in a defeat for the government forces. In this picture government snipers are in position on the Brandenburg Gate, looking down the Charlottenburger Chaussee, along which a large proportion of the revolutionaries approached the Reichstag on 9 November.

group of armed demonstrators occupied the building of the Social Democratic newspaper *Vorwärts*, along with other publishing houses in Berlin's newspaper district. On the evening of 5 January, these spontaneous actions were followed by the formation of a 'Revolutionary Committee', while Liebknecht further escalated the situation by once more demanding the 'overthrow of the Ebert–Scheidemann government'.[21]

On 5 January 1919, some 100,000 people demonstrated on the streets of Berlin against Eichhorn's dismissal. The high point of the protest was a speech by Liebknecht at the police headquarters. Liebknecht announced that 'now is the time for the most determined struggle of the revolutionary proletariat, it must do more than protect the gains of the revolution…it must make this revolution into a socialist revolution, which must become world revolution.'[22]

Harry Graf Kessler attended the event as an onlooker, primarily to understand Liebknecht's appeal to the far Left: 'When he ended there was a roar of approval, red flags were flourished, and thousands of hands and hats rose in the air. He was like an invisible high priest of the Revolution, a mysterious, resounding symbol, to which these people looked up. The demonstration seemed halfway between a Roman mass and a Puritan prayer meeting. The wave of Bolshevism coming in from the East resembles the invasion by Islam in the seventh century...'[23]

Käthe Kollwitz also followed developments with increasing concern: 'On Sunday 5 January, demonstration gatherings against Eichhorn's dismissal. Hans [her son], who is in the student assembly in the evenings and comes home late, tells me that the *Vorwärts* has once again been occupied by Spartacus. All the agitation material for the National Assembly has been burnt on the street.'[24] The following day, she added: 'Went to the studio to work. Back through the city, because the tram was interrupted. Everywhere masses of people in excitement. At Alexanderplatz I saw a procession of around 100 armed workers marching, some miserable-looking, raggedy soldiers among them. The men are lean, gloomy, determined, followed by adolescents.'[25]

Liberal Germans were also fearful of the ensuing chaos and disruption in Berlin that January. Corresponding with her son Gerhard (who would later, after changing his first name to the biblical 'Gershom', gain fame as a scholar of Jewish mysticism), Betty Scholem complained that the family's printing shop in Berlin was suffering from the strikes and demonstrations outside. She explained to her son, who had recently started university in Switzerland, that she worried about the armed conflicts in the streets and the absence of electricity.[26] But worse was yet to come. 'We have an unbelievable week behind us, dismal to the highest degree.... [Spartacus'] reign of terror was frightful.'[27]

Even if the actual power base of the Spartacus League was small, its very existence raised concerns among the leading Majority Social Democrats. Ebert took the threat very seriously. In his view (and in this he was not alone) the communist uprising in Berlin in January 1919 bore more than a fleeting resemblance to the Bolsheviks' successful bid for power in the autumn of 1917. He was utterly determined to prevent the events in Petrograd from repeating themselves in Berlin, with force if necessary.[28] During the night of 5–6 January, Ebert and his government had issued a strongly worded statement condemning the far Left's actions and calling on their followers to assemble at the Reich Chancellery in the Wilhelmstraße and to protect the government.[29]

The following morning, Philipp Scheidemann addressed the crowd of MSPD supporters that had answered Ebert's call and gathered outside the Reich Chancellery: 'It cannot be tolerated that a small minority rules the people, today that's just as unacceptable as before . . . the minority must give way to the will of the majority. That's why we are demanding the National Assembly. . . . We appeal to the entire people, especially those who are armed, the soldiers, that they remain available to the government. For the moment, we can only ask you to wait here, and to declare your support for us by calling out: long live freedom, equality, solidarity!'[30]

Ebert then spoke from a window of the same building. Drawing on the by then constant references to Russia, he warned that Karl Radek, who had illegally entered Germany from Russia, was liaising with Eichhorn about bringing Russian soldiers to the Rhine to fight in a new coalition against the British and French. He also accused the Spartacists of further escalating the spiral of violence:

There will be further loss of blood. It was difficult for us to declare ourselves in agreement, when we know that there will be shooting at women and children, shooting at fathers and mothers. But the Spartacist gang will have it no other way, and now we too must act! . . . Soldiers, those of you who did your duty out there in the field, you have to realize that it is now your duty to see to it, that order returns to Berlin, that we obtain peace and that you can finally take off the rags which you had to wear for four and a half years! . . . Finally, now is the time to bring things to an end! Women and children, go home, don't be like the Spartacists who push women and children to the front. Now the work of the men has begun![31]

A central figure in this situation was the MSPD's military expert, Gustav Noske, who had previously played a central role in containing the revolution in Kiel in November 1918. Now, following the departure of the USPD from the Council of People's Deputies, he had assumed responsibility for the army and navy within the government. With the famous words '[s]omebody has to be the bloodhound, and I do not shrink from this responsibility', Noske assumed command of the government troops in and around Berlin.[32] In his mind, the task ahead was to re-establish 'law and order' with all available means. For this purpose, he did not rely on regular troops alone, but also, even mainly, on *Freikorps* volunteers. It was no coincidence that many of these right-wing formations called themselves 'Freikorps'—a name coined during the anti-Napoleonic 'Wars of Liberation' (1813–1915) when German volunteers, spurred on by Prussia's military humiliation at the hands of the French, made a significant contribution to Napoleon's eventual defeat. The *Freikorps* of the early Weimar years had a different purpose. What united them was a profound hatred of communism and, more often than not, of the republican system which they were now called upon to defend against 'Bolshevism' (Figure 9.3).[33]

In calling on these volunteers to terminate the apparent threat of Bolshevism hanging over the German capital, Noske was enlisting those members of German society who had loathed and opposed the revolution from the very beginning, and who had been waiting for an opportunity to settle scores for the past two months. They were not fighting *for* the republic, but against 'Bolshevism'. Within the *Freikorps*,

Figure 9.3 'A spectre is haunting Europe…' The fear of Bolshevism spreading westwards, which the poster shown here is designed to stoke, was a widespread fear of the time, and it had a significant influence on political developments.

former front-line soldiers, infuriated by defeat and the subsequent revolution, joined forces with untested cadets and right-wing students, who compensated for their lack of combat experience by often surpassing the war veterans in terms of radicalism, activism, and brutality.

For many of these younger volunteers, who had come of age in a bellicose atmosphere saturated with tales of heroic bloodshed but had missed out on a first-hand experience of the 'storms of steel', the militias offered a welcome opportunity to live a romanticized warrior existence. As one militia leader observed, many younger volunteers tried to impress their superiors through 'rough militarist behaviour', which was 'nurtured as a virtue in large parts of the post-war youth', and which deeply affected the general tone and atmosphere within paramilitary organizations after 1918.[34] Once they had joined paramilitary units dominated by former shock-troop officers, younger volunteers were keen to prove their worthiness within a community of often highly decorated warriors and 'war heroes'.[35]

Together the battle-hardened veterans of the Great War and the younger 'romantic' volunteers formed explosive all-male subcultures in which brutal violence was an acceptable, if not desirable, form of political expression. Action, not ideas, was the defining characteristic of these groups. They were driven forward not by a revolutionary vision of a new political utopia, but by a common rhetoric of restoring order and an interlocking series of social antipathies.[36]

A central part of this was anti-feminism. Even before the war, the rise of a large and vociferous feminist movement had raised concerns among conservatives who feared the 'feminization' of German society, fears that were cemented by female suffrage in 1918. After 1918, with a female majority among German voters, this 'nightmarish' vision had become a reality and it fed into a general perception that order and discipline had been swept away by the revolution, and that moral degeneracy was taking over society. Prominent female activists of the far Left such as Rosa Luxemburg were particularly hated by the far Right, as were gay people who felt much liberated by the revolution and became much more outspoken after November 1918.[37]

Even if the abolition of the infamous 'gay paragraph', Section 175 of the penal code, was not raised during or immediately after the revolution—it was only scrapped by the Reichstag's penal review committee in 1929, but the reform was never implemented—many homosexuals regarded the revolution as a great liberation, notably for those living in the German capital. Berlin had been a centre for a variety of social and sexual subcultures long before 1914, but nothing compared to the post-war period.[38] Homosexual emancipation activists hoped that the new age of democracy would bring about a new dawn for sexual liberation and gay rights emancipation. The coming of democracy did bring limited press freedom:[39] new magazines for gay men, lesbians, and transvestites were put on the market and sold at street kiosks and by subscription all over Germany, causing 'an absolute tidal wave of homosexual journals', in Magnus Hirschfeld's words.[40]

Needless to say, these limited freedoms alarmed the far Right, which was anyhow under the impression that the world had been turned upside down by the revolution of 1918. In marked contrast to the hostile world that surrounded them, the militias offered clearly defined hierarchies, and a familiar sense of belonging and purpose. The paramilitary groups viewed themselves as fortresses of soldierly camaraderie, masculinity, and 'order' in what the activists perceived as a hostile world of democratic egalitarianism, communist internationalism, feminism, and gay rights campaigners. It was this spirit of camaraderie, coupled with the desire to be part of a post-war project that would imbue meaning in what now seemed the pointless experience of mass death and defeat during war, which held these groups together. They perceived themselves to be the nucleus of a 'new society' of warriors, representing both the eternal values of the nation and new authoritarian concepts for a state in which that nation could thrive.[41]

One of them, Ernst von Salomon, who had experienced the post-war Revolution of 1918 as a 16-year-old cadet, described his (retrospectively stylized) perception of the revolution in his autobiographical novel *Die Geächteten* (*The Outlaws*):

Behind the (red) flag tired crowds surged in a disorderly fashion. Women marched in front. They shoved their way ahead with their broad skirts, the grey skin of their faces hanging in wrinkles over sharp bones.... The men, old and young, soldiers and workers, and many petty bourgeois in between them, strode with dull, worn faces.... Thus they marched, the champions of the revolution. Was it from this black crowd that the glowing flame of revolution was to spring, that the dream of blood and barricades was to be realized? Impossible to capitulate before them.... I sneered at their claims which knew no pride, no confidence in victory... I stood up straight and thought 'rabble', 'pack', 'scum', and squinted as I watched these hollow, destitute figures; like rats, I thought, carrying the dust of the gutter upon their backs...'[42]

Just like von Salomon, many former front-line soldiers bitterly resented the outbreak of revolution in 1918 and felt that their sacrifices had been betrayed by the home front. One experience commonly recounted in the memoirs and diaries of right-wing veterans was the humiliation of being stripped of their medals and epaulettes by the supporters of the workers' and soldiers' councils.

On 15 November 1918 I was on the way from the hospital at Bad Nauheim to my garrison at Brandenburg. As I was limping along with the aid of my cane at the Potsdam station in Berlin, a band of uniformed men, sporting red armbands, stopped me and demanded that I surrender my epaulettes and insignia. I raised my stick in reply; but my rebellion was soon overcome. I was thrown down, and only the intervention of a railroad official saved me from my humiliating position. Hate flamed in me against the November criminals from that moment. As soon as my health improved somewhat, I joined forces with the groups devoted to the overthrow of the rebellion.[43]

Others felt unwelcomed by their relatives on arrival back home because their long absence and corresponding loss in family income had not been vindicated by victory—a theme explored in Joseph Roth's famous and remarkably perceptive 1923 novel *The Spider's Web*. Roth's novel centres on the post-war upheavals in Berlin: the protagonist of the book, Lieutenant Theodor Lohse, is one of the many demobilized officers of the Central Powers, for whom defeat in the Great War serves as a major source of political mobilization against the post-war order. Forced to earn a meagre living as a private tutor in the household of a wealthy Jewish businessman, Lohse soon despairs over the perceived national humiliation caused by military collapse and the hostility with which his own family greets his return from the battlefields of Flanders: 'They couldn't forgive Theodor—he who had twice been mentioned in dispatches—for having failed to die a hero's death as a lieutenant. A dead son would have been the pride of the family. A demobilized lieutenant, a victim of the revolution, was a burden to his womenfolk. . . . He could have told his sisters that he was not responsible for his own misfortune; that he cursed the revolution and was gnawed by hatred for the socialists and the Jews; that he bore each day like a yoke across his bowed neck and felt himself trapped in his epoch as in some sunless prison.'[44]

The only escape route for Lohse from the 'sunless prison' of an invalidated existence is the possibility of continuing the war through other means. In consequence Lohse quickly joins one of the many paramilitary organizations that mushroomed in post-war Europe and which embodied a major problem facing most of the Continent in the years immediately after 1918: the inability of many to leave the war behind them and to accept the arrival of peace. As one of the more prominent real-life *Freikorps* men, Friedrich Wilhelm Heinz, put it in his memoirs: 'When they told us that the war was over, we laughed, because we *were* the war. Its flame continued to burn in us, it lived on in our deeds surrounded by a glowing and frightful aura of destruction. We followed our inner calling and marched on the battlefields of the post-war period...'[45]

The absence of Allied soldiers on German soil before the official end of hostilities on 11 November appeared to give plausibility to a conspiracy theory first propagated by Ludendorff and Hindenburg in the autumn of 1918: that the German army had not actually been defeated from outside but had only collapsed as a result of a 'stab-in-the-back' by subversive elements on the home front. Those who promoted the idea of the army having been 'undefeated in the field' could build on older and well-established narratives of betrayal, notably the medieval legend of the Nibelungs, in which the Germanic hero Siegfried is callously stabbed in the back with a spear. Its modern, post-1918 version emphasized rootless internationalist conspiracies and betrayal on the home front as the primary cause of Germany's defeat, an idea that was to become a cornerstone of right-wing belief in interwar Germany.[46]

The myth of the 'undefeated' German army allegedly betrayed by the revolution travelled fast, even beyond the German borders and into far-flung PoW camps. The German-language journal of the Japanese prisoner camp Bandō (where some 1,000 German and a handful of Austro-Hungarian PoWs had been interned since 1917) noted in early December: 'While the troops on the western front, largely unshaken, still continued the unequal struggle, the house behind the front had been engulfed in bright flames. We now lie defenceless before the enemy; again, as once before after Jena and Auerstedt [the twin battles of 1806, during which Prussia suffered a crushing military defeat at the hands of Napoleon], our fatherland must wade through insult and disgrace.'[47]

Central to the stab-in-the-back myth was the sometimes implicit, but more often explicit, notion that the betrayal had to be avenged on a 'day of reckoning' when the 'enemy within' would be combated ruthlessly and without mercy. As the notorious German *Freikorps* leader, former naval officer and future Nazi Ambassador to Bucharest Manfred von Killinger emphasized in a letter to his family: 'I have made a promise to myself, Father. Without armed struggle, I have handed over my torpedo boat to the enemies and watched my flag go down. I have sworn to take revenge against those who are responsible for this.'[48]

Noske's decision to recruit men like Killinger in an attempt to suppress the perceived Bolshevik threat thus offered such men a state-sanctioned opportunity to act on their fantasies of violent retribution. It was in Berlin in January 1919, during the suppression of the 'Spartacus Uprising', that the pent-up hatred towards the November Revolution and its backers exploded. Fired by the government's official statement of 8 January announcing that 'violence can only be met with violence' and that the 'hour of revenge draws near',[49] the *Freikorps* marched on Berlin, joining forces with regular troops. On 11 January, they stormed the newspaper district. Using artillery fire and machine guns, they attacked the rebels' stronghold in the *Vorwärts* building. Despite surrendering, seven of the occupiers of the *Vorwärts* building were brutally murdered by the *Freikorps*. Others, such as Hilde Steinbrink, who had manned the last machine gun with which the Spartacists sought to defend themselves against the *Freikorps* troops, were arrested and interned.[50] Overall, some 200 people were killed during the January Uprising, and a further 400 arrested. That afternoon, Noske led a military parade of 3,000 troops through central Berlin to celebrate the victory of his 'forces of order' over their communist adversaries. By 12 January, all remaining pockets of resistance had been eliminated.[51]

To left-liberal and social democratic observers, the killing of German workers was deeply regrettable, but this feeling was not shared by everyone: 'Great joy among the bourgeois public over the storming of the police headquarters, which succeeded last night. I am devastated, very much so, even if I am content that Spartacus has been pushed back. But I have the eerie feeling that the troops have not been called in for that alone; the reaction is on the march. In addition, this raw application of power, this shooting of comrades—of those who should be comrades—is horrible.'[52]

Even more conservative contemporaries such as the prominent historian Friedrich Meinecke, who lived in the affluent Berlin suburb of Dahlem, where the *Freikorps* had gathered before moving into the city, expressed concern that the Ebert government had unleashed forces that it might not be able to control: 'The Spartacus terror, that kept us on edge for eight days, now appears to be broken. It was essential to deploy a small but reliable force against this spectre, which emanated from a cowardly rabble.... But will these young lieutenants, who have once more put on their uniforms and who are marching in rank and file with their guns, also have the tact to understand the new era?... After all, there is but a tender band between the Ebert government and these helpers from the bourgeoisie and the reserve officers.'[53]

Luxemburg and Liebknecht, the two most prominent members of the Central Committee of the Communist Party, tried to escape the ongoing revenge killings in Berlin by hiding in constantly changing quarters in the capital. Both had done little to de-escalate the situation even when it had become clear that the rebels were doomed to fail. If she had private doubts about the far Left's ability to seize power from the government, Luxemburg still publicly reiterated her firm conviction that the Ebert government had to be toppled with force. On 8 January she wrote in *Rote Fahne*: 'The lessons of the last three days clearly urge the working class: Do not talk! Do not discuss things forever! Do not negotiate! Act!'[54]

After several days on the run, Luxemburg and Liebknecht reached their last hiding place in a flat in the affluent suburb of Wilmersdorf. Here they wrote their final articles for the *Rote Fahne*. Liebknecht published his ardent text '*Trotz alledem!*' ('Despite it all!'), in which he admitted temporary defeat but called on his followers to persevere. The time had not been quite ripe for a communist revolution to succeed, he wrote: 'The horrendous counter-revolutionary mudslide from backward elements of the people and the propertied classes drowned it.' And yet: 'The defeated of today will be the victors of tomorrow.'[55] Luxemburg seconded these sentiments in a powerful essay, sarcastically entitled 'Order restored in Berlin': 'You stupid henchmen! Your "order" is built on sand. Tomorrow the revolution will once again "raise itself with a rattle" and announce with fanfare, to your terror: "I was, I am, I will be!" '[56]

In the evening hours of 15 January 1919, right-wing paramilitaries broke into the flat. Liebknecht and Luxemburg were arrested and— together with another communist activist, Wilhelm Pieck, the future President of the German Democratic Republic, they were handed over to the 'Garde-Kavallerie-Schützen-Division', an elite unit of the old

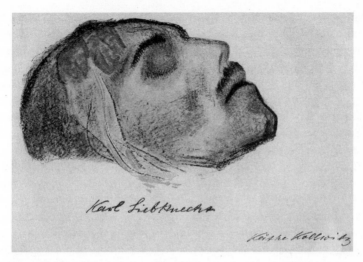

Figure 9.4 Karl Liebknecht, the leader of the far Left of the German revolutionary movement, on his deathbed. His head is held together with a bandage, having been shot in his brutal murder at the hands of *Freikorps* soldiers. This drawing of the dead revolutionary was produced by Käthe Kollwitz.

imperial army, now under the command of a notorious anti-Bolshevik, Captain Waldemar Pabst.[57] At the division's temporary headquarters in the up-market Hotel Eden, Pieck, for reasons that have never been fully clarified, managed to convince Pabst to let him go (possibly in exchange for information on the hiding places of other Spartacists, as Pabst himself claimed in a post-1945 interview).[58] Liebknecht meanwhile was assaulted, spat upon, and struck down with rifle butts. At 10.45 that night, the unconscious communist leader was driven to the largest park in central Berlin, the Tiergarten, where he was shot three times at close range (Figure 9.4). The killers then dropped Liebknecht's body unceremoniously at a close-by ambulance station, claiming that they had found 'an unidentified body'.[59]

According to the official report filed by the division, Luxemburg was in the meantime taken away from her guards by an 'outraged crowd'. In reality, Luxemburg sat in Pabst's temporary office reading Goethe's *Faust* when the soldiers returned to the hotel. She was also struck twice in the face by a rifle butt. Bleeding heavily, she was thrown into a car. After a short drive, a lieutenant jumped onto the left running board and killed Luxemburg with a single shot to the head. Her corpse was thrown into the Landwehr Canal, and her decomposed body was only found several weeks later, in May 1919.[60] When Liebknecht and another thirty-one murdered Spartacists were buried on 25 January 1919, more than 100,000 people took to the streets and participated in the procession, many of them people who had not backed the rising, but regretted the killings. The marches were accompanied by a heavy police and military presence, including some of the very same *Freikorps* soldiers who had murdered Liebknecht and Luxemburg. As the artist Käthe Kollwitz noted in her diary that day: 'Karl Liebknecht was buried today.... I was permitted to make a sketch of him and went to the morgue early in the morning. There, in the hall, alongside the other coffins, he lay in state. Red flowers had been laid around his shattered forehead, his face proud, his mouth slightly open and distorted with pain, a somewhat surprised expression upon his face. His hands lay alongside each other, a couple of red flowers on his white shirt.' She then proceeded to describe the funeral: 'The entire centre of the city is closed off; the enormous column of marchers has been diverted... From Friedrichshain the column marched behind the coffins... How petty and false these measures are. If Berlin—a large part of Berlin—wishes to bury its fallen, then that is not a revolutionary matter. Even between battles there are hours of rest set aside to bury the dead. It is unworthy and provocative to hassle those who wish to follow Liebknecht to his burial with military means. And it is a sign of the government's weakness that it must endure that.'[61]

The murder of these two revolutionary leaders was a prominent example of the brutalization of political life as a result of the war and its legacies. It continued for years to come, as became evident, for example, when the USPD leader Hugo Haase was shot and killed in 1919 by an allegedly insane leatherworker, Johann Voss, as Haase tried to enter the Reichstag building. A few years later, in 1922, German Foreign Minister Walther Rathenau was assassinated by members of the far-right 'Organisation Consul'. Only two weeks earlier, an attempt by the same secret organization to kill the former SPD-Chancellor and then mayor of Kassel, Philipp Scheidemann, with prussic acid had failed.[62] But this brutalization did not only affect Germany. Political murders were widespread in Europe during the immediate post-war period. In Ireland, men like Michael Collins fell victim to one during the civil war. In Hungary, the left-liberal star columnist Béla Bacsó and the editor-in-chief of the social democratic daily newspaper Népszava,

Béla Somogyi, were also murdered. Nor did the wave of politically motivated murders wane after 1919. On 15 March 1921, for instance, the Armenian student Soghomon Tehlirian shot the former Interior Minister of the Ottoman Empire, Talat Pasha, one of those chiefly responsible for the Armenian genocide that unfolded from the spring of 1915 onwards and during which up to 1.5 million Ottoman Armenians had been systematically killed. In 1925, a dental technician in Vienna with ties to the Austrian Nazi Party murdered the novelist Hugo Bettauer, who, as a converted Jew with liberal political opinions, fitted into the radical Right's concept of the enemy. A few years later, the Yugoslav King Alexander I suffered the same fate in Marseille. His assassin was a member of the Croatian Ustasha, which felt suppressed by the Serb majority. Murder as a means of political conflict was no longer an exception, but rather an integral feature of post-war European culture.

In Germany's case, the murders of Luxemburg and Liebknecht would have long-term consequences for the relationship between communists and Social Democrats. Horrified by Noske's decision to unleash the forces of counter-revolution on German workers, one of the most prominent women's rights activists in Germany, Clara Zetkin, was prompted to break all remaining ties with the Social Democrats.[63] Zetkin, who had not previously followed her close friend Luxemburg into the newly founded Communist Party, now—at the age of 62— decided to join the KPD: 'As old as I am . . . I nevertheless want to use the time in which I can still be active to stand and fight where life is and not where decay and weakness are staring at me.'[64]

The gap that had opened up within the socialist workers' movement before and during the First World War and that had widened in the Blood Christmas of 1918 now became an insurmountable chasm. For the far Left—the supporters of the USPD and the KPD—it was clear that the leadership of the Majority Social Democrats bore responsibility for the violent events of January 1919, which overshadow the relationship between the Left party and the SPD to this day. By contrast, Ebert and Noske were convinced that they had preserved Germany from Bolshevism and 'Russian conditions' through consistent action—an issue that also played a large role in the election campaign for the National Assembly in January 1919.

10

The triumph of liberalism

Amid an atmosphere of revolutionary turmoil and violence in January 1919, the German public was called to elect a National Constitutional Assembly, the German interim parliament assembled to draw up a new constitution for the Reich. On election day, the voters turned out in unprecedented numbers and returned an overwhelming majority of 76 per cent for the three parties that firmly stood for a *democratic* renewal of Germany: the Majority Social Democrats (37 per cent), the liberal German Democratic Party or DDP (18.5 per cent), and the Catholic Centre Party (19.7 per cent). In other words, the MSPD gained 3.1 per cent in comparison to the last general elections of 1912, despite the fact the more radical USPD had split from the main party. The largest opposition party, with a share of just over 10 per cent, was the nationalist DNVP, followed by the USPD (7.6 per cent) and the national-liberal DVP.[1] The result was unequivocal: the great majority of Germans wanted a new democratic beginning and not the kind of socio-economic revolution that elements of the USPD and the newly founded KPD demanded. The latter had called for a boycott of the general election, most likely because they realized that the election results would reveal their weakness.

One of the most important changes in these elections, the first fully democratic elections in Germany, was that all adults over the age of 20 were enfranchised. For the first time in German national elections, women had full and equal suffrage and were able to vote and stand for election at the local and national level—a turn of events that is even more remarkable given that both the Reichstag and the Prussian Landtag had rejected suffrage petitions just weeks before the revolution.[2] Germany was, of course, by no means the first country where women had won the right to vote: New Zealand's women had gained that right in 1893. In Europe, Finnish women won full civil rights in

1906, Norwegian women in 1913, and Danish women in 1915. Yet Germany was the first major highly industrialized country in the world to enfranchise women.

As early as 12 November 1918, the Council of People's Deputies had released the following decree: 'All elections to public bodies shall henceforth be conducted according to equal, secret, general voting rights on the basis of the proportional election system for all male and female persons of at least twenty years of age.'[3] Less than three weeks later, on 30 November, the new National Voting Act came into force, granting active and passive voting rights for women. This cleared the path for the first nationwide elections with female participation: the elections for the National Assembly on 19 January 1919 in which women were allowed to vote and be elected for public office. Prior to this, there had already been some state parliament elections in which women were permitted to use their voting rights: In Baden, women first exercised this basic democratic right on 5 January 1919, and in Württemberg on 12 January 1919. The women's rights activist Marianne Weber (DDP), who was married to the sociologist Max Weber, became the first woman ever to take the floor in a German parliament. In her maiden speech in the Karlsruhe *Ständehaus*, she addressed her colleagues and pointed out that: 'We women express our great joy and satisfaction that we have been called to join in this task, and I believe I may be able to say that we are better prepared for it than most of you might believe.'[4]

Conservative female politicians also welcomed universal suffrage, albeit for different reasons as one of the most prolific DNVP delegates in the Constituent Assembly in Weimar, Käthe Schirmacher, made clear. Schirmacher was born in Danzig in 1865 as the daughter of a wealthy merchant and had been one of the first women in Germany to obtain a Ph.D. Openly gay, a vocal supporter of the progressive feminist movement before 1914, and one of the co-founders of the International Woman Suffrage Alliance, she gradually moved politically from the Left to the far Right. During the Great War, she had become a supporter of the nationalist Fatherland Party, and a role-model, in the eyes of like-minded women, for female participation in public affairs. After 1918, Schirmacher came to emphasize female involvement in politics as a crucial precondition for a rejuvenation of the German nation, a nation thrown into deep crisis by the men's failure to secure victory in 1918.[5]

Weber's and Schirmacher's self-confidence partly stemmed from the knowledge that women now composed the majority of Germany's voters. Because of the war-induced population changes—notably the deaths of some two million German men, the majority of eligible voters—there were 2.8 million more female voters (17 million in total) than male voters.[6] And the vast majority of them exercised their right to vote: in the general elections for the National Assembly in January 1919, more than 82 per cent of all eligible female citizens over the age of 21 cast their vote—an extremely high level of political participation in a period of general tension and unrest (Figure 10.1). The majority of them did not vote for political parties of the Left (which tended to be more strongly supported by men), but for the Centre-Right and nationalist Right.[7]

At the same time, 300 women used their newly won right to stand for election. In the end, there were 39 elected female members of the National Assembly (including Marie Behnke and Helene Grünberg, who succeeded two deputies upon their deaths). Despite their inclination to vote for centrist parties or for the Conservative Right, female representation within the National Assembly was strongest in the parties of the Left, notably in the two Social Democratic parties, the MSPD and the USPD, who together had twenty-one female MPs in the National Assembly.[8] One of them, the 40-year-old Majority Social Democrat Marie Juchacz, a trained tailor who had been a member of the MSPD party leadership since 1917, became the first female elected representative of the people in a German national parliament to give a speech.[9] On 19 February 1919, she noted 'that it was the revolution that helped to overcome old prejudices here in Germany'. The revolution had given women 'what had hitherto been wrongly kept from them'.[10] There were other indicators of a huge increase in political activity among German women, too. The number of female members in the free trade unions rose dramatically from 500,000 in 1918 to 1.7 million in 1920, while membership in the MSPD among women rose from 66,000 to over 200,000 in the same period.[11]

Whatever drove an individual's election choice, the results paved the way for a more formal coalition of those parties that had supported the 1917 'Peace Resolution': The MSPD, the liberal German People's Party (DDP, which had become the successor party of Imperial Germany's Progressive People's Party), and the Catholic Centre Party. These three parties were soon to form the so-called 'Weimar coalition'.[12] The Weimar coalition gained its name from the central German city in which the National Assembly convened. It was here, in the National Theatre, that the constituent met from February 1919 onwards.

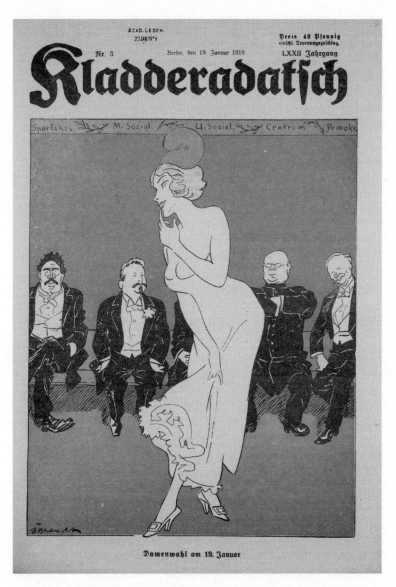

Figure 10.1 The satirical magazine *Kladderadatsch* refers to the election of 19 January 1919 as 'Ladies' Choice'. It was the first time that women in Germany had the right to vote in national elections. Female voters significantly outnumbered male voters in 1919.

Weimar had been chosen as the gathering place for the work on the new constitution not only because the situation in the capital was still considered unsettled after the 'Spartacist Rising', but also for symbolic reasons. The government thought that the 'spirit of Weimar'—the symbol of classical, humanistic German culture long associated with the life and work of the eighteenth- and early nineteenth-century German writers and sometime Weimar residents Johann Wolfgang von Goethe and Friedrich Schiller, would demonstrate a new beginning to both fellow Germans and the Allies. Apart from signalling a symbolic departure from the militaristic culture of Imperial Germany, the decision to draft the constitution in Weimar was also a concession to strong anti-Berlin sentiments in other parts of Germany (notably in Bavaria and in the Catholic Rhineland), whose populations felt that too much power was concentrated in Prussia and the capital.[13]

On 6 February 1919, the day of the formal opening of the National Assembly (and the day that also marked the twenty-third birthday of her fallen son, Peter, who had died in 1914), Käthe Kollwitz wrote in her diary: 'It is a beautiful day. For the first time after a long period I once again feel that I can achieve something. . . . I have sketched the mother who is clasping her two children; it is me with my own children, my Hans and my Peterchen. And I have managed to do it well. . . . In the evening we drank wine. To the boy's memory. And to the National Assembly.'[14]

It was Friedrich Ebert who gave the opening address to the National Assembly that day. Placing the revolution and the new political beginnings marked by the opening of the National Assembly in the context of the German liberal 'freedom movement' of the first half of the nineteenth century,[15] Ebert also repeated his pleas for order, discipline, and hard work to safeguard what had already been achieved. He absolved the revolution of responsibility for Germany's military defeat and its consequences. Those were, instead, the results of the war, the mistaken policies of the old elites, and the vengeful attitudes of the Entente powers. Like many of his fellow citizens, Ebert was still adamant that a Wilsonian peace ought to be the outcome of the Allied talks in Paris:

The war not only exhausted us. It also tremendously exhausted *our opponents.* And from this feeling of exhaustion comes their efforts to recover their losses from the German people and to bring the idea of exploitation into the work of peace. These revenge and rape plans require the strongest protest. (Bravo!) The German people cannot be made the wage slaves of other countries

for twenty, forty, or sixty years.... The German people are resolved to hold
responsible those who can be proven to have committed any intentional
wrongs or violations. But one should not punish those who were themselves
victims, victims of the war, victims of our previous lack of freedom.[16]

There was still an additional demand that Ebert raised on 6 February,
this time addressing his fellow parliamentarians: he asked the National
Assembly to authorize the government to immediately begin negotiations with the government of neighbouring German-Austria about a
unification of the two states. In doing so, Ebert suggested, the republic
would return to the Greater German aspirations of the first half of
the nineteenth century and 'reknit the bond that the violence of 1866
once tore asunder', by which he meant the Battle of Königgrätz
between Prussia and the Habsburg Empire. As a result of Prussia's victory in 1866, the German Question was decided in favour of the Small
German solution, a 'larger Prussia', as many critics—including the
SPD under its long-time leader August Bebel—had long argued.[17]

Ebert's demand for the *Anschluss* of Austria at the opening of the
German National Assembly requires some explanation, not least
because it appears highly naive in retrospect. However, in the winter of
1918–19 more than a few Germans hoped that the German Reich
would soon compensate for its military defeat and the anticipated loss
of Alsace-Lorraine by incorporating German-Austria, the truncated,
German-speaking state left over after the disintegration of the
Habsburg Empire.[18]

The debate on the *Anschluss* of Austria had already begun on 12
November 1918, when the Provisional Government in Vienna declared
German-Austria to be 'part of the German Republic'.[19] Ebert and the
Council of the People's Deputies were initially sceptical as to whether
or not the Allies would ever agree to such a fait accompli,[20] but the
six members of the revolutionary government certainly regarded it as
worth striving for.[21] They appealed to the Wilsonian principle of self-
determination of peoples, on which—at least that's what most
Germans believed until the spring of 1919—the Versailles Peace Treaty
would be based.

The widespread hope for a 'peace of reconciliation' and the imminent
union of Germany and German-Austria were all part of the initially
optimistic mood that characterized the first post-war months in
Germany. In the view of the German sociologist Max Weber, the revolution appeared to be the 'most certain way of bringing the Greater

German problem that now stands before us to a solution'.[22] Particularly
in the first weeks following the armistice, many believed the time for
the Greater German Republic, which the revolutionaries of 1848 had
strived for in vain, had finally arrived. 'Proudly and upright we stand
here and place upon the grave of the old Reich the hope for a Greater
Germany,' commented Wilhelm Heile, a DDP supporter and leading
pan-Europeanist, in an editorial for the left-liberal magazine *Die Hilfe*
in late autumn 1918. 'Now, unlike our fathers in 1871, we can build
ourselves a new house from the ground up.'[23]

Eminent German historians also supported the rebirth of the
Greater German idea with enthusiasm, despite the fact that most of
them had previously welcomed Bismarck's Small German solution of
1871 as the fulfilment of German history, a 'developmental process that
led from Luther and the Reformation and the Great Elector and
Frederick the Great all the way to the Prussian reform era, only to find
its crowning conclusion in the work of Bismarck'.[24] Now, following
the collapse of Imperial Germany, this conception of history was
widely regarded as obsolete. The national-liberal *Vernunftrepublikaner*
['republican by reason alone'], Hermann Oncken, suddenly argued
that the disintegration of the multi-ethnic Austro-Hungarian Empire
had made a unification of the Reich with the German-speaking parts
of Austria both possible and essential. In the changed geopolitical
situation of 1918, Oncken believed, there was only one foreign policy
objective to which the German Republic ought to fully and completely commit itself: 'The return of the Greater German idea. That, for
us, is the opportunity resulting from the world crisis... Greater
Germany has now become possible because the Austrian dynastic state
no longer exists, and it has become necessary because German-Austria
cannot survive alone. Not only has the theoretical basis for the Small
German idea of 1848/66 become obsolete; the Small German Reich
itself which has existed from 1871 has lost its justification for existence.
The Small German idea... must automatically transform itself into the
Greater German idea.'[25]

For Oncken and many others, the common language and the shared
history, as evidenced most recently by the German–Austrian alliance
during the First World War, made unification in one nation-state a
logical next step. According to Oncken, the lost war and the collapse
and implosion of the Habsburg Empire and Germany's defeat even
possessed a 'historical meaning', namely that they provided for a unique

historical moment in which 'Germany's destiny' might be fulfilled through the *Anschluss* of Austria.[26] From an Austrian perspective, too, *Anschluss* made perfect sense given that Vienna had lost its empire, and the Republic of German Austria was deemed economically unviable by most contemporaries.

The broad public consensus regarding this Greater German expansion of the Reich after the war led to the founding of a whole series of non-partisan associations, such as the 'German-Austrian People's League' (Deutschösterreichischer Volksbund).[27] Its leadership reflected the breadth of the cross-party support for *Anschluss* in 1918–19: its first chairman was the Majority Social Democrat Paul Löbe, with the German Nationalist Otto Hoetzsch as his deputy. In consequence, Ludo Hartmann, the German–Austrian Ambassador to Berlin, could therefore count upon the broad support of the National Assembly when, in early February 1919, he asked the German government to make a formal commitment to Greater Germany.[28]

That a range of democratic politicians—most prominently, Ebert himself—were pushing for *Anschluss* in early 1919 had several reasons. First, a successful incorporation of German-Austria into the Reich would have been proof of the republic's ability to bring about a more 'comprehensive' solution to the German question than even Otto von Bismarck had been capable of after his victory in the Franco-Prussian War of 1870–1.[29] Second, the parties that represented the clear majority in the National Assembly after the elections could have demonstrated through their support for the *Anschluss* movement that the republic was deeply rooted in the liberal-nationalist traditions of the German past. It was therefore no coincidence that Hugo Preuß, a liberal professor of constitutional law and the 'father' of the Weimar Constitution, emphasized that his first draft of the constitution—including the provisions for *Anschluss*—was based on the ideals of the Paulskirche parliament of 1848/9.[30]

In Preuß's view, these ideals contained both the principles of parliamentary democracy *and* the striving for a Greater German fatherland. Article 2, Section 1 of the Weimar Constitution therefore provided for new territories joining the Reich if this corresponded to the desires of the population residing there. Section 61, paragraph 2 additionally allowed German-Austria to take a seat in the Reichsrat (the second legislative body in the Weimar Republic, similar to the upper house in other constituencies, but with elected representatives of the

German states). Initially, German-Austria was to be represented in an advisory function until the day it became part of 'unified' Germany.[31]

All of these constitutional preparations became obsolete in May 1919, when the victorious powers presented the German delegation with the draft treaty terms.[32] There they made it unmistakably clear that they would not tolerate any territorial expansion of Germany. The treaty even contained a clause that expressly forbade *Anschluss*. Germany was thereby forced to recognize (in Article 80 of the Versailles Treaty) that the independence of Austria 'is immutable, unless the Council of the League of Nations agrees to an amendment'.[33] Since Britain and France were among the permanent members on the League of Nations' Council and decisions there had to be made unanimously, any agreement of this kind was highly unlikely in the foreseeable future. Germany's defeat in the struggle over a democratically legitimized *Anschluss* on the basis of Austria's right to self-determination was a bitter foreign policy blow for the government, and one that was to haunt Germany in the following years as *Anschluss* moved from being a left-wing project to one increasingly associated with the far Right.

Yet the failure to deliver on *Anschluss* should not conceal the fact that the constituents achieved a great deal in the face of countless challenges and internal disagreements. Formally proclaimed on 11 August 1919, the Weimar Constitution was a remarkable document, written in the spirit of liberalism, which protected basic liberties like freedom of speech and the press, declared the equality of women and men, and established free and equal voting rights for all adult German citizens. Moreover, it formalized the demands—many of which had already been established during the revolutionary period and subsequently implemented—for the equality of women and their access to the higher echelons of the administration, from the judiciary to all areas of public administration and government. Even if, in reality, progress on matters of gender equality was slow, it was a huge step to have these rights enshrined in the constitution. The same applied to areas such as continued payment of salaries during maternity leave, the reform of abortion laws, the equal status of marriage partners, the abolition of celibacy for public servants, the re-regulation of the alimony issue, the introduction of free schools, and co-education for everyone.[34] Yet, the deeply politicized debates around a reform of paragraph 218 of the penal code that regulated abortions showed that female bodily autonomy remained a hugely controversial subject.[35] Nonetheless, during the Weimar Republic, women's reproductive rights expanded significantly, leading to greater sexual liberation and better access to birth control. While the availability of reliable forms of contraception allowed families to practise family planning, sex reformers disseminated manuals encouraging middle-class families to express their sexuality. Eventually, in 1926, the abortion laws were reformed, making it a 'misdemeanour' rather than a more serious criminal offence.[36] Obviously, there were significant differences between opportunities for those living in larger cities and those living in the countryside. Women in rural areas did not enjoy the same opportunities as those living in urban areas.[37]

Although Germany remained a federal state, the central state had more power than was the case in the Kaiserreich and some small states were consolidated. The power of Prussia—a state that was home to three-fifths of the overall German population—was somewhat curbed compared to the times before 1918, because Prussia now only commanded two-fifths of the seats in the Reichsrat, thus losing its previous majority in the Upper House.[38]

The government, headed by the Reich Chancellor, was responsible to parliament (the Reichstag), which was elected through a proportional voting system. This meant that each party's number of seats in the Reichstag would precisely correspond to the proportion of votes it received in the election.[39] A president was to be elected by popular vote every seven years, and he had the power to name and dismiss the chancellor and the cabinet and, in extreme circumstances, to invoke emergency powers that would allow the chancellor to govern by decree. The President was also allowed to dissolve parliament. This was particularly important in cases when the Reichstag voted down the President's emergency decrees, as it was entitled to do. The President was also granted extensive emergency powers under the constitution's Article 48 which gave the President the right to rule by decree and use the army to restore law and order in any federated state if he thought the existing order was under threat. Friedrich Ebert used Article 48 a remarkable sixty-three times in 1923–4 alone when Germany was fighting an economic emergency and serious threats from the far Left and the far Right.[40] Against the backdrop of the crisis of Weimar in the 1930s and the rise of Hitler, the Reich President's extensive powers have frequently been criticized—always, however, with the knowledge of what happened in January 1933. The severe economic and government crisis that set in from late 1929 could not have been foreseen by anyone in 1919.

Significantly, a majority of delegates in the National Assembly felt that some continuity should be preserved when they decided that the name of the state whose constitution they were drafting should remain the German Empire, rather than the German Republic. Liberal politicians in particular were at pains to emphasize that the name 'Reich' linked the new republic to the democratic traditions of 1848, not the semi-authoritarian regime of Wilhelm II. It should have been possible to foresee at this point that the issue would cause problems in the coming years when supporters of the republic started to refer to their state as the 'German Republic' while right-wing politicians reappropriated the name 'Reich' for an alternative vision of Germany's future. Ultimately, it was Hitler who, in 1929, first spoke of a 'Republic of Weimar' as a negatively connoted state he wanted to overcome.[41]

Already on 10 February, one day before Ebert's election as the first Reich President of the Weimar Republic, the National Assembly approved the basic principles of the draft constitution, which brought the German political system more in line with liberal Western and Northern Europe, while also going well beyond those models in some cases. The proportional voting system allowed for representation in the Reichstag of every party that attracted 60,000 votes in a general election. Unlike a first-past-the-post voting system, proportional representation was a direct reflection of the will of the people as it guaranteed a distribution of seats that exactly mirrored the voters' preferences. Moreover, allowing for referenda and plebiscites—along with a directly elected president—were strong indicators of direct democracy.[42]

All in all, Weimar Germany's constitution was significantly more democratic and liberal than the constitutions of most other countries in the 1920s. Not without justification did the German Minister of the Interior, Eduard David (MSPD), claim in a parliamentary speech of 31 July 1919 that no other state had a comparably democratic constitution. The Weimar Republic, or so he argued, was now 'the most democratic democracy in the world'.[43]

The strong liberal imprint on the constitution was largely the work of members of the DDP such as Hugo Preuß and Marie-Elisabeth Lüders, who identified with the ideals of left-liberalism and whose optimism about the future left its imprint on the text. In hindsight, though this initial optimism of what the German theologian and philosopher Ernst Troeltsch called 'the dreamland of the armistice period' between November 1918 and early summer 1919 must seem naive, it was a powerful sentiment at the time.[44] Käthe Kollwitz, for example, highlighted the difference between a past of wartime anxieties and a future of peace and democracy when she wrote in her diary:

The past five years were pointed backwards. They were full of pain, mourning, the longing for peace... Now everything is pointing towards the future. A future that we want to be bright, beyond the next darkness. Today one does not want to be alone, one wants to encourage oneself, to strengthen and express one's faith.... 1918 ended the war and brought the revolution. The horrific, ever more intolerable pressure of the war is gone and our breathing has become easier. No one believed that good times would come immediately, but the narrow shaft in which we were stuck, where we could not move, has been crawled through, we see light and breathe air...[45]

From Kollwitz's vantage point, and that of many others, it looked as if moderate revolutionaries had triumphed, while the perceived supporters of a Bolshevik-style revolution had been marginalized. The new government conveyed its firm belief to the peacemakers in Paris that Germany had broken with the autocratic traditions of the past, thus fulfilling the key criteria of Wilson's Fourteen Points for a 'just peace'.

It is easy to retrospectively dismiss this sentiment as naive. Yet many policy-makers in Germany firmly believed that they had delivered where the liberal revolutionaries in 1848 had failed. It was not a coincidence that the Weimar Republic was to adopt the black-red-and-golden banner of the 1848 revolution as its national flag.[46] The meaning of this symbolism was obvious to everyone: the moderate revolutionaries of 1918 were correcting the erroneous political developments since 1848. Liberal democracy, which had failed to come into existence then, had finally emerged triumphant.

In fact, at this point in time, the revolution had already achieved immense things: the replacement of the Kaiser and his imperial order with a modern democracy and a National Assembly that created the most progressive constitution and the most far-reaching social welfare laws that had ever existed in Germany. Three-quarters of the delegates in the National Assembly supported the democratic government under Philipp Scheidemann, who succeeded Ebert when the latter was elected as Reich President. Hardly any other country in the world at the time had a more liberal constitution and more progressive social legislation. What overshadowed these considerable achievements was the continuing refusal of small minorities on the extreme Left and Right to accept that the moderate revolution of November 1918 had the backing of the vast majority of Germans, sometimes out of conviction or because they felt that the only alternative to a republic run by moderates was the gloomy prospect of Bolshevism. While such pragmatism was certainly important for many who voted for the parties of the moderate Left and Centre, the idea that Weimar was a republic without republicans (or at best a state in which there were some 'republicans by reason') has certainly been exaggerated.[47] There were, in fact, plenty of 'republicans at heart' throughout the 1920s who recognized that constant effort was required to make democracy work in Germany. As the SPD's Hermann Müller, Weimar's two-time Chancellor, put it in 1928: 'I am the last person to deny that a lot more needs to be done until all institutions of the German Republic are filled by a truly republican spirit and a strong democratic tradition has been established in Germany.' Yet, Müller insisted, Germany had already come a long way within a brief space of time: 'Before the war, the Wilhelmine Reich—drawing its strength from the most advanced military machine in the world—was the only stable state among those governed by autocrats. On 9 November 1918 Prussian-German militarism surrendered to the German people. It marked the end of an autocratic regime. The people took their destiny into their own hands. Does this regime change in itself not deserve to be called a successful revolution?'[48]

People like Müller and his sizeable group of supporters acknowledged that democratization required more than the enactment of progressive legislation. Hence, they discussed and probed how to stage and visualize republican politics, how to invent or recreate powerful symbols of popular participation and to perform the nation in parades and spectacles. The office of the Reichskunstwart and its ambitious head, Edwin Redslob, who was responsible for the official symbols and national celebrations of the republic, is just one important example of the many groups and institutions that were devoted to the performative aspects of a distinctively democratic form of politics.[49] By 1928, when Müller wrote his book on the November Revolution and he was re-elected as Chancellor, it must have looked as if the efforts of the previous ten years had paid off.

11

Democracy besieged

The establishment of the National Assembly did little to end the latent, and at times open, civil war on the streets of Germany's cities. Instead, that spring witnessed the start of a second, more radical phase of the revolution, which was characterized by large strikes in the Ruhr district and in central Germany, and by street battles in Berlin, Bremen, and Munich. This time, violence was not directed against an autocratic regime but against parliamentary democracy. In Bremen, the USPD and the KPD proclaimed a soviet republic on 10 January, thus seeking to unseat the MSPD-dominated workers' council and the city's senate. Martial law and press censorship were imposed by the insurgents, who sought to force the political concepts of a minority on the city's majority. The national government responded with force and bloodily crushed the putsch with the help of *Freikorps* soldiers. At the same time, in the industrial heartlands of the Ruhr district and central Germany, some 300,000 mine workers went on a general strike and demanded the immediate nationalization of the pits. Here too, violence ensued when *Freikorps* soldiers sought to terminate the strikes. In Dresden, the War Minister of Saxony, Gustav Neuring, was thrown into the River Elbe, and shot dead as he swam and tried to reach the bank. When, on 9 March 1919, in response to the KPD's declaration of a general strike and violent disorder in Berlin, Gustav Noske ordered that 'every person who is found fighting with arms in the hand against government troops is to be immediately shot', his men caused mayhem in the capital (Figure 11.1).[1] The already tense situation was made worse by rumours about an alleged communist massacre in which up to 200 policemen had been brutally murdered in the rebellious east of the city. None of this was true, but rumours fuelled the anger of those charged with putting down the rising.[2] Using machine guns, tanks,

Figure 11.1 The March Battles in Berlin were suppressed with extreme brutality by the government. More than 1,000 'insurgents' were killed, and numerous sympathizers arrested. Here a suspected female supporter of the rebels is led away to an uncertain fate in the Berlin district of Friedrichshain.

and even aeroplanes to drop a few bombs, government forces—both regular soldiers and *Freikorps* troops—descended on their opponents, leaving 1,000 of them dead. The March Uprising also provided a welcome excuse for a long-anticipated reckoning, as government soldiers murdered Leo Jogiches, Luxemburg's former lover and her successor as editor of *Die Rote Fahne*, as well as thirty-one members of the People's Navy Division, which had caused their humiliating defeat in the Battle of Christmas Eve in 1918.[3]

Unrest also spread in Munich, where the initially bloodless revolution of November 1918 radicalized in the spring of 1919. Over the previous months, Eisner had proved himself to be firmly committed to further-ing revolutionary change but also unable to provide adequate food supplies and jobs. The Bavarian peasantry were withholding foodstuffs, and the Allies had requisitioned most of the railway locomotives. Workers began to heckle Eisner and shout him down at meetings. In cabinet, Eisner was angrily told by one of its members: 'You are an anarchist...You are no statesman, you are a fool...We are being ruined by bad management.'[4] In the eyes of Bavaria's nationalist middle classes, he had also betrayed the sacrifices of those who died in the war when, as Prime Minister of Bavaria, he leaked state documents which he believed proved that the war in 1914 had been caused by 'a small horde of mad Prussian military' men as well as by 'allied' industrialists, capitalists, politicians, and princes.[5] At an international conference of socialists, held in the Swiss city of Bern in February 1919, he attacked Ebert's government for refusing to acknowledge Germany's guilt in starting the war in 1914. Both the message itself and its timing (at the start of the Paris Peace Conference) did not help to endear conservative circles to Eisner's rule.[6]

Although a firm believer in radical reform, Eisner was not opposed to the principles of democracy and called for general elections for the Bavarian parliament on 12 January 1919, during which his Independent Social Democrats suffered a crushing defeat, winning no more than 2.5 per cent of the popular vote, or 3 out a total of 180 seats.[7]

The election result increased the feeling of uncertainty over the future among many Bavarians. When, one week after the Bavarian elections, Prince Leopold von Bayern, the former Commander in Chief of Germany's troops in the east, returned to Munich from his former headquarters in Kaunas, he naturally complained about what the two months of Eisner's rule had done to the city from which his family had ruled over Bavaria for nearly a millennium: 'But how did my dear home city, the capital and Bavaria's seat of royal power look?' Driving through the city in his Field Marshal's uniform, Leopold von Bayern felt that 'The city itself looked sad enough; the streets dirty and poorly attended to, little life in the city; the few soldiers which one saw were sloppy and disorderly. It tears at one's heart. At the Residence, the ministry of war and all public buildings, there were now red flags, and naturally, there was no one guarding my house any more.'[8]

Von Bayern was not alone and some fellow nationalists went further than him. As Eisner was walking to parliament to submit his resignation on 21 February, he was shot in the back twice by a 22-year-old nationalist law student, Count Anton Arco-Valley.[9] Eisner's guards immediately returned fire and wounded Arco-Valley, who was almost lynched on the spot by an angry crowd. One of Eisner's socialist followers, Alois Lindner, walked into parliament shortly afterwards, drew a gun, and, in full view of all the other deputies in the debating chamber, fired two shots at Eisner's severest critic, the Majority

Social Democratic leader Erhard Auer, leaving him severely injured and two others dead.[10]

Following Eisner's assassination and the attempted murder of Auer, the Bavarian Majority Social Democrats declared themselves the legitimate government. A coalition cabinet headed by Eisner's former Minister for Culture, the Majority Social Democrat Johannes Hoffmann, was formed, but it was unable to restore order as massive street demonstrations followed Eisner's funeral. The far Left was unwilling to accept the new government. On 3 April, socialists in the city of Augsburg called for the creation of a Bavarian Council Republic, a move inspired by recent events in Hungary, where, on 22 March, the Hungarian Communist leader, Béla Kun, had proclaimed a soviet republic, simultaneously calling on Bavarian and Austrian radicals to follow his example.[11]

As Victor Klemperer noted, both the murder of Eisner and the proclamation of the Hungarian Soviet Republic had an immediate radicalizing effect on Munich: 'The city took on a more threatening appearance as trucks arrived, red flags fluttering from them, crammed full of standing soldiers holding their weapons at the ready or ostentatiously loading them...Flyers called for the suppression of the bourgeois press, for a general strike, for a "second revolution".'[12]

Other contemporaries agreed that the mood in Munich had radically shifted in the spring of 1919. 'The news from Hungary hit Munich like a bomb', wrote the anarchist essayist and poet Erich Mühsam in the Bavarian capital.[13] Bavaria returned to a state of revolutionary unrest. Under the leadership of a former schoolteacher, Ernst Niekisch, the Central Council of the Bavarian Republic announced that the elected government under Johannes Hoffmann had come to an end and instead proclaimed the state a soviet republic. From the start, however, the Munich Soviet Republic could build on little support in the largely agrarian, conservative, and Catholic state of Bavaria. The new regime's leadership was dominated by urban (and often Jewish) literati from Schwabing, such as the 25-year-old Bohemian poet Ernst Toller (Figure 11.2) or the anarchist writer and translator of Shakespeare, Gustav Landauer. Their revolutionary agenda was as ambitious as it was unrealistic: it could only have been imposed in a far more dislocated and broken state than Bavaria. Banks and large industrial concerns were to be nationalized; 'free money' would be issued to abolish capitalism; universities were to be run by the students and professors

Figure 11.2 A 'wanted' poster for the socialist playwright Ernst Toller in the wake of the bloody suppression of the Munich 'Räterepublik'. Toller, who had briefly led the Bavarian Independent Social Democrats, was threatened with the death penalty after his arrest. In the end he was sentenced to five years' imprisonment for high treason.

stripped of their titles. The press was to be subjected to censorship by Landauer's Office of Enlightenment and Public Instruction.[14] The subject of history was abolished at Munich University as it was deemed hostile to civilization. Franz Lipp, the Commissar for Foreign Affairs, switzerlandtelegraphed to Moscow to complain that the 'fugitive Hoffmann has taken with him the keys to my ministry toilet', and declared war on the neighbouring state of Württemberg and on Switzerland because 'these dogs have not at once loaned me sixty locomotives. I am certain', he added, 'that we will be victorious.'[15] As the anarchist writer Gustav Landauer noted on a postcard sporting his face, sent to the novelist and literary critic Fritz Mauthner in April 1919: 'The Bavarian Council Republic has honoured me by making my birthday a national holiday. I am now the "people's delegate" for propaganda, education, science, arts, and a few other things. If I have a few weeks, I hope I can achieve something; however, it is very likely that it will only be a few days, and then all this will have been but a dream.'[16]

Support for the new government was mainly confined to industrial workers and a handful of left-leaning intellectuals, while middle-class conservative residents of Munich such as Victor Klemperer clearly had little sympathy for the dominant figures of the new regime such as Landauer ('Eisner reincarnate, not one bit smarter, but a good bit more radical'). Their revolutionary agenda was as ambitious as it was unrealistic—'miles removed from all political necessities', in Klemperer's words. Instead of regular courts, 'revolutionary tribunals' were created, as Klemperer noted with sarcasm: 'Revolutionary Tribunal in the Palace of Justice. With the lavish rococo decoration of its ornate staircase, the Palace of Justice fits splendidly with tableaux from 1792, the age of Danton; I would bet that the artistic directors of our Munich revolution very much took this into consideration. Landauer is an expert, after all, on ... the French Revolution.'[17]

Klemperer—a liberal conservative German patriot even after the Nazis had forced him out of his job and into an increasingly threatening social isolation—made no secret of what he thought of the radical Left: he once attended one of their meetings out of curiosity, only to be disappointed. 'About 250 people sat tightly packed at two long tables, smoking and drinking beer, most of them men of various ages, the majority probably workers. . . . It could have well been a regular meeting of railroad workers, or a presentation by a rabbit-breeders' club—except for the content of the speeches which insisted on the "necessity of civil war". . . Abominable waste of time, I thought, and I left. I did not sympathize in the least with these people.'[18]

By contrast, news of the events in Munich was welcomed by Russian Bolsheviks as a sign that a communist revolution in all of Germany was imminent. From Moscow, the Bolshevik Politburo member and chairman of the newly founded Comintern, Gregory Zinoviev, cabled an enthusiastic message: 'We are deeply convinced that the time is not far off when the whole of Germany will be a soviet republic. The Communist International is aware that you in Germany are now fighting at the most responsible posts, where the immediate fate of the proletarian revolution throughout Europe will be decided.'[19]

Other contemporaries agreed, even if they objected to communism. The politically conservative future Nobel Laureate Thomas Mann, himself living in Munich at the time, was convinced that the Bolshevik revolution was bound to spread: 'It may be assumed that the rest of Germany will follow', Mann noted in his diary on 7 April 1919.[20]

From Paris and other Western capitals, the Allies were observing the unfolding events in Bavaria and Hungary with growing concern. Robert Lansing, US Secretary of State, stated on 4 April 1919 that 'Central Europe is aflame with anarchy; the people see no hope; the Red Armies of Russia are marching westward. Hungary is in the clutches of the revolutionists; Berlin, Vienna and Munich are turning towards the Bolsheviks.'[21]

In the meantime, the Hoffmann government had fled Munich for the safety of Bamberg in northern Franconia, just as the German National Assembly had fled Berlin for Weimar. However, Hoffmann was not going to accept the putsch in Munich without a fight. On Palm Sunday, 13 April 1919, a Bavarian republican militia loyal to the Hoffmann government attempted to topple the Munich Soviet Republic by force, but failed in the face of stiff resistance from the 'Red Army', recruited from the armed members of the workers' and soldiers' councils.[22] Hoffmann's attempt to violently reinstate the legitimate Bavarian government had an immediate radicalizing effect. In Munich, the Bavarian Councils' Republic moved significantly to the left, as Max Levien and Eugen Leviné, two Russian-born revolutionary activists who had long toiled for radical political change, pushed the 'coffee house anarchists' aside and took over the leadership of what became known as the Second Munich Soviet Republic.[23]

Without waiting for the approval of the German Communist Party, they established a Bolshevik regime in Munich and opened communications with Lenin, who enquired whether they had managed to nationalize the banks yet. Levien, who had been accidentally caught in Germany at the outbreak of war in 1914 and drafted into the German army, followed Lenin's instructions, and began arresting members of the aristocracy and the upper middle classes as hostages. While the main church in Munich was turned into a revolutionary temple presided over by the 'Goddess Reason', the communists set about expanding and training a Red Army, which soon numbered 20,000 well-armed and well-paid men. A series of proclamations announced that Bavaria was going to spearhead the Bolshevization of Europe; workers had to receive military training, and all weapons in private possession had to be surrendered on pain of death.[24]

The developments in Munich, their defeat of Palm Sunday, coupled with another failed military intervention at Dachau on the outskirts of Munich three days later, also led to a radicalization of the anti-Bolshevik forces.[25] Hoffmann, who had been reluctant at first to enlist anti-republican volunteers or to seek support from the national government in Berlin, now had a change of heart. He publicly appealed to all anti-Bolshevik forces in Bavaria to crush the Councils' Republic:

Bavarians! Countrymen! In Munich rages a Russian terror, unleashed by foreign elements. This insult to Bavaria cannot be allowed to last another day, not even another hour. All Bavarians must immediately help, regardless of party affiliation...Munich calls for your aid. Come on! Step forward! Now! The Munich disgrace must be wiped out.[26]

Hoffmann's call naturally appealed to men who were ultra-nationalist and anti-democratic, and who appreciated the opportunity to settle scores with the forces of Bolshevism. Many were militantly monarchist and eager to restore the old order, like Major General Franz Ritter von Epp, a former commander of the Bavarian Life Guards, who led the *Freikorps* Oberland, or his adjutant, the highly decorated 31-year-old war hero and future head of the Nazi SA, Ernst Röhm. In total, some 15,000 men from Bavaria answered Hoffmann's call to arms.[27]

In addition to locally recruited forces, the government in Berlin sent some 15,000 regular troops, under the command of the Prussian Major General von Oven, to put an end to communist rule in Munich.[28] As the troops poured into Bavaria from mid-April, rumours spread that the Councils' Republic had released from prison and armed large numbers of criminals as well as enlisting former Russian PoWs to strengthen the ranks of their armed forces.[29] Before government soldiers had reached the city of Munich, a communiqué jointly signed in the name of the military command and Hoffmann's Bavarian government announced: 'Anyone who takes up arms against government troops will be punished by death ../. Every member of the Red Army will be treated as an enemy of the Bavarian people and the German Reich.'[30]

The Battle for Munich that began on 1 May was brief but bloody. One day before fighting in the city started, some members of the

Bavarian 'Red Army' unwisely chose to shoot ten hostages, including one woman, in the Luitpold-Gymnasium in Munich. The ruthless killing of hostages, many of them aristocrats and members of the ultra-right-wing 'Thule' Society was quickly exploited for propaganda purposes.[31] Well beyond Bavaria, the shooting of the Munich prisoners became the most important symbol of the 'Red Terror' that supposedly threatened Germany from all sides. The suggestive photos of the corpses, taken by Hitler's future private photographer Heinrich Hoffmann at the scene of the crime, were immediately distributed in newspapers and on postcards across Germany. They were part of a modern propaganda machinery designed to communicate the impression that, as one newspaper put it, the revolution had long since surpassed 'the disgraceful acts of the French Revolution' and had opened wide 'the gates of hell'.[32] The fact that the murdered woman was a relative of one of the *Freikorps* commanders, and that she was rumoured to have been subjected to sexual violence before her execution, did not improve the situation. The execution was a grave mistake, since it gave the counter-revolutionaries the ideal excuse for righteous indignation and vicious retribution.[33]

Victor Klemperer observed the end of the Munich Soviet first hand from 1 May onwards: 'today, as I'm writing these lines, a veritable battle is raging. A whole squadron of planes is flying over Munich, firing and being shot at, dropping flares . . . Infantry fire is rattling. More and more troops march or drive or ride down Ludwig Street with mortars and artillery . . . and from the safety of the street corners, where it is safe and the view is good, crowds of spectators watch on, often with opera glasses in hand.'[34]

As the army and *Freikorps* troops moved into the city, more than 600 people were killed during the fighting, many of them civilian bystanders. Summary executions of prisoners, including Gustav Landauer and the Councils' Republic War Commissar Rudolf Egelhofer, continued on 2 and 3 May. Only a few weeks earlier, on 14 March, Landauer had written to his friend Ludwig Berndl: 'Be not concerned about my life! Of the three dimensions, length was always the one I was least worried about . . . .'[35]

Coming across a gathering of a Catholic craftsmen's society on 6 May, members of a *Freikorps* unit, assuming that they had stumbled across a meeting of socialist revolutionaries, took them to a nearby cellar, beat them up, and killed a total of twenty-one men.

Furthermore, fifty-three Russians who had served in the Red Army were tortured and shot on the outskirts of Munich.[36] One of the officers involved in the 'liberation' of Munich, Manfred von Killinger, would later gleefully relate in his stylized memoirs how a band of marauding soldiers under his command had restored 'order' in Red Munich in 1919. A prisoner received a hand grenade 'in the gills', 'gurgled' in his blood, and 'staggered off'. A captured woman, whom Killinger portrays as a 'Schwabing painter wench', is beaten and whipped by several men 'until not a single white spot is left on her backside'. Killinger himself showed little remorse about his actions and those of his men: '"Brutish", some people will say. True, but appropriate. The rabble would have interpreted anything else as wimpishness.'[37]

The restoration of 'order' continued long after the fighting had ended. Over the following weeks, some 2,200 supporters of the Councils' Republic were sentenced to death or long prison terms, while a total of 5,000 court cases were concerned with crimes committed during the Soviet Republic.[38] 'In my mind, I look around and see nothing but the dead, lots of murder victims…', the anarchist Erich Mühsam wrote in his prison cell on 7 May, having been sentenced to fifteen years' imprisonment. 'And that is the revolution that I have been cheering for. After only half a year, there is now a pool of blood: I am horrified.'[39]

The cataclysmic events in and around Munich had a lasting effect on a city that previously prided itself on being a largely peaceful and deeply bourgeois metropolis. Untouched by the Great War—except through economic deprivation and the manifold deaths of the city's sons on far-flung fronts—Munich had suddenly experienced revolutionary turmoil, street fighting, and even artillery fire and aerial bombardment. As Thomas Mann recorded in his diary on 1 May, the citizens of Germany's second city were horrified, although middle-class observers tended to attribute blame for the escalation of violence and disorder one-sidedly to the Reds. Mann, a resident of the affluent residential district of Bogenhausen, was kept abreast about events in the city centre through the mother of his wife Katia, who lived closer to the government district: 'K's mother called in the morning; apparently a white flag was flying over the Wittelsbach Palais, the Reds had surrendered at 4 a.m. Turns out this was untrue. A handover is not yet on the cards, and the shooting continues intermittently. In the city…there is a mighty uproar: during the night, the middle-class and aristocratic hostages interned in the Luitpoldgymnasium...have been mutilated and executed...Incredible outrage among the middle-class citizens. All red armbands have suddenly disappeared.'[40]

The profound sense of living in a world in which established social orders and hierarchies had been violently overturned prompted a right-wing backlash in Bavaria. After the bloodbath, moderates such as Hoffmann's Social Democrats, despite having commissioned the action, did not stand much of a chance in Munich. A 'White' counter-revolutionary government eventually took over. Munich in particular was to become the most staunchly nationalist and anti-Bolshevik city in Weimar Germany and it was not a coincidence that it was the Bavarian capital that became the birthplace of Nazism.[41]

12

Undermining Weimar

In early 1919, while Germany was still experiencing revolutionary unrest and German politicians were drafting the constitution in Weimar, the leaders of the victorious Allies convened in Paris in order to decide on the future of the vanquished. For most Germans, the most pressing question was whether Wilson's promise—a peace without annexations and indemnities, a world made safe for democracy—would be fulfilled. They were to be bitterly disappointed.

As the British Prime Minister, David Lloyd George, acknowledged in 1919, the nature of the peace conference in Paris differed in a number of significant ways from the negotiations that had taken place at the great European peace conference of the previous century: the Congress of Vienna of 1814–15. First, and most importantly, the defeated imperial powers and their successor states—Germany, Austria, Hungary, Bulgaria, and the Ottoman Empire—were not invited to the negotiations, whereas France had been a central actor in the Vienna discussions about the creation of a new international order. The defeated powers were to be summoned only when the various peace treaties to be imposed on them had been finalized. Russia—Britain and France's key ally between 1914 and 1917—was also not represented in Paris, largely because Britain and France were still actively involved in trying to bring down Lenin's Bolshevik government by offering logistical and military assistance to its White opponents. A second difference lay in the number of participating countries: five at the Congress of Vienna in 1815, but more than thirty allied and associated states in Paris.[1] Obviously, not all participants had equal rights and say in the discussions. At the top of the hierarchical pyramid stood the 'Council of Ten', which, from late March 1919, gave way to the 'Council of Four', with the conference's host, French Prime Minister Georges Clemenceau, as chairman. Apart from Clemenceau, US President Woodrow Wilson and the British Prime Minister, David Lloyd George, were the key actors, even if Italy's head of government, Vittorio Emanuele Orlando, also sat on the 'Council of Four'. From late April, as Italy temporarily withdrew from the conference in anger over Rome's unresolved territorial claims on the Adriatic port of Fiume, it was essentially the 'Big Three'—Clemenceau, Wilson, and Lloyd George—who made the decisions. During their deliberations, they were advised by a total of fifty-two expert commissions dealing with complex issues such as reparations and new borders.[2]

Soon after the opening of the Peace Conference, it became clear that each delegation leader had come to Paris with his own objectives, which often proved incompatible with those of other Allied delegations. For France, the future containment of its eastern neighbour, Germany, was the single most important issue on the agenda. Clemenceau deliberately decided to open the conference on 18 January, the forty-ninth anniversary of the founding of the German Reich in Versailles after France's humiliating defeat in the Franco-Prussian War of 1870–1. Finding a solution to the 'German problem' that had haunted Paris ever since was considered a matter of both collective security and justice: during the Great War, ten French *départements* had suffered directly from battle or occupation, leaving vast areas in the west of the country in ruins. Even worse, the country had lost a quarter of its male population between the ages of 18 and 27. Of all the western allies, France was the country most profoundly and directly affected by the conflict. Clemenceau knew all too well that the overwhelming majority of his people demanded punishment for the perceived main culprit, Germany, and due compensation for France. In order to ensure that Germany would never threaten France again, various plans were contemplated by Clemenceau and his advisers: a complete break-up of the Reich, the occupation of much of the Rhineland, and the creation of strong allied states on Germany's eastern border.[3]

For the British—then, as before the war, concerned about the 'balance of power' on the Continent—the prospect of a potential French hegemony was as alarming as had been the pre-war threat of German dominance. Instead of backing all of the French demands, Lloyd George sought to reconcile what he considered a 'just' punishment for the war crimes committed by the Central Powers with maintaining economic harmony in Europe. Germany's global importance was to be minimized (by taking away her overseas colonies and scuppering the German High Seas Fleet), but not to the extent that overseas trade would cease altogether. Germany had been a major trading partner for Britain before the war and a completely impoverished, potentially even Bolshevik, Germany was simply not in London's best interest. At the same time, however, and against the backdrop of general elections to be held in December 1918, Lloyd George found himself under significant domestic pressure to impose a harsh peace on Germany, notably from conservative papers, such as Lord Northcliffe's *Daily Mail* and *The Times*, which demanded large reparations as well as the trial for war crimes (and potential execution) of Kaiser Wilhelm II. Britain's interests also clashed with those of France in the Middle East where vital strategic and economic interests were at stake.[4]

US President Wilson, by contrast, had always maintained that the result of the conference should be a 'just peace', leading to a redesigned system of international relations based on a radically new interpretation of popular sovereignty with global application. Rational, morally accountable individuals would elect sovereign governments everywhere. The subjects closest to his heart—the realization of the principle of national 'self-determination' (by which he meant government derived from popular sovereignty) and the creation of a League of Nations that would make future wars unlikely, if not impossible, by guaranteeing collective security and international peace—featured particularly prominently on his agenda.[5] Wilson, like so many American presidents before and after him, had the US example in mind which he sought to universalize and apply to Europe in particular. Within the successor states to Europe's empires, some forms of difference, such as religion and ethnicity, could be recognized and legitimized, but would remain bounded by the values of the wider community.[6] Behind his lofty idealism, however, lay a calculated aim: if the Great War and the Allied victory had shifted the global balance of power away from Europe and towards the USA, the new world order he promoted would cement his country's global dominance, both politically and economically.[7]

Navigating between the Allies' conflicting positions while also keeping the delegations of smaller countries in Paris happy was an almost impossible task. Even if the Western Allies' political leaders were reluctant to admit it, they were fully aware from the start of the deliberations in Paris that the final versions of the peace treaties were going to be a compromise—not between the victors and the vanquished, but between the key actors among the victorious Allies.[8]

The victors summoned Germany's representatives to Versailles at the end of April 1919, subjecting the German delegation to some humiliation along the way. As their train arrived in Paris after a long journey through the bombed-out French countryside, they were 'brusquely loaded onto buses and sent under heavy escort to Versailles; their luggage had been unceremoniously dumped in the hotel courtyard and they were told rudely to carry it in themselves'.[9] The head of the German delegation, Foreign Minister Count Ulrich von Brockdorff-Rantzau, had been an advocate of a compromise peace during the war and supported the new democratic German government. But he also looked and acted like a stereotypical north German aristocrat who assumed that he would be welcomed in Paris as an equal negotiation partner. Like most Germans, Brockdorff-Rantzau believed that the Wilsonian promise of a negotiated peace without winners and losers would be kept. He fully expected that Germany would suffer some territorial losses but was also prepared to make a case for the principle of self-determination to be honoured. His delegation had brought a large number of maps to show that some disputed territories were unquestionably German because of their history and their ethnic composition.[10]

On 7 May 1919 the German delegation was summoned to a meeting at the Trianon Palace Hotel in Versailles. Clemenceau opened the meeting. 'The hour has struck for the weighty settlement of our account. You asked for peace. We are disposed to grant it to you.'[11] When Brockdorff-Rantzau was asked to speak, he decided to remain seated in a deliberate act of protest. He insisted that Germany stood wrongly accused of starting the war, denied that war crimes had been committed, and insisted that the Allies had to end the economic blockade now that the fighting was over. Brockdorff-Rantzau's speech, presumably driven by the desire to assure domestic audiences back home that the delegation was fighting for Germany's interests, annoyed the Allied leaders further. After the German foreign minister had left the room, Wilson, Clemenceau, and Lloyd George were dismayed. Wilson said, 'This is the most tactless speech I have ever heard. The Germans are really a stupid people. They always do the wrong thing.'[12]

By evening, when they had had a chance to read the provisions laid before them, the German representatives reacted with disbelief. The terms of the treaty were quickly published in the German press, and greeted with horror throughout the Reich: Germany lost a tenth of its population (some 6.5 million people) and about one-seventh of its territory (roughly 43,000 square kilometres). In the west, Alsace-Lorraine was handed back to France after nearly half a century under German rule, along with the border territories of Eupen and Malmedy, which were ceded to Belgium. Between 200,000 and 300,000 ethnic Germans left Alsace and Lorraine as a consequence, either voluntarily or as a result of expulsions.[13] At least temporarily, Germany also lost sovereignty over a 50-kilometre-wide strip of land east of the Rhine, a territory that was to be demilitarized and 'secured' through three Allied bridgeheads across the river, largely to appease French security concerns. These were to be removed in the future if Germany fulfilled its treaty obligations. The Saar region, a major coalmining and manufacturing area on the Franco-German border, fell under the administration of the League of Nations with special permission given to France to exploit the region's coal mines for fifteen years in compensation for German damage caused to northern France.[14]

The largest and most contested territorial transfers, however, were in the east, where the Allies delivered on their promise to create an independent Poland. France had endorsed the idea of an independent Poland in the autumn of 1917 and Woodrow Wilson had envisaged, in the thirteenth of his Fourteen Points, that a reconstituted Poland should receive territory that was 'indisputably' Polish while also gaining 'free and secure access to the sea'.[15] The impossibility of simultaneously fulfilling these promises without violating the right to self-determination of the very sizeable German community in the now Polish territory illustrates the challenge of creating a new functioning successor state with undisputed borders in East-Central Europe. For Germany, the creation of a Polish nation-state meant the loss of Posen (Poznań), much of west Prussia, and parts of Upper Silesia. Danzig, the Baltic port at the mouth of the Vistula with an overwhelmingly German population, became a 'Free City' under the nominal control of the newly founded League of Nations, of which Germany was initially not allowed to be a member. In order to give Poland access to the Baltic Sea, as promised in Wilson's Fourteen Points, the Allies created a 'corridor' of land separating east Prussia from the rest of Germany. Of the 1.1 million Germans who had resided in the Polish Corridor in 1919, 575,000 had six years later moved to the new German Republic.[16]

In some disputed cases, the Allies allowed for plebiscites, calling on the inhabitants of the regions in question to decide to which state they wished to belong. The most important of these was held in the coal-rich region of Upper Silesia, one of three disputed ethnically mixed German border regions in which plebiscites were prescribed by the Versailles Treaty (the others being north Schleswig and the small districts of Allenstein and Marienwerder, where Poles and Germans lived side by side).[17] Upper Silesia mattered to both Berlin and Warsaw not just because of the population that lived there, but also because of its mines, and iron and steel mills. The Silesian mines were the source of almost a quarter of Germany's annual output of coal, 81 per cent of its zinc, and 34 per cent of its lead. The German government argued that the people of Upper Silesia were overwhelmingly German; that the territory had been German for centuries; and that its prosperity owed everything to German industry and German capital. If Germany lost Upper Silesia, the German note concluded, it would not be able to fulfil its other obligations under the treaty.[18]

After the referendum on 20 March 1921, which was preceded and accompanied by significant outbursts of violence, the final delineation of the new Polish–German frontier came in October 1921, when the Supreme Council of the Paris Peace Conference adopted a partition which gave Poland a third of the Upper Silesian territory and 43 per cent of the population, including the cities of Kattowitz (Katowice) and Königshütte (Chorzow), both of which had overwhelmingly voted to remain in Germany, as well as four-fifths of the industrial triangle in the east—a result widely decried in Germany as an act of 'victor's justice'.[19]

In addition to losing significant territories in the east, Germany also had to hand over its overseas colonies (territories with a combined size of 1.6 million square kilometres) which were redistributed between the victor states under mandates from the League of Nations. The loss of German Kamerun (Cameroon), Togoland (the western part of which now forms the Volta region of Ghana), Ruanda-Urundi, German South West Africa (Namibia), and the German Pacific islands meant that Germany was deprived of the material attributes of empire.[20]

Most of the former German colonies in Africa were to become so-called Class B mandates under the League of Nations. These B mandates were territories that, in the eyes of the Western leaders in Paris, required firm guidance by their mandatory power (mainly

Britain and France), but with a view to being released into independence
at some indefinite point in the future. Still other formerly German-
controlled territories, notably the former German South West Africa
(today's Namibia) and the South Pacific islands formerly occupied by
Germany, became Class C Mandates. These most closely resembled
colonies of old, 'best administered under the laws of the Mandatory as
integral portions of its territory'.[21] Unlike the former imperial territories in Europe, inhabited by whites, so ran the emphatically racist
rationale that guided the entire mandate system of the Paris peace
treaties, the colonial peoples of colour were not ready to look after
their own affairs.[22]

Set against the complex backdrop of contemporary expectations,
the Paris Peace Treaties almost inevitably disappointed everyone
involved. With the benefit of hindsight, historians such as Margaret
MacMillan and others have been somewhat kinder than contemporaries
in their assessment of the treaties, acknowledging that the peacemakers
in Paris were often forced to accept new realities that had already been
created on the ground, confining their role to adjudicating between
conflicting ambitions of various actors.[23] Yet not all historians are persuaded that the peacemakers made the best of a bad job, emphasizing
instead that the Paris conference fell short of its ultimate objective: the
creation of a secure, peaceful, and lasting world order.[24]

The unravelling of the order established in Paris within less than
two decades owed much to the rise of strong revisionist and nationalist
forces in the vanquished states of Europe, not least in Germany, where
the economic turmoil in the wake of the Great Depression after 1929
played into the hands of Hitler's Nazi movement, which had always been
adamant that it would tear apart the 'dictated peace' of Versailles,
with force if necessary. Precisely because of the rise of Nazism, historians and the general public alike have devoted far greater attention to the
Versailles Treaty than to any other aspect of the peacemaking process.
Yet it could be argued that the focus on Versailles (and notably on the
reparations question and the 'war guilt' clause, attributing sole responsibility for the outbreak of hostilities to Berlin) has narrowed our
understanding of the Paris Peace Conference and somewhat marginalized the single biggest issue at stake at the time: the transformation of
an entire continent previously dominated by land empires into one
composed of 'nation-states'. This issue had only become central to the
war in the final stages of the conflict. Neither London nor Paris had

gone to war in 1914 with the aim of creating a 'Europe of nations' and it was only from early 1918 onwards that the destruction of the land empires became an explicit war aim.[25]

It is worth recalling the scale of this transformation: when the First World War formally ended with an Allied victory, three vast and centuries-old dynastic land empires—the Ottoman, Habsburg, and Romanov empires—completely vanished from the map. A fourth, Imperial Germany, which had become a major land empire during the Great War when it gained enormous territories in East-Central Europe, was significantly reduced in size, stripped of its overseas colonies, and transformed into a parliamentary democracy with what Germans across the political spectrum referred to as a 'bleeding frontier' towards the east.[26]

The German Reich had been a major player in the great imperial game before 1914, and it is not possible to understand the loss of status keenly felt by many Germans at the time without recognizing the scale of the German Empire that fought the war, and its dismantling in its aftermath. Indeed, without recognizing the imperial dimensions and aspirations of the *Kaiserreich* it is not possible to fully understand the reasons why the Weimar Republic appeared such a mutilated state to German nationalists in the interwar period, during which right-wing groups protested vigorously at Germany's loss of eastern territory in the wake of the Treaty of Versailles and—to a lesser extent—the 'theft' of Germany's colonies.

In East-Central Europe the implosion of imperial structures was felt most keenly and most immediately. As the continental empires disintegrated, ten new states emerged from their ruins: Finland, Estonia, Latvia, Lithuania, Poland, Czechoslovakia, German-Austria, Hungary, Yugoslavia, and Turkey, now firmly based in Asia. Meanwhile, in the Arab Levant, which had been ruled for centuries by the Ottomans, Britain and France invented new 'states': Palestine, Transjordan (Jordan), Syria, Lebanon, and Mesopotamia (Iraq) were to become League of Nations' 'mandates' administered by London and Paris until an uncertain point in the future when they were to be released into independent statehood.[27]

At the centre of contemporary German indignation, however, stood not the loss of the country's overseas empire but Articles 231 and 232 of the treaty, which obliged Germany to accept the sole responsibility for the outbreak of the war in 1914. Article 231 assigned responsibility for the damages suffered by the Allies to Germany and the Central Powers, while Article 232 reached the conclusion that a guilty Germany owed reparations for the damage that it had caused. To the Germans, Articles 231 and 232 were seen as a form of moral condemnation that added to the humiliation of defeat, and accompanying territorial and material losses.

The real purpose of Article 231, however, was to legitimize the imposition by the Allies of punitive financial reparations on Germany in order to compensate the French and the Belgians for the damage caused by over four years of German occupation. Germany's 'war guilt' and responsibility for massive destructions—particularly during the German strategic retreat in 1917 to the heavily fortified 'Siegfried Line' between Arras, Saint-Quentin, and Vailly, when the army implemented a scorched earth policy—made the country liable for 'all losses and damages' suffered during the war. The Allies realized that such a broad definition of financial liability, which theoretically encompassed the cost for every bullet and every orphan pension, was likely to lead to unrealistic claims beyond Germany's ability to pay. Yet they were also aware that any concession on the reparation issue would outrage their domestic electorates, still reeling from the devastations of the war. The French public in particular had also not forgotten about Berlin's imposition of vast indemnities in 1871 (which did not even have the justification of immense property damage). As it proved impossible to agree on a definitive sum, the exact amount of reparations to be paid by Germany was deferred to a later point in time. However, since the amount of reparations was not established in the treaty, as most Germans viewed it, they were told to essentially sign a blank cheque.[28]

The final reparations figure agreed on in the 1921 London Schedule of Payments was 132 billion Gold Marks, structured in three types of bonds ('A', 'B', and 'C' bonds). However, a large share of this seemingly enormous sum, the so-called 'C' bonds that amounted to 82 billion Gold Marks, was never expected to be repaid. C bonds were mainly included to mollify Allied public opinion. Instead, the Germans would pay reparations by servicing the so-called 'A' and 'B' bonds, which together totalled 50 billion Gold Marks, to be paid over thirty-six years. German experts were secretly convinced that these payments were manageable, even if they would never have admitted this in public.[29]

The Allies further sought to ensure that Germany would not be in a position to wage war again by demanding the handover of large quantities of weapons and war materiel. The treaty also required the German army to be restricted to a maximum strength of 100,000 men and banned it from having tanks, aeroplanes, and submarines.[30] The German navy, reduced to a total of 15,000 men, was effectively dismantled and barred from building any large new ships. The great High Seas Fleet, whose expansion before 1914 had contributed strongly to the rise of Anglo-German tensions, had been interned in Scapa Flow in the British Orkneys since November 1918. Eleven days before the German emissaries in Paris signed the Versailles Treaty, the German commander of the fleet, Admiral Ludwig von Reuter, decided to scuttle his seventy-four vessels, from battleships to destroyers, to prevent them from being distributed among the victorious Allies.[31]

The Germans were given two weeks to reply, and in that brief interval, only modestly extended, they managed to assemble detailed documentation and reasoned arguments protesting the harsh terms of the treaty. Yet, the provisions of the treaty were not changed in any substantial way. The public debate, meanwhile, was vicious. The provisions of the treaty were condemned as outrightly criminal by most Germans from the moment the draft was handed to the government in Berlin in May 1919. Post-imperial Germany, internally divided over pretty much everything else, was united in its shared fundamental opposition to the terms of the Treaty of Versailles. Even members of the governing coalition recklessly advocated refusal. The risk, though, was very great. It was all but certain that Allied armies would march in and occupy Germany should the government refuse to sign the treaty. Meanwhile, the economic blockade of Germany was still in place to ensure Berlin's 'cooperation', causing significant hardship to ordinary Germans.

Chancellor Philipp Scheidemann's speech in the German National Assembly on 12 May 1919 was indicative of the general mood. Speaking against the severing of German territories and populations through new borders, he said: 'We are of one flesh and one blood, and whoever tries to separate us cuts with a murderous knife into the living body of the German people.' Scheidemann persisted in his overheated rhetoric: the treaty signified 'pitiless dismemberment', 'enslavement', 'the creation of helots'. 'Sixty million [Germans] behind barbed wire and prison cages, sixty million at forced labour . . . [with] their own land made into a prison camp!' 'The foot on the neck and the thumbs in the eye'— that was the meaning of the treaty. The stenographer recorded 'stormy

applause' and 'active agreement'. His speech culminated in the since
famous words: 'Which hand would not wither that binds itself and us
in these chains?' According to the minutes, the speech of Germany's
first democratically elected head of government was greeted 'with several minutes of emphatic applause' from fellow parliamentarians across
the political divide.[32] However, he also said: 'Thrice woe upon those
who delay a genuine peace by only one day', and received 'minutes of
thunderous applause in the house and in the galleries'. The sentiment
expressed in Scheidemann's speech, namely that peace had to be
obtained, if necessary at any cost, was shared by the overwhelming
majority in Germany.[33]

Nevertheless, the nationalist right naturally went further in its criticism of the draft treaty. The speaker for the German National People's
Party (DNVP), Arthur Graf von Posadowsky-Wehner, was particularly
scathing in his attack on the treaty. The former Minister of the Interior
and Vice-Chancellor of Imperial Germany, Posadowsky-Wehner portrayed the treaty as an unprecedented crime against the German
nation. The "theft" of "undeniably" German territory, the restrictions
on the size of the military, the ban on union with Austria, the demand
that the Kaiser and his generals and officials be turned over to the
Allies—all of this seemed incompatible with international conventions
and principles of sovereignty. The seizure of Germany's overseas telegraph and telephone cables and radio transmitters served as further
examples of Allied 'vengefulness'. Posadowsky-Wehner knew that a
refusal to sign would lead to a 'temporary evil of continued warfare',
but Germany would retain its honour; and even if this meant the death
of the German people 'after death, in our belief, comes resurrection'.
As a devout Christian, he believed in life after death: 'He therefore called
upon his fellow Germans to have 'the ultimate courage [*Todesmut*]' to
bear the consequences for the sake of future generations. Posadowsky-
Wehner also accused the Allied governments of hypocrisy. Referring
to India and Ireland, he insisted that London's commitment to self-
determination was questionable. Belgium should be ashamed of itself
for accusing Germany of mishandling its colonies. But the main culprit, in Posadowsky-Wehner's view, was US-President Wilson who had
lured Germany into signing an armistice with false promises of a just
peace. 'This treaty is a Shylock treaty', he thundered to great applause,
and Wilson was now looking for a pound of German flesh.[34] The most
the treaty supporters could muster in response was that Germany

would suffer terrible consequences, including an Allied occupation of the country should Germany refuse to sign.

Nevertheless, the Scheidemann government resigned over the matter, making way for a new cabinet under Gustav Bauer, a former office clerk from East Prussia who had risen through the ranks of the trade unions in Imperial Germany to become one of the chairmen of its 'General Commission'. In Germany's first democratic government under Scheidemann, Bauer had served as Labour Minister. The new government was backed by the Social Democrats and the Centre Party while the liberal DDP, which had previously formed part of the Weimar coalition, categorically refused to be part of any government that would sign the Versailles Treaty. Bauer was not enthusiastic about the prospect either, but saw no viable alternative, particularly after Groener and other senior generals had ruled out the possibility of resuming hostilities. Bauer appreciated though that Scheidemann and the other parliamentarians had just reason to feel deeply aggrieved, most notably with Wilson, on whom they had placed their high hopes for a 'just peace'. The American President had indicated in speeches and in his responses to the Central Powers' peace notes in 1918 that his war was with autocrats, while a genuinely representative government could expect 'peace negotiations' on the basis of the Fourteen Points. Half a year later, following a democratic revolution in Germany, representatives of the new government had not been invited to the peace negotiations. Instead they were now offered a 'Diktat', a 'dictated' treaty with no opportunity to discuss any of the provisions put in front of them.[35]

German efforts to have the conditions moderated, and the 'war guilt' clause deleted, prompted the Allies to declare that Germany had 'wanted and unleashed the war' and was responsible for the 'raw and inhuman manner in which it was carried out'.[36] In a desperate attempt to prevent the Allies from distributing the warships of the German High Seas Fleet among themselves, Admiral Ludwig von Reuter ordered the scuttling of the entire fleet on 21 June. The Allies gave Germany another ultimatum on 22 June to accept the terms within five days or face a continuation of war. With the threat of an invasion hanging over their heads, the government and the military command signalled their acquiescence, and the Constitutional Convention agreed to sign the treaty under protest.[37]

At 3 p.m. on 28 June 1919, exactly five years after the assassination of Archduke Franz Ferdinand, the Bauer government's two emissaries

Figure 12.1 On 22 May 1919 the National Constituent Assembly authorized the German government to sign the Versailles Treaty. An overwhelmingly female audience here follows the speeches and debates, which led up to this decision, from the viewers' gallery.

charged with signing the peace treaty—Foreign Minister Hermann Müller and Johannes Bell, the Minister for Transport—were led into the Hall of Mirrors in Versailles and advanced to the centre of the room, escorted by Allied soldiers. The venue had been carefully chosen by the elderly French Prime Minister and host of the Paris Peace Conference, Georges Clemenceau: it was the very same place where, after France's defeat in the Franco-Prussian War of 1870–1, Wilhelm I had been proclaimed Kaiser of a unified German nation-state. Normally more level-headed, the then Prussian Prime Minister and soon-to-be Chancellor of the Reich, Otto von Bismarck, had consciously chosen the Palace of Louis XIV as the stage for a symbolic humiliation of a recently defeated France.

Now, almost half a century later, the opportunity had arisen for France to avenge the humiliation. The two German emissaries chosen to sign the peace treaty had to proceed past a long line of permanently disfigured French veterans, who had been brought to the signing ceremony as living reminders of the crimes committed by Germany.[38] 'The whole affair was elaborately staged and made as humiliating to the enemy as it well could be', noted Colonel Edward House, the key diplomatic adviser to US President Wilson.[39] According to a British observer, the German dignitaries looked like 'prisoners led in to hear the reading of their sentence'.[40] Müller and Bell returned to Berlin the same evening, while in Paris, people celebrated in the streets.

The general population in Germany, by contrast, continued to be outraged. Spontaneous demonstrations were held across the Reich to protest the injustices of a peace treaty that seemed intent on perman- ently expelling Germany from the ranks of the Great Powers. The fact that Britain and the United States had gone to considerable lengths to preserve German unity and independence, notably in opposing French efforts to detach the Rhineland, was generally overlooked. Instead, the enthusiasm with which so many Germans had welcomed the advent of democracy in 1918 turned into a sense of fundamental betrayal and resentment at the terms of peace less than a year later.[41] A significant proportion of the population came to associate the peace treaty with the revolution of 1918 and its outcome, the Weimar Republic. Some, notably on the far Right, referred to the Versailles Treaty as 'the real constitution' of Weimar—an externally enforced 'un-German' form of state, whose sole purpose was to enslave the German people for generations.[42]

Negative views of Versailles were further reinforced by John Maynard Keynes's polemical attack on the treaty, articulated in his best-selling book *The Economic Consequences of the Peace*, published in December 1919. Keynes had been a British Treasury expert during the Peace Conference in Paris, specializing in the issue of German financial responsibility. Like millions in Europe and further afield, he had been an ardent supporter of Wilsonianism and hoped that the Paris Peace Conference would produce a treaty based on Wilson's Fourteen Points. Later, appalled at the draft treaty with Germany, he resigned from the British delegation before the ceremonial signing on 28 June 1919. He immediately set to work on his book, which was published in December 1919, and virtually over night made Keynes a transatlantic public intellectual.

Keynes portrayed the Versailles Treaty as a Carthaginian peace, intent on ruining Germany as effectively as Rome had destroyed Carthage in 146 BC. He insisted that the Treaty of Versailles had artificially

Figure 12.2 Hostility towards the demands of the Treaty of Versailles united the otherwise deeply divided political parties of the Weimar Republic. There were mass public protests in many German towns and cities. Here Marie Juchacz, Majority Social Democrat deputy to the National Constituent Assembly, speaks to demonstrators on Berlin's Wilhelmplatz.

weakened Germany, well below its material capabilities. Sooner or later, post-war Germany would restore its security, first through military equality and eventually through military superiority.[43]

However, what was generally ignored, then and since, was that Germany had actually fared better in Paris than all of the other Central Powers.[44] In the Treaty of Saint-Germain-en-Laye, signed in September 1919, for example, the German–Austrian rump state was forced to cede south Tyrol to Italy, southern Styria to the Kingdom of Serbs, Croats and Slovenes, and Feldsberg and Böhmzell to Czechoslovakia. Habsburg Galicia had already been claimed by Poland while Bohemia, with its three million German speakers, had become part of Czechoslovakia. The treaty also stipulated that Austria (along with Hungary) would have to carry most of the old empire's war debt, as well as paying reparations. Setting the exact figures for reparations was eventually turned over to the reparation commission.[45]

German-Austrians who, like their German counterparts, had hoped for *Anschluss*—the voluntary union of Austria with the Reich—as a realization of liberal nationalists' aspirations during the 1848 Revolution, were bitterly disappointed.[46] Ever since the military defeat and the disintegration of the empire, the Austrian Left (and their German counterparts) had promoted the idea that a union between the two states would comply with Wilson's idea of self-determination while also offering a major boost of legitimacy for the emerging Weimar Republic. There was also a clear economic rationale for such a move: almost nobody considered the Austrian state, now stripped of its breadbaskets in the fertile lands of Hungary or Bohemia, capable of feeding its six-million-strong population. Agrarian production in Austria immediately after the war's end only reached half of the pre-war levels, leaving the country's capital, Vienna, dangerously exposed to the threat of starvation.[47]

In Germany, nobody had supported the *Anschluss* more fiercely than the Majority Social Democrats, who pointed to the fact that the ban on 'unification' represented an egregious violation of the right to national self-determination. As late as 18 March 1919, the *Vorwärts* declared: 'Bismarck's Lesser German Reich has tottered into the disaster of the World War, but the Greater German idea of 1848, whose goal was the union of all Germans, including the German-Austrians, is marching and completing itself in our own times under the symbol of the black-red-golden banner, the revolutionary flag of 1848.'[48]

The *Anschluss* ban was thus widely seen as a major defeat for Ebert and his party and the political Right was quick to instrumentalize this. The arch-conservative weekly *Die Tradition* had already proclaimed in early April 1919 that the Social Democrats' expressed hope for a peaceful revision of the German frontiers of 1871 was unrealistic. 'If it were possible to create empires out of words and warm German hearts, then the idealists of Frankfurt's *Paulskirche* would already have created the Greater German fatherland, stretching from the Belt to the Adriatic, some seventy years ago.'[49] Following the *Anschluss* ban, Kuno von Westarp, editor-in-chief of the *Kreuzzeitung* and later chairman of the DNVP, saw this assessment confirmed. In his view, the fathers of the Weimar Constitution had 'not succeeded... in realizing the plan of a Greater Germany, for the sake of which, at the start of the negotiations [over the Constitution], they had felt so enormously superior to Bismarck'.[50]

The MSPD knew all too well the implications of its diplomatic failure, and thus stubbornly refused to admit to the fiasco of its Greater German efforts. On 22 June 1919, when the National Assembly finally approved the signing of the Versailles Peace Treaty after long and heated debates, Paul Loebe assured the plenum that the republic would continue to advocate Greater Germany—'for the unity of all those... who, from the Danube to the Adige, as from the mouths of the Weser and Elbe, the Oder and Vistula, have learned to speak from a German mother'.[51] But following the Allied *Anschluss* ban, the Majority Social Democrats' promise lacked one decisive element: credibility. If, in 1918–19, *Anschluss* had been a democratic project of the Left, its non-realization was soon used by the extreme Right in both Austria and Germany as 'proof' of the inability of the republican state to deliver on promises.[52]

If Austrians thought they were hard done by, Hungarians had even more reasons to complain. Altogether the country lost two-thirds of its pre-war territory and more than 73 per cent of its population, according to the provisions of the Treaty of Trianon, which—due to political upheaval in Budapest and the Romanian invasion of Hungary—was only finalized in 1920.[53] Wrecked by four years of war, revolution, and counter-revolution, as well as foreign invasion in 1919, the country was economically in ruins even before it signed the Trianon Treaty, with production levels in Hungary's consumer goods industry at about 15 per cent of their pre-war levels.[54]

Compared to Hungary's staggering territorial losses, those of Bulgaria, the one Balkan nation to have fought alongside the Germans, Habsburgs, and Ottomans, were slightly less dramatic, even if the Bulgarians did not see it that way. Like the other vanquished powers, Bulgaria was not represented at the Peace Conference. Similar to other leaders of the Central Powers, the new government in Sofia had initially hoped that the principle of self-determination would be applied after the country's new borders were settled in Paris, as Bulgarians were in a majority in three areas outside its new notional borders: in the southern Dobrudja along the west coast of the Black Sea, in western Thrace at the top of the Aegean, and in parts of Macedonia. The problem was that all three territories were also claimed by other states—states that were considered friends of the Allies: Romania insisted on the southern Dobrudja (even if there were fewer than 10,000 Romanians living there, out of a population of almost 300,000); the Kingdom of Serbs, Croats, and Slovenes claimed Macedonia; and Greece demanded western Thrace.[55]

When the draft treaty was finally delivered in September 1919, its content surpassed even the gloomiest predictions. In relative terms, the Treaty of Neuilly of November 1919 was certainly harsher than the Versailles Treaty imposed on Germany. The treaty forced Sofia to cede a total of 11,000 square kilometres of territory, including western Thrace (handed over to Greece), and four border areas, including the strategically important towns of Strumica, Caribrod, and Bosilegrad with their surroundings (amounting to 2,500 square kilometres) to the new Kingdom of Serbs, Croats, and Slovenes. Given that Sofia had already lost all of the territorial gains made during the First Balkan War of 1912–13 when Bulgaria's former allies, Romania, Greece, and Serbia, defeated her in the Second Balkan War later that year, the sense of national tragedy was overwhelming.

The treaty also imposed upon Bulgaria a staggering reparations bill of 2,250 million gold francs, to be paid over thirty-seven years. In addition, Sofia had to agree to the transfer of large quantities of live-stock and railroad equipment to Greece, Romania, and the Kingdom of Serbs, Croats, and Slovenes, which also was to receive annual deliveries of 50,000 tons of coal from Sofia. Proportionate to its size and GDP, Bulgaria faced the highest reparations bill of all the Central Powers.[56]

Finally, the armed forces were severely slashed; the army was to be a mere police force of 20,000. When the details of the treaty were published, there was talk in Sofia of resistance but the successor to Teodor Teodorov as Bulgarian Prime Minister, Aleksandar Stambolijski, said that he would sign 'even a bad peace' for lack of alternatives.[57] On 27 November 1919 he did this, during a brief ceremony in the old town hall in Neuilly. It looked, said an American present that day, 'as if the office boy had been called in for a conference with the board of directors'. Among the observers was the Greek Prime Minister, Venizelos, 'endeavouring not to look too pleased' at having gained western Thrace for his country.[58]

In the eyes of most Bulgarians, and not without reason, the Treaty of Neuilly symbolized the lowest point of their national existence as an independent state. The redrawing of borders left Bulgaria without agriculturally fertile areas (such as Dobrudja and Thrace) and without access to the Aegean Sea—a major issue as trade via ships was a decisive factor for whole sectors of the Bulgarian economy.[59] Prompted by the redrawing of borders, Bulgaria experienced yet another massive influx of refugees from Macedonia, Thrace, and Dobrudja (as well as from the ceded western borderlands), the second wave of refugees since 1913. Between 1912 and the mid-1920s, Bulgaria had to accommodate roughly 280,000 refugees, which now made up to 5 per cent of the overall population. Around half of these people came from territories that were ceded to Greece (Aegean Macedonia and western Thrace) and 25 per cent from the Ottoman Empire (eastern Thrace). Smaller in number, but no less dramatic, was the influx of refugees from territories that now belonged to the Kingdom of Serbs, Croats, and Slovenes (12.5 per cent) and Romania (11 per cent).[60] Accommodating such a massive population intake at a time of severe economic and social crisis posed one of the most significant challenges to the Bulgarian state for years to come.[61] As Stambolijski put it in a desperate letter to the unsympathetic French Prime Minister, Clemenceau, on 22 November 1919: 'The population of Bulgaria now lives in a truly disturbed state. Its disasters are made even worse by the sufferings of the numerous refugees...These countless refugees, homeless people without any possessions,... will always be a bleeding wound in the relationships in the Balkans.'[62] Stambolijski was right, even if he did not live to see developments after 1923. For much of the interwar period, Bulgaria struggled to come to terms with the human and financial costs of a lost war, economic crisis, and international isolation, leading to deep internal divisions and violent clashes between supporters of different political camps, and rapidly changing governments, often disposed of through putsches.

For Bulgaria's long-time colonial master and wartime ally until 1918, the Ottoman Empire, the process of disintegration had begun well before the armistice, when the great retreat of Ottoman forces and the advance of British troops and local auxiliaries 'liberated' all of its Arab territories. Even before the convening in January 1919 of the Paris Peace Conference—at which the Turks were the only representatives of the Ottoman Empire's peoples excluded from the deliberations—it had become clear that the fate of the empire lay in the hands of Britain and France, as US President Woodrow Wilson displayed little interest in getting involved in implementing a post-war order in the Middle East. The United States had never declared war on the Ottoman Empire and Wilson's departure from Paris on the very day of the signing of the Versailles Treaty was indicative of his lack of interest in the peace settlement with Constantinople. Britain and France, by contrast, were intent on dividing most of the Ottoman Empire's Arab provinces between them.

Yet while realists in Constantinople had long given up on the Arab territories in the Middle East, there were some Ottoman statesmen who optimistically hoped for a strict application of the twelfth of Wilson's Fourteen Points, which advocated 'a secure sovereignty' to the 'Turkish portion of the present Ottoman Empire', namely Anatolia in Asia Minor and eastern Thrace in Europe.[63] On 17 June 1919, the liberal Turkish Prime Minister, Damad Ferid, argued along similar lines to his counterparts in the other defeated states when he assured Clemenceau, Lloyd George, and Wilson in Paris that his government had nothing in common with the wartime rulers of the Committee of Union and Progress who were to blame for the Ottoman Empire's entry into the war and the terrible fate of the Armenian Christians. If the Wilsonian principle of self-determination was to be applied, Anatolia in particular had to remain Turkish. The problem was that parts of Anatolia were now also claimed by others. Thanks to vague promises made in early 1915 by Sir Edward Grey, the British Foreign Secretary, Greece, which went on to fight on the Allied side for the last eighteen months of the war, felt entitled to make claims on western Anatolia, which was home to substantial Greek communities. The Greeks enjoyed traditional sympathies in the West as fellow Christians, while the Ottomans could expect little support in either Britain or France. Lloyd George famously dismissed the Turks as 'a human cancer, a creeping agony in the flesh of the lands which they misgovern, rotting away every fibre of life'.[64]

Other existing or emerging states also had their designs on parts of Anatolia. Italy sought to establish a permanent foothold in western Anatolia, having previously gained the formerly Ottoman Dodecanese Islands in 1911. Having received vague assurances in the 1915 London Treaty that if the Ottoman Empire was to be broken up Rome would receive its 'fair share', Italian diplomats further pushed for a sphere of influence in Anatolia. Meanwhile, Kurds—dreading the prospect of minority status under Armenian, Arab, or Turkish rule—also demanded independence or autonomy with foreign protection. Likewise, former Russian Armenia, which had become the Democratic Republic of Armenia in May 1918, pressed for the annexation of a number of Ottoman provinces in the east. Violence here had escalated in the spring of 1918, when survivors of the *Aghet* exacted revenge against local Muslim civilians, notably in massacres in Erzinjan and Erzurum from late January to mid-February 1918, where close to 10,000 Muslim Turks were estimated to have been butchered.[65]

Territorial demands and violence further worsened the situation in a country already devastated by the Great War, as British fact-finding missions clearly demonstrated. One of the officers dispatched into the interior from Constantinople, Lieutenant Clarence Palmer, who had spent most of the war in an Ottoman PoW camp, visited various towns and villages in north-western Anatolia, from where he reported back to his superiors. As he travelled from Eskişehir to Konya, he witnessed towns and villages ravaged by hunger, sickness, and material shortages. Displaced Armenians, he noted, had sold their children for food while the absence of fallen men and the requisitioning of farm animals meant that agricultural production and manufacturing had come to a standstill.[66]

In August 1920, more than a year after the conclusion of the Treaty of Versailles, the victorious Allies finally signed a peace treaty with the Sultan's government under Damad Ferid. The Treaty of Sèvres, signed in the show room of a porcelain factory in August 1920, confirmed that the Turks would be left with as little as one-third of Anatolia. A substantial portion of Anatolia was awarded to Greeks, Armenians, and Kurds while allowing foreign spheres of influence and domination in much of the rest.[67] Greece was allocated Smyrna and its environs, subject to a plebiscite within five years. The Armenians received vast areas of eastern Anatolia, stretching from Trabzon to Lake Van, and Kurdistan was to become an autonomous region. The Straits of Bosporus were placed under international administration. France and Italy each retained spheres of influence in Anatolia.[68] Post-imperial Turkey would also have to pay indemnities. According to Article 231 of the treaty, Turkey had caused 'losses and sacrifices of all kinds for which she ought to make complete reparation'. As with the German *Kriegsschuld* clause, the Allies recognized it would be well beyond the capacity of post-imperial Turkey to pay this kind of reparation. Accordingly, the treaty set up a Financial Commission comprising one representative each from France, the British Empire, and Italy, with a Turkish representative serving in a purely consultative capacity. No other defeated Central Power had to subject itself to such a compromise of its sovereignty and for Turkish nationalists it continued, in an even more extreme form, the humiliating European interference in Ottoman affairs during the nineteenth century.[69]

In order to understand the Allies' apparently vengeful attitude towards the defeated Central Powers in 1918–20, it is important to take

into account the moral climate of the post-war period and the degree
to which the war had created a climate of bitterness.[70] The lingering
memory of German atrocities in Belgium in 1914, the damage caused
by the German troops during their strategic withdrawal in 1917, the
offensives of 1918, and the despair and anger over lost relatives and
friends killed in the field featured prominently on the minds of heads
of state and diplomats at the Paris conference. The passions of war had
not yet subsided and the Allied leaders, dependent on popular support,
were aware that soldiers, as well as their families, were looking for
compensation from the enemy in order to validate their sacrifices. In
the eyes of the Allies, the Germans had also done themselves great
damage by suddenly talking about a 'just peace' when—only a few
months earlier—they had imposed draconian terms on Russia and
Romania in the 1918 treaties of Brest-Litovsk and Bucharest. And then
there was, of course, the issue of collective security: the victorious
Allies feared a military revival of their defeated opponents, especially
that of a resurgent Germany. Depriving Berlin of the means to wage a
revenge war was central to the maintenance of a general peace, and to
France's territorial integrity in particular.

None of this mattered, of course, to Germans in 1919. The resentment against the Treaty of Versailles was not only fuelled by the
perceived humiliation of defeat. There was also the issue of perceived
hypocrisy, as Wilson's idea of self-determination was clearly applied to
peoples considered allies of the Entente (Poles, Czechs, south Slavs,
Romanians, and Greeks), but not to those viewed as enemies. Worse
still, the application of the principle of national self-determination to
territories of mind-boggling ethnic complexity was at best naive and,
in practice, an invitation to transform the violence of the First World
War into a multitude of border conflicts and latent or open civil wars.[71]

All of the new states, supposedly founded on the principle of
national self-determination, had within their borders large and vocal
national minorities, which (most notably after the onset of the Great
Depression) began to demand reunification with their 'homelands'.
The territory transfers and refusals to permit German speakers to 'self-
determine' and join with Austria or Germany, for example, left some
13 million ethnic Germans (including German Austrians) outside the
Reich's borders.[72]

The problem of irredentism continued to haunt European politics
for decades.[73] Those who now found themselves as a minority in

ethnically mixed successor states often succumbed to nationalist agitation. In contested Silesia, for example, the Friedrich-Wilhelms-University in Breslau became a hotbed of German nationalist agitation. Reflecting the city's multi-ethnic composition, it had traditionally been one of Germany's most cosmopolitan educational institutions, and through-out the nineteenth century had boasted Polish fraternities, as well as large numbers of Jewish students.[74] After 1918, however, the atmos-phere was deeply hostile to inter-ethnic cohabitation. Young German nationalists from across the region flocked to hear faculty members such as Walter Kuhn, a self-proclaimed expert in the increasingly fash-ionable field of *Ostforschung* (or 'Research of the East'), give lectures on the need to reverse the Versailles Treaty and recover 'lost' German populations in Poland and East-Central Europe more generally.[75] Such ideas fell on fertile ground. Generally speaking, Germans who lived in ethnically mixed border areas were disproportionately more likely to support parties of the radical Right, and eventually end up in one Nazi formation or another, than those who inhabited the urban centres further west.[76] For all its hatred of the Paris Peace Conference, Nazi Germany and its overtly exterminationist imperial project of the later 1930s and early 1940s owed much to the logic of the successor state created by the Paris treaties.[77]

Versailles made the Weimar Republic more ethnically homogeneous than Germany had ever been since unification in 1871, notably through the near-complete loss of its sizeable French- and Polish-speaking minorities. Yet at the same time, it created a sizeable community of ethnic Germans living outside the borders of the Reich. The popula-tion of the Kingdom of Serbs, Croats, and Slovenes (soon to be renamed Yugoslavia) contained 14 per cent ethnic Germans, while the new Czechoslovak state contained more ethnic Germans (23 per cent of the overall population) than Slovaks.[78]

Theoretically, the rights of these large minorities were to be pro-tected by the so-called Minorities Treaties, a series of bilateral agree-ments signed by each of the new states as a precondition for their international recognition as sovereign entities within the League of Nations.[79] Post-imperial Poland was supposed to provide the model. The Polish Minorities Treaty, or 'Little Versailles' Treaty, signed on the same day as its better-known namesake, would guide all subsequent statements from the conference on the subject, and similar agreements would bind no fewer than seven additional successor states.[80]

The Minorities Treaties sought to protect the collective rights of all ethnic or religious minorities who were now living inside the successor states of East-Central Europe.[81] The new nation-states had to guarantee the rights of political organization and representation, and the use of minority languages in courtrooms and schools, as well as compensation for land transfers. In Czechoslovakia, for example, international treaties guaranteed minority groups collective rights. In areas where they made up at least 20 per cent of the population, Germans had the right to obtain an education and deal with state authorities in their own language. As ethnic Germans tended to be clustered in certain regions, this effectively meant that 90 per cent of them were able to avail themselves of this concession.[82]

Alleged violations of the treaties could be brought to the League Council and the International Court of Justice. Significantly, parties outside the national boundaries could make representations on behalf of beleaguered minorities. The Hungarian government, for example, might sue on behalf of Magyars in Slovakia, or Weimar Germans on behalf of the Sudeten Germans. It was one of the Peace Conference's most significant achievements, as it provided a legal framework through which aggrieved minorities could (and did) seek redress against treaty violations.[83]

From the perspective of many Germans, however, the Minorities Treaties were merely a fig-leaf to cover up the blatant breach of the fundamental principle of self-determination, which they had wrongly assumed would underpin the Versailles Treaty. Many, notably on the Right, felt that the 'lost' minorities had to be 'returned' at all cost, putting treaty revisionism high up on the political agenda long before the Nazis entered the scene.[84]

The situation was even less clear when it came to minorities that had no national state to represent their interests, such as the several million Jews living in the Pale of Settlement in the western borderlands of the collapsed Romanov Empire and in the eastern half of the former Habsburg Empire. Accused of being both Bolsheviks and antinational by many in their new national homelands, and confronted with pogroms in Ukraine, Russia, and even Poland, their situation after 1918 was even more precarious, and much more frequently threatened by violence than had been the case before 1914.[85] As the German Jewish war veteran and novelist Arnold Zweig noted in 1920, in response to a particularly well-documented pogrom in Pinsk: 'Poles and pogroms have befallen the eastern Jewish people who live piled together in the big cities and scattered through towns and villages. From the big cities comes shocking news, but the towns and villages, without railroads, without telegraph offices, have long been mute. Slowly one hears what is happening there: murder and massacre.'[86]

Many Jews threatened by the increasingly hostile conditions in East-Central Europe fled west, quite a few of them to Germany. There were perhaps 80,000 'Eastern Jews' in Germany before the First World War. After the war there was a renewed influx, as the Russian Civil War raged on, prompting anti-Semitic pogroms and murders on a huge scale by the revolution's tsarist opponents.

The arrival of tens of thousands of *Ostjuden* also fanned anti-Semitism among those Germans who had long regarded their fellow German citizens of Jewish faith as second-class citizens, and who felt their long-standing preconceptions of Jewish 'otherness' confirmed and reinforced when eastern Jews with their different dress, cultural traditions, and languages arrived.

Even some German Jews shared notions of cultural superiority over Orthodox Jews. Victor Klemperer, the son of a rabbi in the extremely liberal Reform Synagogue in Berlin, but baptized as a Protestant, displayed a not uncommon air of superiority towards, if not disdain for, Orthodox Jewry of the East, or *Ostjuden*, as they were commonly referred to at the time. During a longer visit to the also German-occupied city of Vilnius in 1917, Klemperer had frequently encountered Orthodox Jews, and dismissed Orthodoxy as 'repulsive fanaticism'. After a visit to the local Talmud Torah school, he stepped onto the courtyard in front of it and 'took a deep breath, as if I had swum under water. No, I did not belong to these people, even if it was proven a hundred times that they were blood relatives. I did not belong to them even if my own father had studied with them. I belonged to Europe, to Germany, I was nothing other than German and I thanked my creator for being German.'[87] German Jews had since the early nineteenth century developed notions about the 'otherness' of Eastern European Jews in order to exhibit a sense of social distance and reinforce their own qualities of culture and refinement.[88] Ironically, Jewish liberals and German anti-Semites alike shared stereotypes of Eastern Jews as a wild and primitive people. At the end of the nineteenth century, German Zionists were the only ones to idealize Eastern European Jews as a community rooted in authentic Jewish traditions. When masses of Eastern Jews settled in Germany after the Great War, many German Jews feared that these new immigrants would threaten their assimilation into German society. The German Jewish communities accepted responsibility for the Eastern Jews but believed that post-war Germany was in no position to absorb more workers.[89]

If some German Jews viewed the *Ostjuden* with suspicion, German anti-Semites naturally went much further. When Lina von Osten, the future wife of the chief organizer of the Holocaust, Reinhard Heydrich, first encountered Orthodox Jewish refugees, she felt nothing but disgust. Von Osten, who introduced Heydrich to Nazism in the late 1920s, recalled in her memoirs that she had regarded the Eastern Jews who arrived in Germany in large numbers after 1918 as 'intruders and unwelcome guests', and had felt so 'provoked' by their mere presence that she just 'had to hate them': 'We compared living with them to a forced marriage, in which one partner literally cannot bear the smell of the other.'[90]

The Russian Revolution added another layer to anti-Semitism, both in Germany and beyond. In Munich, the Baltic German refugee (and future Nazi Minister for the Occupied Eastern Territories) Alfred Rosenberg commented in an article of May 1919: 'Lenin is the only non-Jew among the peoples' commissars; he is, so to speak, the Russian storefront of a Jewish business.... But one can observe, and all recent news confirms it, that the hatred against the Jews in Russia is constantly spreading despite all terror.... If the present government falls, no Jew will remain alive in Russia; one can say with certainty that those not killed will be driven out. Where to? The Poles are already keeping them at bay, and so they will all come into old Germany, where we love the Jews so much and keep the warmest seats ready for them.'[91]

The notion of Jews as the main drivers and beneficiaries of Bolshevism clearly originated from Russia, most notably from White propaganda, but the idea spread quickly across Europe. The fact that a relatively high number of Jews had played prominent roles in the subsequent Central European revolutions of 1918/19—Rosa Luxemburg in Berlin, Kurt Eisner in Munich, Béla Kun in Hungary, Victor Adler in Vienna—seemed to make such accusations plausible, even for observers in Britain and France.

Such views were further fuelled by the broad international circulation of the fabricated *Protocols of the Elders of Zion*, the alleged minutes of a late-nineteenth-century meeting of Jewish leaders to discuss how to achieve global domination for the Jews. The *Protocols* were translated into Western European languages from 1919 onwards, often funded by wealthy private individuals such as the American industrialist Henry Ford, who provided the printing cost for over 500,000 copies to be distributed in the USA. Its exposure as a forgery in 1921 did not reverse the *Protocols'* enormous impact on the counter-revolutionary imagination. Yet the unholy marriage of anti-Semitism and anti-Bolshevism produced very different results in different European settings. It was only east of the River Rhine (and more dramatically east of the River Elbe) that anti-'Judaeo-Bolshevism' would lead to the pogroms and mass murders of Jews that were such a terrible feature of the years 1917–23, and again of the years after 1939.[92]

Allegedly representing everything the far Right despised, the Jews could simultaneously (and paradoxically) be portrayed as the embodiment of a pan-Slavic revolutionary menace from 'the East' that threatened the traditional order of Christian Central Europe, as 'red agents' of Moscow, and as representatives of an obscure capitalist 'Golden International' and force of Western democratization. What these accusations had in common was the assumption that Jews were inherently rootless, with a 'natural' internationalist animus against the nation-state and their 'host peoples'.

Even before the war, right-wing groups such as the Pan-German League had constantly levelled such accusations. The notion that Jews were patriotically 'unreliable' also drove the so-called Jewish census of October 1916, ordered by senior army officers who hoped it would give them support in refusing Jews admission to the officer corps once the war was over. The aim was to reveal the cowardly and disloyal nature of the Jews by showing statistically that Jews were underrepresented in the army, and that those who had joined up were overrepresented in desk jobs. In fact, it showed the reverse: many Jewish Germans were nationalist to the core, and identified strongly with the Reich. German Jews were over- rather than underrepresented in the armed forces and at the front. This confounded the expectations of anti-Semitic officers to such a degree that the results of the census were suppressed. But the knowledge that it had been ordered caused a great deal of anger among German Jews, even if the attitudes it revealed were not shared by the majority of rank-and-file troops.

Alongside extreme right-wing propaganda scapegoating Jews for the military defeat and revolution of 1918–19, there also emerged a more popular form of anti-Semitism, directed particularly at war profiteers and the small number of financiers who managed to get rich during the war or in the post-war years of inflation. A fresh source of conflict arose in the gathering pace of immigration on the part of impoverished Jewish refugees fleeing anti-Semitic violence and civil war in Russia.

The civil war in Russia also prompted others to move to Germany, including large numbers of non-Jewish Russians trying to escape the Bolsheviks. Hundreds of thousands of Russian refugees fled the carnage of the civil war by moving westwards. Desirable European destinations for Russian refugees included London, Prague, and France.[93] But the largest number of refugees, among them the political leaders of emigrant communities, made their way to Germany, the closest Central European country where they might be able to find safety. They numbered 560,000 in the autumn of 1920. Berlin—and notably the districts of Schöneberg, Wilmersdorf, and Charlottenburg (which then acquired its nickname 'Charlottengrad')—became a major centre of settlement for Russia's exile community, which created some seventy-two Russian publishing houses in the German capital by 1922. While some integrated easily, others found it hard to find work and were correspondingly perceived as a burden by many Germans.[94]

Although unintentional, the reshuffling of borders in Paris and the tumultuous events in Russia thus contributed to furthering xenophobia and anti-Semitism in Germany at a time when the country was also holding its breath over the continuum of violence on German streets and the persistent fears of an open civil war.

Epilogue

The defiant republic: Germany, 1919–1923

Revolutionary and counter-revolutionary turmoil in Germany continued after the fall of the Munich Soviet in 1919. In March of the following year, prompted by the Versailles Treaty's stipulation of a reduction of the German armed forces to 100,000 men and the German government's subsequent order to *Freikorps* units to disband, the German Right staged a coup in Berlin. One of the key figures behind the putsch, General Walther von Lüttwitz, refused to obey the orders and was dismissed from his post. The government intended to charge him with treason after the discovery of documents that clearly demonstrated his involvement in the conspiracy. Lüttwitz, however, had the support of many *Freikorps* soldiers, notably that of the notorious Ehrhardt Brigade, named after its leader, the naval captain Hermann Ehrhardt. Assured of their loyalty, Lüttwitz sent an ultimatum to President Ebert, demanding a halt to the demobilization of both army and *Freikorps*, the immediate dissolution of parliament and the forcible suppression of all strikes.[1] When Ebert rejected the ultimatum, the Ehrhardt Brigade marched on Berlin. On 13 March, Lüttwitz and Dr Wolfgang Kapp, an East Prussian civil servant and co-founder of the extreme-right wartime Fatherland Party, proclaimed that the Reich government had been deposed.[2]

Ebert and his government fled Berlin for Dresden before moving on to Stuttgart, having failed to persuade the Reichswehr's Chief of the General Staff, Hans von Seeckt, to provide military support for the government from the regular Reichswehr units. To be sure, there were some high-ranking officers who were supportive of the republic (if only for pragmatic reasons) such as General Walther Reinhardt, the first head of the republican Reichswehr, who was ready to militarily intervene against the Kapp putsch.[3] Yet Ebert chose to pursue a different strategy to fight Kapp and his fellow putschists. Together with the trade unions, and supported by the Independent Social Democrats, the government called a general strike:

> Workers! Comrades! We did not make a revolution in order to submit our-
> selves today to a bloody regime of mercenaries. We will not collaborate with
> these Baltic criminals!... Everything is at stake! That is why the most extreme
> means of resistance are called for.... Lay down your work! Strike! Cut off this
> reactionary clique's air supply! Fight with all means to preserve the republic!
> Lay all discord aside.... Paralyse all economic life! Not a single hand should
> move! No proletarian should help the military dictatorship! General strike all
> down the line! Proletarians, unite! Down with the counter-revolution![4]

Even the KPD joined in on 14 March and called on their supporters to back the general strike. In an impressive demonstration of Social Democracy's grassroots strength, workers across Germany downed their tools. Public transport shut down completely, factories and all public institutions remained shut. Even the gas- and waterworks in the German capital ceased operations. It was the largest strike in Germany's history, and it brought everyday life in Germany to an abrupt standstill. After four and a half days the putschists gave up.[5]

Yet even after the collapse of the Kapp putsch, the workers refused to call off the strike. Emboldened by their victory over the far Right, the left-wing advocates of radical change saw a renewed opportunity, as the flames of revolution flared up again in various places. As in the autumn of 1918, socialist workers' councils were established in the cities of Leipzig, Hamburg, and Chemnitz. Harry Graf Kessler noted in his diary on 19 March that the Kapp putsch had failed, but that violent clashes had occurred between insurgents and army troops in Berlin, Leipzig, Nuremberg, Chemnitz, Dresden, and in the Ruhr.[6] The following day, he wrote: 'At various points in Berlin, the mob has captured officers of the retreating putschist forces and murdered them. The bitterness of the working classes against the military seems to be boundless; and the successful general strike has greatly increased their sense of power.'[7]

Meanwhile, in the industrial region of the Ruhr, a 50,000 strong 'Red Army' of workers, initially formed by left-wing Social Democrats and communists as a means of self-defence against the right-wing putschists in Berlin, began to advance more radical political demands such as the nationalization of key industries and the introduction of a Councils' Republic.[8] Supported by 300,000 mineworkers and their unions, they seized control of the whole Ruhr valley and demanded nationalization in the mining industry. In order to minimize the risk of a continuous general strike, a new government was formed under the Majority Social Democrat Hermann Müller. Yet, Müller's appointment on 26 March did little to defuse the situation. By the end of the month, the government, supported by President Ebert, dispatched regular troops, supported by *Freikorps* soldiers, into the Ruhr valley. Under the terms of the Versailles Treaty, the Ruhr valley was a demilitarized zone and the German government's decision to despatch troops into that zone was a clear violation of the peace treaty. Yet, Ebert and Müller insisted that they were responding to a national emergency—a revolutionary uprising against their democratically elected government. Under the command of Lieutenant General Oskar von Watters, the government troops and their irregular supporters began to violently suppress the strikers and other supporters of what was now commonly referred to as the March Revolution. Their actions ushered in a civil-war-like situation in which more than 1,000 members of the 'Red Army' and some 250 government troops were killed. Unlike during the Kapp Putsch, the army leadership had no reservation about opening fire on striking workers. Many of the latter saw the crushing of the rising as an opportunity to settle scores with those who had prevented the 1920 right-wing putsch from succeeding. As one young student volunteer serving in the Ruhr joyfully reported in a letter to his parents: 'No pardon is given. We shoot even the wounded. The enthusiasm is tremendous—unbelievable. Our battalion has had two deaths, the Reds two or three hundred. Anyone who falls into our hands gets the rifle butt and is then finished off with a bullet.'[9]

The violent unrest in the Ruhr and elsewhere gave the French government a pretext to occupy the demilitarized zone. This prompted an immediate end to the fighting in that particular region.[10] Yet violence in Germany continued, albeit in different, more targeted ways. On 26 August 1921, the Centre Party politician Matthias Erzberger was shot and killed in the Black Forest.[11] The fact that he had signed the armistice of November 1918 made him, in the eyes of the murderers, a 'November criminal'. An ongoing slander campaign by the DNVP Reichstag deputy member Karl Helfferich added fuel to the fire. The student Oltwig von Hirschfeld had already attempted an assassination of Erzberger in January 1920 which had left the politician critically injured. Erzberger was warned repeatedly that the militant far Right would not give up until he was dead. His murder in the summer of 1921 was carried out by two former navy officers, who had been working on behalf of extremist right-wing secret societies and terror cells like the Organization Consul.[12] For the first time, an elected representative of the young republic had been specifically targeted and killed in a terrorist attack. The following year, on 4 June 1922, the former Reich Chancellor, Philipp Scheidemann, only narrowly survived an acid attack. That same month, on 24 June 1922, Foreign Minister Walther Rathenau was murdered by members of the Organization Consul, including the young ex-*Freikorps* volunteer Ernst von Salomon, on his way to work.[13] It quickly became clear that the same right-wing underground circles which had been responsible for the assassination of Erzberger were also behind the murder of Rathenau. Some of them were former volunteers from the *Freikorps* campaign in the Baltic region and in Upper Silesia, others were nationalist students who wished to prove their commitment through involvement in underground organizations of the extreme Right.[14]

Following the murders of Erzberger and Rathenau, the government introduced several measures to protect the republic and its representatives. President Ebert immediately issued emergency decrees after the assassinations for the 'restoration of public security and order', as provided for under Article 48 of the Weimar Constitution.[15] The emergency decrees made it a punishable offence to denounce the republic or its institutions and representatives, and allowed for the banning of anti-republic press releases and meetings. While the emergency decrees issued in the wake of the attack on Erzberger were lifted again at the end of 1921, the murder of Rathenau saw an increase in popular support for a law for the protection of the republic. In Berlin alone, some 400,000 people took to the streets to protest against the assassination and express their support for the republic. Shortly thereafter, on 21 July 1922, the Law for the Protection of the republic was passed with an initial validity of five years, taking over from the emergency decrees.[16] The law was even supported by the USPD which split that September: while the party's 'right' wing re-merged with the Majority Social Democrats, its left wing joined the German Communist Party. A tiny number of members remained in the USPD which played no role whatsoever in German political history between mid-1922 and its eventual dissolution in 1931.

The murders of Erzberger and Rathenau also put pressure on the parties of the Right, notably the conservative German Nationalist People's Party (DNVP), whose representatives suddenly found themselves accused of supporting terrorism.[17] Chancellor Joseph Wirth of the Centre Party left no doubt that he viewed them as principal enemies of the constitution whose activities had been tolerated for too long. 'The growing terror, the nihilism, which is frequently hidden behind the façade of national ethos can no longer be met with lenience.'[18]

Apart from passing the Law for the Protection of the Republic, which also established the first constitutional court in German legal history, the 'Staatsgerichtshof' in Leipzig, the Reichstag majority approved several further legal instruments to fight radicalism.[19] The most important of them was the Law on the Duties of Civil Servants which demanded their loyalty to the republic as a precondition for employment. To be sure, loyalty to the republic was not something that could easily be decreed by law. It depended on economic and political circumstances that were often beyond the state's control. In order to emotionally attach German citizens to their state, the government had created the office of the Reich Art Protector (Reichkunstwart), whose duties included the organization of annual state celebrations of Weimar's national holiday, Constitution Day (11 August), and new republican symbols. Even if the results of the efforts of the Reichskunstwart, Edwin Redslob, are difficult to quantify, there can be little doubt that the republic managed to stabilize its support base in the 1920s.[20] In 1928, in the last general elections before the Great Depression, a clear majority of voters supported political parties that were not hostile to the republic. The main winner of that election was the SPD, the party that identified most strongly with the republic.

Yet there were clear regional differences in this general picture. Notably in Bavaria where fears of further left-wing revolutionary threats like those of 1919 had become particularly entrenched, politics became dominated by the conservative right. Munich, in particular, became a magnet for extreme nationalists from all over Germany. It was no coincidence that it was here that Adolf Hitler fully developed the ideological basis for Nazism.[21]

The impoverished son of a customs inspector from the Austrian town of Braunau am Inn, Hitler had spent the war serving on the

Western front as a dispatch runner. The war or, more specifically, the Central Powers' defeat in November 1918 had radicalized Hitler, but he was not quite sure whether his extremism was of the Left or the Right.[22] Indeed, when he returned to Munich, he briefly served as a representative (*Vertrauensmann*) of his army unit liaising with the propaganda department of Eisner's revolutionary government, charged with training fellow soldiers in democracy, before being elected in April 1919 to a soldiers' council.[23] Hitler was not the only future senior figure of the Third Reich who initially sympathized with the Left. Sepp Dietrich, later a general in the Waffen-SS and head of Hitler's SS-Leibstandarte, was elected chairman of a soldiers' council in November 1918.

Yet Hitler's interest in socialism was short-lived and he soon converted to the extreme Right. He first attended a beer hall meeting of the radical right-wing German Workers' Party (*Deutsche Arbeiterpartei* or DAP) in September 1919, joined the party later that month, and quickly took control of it before it renamed itself as the National Socialist German Workers' Party (NSPAD) in February 1920. Hitler's extreme worldview of later years, with its distinct emphasis on racial doctrine, biological anti-Semitism, and violent expansionism, was not fully articulated at this point. What shaped him at this time was the experience of perpetual crisis, from war to defeat to revolution, and the common contemporary assumption that Germany was on the verge of civil war.[24]

Hitler found small but susceptible audiences for his radical messages of anti-Bolshevism and national renewal. Yet his premature attempt to follow Mussolini's example and seize power in 1923 failed miserably. At midday on 9 November, Bavarian police opened fire on his supporters as they marched through Munich, killing sixteen of them. Hitler himself managed to escape, but was arrested two days later.[25] Only a few weeks earlier plans devised in Moscow for a 'proletarian uprising' in Germany—a 'German October'—had failed because of a lack of public support.[26]

Although often labelled a 'weak democracy', the Weimar Republic had by late 1923 managed to fend off some serious challenges from both the Left and the Right—far more serious challenges, in fact, than those faced by the Federal Republic of Germany in the 1970s and 1980s (without the FRG being considered a 'weak democracy' by anyone). By late 1923, the Weimar Republic seemed more politically stabilized than ever.

The same applies to the extreme economic problems that the republic had partly inherited from Imperial Germany. Reparations were an additional burden for the state at a time when the country was still servicing its wartime debts and Germany's industrial capacity was diminished. Important industrial areas such as Lorraine and parts of Upper Silesia were lost. Industrial and agricultural production stood at less than half of its pre-war level, while the state had to cover significant additional costs for injured veterans and the dependants of the fallen of the war.

Meanwhile, the inflation seemed unstoppable. It took more than 1,000 Marks to buy a US dollar in August 1922, 3,000 in October, and 7,000 in December. As Richard Evans has pointed out, the depreciation of the German currency had dramatic political consequences: 'The German government could not make the required reparations payments any longer, since they had to be tendered in gold, whose price on the international market it could no longer afford to meet. Moreover, by the end of 1922 it had fallen seriously behind in its deliveries of coal to the French, another part of the reparations programme. So French and Belgian troops occupied Germany's leading industrial district, the Ruhr, in January 1923 in order to seize the missing coal and force the Germans to fulfil their obligations under the treaty. The government in Berlin almost immediately proclaimed a policy of passive resistance and non-cooperation with the French in order to deny the occupiers facilities to garner the fruits of Ruhr industrial production for themselves. The struggle was only called off towards the end of September. Passive resistance made the economic situation worse. Anyone who wanted to buy a dollar in January 1923 had to pay over 17,000 Marks for it; in April 24,000; in July 353,000. This was hyperinflation on a truly staggering scale.' And it got a lot worse before it got better: by October 1923, the price for one dollar was 25,260,000,000 Marks, and 4,200,000,000,000 Marks in December.[27]

Yet Weimar eventually mastered this challenge as well and was brought back from the brink when Germany's new government decided to resolve the crisis through negotiations and financial reforms. Gustav Stresemann, who combined the office of Foreign Minister with the Reich chancellorship for a few months in 1923, negotiated the withdrawal of the French from the Ruhr in September in return for a guarantee that Germany would meet its reparations payments in future.

On 25 October, the government in Paris—'incentivized' by the United States government—signalled its willingness to have the reparations issue reviewed by an international commission of experts under the chairmanship of the American banker Charles Dawes. This introduced a period of détente, within the framework of which the withdrawal of French and Belgian troops from the Ruhr district occurred. In return, Germany vowed to honour its commitments under the new payment plan, which was approved the following year.[28]

So as to stabilize the financial situation, the cabinet agreed to introduce a new currency, the Rentenmark, whose value was expressed in gold, thus serving as an obstacle to inflationary policies. The idea was to restore international confidence in the currency to prompt foreign investment. In mid-November the new money was issued, and the 'miracle of the Rentenmark' proved a success.[29] The exchange rate to the dollar was stabilized at pre-war level. The Reichsbank president managed to protect the temporary Rentenmark from speculation and finally replace it with the new 'Reichsmark'. The hyperinflation was thus over and the republic was financially more stable than ever before.[30]

The end of the Franco-Belgian Ruhr occupation and the consolidation of the German economy at the end of 1923 inaugurated a phase of stabilization, which was also reflected in international relations. Already in 1922, Germany had normalized its relations with the Soviet Union in the Treaty of Rapallo. Two years later, with the Dawes Plan, the German reparations payments were placed on a more solid financial footing. International loans—particularly from the United States— helped to stimulate the German economy. And in 1925, the Treaty of Locarno, in which Germany recognized its new western frontiers, reflected the clear easing of tensions in Berlin's relationship with Paris and London. For this change of course in international relations, the main architects of the Treaty of Locarno—British Foreign Minister Austen Chamberlain along with his colleagues, the German Gustav Stresemann and the Frenchman Aristide Briand—were honoured with the Nobel Peace Prize in 1925 and 1926.

Already by late 1923, it was difficult to deny that the republic had asserted itself under the most difficult of circumstances. Germany had a democratic government, a liberal constitution that granted its citizens wide-ranging basic political and economic rights, and a noticeably

improving economy. The government crisis of autumn 1923 had been
overcome. Extremist minorities on the political Left and Right had
been marginalized, and their attempts to violently topple the republic
had failed. Despite its territorial losses, the Reich had been preserved
as a unified nation-state—counter to French ambitions and the efforts
of small separatist movements inside Germany. In view of the great
number of challenges that the young republic had been exposed to
between 1918 and 1923, German democrats could have looked back
on their achievements with a certain degree of pride.

That the supporters of parliamentary democracy in Germany did
not present these highly remarkable successes more aggressively had a
lot to do with the unrealistic expectations that many Germans had
harboured since the last year of the war. A German victory had still
appeared within grasp in the first half of 1918. After the reversal of
military fortunes in the second half of that year, many contemporaries
still expected a compromise peace. Furthermore, they assumed that the
new political order would provide instant solutions for the problems
that the republic had inherited from its legal predecessor in 1918. Worse
still, there existed irreconcilable ideals as to how the political future of
Germany should look. While the republic was regarded by the Right
as an 'un-German' form of government that had been forced on them
by the Allies, a minority on the far Left mourned the 'lost opportunities' that a 'true revolution' would have brought. More incisively than
most, the great Weimar social critic and satirical essayist Kurt Tucholsky
pointed to that tension between illusion and real life in his satirical
poem 'Ideal and Reality' (1929):

> In still nights and monogamous beds
> you dream of what you're missing in life.
> Your nerves are crackling. If only we had
> that which, because it is not there, quietly torments us.
> (…)
> We dreamt, under imperial restraint,
> of a Republic and now it's this one!
> One always desires the tall and slender ones,
> and ends up with the little fat one—
> C'est la vie![31]

Yet even Tucholsky, who continually railed against the democratic
deficit in the army and the justice system during the 1920s, would have
found it difficult to deny that, from a democrat's perspective, the 'little

fat one' offered clear benefits when compared to the political conditions that had prevailed under the empire. Historians have repeatedly and justifiably pointed to the many weaknesses of Weimar—weaknesses which, however, have only proven to be such in retrospect. Yet they are being continuously referred to when historians assess the nature and success (or lack thereof) of the revolution. This has led to a very one-sided image of Weimar as a stillborn republic—a perception that is certainly not reflected in the views of most people in 1918 or even in 1923. In fact, in late 1923, the failure of democracy would have seemed far less probable than its consolidation. At that point, the future of the Weimar Republic was wide open.

Notes

'LIKE A BEAUTIFUL DREAM'

1. John C. G. Röhl, *Wilhelm II.: Der Weg in den Abgrund, 1900–1941* (Munich, 2008), 1246–7.
2. Ibid. 1247. On the ways in which Wilhelm's behaviour was discussed by contemporaries, see: Martin Kohlrausch, *Der Monarch im Skandal: Die Logik der Massenmedien und die Transformation der wilhelminischen Monarchie* (Berlin, 2005).
3. Richard Bessel, *Germany after the First World War* (Oxford, 1993), 1.
4. Geoff Eley, Jennifer L. Jenkins, and Tracie Matysik (eds), *German Modernities from Wilhelm to Weimar: A Contest of Futures* (London, 2016); Frank-Lothar Kroll, *Geburt der Moderne: Politik, Gesellschaft und Kultur vor dem Ersten Weltkrieg* (Berlin, 2013); Sven O. Müller and Cornelius Torp (eds), *Das Deutsche Kaiserreich in der Kontroverse* (Göttingen, 2009); Geoff Eley and James Retallack (eds), *Wilhelminism and its Legacies: German Modernities, Imperialism, and the Meaning of Reform, 1890–1930: Essays for Hartmut Pogge von Strandmann* (Oxford, 2003); Matthew Jefferies, *Imperial Culture in Germany, 1871–1918* (Houndmills and New York, 2003); Wolfgang König, *Wilhelm II. und die Moderne: Der Kaiser und die technisch-industrielle Welt* (Paderborn, Schöningh-Verlag, 2007); Eberhard Straub, *Kaiser Wilhelm II. in der Politik seiner Zeit: Die Erfindung des Reiches aus dem Geist der Moderne* (Berlin, Landt-Verlag 2008). See, too: Robert Gerwarth and Dominik Geppert (eds), *Wilhelmine Germany and Edwardian Britain: Essays on Cultural Affinity* (Oxford and New York, 2008).
5. Jeffrey R. Smith, *A People's War: Germany's Political Revolution, 1913–1918* (Lanham, Md, 2007), 25–49.
6. Richard Bessel, 'Revolution', in Jay Winter (ed.), *The Cambridge History of the First World War*, vol. 2 (Cambridge, 2014), 127.
7. Jeffrey Verhey, *The Spirit of 1914: Militarism, Myth, and Mobilization in Germany* (Cambridge, 2000).
8. Holger Afflerbach, *Falkenhayn: Politisches Denken und Handeln im Kaiserreich* (Munich, Oldenbourg, 1994), 171; Barbara Tuchman, *August 1914* (Bern, Munich, Vienna, 1960), 150; Richard Dehmel, *Zwischen Volk und Menschheit: Kriegstagebuch* (Berlin, 1919), 9–13; 24.

9. *For a new total history of the First World War, see: Joern Leonhard, Pandora's Box: A History of the First World War (Cambridge, Mass., 2018).*

10. Alexander Watson, *Ring of Steel: Germany and Austria-Hungary at War, 1914–1918* (London, 2015).

11. For a recent narrative account, see: Joachim Käppner, *1918: Aufstand für die Freiheit: Die Revolution der Besonnenen* (Munich, 2017).

12. *Berliner Tageblatt*, 10 November 1918.

13. Ibid.

14. See, for example, Eric Weitz, *Weimar Germany: Promise and Tragedy* (Princeton, 2007). See also, for a critical engagement with the 'crisis' paradigm: Moritz Völlmer and Rüdiger Graf (eds), *Die 'Krise' der Weimarer Republik: Zur Kritik eines Deutungsmusters* (Frankfurt am Main, 2005). Scholars have also emphasized that the notion of a 'Republic without Republicans' is misleading. See Andreas Wirsching and Jürgen Eder (eds), *Vernunftrepublikanismus in der Weimarer Republik: Politik, Literatur, Wissenschaft* (Stuttgart, 2008).

15. Dieter Gosewinkel, *Einbürgern und Ausschließen: Die Nationalisierung der Staatsangehörigkeit vom Deutschen Bund bis zur Bundesrepublik Deutschland* (Göttingen, 2001), 345.

16. Volker Ullrich, 'Kriegsalltag: Zur inneren Revolutionierung der Wilhelminischen Gesellschaft', in Wolfgang Michalka (ed.), *Der Erste Weltkrieg. Wirkung—Wahrnehmung—Analyse* (Weyarn, 1997), 610–11. Also see Florence Hervé, *Geschichte der deutschen Frauenbewegung* (Cologne, 1995). Richard Evans, *Sozialdemokratie und Frauenemanzipation im Kaiserreich* (Berlin and Bonn, 1979) has demonstrated that the SPD was much more equivocal on the issue than was previously assumed, for example by: Willy Albrecht, Friedhelm Boll, Beatrix W. Bouvier, Rosemarie Leuschen-Seppel, and Michael Schneider, 'Frauenfrage und deutsche Sozialdemokratie vom Ende des 19. Jahrhunderts bis zum Beginn der zwanziger Jahre', *Archiv für Sozialgeschichte* 19 (1979), 459–510.

17. Adele Schreiber, *Revolution und Frauenwahlrecht: Frauen! Lernt wählen!* (Berlin, 1919), 14–15.

18. Kathleen Canning, ' "Sexual Crisis," the Writing of Citizenship, and the State of Emergency in Germany, 1917–1922', in Alf Lüdtke and Michael Wildt (eds), *Staats-Gewalt: Ausnahmezustand und Sicherheitsregimes: Historische Perspektiven* (Göttingen, 2008), 167–213. On the formation of new publics during the Weimar era, see: Kathleen Canning, Kerstin Barndt, and Kristin McGuire (eds), *Weimar Publics/Weimar Subject: Rethinking the Political Culture of Germany in the 1920s* (New York, 2010).

19. Kathleen Canning, 'Das Geschlecht der Revolution: Stimmrecht und Staatsbürgertum 1918/1919', in Alexander Gallus (ed.), *Die vergessene Revolution von 1918/19* (Göttingen, 2010), 84–116.

20. James D. Steakley, *The Homosexual Emancipation Movement in Germany* (New York, 1975); John C. Fout, 'Sexual Politics in Wilhelmine Germany:

The Male Gender Crisis, Moral Purity, and Homophobia', *Journal of the History of Sexuality* 2 (1992), 388–421.

21. Magnus Hirschfeld, 'Situationsbericht', *Jahrbuch für sexuelle Zwischenstufen mit besonderer Berücksichtigung der Homosexualität* 17 (1918), 159–60.

22. Adam Seipp, *The Ordeal of Peace: Demobilization and the Urban Experience in Britain and Germany, 1917–1921* (Farnham, 2009); Scott Stephenson, *The Final Battle: Soldiers of the Western Front and the German Revolution of 1918* (Cambridge and New York, 2009), 320–6; Bessel, *Germany after the First World War*, 47, 74–6.

23. Karl Hampe, *Kriegstagebuch 1914–1919*, ed. Folker Reichert and Eike Wolgast (second edition, Munich, 2007), 775 (entry of 10 November 1918).

24. Ernst Troeltsch, 'Die Revolution in Berlin. 30.11.1918', in Ernst Troeltsch, *Die Fehlgeburt einer Republik: Spektator in Berlin 1918 bis 1922* (Frankfurt am Main, 1994), 5–11, here 10.

25. Elard von Oldenburg-Januschau, as quoted in: Stephan Malinowski, *Vom König zum Führer: Sozialer Niedergang und politische Radikalisierung im deutschen Adel zwischen Kaiserreich und NS-Staat* (Berlin, 2003), 207.

26. Eberhard Straub, *Albert Ballin: Der Reeder des Kaisers* (Berlin, 2001), 257–61.

27. Heinrich August Winkler, *Weimar 1918–1933: Die Geschichte der ersten deutschen Demokratie* (Munich, 1993), 25f. and 87ff.

28. Lida Gustava Heymann and Anita Augspurg, *Erlebtes—Erschautes: Deutsche Frauen kaempften fuer Freiheit, Recht, und Frieden 1850–1950*, ed. Margit Twellmann (Frankfurt am Main, 1992), here 178.

29. Hermann Müller, *Die Novemberrevolution: Erinnerungen* (Berlin, 1928, 2nd edn 1931), 41.

30. Leonhard Frank, *Links, wo das Herz ist* (Berlin, 1952), as quoted in: Günther Albrecht (ed.), *Erlebte Geschichte von Zeitgenossen gesehen und geschildert. Erster Teil: Vom Kaiserreich zur Weimarer Republik* (East Berlin, 1967), 188–90.

31. Martin Buber (ed.), *Gustav Landauer: Sein Lebensgang in Briefen*, 2 vols (Frankfurt am Main, 1929), 322f.

32. *Kreuzzeitung*, 12 November 1918.

33. Detlef Lehnert, *Sozialdemokratie und Novemberrevolution: Die Neuordnungsdebatte 1918/19 in der politischen Publizistik von SPD und USPD* (Frankfurt am Main, 1983), 18. See, too: Susanne Miller and Gerhard A. Ritter, 'Die November-Revolution im Herbst 1918 im Erleben und Urteil der Zeitgenossen', *Aus Politik und Zeitgeschichte* 18 (1968), 3–40.

34. Reinhard Rurüp, 'Problems of the German Revolution 1918–19', *Journal of Contemporary History* 3 (1968), 109–35; Eberhard Kolb, '1918/19: Die steckengebliebene Revolution', in Carola Stern and Heinrich August Winkler (eds), *Wendepunkte deutscher Geschichte 1848–1990* (new revised edn, Frankfurt am Main, 2001), 100–25; Frances L. Carsten, *Revolution in Central Europe 1918–19* (London, 1972); Heinrich August Winkler,

Die Sozialdemokratie und die Revolution von 1918/19: Ein Rückblick nach sechzig Jahren (Berlin, 1979).

35. Eric J. Hobsbawm, 'Revolution', in Roy Porter and Mikulas Teich (eds), *Revolution in History* (Cambridge, 1986), 5–6.

36. Kolb, '1918/19: Die steckengebliebene Revolution', 87f.

37. Oskar Lafontaine, 'Rede auf dem Parteitag in Cottbus am 24./25. Mai 2008', <https://archiv2017.die-linke.de/fileadmin/download/disput/2008/disput_juni2008.pdf> (last accessed 22 November 2017).

38. Andreas Wirsching and Jürgen Eder (eds), *Vernunftrepublikanismus in der Weimarer Republik: Politik, Literatur, Wissenschaft* (Stuttgart, 2008).

39. Albert Einstein, *Einstein Papers*, vol. 7: *The Berlin Years: Writings, 1918–1921* (Princeton, 1998), 946.

40. Ernst Troeltsch, 'Die Revolution in Berlin 30.11.1918', in Ernst Troeltsch, *Die Fehlgeburt einer Republik: Spektator in Berlin 1918 bis 1922* (Frankfurt am Main, 1994), 5–11, here 9.

41. Thomas Mann, *Tagebücher 1918–1921*, ed. Peter de Mendelssohn (Franfurt am Main, 1979), 67 (diary entry of 10 November 1918).

42. Adolf Hitler, *Mein Kampf: Eine kritische Edition*, ed. Christian Hartmann, Thomas Vordermayer, Othmar Plöckinger, and Roman Töppel (Berlin and Munich, 2016), vol. 1, 553.

43. Gerhard Pau, 'Der Sturm auf die Republik und der Mythos vom "Dritten Reich"', in Detlef Lehnert and Klaus Megerle (eds.), *Politische Identität und nationale Gedenktage. Zur politischen Kultur der Weimarer Republik* (Opladen, 1989), 255–79, particularly 270–9.

44. Alfred Rosenberg, *Dreißig Novemberköpfe* (Munich, 1927), 7.

45. Michael Geyer, 'Endkampf 1918 und 1914: German Nationalism, Annihilation, and Self-Destruction', in Alf Lüdke and Bernd Weisbrod (eds.), *No Man's Land of Violence: Extreme Wars in the 20th Century* (Göttingen, 2002), 37–67.

46. Niess, *Geschichtsschreibung*; Institut für Marxismus–Leninismus beim ZK der SED (ed.), *Vorwärts und nicht vergessen: Erlebnisberichte aktiver Teilnehmer der Novemberrevolution 1918/19* (East Berlin, 1958); Arbeitskreis verdienter Gewerkschaftsveteranen beim Bundesvorstand des FDGB (ed.), *Erinnerungen von Veteranen der deutsche Gewerkschaftsbewegung an die Novemberrevolution* (2nd edn, East Berlin, 1960); Jakov S. Drabkin, *Die Novemberrevolution in Deutschland* (East Berlin, 1968); Institut für Marxismus–Leninismus beim ZK der SED (ed.), *Illustrierte Geschichte der deutschen Novemberrevolution 1918/19* (East Berlin, 1978).

47. See, for example: Arthur Rosenberg, *Entstehung und Geschichte der Weimarer Republik* (Frankfurt am Main, 1955); Friedrich Stampfer, *Die 14 Jahre der Ersten Deutschen Republik* (Offenbach, 1947; 3rd edn Hamburg 1953); Ferdinand Friedensburg, *Die Weimarer Republik* (Berlin, 1946, 2nd edn 1957); Leopold Schwarzschild, *Von Krieg zu Krieg* (Amsterdam, 1947); Erich Eyck, *Geschichte der Weimarer Republik*, vol. 1, *Vom Zusammenbruch des*

Kaisertums bis zur Wahl Hindenburgs (Zurich, 1954), vol. II: *Von der Konferenz von Locarno bis zu Hitlers Machtübernahme* (Zurich, 1956). Friedrich Meinecke, *Die Deutsche Katastrophe* (Wiesbaden, 1947), 88, speaks of a 'Notbau', an improvised construction built out of necessity rather than conviction.

48. Friedrich Balke and Benno Wagner (eds), *Vom Nutzen und Nachteil historischer Vergleiche: Der Fall Bonn—Weimar* (Frankfurt am Main, 1997); Christoph Gusy (ed.), *Weimars langer Schatten: 'Weimar' als Argument nach 1945* (Baden-Baden, 2003); Sebastian Ullrich, *Der Weimar-Komplex: Das Scheitern der ersten deutschen Demokratie und die politische Kultur der frühen Bundesrepublik 1945–1959* (Göttingen, 2009).

49. On larger trends in the historiography, see: Eberhard Kolb, *Die Weimarer Republik* (6th edn, Munich, 2002), 166–77; Ursula Büttner, *Weimar: Die überforderte Republik 1918–1933* (Stuttgart, 2008). See, also: Anthony McElligott (ed.), *Weimar Germany* (Oxford and New York, 2nd edn, 2011).

50. Karl Dietrich Erdmann, 'Die Geschichte der Weimarer Republik als Problem der Wissenschaft', *Vierteljahrshefte für Zeitgeschichte* 3 (1955), 1–19, here 6–8.

51. Ulrich Kluge, *Soldatenräte und Revolution: Studien zur Militärpolitik in Deutschland 1918/19* (Göttingen, 1975); Eberhard Kolb, *Die Arbeiterräte in der deutschen Innenpolitik 1918/19* (Düsseldorf, 1962; 2nd edn 1978); Walter Tormin, *Zwischen Rätediktatur und sozialer Demokratie: Die Geschichte der Rätebewegung in der deutschen Revolution 1918/19* (Düsseldorf, 1959); Peter von Oertzen, 'Die großen Streiks der Ruhrbergarbeiterschaft im Frühjahr 1919', in *VfZ* 6 (1958), 231–62; Peter von Oertzen, *Betriebsräte in der Novemberrevolution: Eine politikwissenschaftliche Untersuchung über Ideengehalt und Struktur der betrieblichen und wirtschaftlichen Arbeiterräte in der deutschen Revolution 1918/1919* (Düsseldorf, 1963; 2nd edn Berlin, 1976); Erich Matthias, *Zwischen Räten und Geheimräten: Die deutsche Revolutionsregierung 1918/19* (Düsseldorf, 1970); Reinhard Rürup, *Probleme der Revolution in Deutschland 1918/19* (Wiesbaden, 1968); Reinhard Rürup (ed.), *Arbeiter- und Soldatenräte im rheinisch-westfälischen Industriegebiet: Studien zur Geschichte der Revolution 1918/19* (Wuppertal, 1975). This controversy was already reflected in the earliest accounts of the revolution by people actively involved in shaping it. See, for example: Emil Barth, *Aus der Werkstatt der deutschen Revolution* (1919); Eduard Bernstein, *Die deutsche Revolution* (1921).

52. Haffner, 'Verratene Revolution' (1969). The English translation oddly carries the title 'Failure of a Revolution'—a more appropriate translation would be 'The Betrayed Revolution'.

53. Kolb, *Weimarer Republik*, 22. On the notion of an 'arrested revolution' ('gebremste Revolution'), see: Winkler, *Weimar*, 33–68; and Wolfgang Schieder, 'Die Umbrüche von 1918, 1933, 1945 und 1989 als Wendepunkte deutscher Geschichte', in Dietrich Papenfuß and Wolfgang Schieder (eds), *Deutsche Umbrüche im 20. Jahrhundert* (Cologne, Weimar, and Vienna, 2000), 3–18.

54. Gallus, *Vergessene Revolution*; Wolfgang Niess, *Die Revolution von 1918/19: Der wahre Beginn unserer Demokratie* (Berlin et al., 2017), 589. New approaches to key aspects of Weimar history are presented in Anthony McElligott and Kirsten Heinsohn (eds), *Germany 1916–23: A Revolution in Context* (Bielefeld, 2015).

55. See, for example, Hans Ulrich Gumbrecht's literary history of the year 1926 which impressively avoids the danger of reading history backwards from 1933. Hans Ulrich Gumbrecht, *1926: Living on the Edge of Time* (Cambridge, Mass., 1997). For two recent, and more positive, accounts, see: Niess, *Die Revolution von 1918/19* and Joachim Käppner, *1918: Aufstand für die Freiheit. Die Revolution der Besonnenen* (Munich, 2017).

56. On this context-bound interpretation of the term 'crisis' in Weimar discourses, see, for example, Wolfgang Hardtwig, *Ordnungen in der Krise: Zur politischen Kulturgeschichte Deutschlands 1900–1933* (Munich, 2007), notably the essays by Rüdiger Graf, 'Optimismus und Pessimismus in der Krise— der politisch-kulturelle Diskurs in der Weimarer Republik', 115–40, and Peter Fritzsche, 'Historical Time and Future Experience in Postwar Germany', 141–64. See also Martin H. Geyer, ' "Die Gleichzeitigkeit des Ungleichzeitigen": Zeitsemantik und die Suche nach Gegenwart in der Weimarer Republik', in Wolfgang Hardtwig (ed.), *Utopie und politische Herrschaft im Europa der Zwischenkriegszeit* (Munich, 2005), 75–100. Moritz Föllmer and Rüdiger Graf (eds), *Die 'Krise' der Weimarer Republik: Zur Kritik eines Deutungsmuster* (Frankfurt am Main, 2005). See, too, McElligott, *Weimar*, 8ff.

57. For an excellent survey on this subject, see: Heather Jones, 'The German Empire', in Robert Gerwarth and Erez Manela (eds), *Empires at War, 1911–1923* (Oxford, 2014), 52–72.

58. Kristin Kopp, 'Gray Zones: On the Inclusion of "Poland" in the Study of German Colonialism', in Michael Perraudin and Jürgen Zimmerer (eds), *German Colonialism and National Identity* (New York and London, 2011); Robert Lewis Koehl, 'Colonialism inside Germany: 1886–1918', *The Journal of Modern History* 25 (1953), 255–72. For the figures on population, see: Ernest Barker, *The Submerged Nationalities of the German Empire* (Oxford, 1915), 7. Germany also had a population of 150,000 Danes in North Schleswig. On discrimination, see: Watson, 'Fighting for Another Fatherland'; Alan Kramer, 'Wackes at War: Alsace-Lorraine and the Failure of German National Mobilization, 1914–1918', in John Horne (ed.), *State, Society and Mobilization in Europe during the First World War* (Cambridge, 1997), 110–21. Kramer, 'Wackes at War', 110–21.

59. Roger Chickering, *We Men Who Feel Most German: A Cultural Study of the Pan-German League, 1886–1914* (London, 1984).

60. Gregor Thum (ed.), *Traumland Osten: Deutsche Bilder vom östlichen Europa im 20. Jahrhundert* (Göttingen, 2006); Philipp Ther, 'Deutsche Geschichte als imperiale Geschichte: Polen, slawophone Minderheiten und das

Kaiserreich als kontinentales Empire', in Sebastian Conrad and Jürgen Osterhammel (eds), *Das Kaiserreich transnational: Deutschland in der Welt, 1871–1914* (second edition, Göttingen, 2006), 129–48.

61. Peter Calvert, *A Study of Revolution* (Oxford, 1970), 183–4.

62. There is now a considerable body of literature on this subject. For an overview, see: Gerwarth, *The Vanquished*. On the refugees and expellees, see: Peter Gatrell, *A Whole Empire Walking: Refugees in Russia during World War I* (Bloomington, 1999); Vejas Gabriel Liulevicius, *War Land on the Eastern Front: Culture, National Identity, and German Occupation in World War I* (Cambridge, 2000); Pierre Purseigle, ' "A Wave on to Our Shores":The Exile and Resettlement of Refugees from the Western Front, 1914–1918', *Contemporary European History* 16 (2007), 432.

63. Peter Holquist, 'Violent Russia, Deadly Marxism? Russia in the Epoch of Violence, 1905–21', *Kritika: Explorations in Russian and Eurasian History* 4 (2003), 627–652, here p. 645.

64. Most studies on that subject are by now fairly outdated. See, for example, Erich Matthias, *Die deutsche Sozialdemokratie und der Osten* (Tübingen, 1954); Peter Lösche, *Der Bolschewismus im Urteil der deutschen Sozialdemokratie 1903–1920* (West Berlin, 1967); Karl-Heinz Luther, 'Die nachrevolutionären Machtkämpfe in Berlin, November 1918 bis März 1919', *Jahrbuch für Geschichte Mittel- und Ostdeutschlands* (1959), 187–222.

65. Käthe Kollwitz, *Die Tagebücher*, ed. Jutta Bohnke-Kollwitz (Berlin, 1989), 375.

I   1917 AND THE REVOLUTION OF EXPECTATIONS

1. Thomas Boghardt, *The Zimmermann Telegram: Intelligence, Diplomacy and America's Entry into World War I* (Annapolis, Md, 2012), 67 and 79.

2. Ibid., 182.

3. On German support for Irish Republicans in 1916, see Jerome aan de Wiel, *The Irish Factor 1899–1919: Ireland's Strategic and Diplomatic Importance for Foreign Powers* (Dublin, 2008); Matthew Plowman, 'Irish Republicans and the Indo-German Conspiracy of World War I', *New Hibernia Review* 7 (2003), 81–105. On support for jihad, see Tilman Lüdke, *Jihad Made in Germany: Ottoman and German Propaganda and Intelligence Operations in the First World War* (Münster, 2005), 117–25; Gerhard Höpp, *Muslime in der Mark: Als Kriegsgefangene und Internierte in Wünsdorf und Zossen, 1914–1924* (Berlin, 1997); Rudolf A. Mark, *Krieg an Fernen Fronten: Die Deutschen in Zentralasien und am Hindukusch 1914–1924* (Paderborn, 2013), 17–42.

4. Jörn Leonhard, *Die Büchse der Pandora: Geschichte des Ersten Weltkriegs* (Munich, 2014), 654. Gerd Koenen, *Der Russland-Komplex: Die Deutschen und der Osten, 1900–1945* (Munich, 2005), 63ff.

5. Reinhard R. Doerries, *Prelude to the Easter Rising: Sir Roger Casement in Imperial Germany* (London and Portland, Ore., 2000); Mary E. Daly (ed.), *Roger Casement in Irish and World History* (Dublin, 2005).

6. Burton J. Hendrick, *The Life and Letters of Walter Hines Page*, vol. 3 *(Garden City, NY*, 1925*)*, 324 *and* 352; *Barbara W. Tuchman, The Zimmermann Telegram (New York*, 1958*)*, 95.

7. David Stevenson, *1917: War, Peace, and Revolution (Oxford*, 2017*)*, 58–9.

8. Friedrich Katz, *The Secret War in Mexico: Europe, the United States, and the Mexican Revolution (Chicago*, 1981*)*, 327–83.

9. Lawrence Sondhaus, *The Great War at Sea: A Naval History of the First World War (Cambridge*, 2014*)*, 157; *Lawrence Sondhaus, German Submarine Warfare in World War I: The Onset of Total War at Sea (Lanham, Md*, 2017*)*, 46–56; *Anne Cipriano Venzon (ed.), The United States in the First World War: An Encyclopedia (New York and London*, 1995*)*, 45–7.

10. For a contemporary assessment, see Kurt Riezler, *Tagebücher, Aufsätze, Dokumente* (Göttingen, 2008), 395; for a good summary of the military situation, see: Leonhard, *Pandora*, 616–17.

11. Joachim Schröder, *Die U-Boote des Kaisers: Die Geschichte des deutschen U-Boot-Krieges gegen Großbritannien im Ersten Weltkrieg* (Bonn, 2003), 428–9.

12. Adam Tooze, *The Deluge: The Great War, America, and the Remaking of the Global Order, 1916–1931* (London, 2015), 39.

13. Günter Wollstein, *Theobald von Bethmann Hollweg: Letzter Erbe Bismarcks, erstes Opfer der Dolchstoßlegende* (Göttingen, 1995), 137.

14. Stevenson, *1917*, 53.

15. Cooper, as quoted in: Decie Denholm, 'Eine Australierin in Leipzig: Die heimlichen Briefe der Ethel Cooper 1914–1919', in Bernd Hüppauf (ed.), *Ansichten vom Krieg* (Königstein im Taunus, 1984), 132–52, 139 (letter of 4 February 1917).

16. Harry Graf Kessler, *Das Tagebuch 1880–1937*, ed. von Roland Kamzelak and Ulrich Ott, vol. 7: 1919–1923 (Stuttgart, 2007), 142 (entry of 1 February 2017).

17. Thomas J. Knock, *To End All Wars: Woodrow Wilson and the Quest for a New World Order* (New York, 1992), 121f.

18. On theological influences on Wilson, see Mark Benbow, *Leading Them to the Promised Land: Woodrow Wilson, Covenant Theology, and the Mexican Revolutions, 1913–1915* (Kent, Oh., 2010); Milan Babík, *Statecraft and Salvation: Wilsonian Liberal Internationalism as Secularized Eschatology* (Waco, Tex., 2013). On Wilson and liberalism more generally, see Niels Aage Thorsen, *The Political Thought of Woodrow Wilson* (Princeton, 1988); Knock, *To End All Wars*, 3–14.

19. Klaus Schwabe, *Deutsche Revolution und Wilson-Frieden: Die amerikanische und deutsche Friedensstrategie zwischen Ideologie und Machtpolitik 1918/19* (Düsseldorf, 1971), 13f.; 16.

20. Ibid. 23f.; 56.

21. Jennifer D. Keene, 'The United States', in John Horne (ed.), *Companion to World War I* (Malden, Mass., 2010), 508–23, 510.

22. Frederick C. Luebke, *Bonds of Loyalty: German Americans and World War I* (DeKalb, Ill., 1974), 29–30.

23. Keene, 'The United States', in Horne (ed.), *Companion to World War I*, 510. Richard Traxel, *Crusader Nation: The United States in Peace and the Great War 1898–1920* (New York, 2006), 147–8.

24. Stevenson, *1917*, 46.

25. Alexander Sedlmaier, *Deutschlandbilder und Deutschlandpolitik: Studien zur Wilson-Administration (1913–1921)* (Stuttgart, 2003), 65f. and 197; Knock, *To End All Wars*, 107.

26. 'Permanent Peace: Address to the United States Senate, January 22, 1917', *War Addresses of Woodrow Wilson* (Boston, 1918), 8.

27. Leonard V. Smith, *Sovereignty at the Paris Peace Conference* (Oxford, 2008), 24–8.

28. Ibid.

29. Robert Service, *Lenin: A Biography* (London, 2000), 256–64. Catherine Merridale, *Lenin on the Train* (London, 2016).

30. Merridale, *Lenin on the Train*.

31. Willi Gautschi, *Lenin als Emigrant in der Schweiz* (Zurich, 1973), 249–56; Helen Rappaport, *Conspirator: Lenin in Exile* (New York, 2010), 286–98.

32. Christopher Read, *Lenin: A Revolutionary Life* (Abingdon and New York, 2005), 30; Hélène Carrère D'Encausse, *Lenin: Revolution and Power* (New York and London, 1982); Service, *Lenin*, 109.

33. Service, *Lenin*, 137.

34. Ibid., 135–42; Read, *Lenin*, 56f.

35. Leonhard, *Pandora*, 652.

36. On Zurich and Switzerland in this period, see: Georg Kreis, *Insel der unsicheren Geborgenheit: Die Schweiz in den Kriegsjahren 1914–1918* (Zurich, 2014); Roman Rossfeld, Thomas Buomberger, and Patrick Kury (eds), *14/18: Die Schweiz und der Große Krieg* (Baden, 2014).

37. On this debate, see: David Priestland, *The Red Flag: A History of Communism* (London, 2009), 52–60; Robert Service, *Comrades! World History of Communism* (Cambridge, Mass., 2007), 36–57.

38. On socialism in 1914, see the classic work of Georges Haupt, *Socialism and the Great War: The Collapse of the Second International* (Oxford, 1972).

39. Bebel's speech in: *Protokoll ueber die Verhandlungen des Parteitages der Sozialdemokratischen Partei Deutschlands, abgehalten zu Mannheim vom 23. bis 29. September 1906* (Berlin, 1906), 232.

40. Eduard Bernstein, *Die Voraussetzungen des Sozialismus und die Aufgaben der Sozialdemokratie* (Stuttgart, 1899), 165.

41. Kautsky as quoted in: Heinrich August Winkler, *Weimar 1918–1933: Die Geschichte der ersten deutschen Demokratie* (Munich, 1993), 16.

42. Walter Mühlhausen, *Friedrich Ebert, 1871–1925: Reichspräsident der Weimarer Republik* (Bonn, 2006), 42f. See, too, Dieter Dowe and Peter-Christian Witt, *Friedrich Ebert 1871–1925: Vom Arbeiterführer zum Reichspräsidenten* (Bonn, 1987).

43. Dieter Engelmann, and Horst Naumann, *Hugo Haase: Lebensweg und politisches Vermächtnis eines streitbaren Sozialisten* (Berlin, 1999).

44. Ernst-Albert Seils, *Hugo Haase: Ein juedischer Sozialdemokrat im deutschen Kaiserreich. Sein Kampf fuer Frieden und soziale Gerechtigkeit* (Frankfurt am Main, 2016).

45. For a survey, see: Eric D. Weitz, *Creating German Communism, 1890–1990: From Popular Protests to Socialist State* (Princeton, 1997); Dieter Engelmann and Horst Naumann, *Zwischen Spaltung und Vereinigung: Die Unabhaengige Sozialdemokratische Partei Deutschlands in den Jahren 1917–1922* (Berlin, 1993).

46. Susanne Miller, *Burgfrieden und Klassenkampf: Die deutsche Sozialdemokratie im Ersten Weltkrieg* (Düsseldorf, 1974), 113–33; Uli Schöler and Thilo Scholle (eds), *Weltkrieg. Spaltung. Revolution. Sozialdemokratie 1916–1922* (Bonn, 2018). Karl Christian Führer, Jürgen Mittag, and Axel Schildt (eds), *Revolution und Arbeiterbewegung in Deutschland 1918–1920* (Essen, 2013).

47. Walter Mühlhausen, 'Die Zimmerwalder Bewegung', in Gerhard Hirschfeldt, Gerd Krumeich, and Irina Renz (eds), *Enzyklopädie Erster Weltkrieg* (Paderborn, 2004), 977–8; R. Craig Nation, *War on War: Lenin, the Zimmerwald Left, and the Origins of Communist Internationalism* (Chicago, 2009); David Kirby, 'Zimmerwald and the Origins of the Third International', in Tim Rees and Andrew Thorpe (eds), *International Communism and the Communist International, 1919–43* (Manchester, 1998).

48. Horst Lademacher (ed.), *Die Zimmerwalder Bewegung: Protokolle und Korrespondenz*, 2 vols. (Paris and The Hague, 1967), vol. 1, pp. 160–9.

49. Mühlhausen, *Zimmerwalder Bewegung*, 977–8.

50. Read, *Lenin*, 36–42.

51. On Russia in this period, see the panoramic studies by Richard Pipes, *The Russian Revolution* (New York, 1990), and Orlando Figes, *A People's Tragedy: The Russian Revolution, 1891–1924* (London, 1996) both of which offer much information and insight into the relationship of war and revolution in Russia. Of great significance for this theme is the path-breaking study by Peter Gatrell, *A Whole Empire Walking: Refugees in Russia in World War I* (Bloomington, Ind., 1999), together with Peter Holquist, *Making War, Forging Revolution: Russia's Continuum of Crisis* (Cambridge, Mass., 2002), and Eric Lohr, *Nationalizing the Russian Empire: The Campaign against Enemy Aliens during World War I* (Cambridge, Mass., 2003). On the collapse of the Russian Army, see A. K. Wildman, *The End of the Russian Imperial Army: The Old Army and the Soldiers' Revolt, March to April 1917* (Princeton, 1980); and A. K. Wildman, *The End of the Russian Imperial Army II: The Road to Soviet Power and Peace* (Princeton, 1987).

52. Peter Holquist, *Making War, Forging Revolution: Russia's Continuum of Crisis* (Cambridge, Mass., 2002), 30, 44. See also Norman Stone, *The Eastern Front 1914–1917* (London, 1975), 291–301.

53. On the February Revolution, see: Helmut Altrichter, *Rußland 1917: Ein Land auf der Suche nach sich selbst* (Paderborn, 1997), 110–40; Manfred Hildermeier, *Geschichte der Sowjetunion 1917–1991: Entstehung und Niedergang*

des ersten sozialistischen Staates (Munich, 1998), 64–80; Peter Gatrell, *Russia's First World War, 1914–1917: A Social and Economic History* (London, 2005), 197–220; Rex A. Wade, *The Russian Revolution, 1917* (Cambridge and New York, 2000); Stephen Smith, *The Russian Revolution: A Very Short Introduction* (Oxford and New York, 2002) chapter 1; Christopher Read, *From Tsar to Soviets: The Russian People and their Revolution, 1917–1921* (Oxford and New York, 1996); Tsuyoshi Hasegawa, 'The February Revolution', in Edward Acton, Vladimir Iu. Cherniaev, and William G. Rosenberg (eds), *Critical Companion to the Russian Revolution 1914–1921* (London, 1997), 48–61; Barbara Alpern Engel, 'Not by Bread Alone: Subsistence Riots in Russia during World War I', *Journal of Modern History*, 69 (1997) 696–721; Allan K. Wildman, *The End of the Russian Imperial Army*, vol. 1: *The Old Army and the Soldiers' Revolt (March–April 1917)* (Princeton, 1980).

54. W. Bruce Lincoln, *Passage through Armageddon: The Russians in War and Revolution* (New York, 1986), 321–5; Richard Pipes, *The Russian Revolution 1899–1919* (London, 1997), 274–5; Hans Rogger, *Russia in the Age of Modernisation and Revolution 1881–1917* (London, 1997), 266–7.

55. Dominic Lieven, *Nicholas II: Emperor of all the Russians* (London, 1994), 226.

56. Douglas Smith, *Former People: The Final Days of the Russian Aristocracy* (New York, 2012), 72; W. Bruce Lincoln, *Passage through Armageddon: The Russians in War and Revolution* (New York, 1986), 331–3; Pipes, *Russian Revolution*, 279–81; Figes, *People's Tragedy*, 320–1.

57. Pipes, *Russian Revolution*, 307–17; Lincoln, *Passage*, 337–45.

58. Lincoln, *Passage*, 334–44; Figes, *People's Tragedy*, 327–49; Robert Paul Browder and Alexander F. Kerensky (eds), *The Russian Provisional Government 1917: Documents*, 3 vols (Stanford, Calif., 1961); William G. Rosenberg, *The Liberals in the Russian Revolution: The Constitutional Democratic Party, 1917–1921* (Princeton, 1974), 114–16.

59. Marc Ferro, *October 1917: A Social History of the Russian Revolution* (London, 1980).

60. Figes, *People's Tragedy*, 323–31.

61. Lenin, 'First Letter from Afar', in James E. Connor (ed.), *Lenin on Politics and Revolution: Selected Writings* (Indianapolis, 1968), here 151–5. Italics in the original.

62. Leonhard, *Pandora*, 655.

63. Service, *Lenin*, 260.

64. Lincoln, *Passage*, 346–71; Altrichter, *Rußland 1917*, 166–70.

65. Joshua Sanborn, *Imperial Apocalypse: The Great War and the Destruction of the Russian Empire* (Oxford and New York, 2014), 205–11.

66. Andrejs Plakans, *The Latvians* (Stanford, Calif., 1995), 108.

67. Wildman, *End of the Russian Imperial Army*, vol. 1, 369; Mark von Hagen, *War in a European Borderland: Occupations and Occupation Plans in Galicia and Ukraine, 1914–1918* (Seattle, Wash., 2007), 84–5.

68. Allan K. Wildman, *The End of the Russian Imperial Army*, vol. 2: *The Road to Soviet Power and Peace* (Princeton, 1987), 225–31; Joshua A. Sanborn, *Drafting the Russian Nation: Military Conscription, Total War, and Mass Politics, 1905–1925* (DeKalb, 2003), 173–4.

69. Figes, *People's Tragedy*, 423–35; Ronald G. Suny, 'Toward a Social History of the October Revolution', *American Historical Review* 88 (1983), 31–52.

70. George Katkov, *The Kornilov Affair: Kerensky and the Breakup of the Russian Army* (London and New York, 1980); Harvey Ascher, 'The Kornilov Affair: A Reinterpretation', *Russian Review* 29 (1970), 286–300.

71. Ascher, 'The Kornilov Affair'.

72. On Trotsky, see: Isaac Deutscher, *The Prophet Armed: Trotsky, 1879–1921* (Oxford, 1954); Robert Service, *Trotsky: A Biography* (Cambridge, Mass., 2009); Geoffrey Swain, *Trotsky and the Russian Revolution* (London and New York, 2014); Joshua Rubenstein, *Leon Trotsky: A Revolutionary's Life* (New Haven and London, 2006).

73. Vladimir Ilyich Lenin, 'The State and Revolution', in Lenin, *Collected Works*, 45 vols (Moscow, 1964–74), vol. 25, pp. 412ff. Heinrich August Winkler, *Age of Catastrophe: A History of the West, 1914–1945* (London and New Haven, 2015), 26–7.

74. Lincoln, *Passage*, 463–8.

75. The situation was different in Moscow where resistance to the Bolsheviks led to much more violence. Leonhard, *Pandora*, 679. Hildermeier, *Geschichte*, 117. Rex A. Wade, 'The October Revolution, the Constituent Assembly, and the End of the Russian Revolution', in Ian D. Thatcher (ed.), *Reinterpreting Revolutionary Russia: Essays in Honour of James D. White* (London, 2006), 72–85.

76. Pipes, *Russian Revolution*, 541–55.

77. Rosa Luxemburg to Marta Rosenbaum, April 1917, as quoted in: Peter Nettl, *Rosa Luxemburg* (Franfurt am Main, 1968), 635.

78. *Vorwärts*, 15 February 1918.

79. Figes, *People's Tragedy*, 492–7; Alexander Rabinowitch, *The Bolsheviks in Power: The First Year of Soviet Rule in Petrograd* (Bloomingdon, Ind., 2007), 302–4.

80. Smith, *Former People*, 118; Lincoln, *Passage*, 458–61; Pipes, *Russian Revolution*, 499.

81. Orlando Figes, *Peasant Russia, Civil War: The Volga Countryside in Revolution, 1917–21* (Oxford and New York, 1989), 296–7.

82. Smith, *Former People*, 134; Graeme J. Gill, *Peasants and Government in the Russian Revolution* (London, 1979), 154.

83. Sean McMeekin, *History's Greatest Heist: The Looting of Russia by the Bolsheviks* (London and New Haven, 2009), 12–13, 24–5, 73–91. For a local case study, see: Donald J. Raleigh, *Experiencing Russia's Civil War: Politics, Society and Revolutionary Culture in Saratov, 1917–1922* (Princeton, 2002).

2 HOPING FOR VICTORY

1. On Brest-Litovsk, see Vejas Gabriel Liulevicius, *War Land on the Eastern Front: Culture, National Identity and German Occupation in World War I (Cambridge and New York, 2000), 204–7; Joshua Sanborn, Imperial Apocalypse: The Great War and the Destruction of the Russian Empire (Oxford and New York, 2014), 232ff.; and the classic account by Winfried Baumgart, Deutsche Ostpolitik 1918: Von Brest-Litovsk bis zum Ende des Ersten Weltkriegs (Vienna and Munich, 1966), 13–92.

2. Baumgart, Deutsche Ostpolitik 1918, 16. See, too, the older but still fascinating account by John Wheeler-Bennett, Brest-Litovsk: The Forgotten Peace. March 1918 (London, 1938), and the more recent account by Borislav Chernev, Twilight of Empire: The Brest-Litovsk Conference and the Remaking of East-Central Europe, 1917–1918 (Toronto, 2017).

3. Cited in Annemarie H. Sammartino, The Impossible Border: Germany and the East, 1914–1922 (Ithaca, NY, 2010), 31.

4. Sammartino, The Impossible Border, 18–44.

5. Gregor Thum, 'Mythische Landschaften: Das Bild vom deutschen Osten und die Zäsuren des 20. Jahrhunderts', in Gregor Thum (ed.), Traumland Osten: Deutsche Bilder vom östlichen Europa im 20. Jahrhundert (Göttingen, 2006).

6. See Hoffmann's account in Karl Friedrich Nowak (ed.), Die Aufzeichnungen des Generalmajors Max Hoffmann, 2 vols (Berlin, 1929), here vol. 2, 190. See, too, the account of another senior German diplomat involved in drafting the Treaty of Brest-Litovsk, Frederic von Rosenberg: Winfried Becker, Frederic von Rosenberg (1874–1937): Diplomat vom späten Kaiserreich bis zum Dritten Reich, Außenminister der Weimarer Republik (Göttingen, 2011), 26–40. Also Baumgart, Deutsche Ostpolitik 1918, 14.

7. Richard von Kühlmann, Erinnerungen (Heidelberg, 1948), 523f.; Leon Trotsky, My Life (New York, 1930); Nowak, Die Erinnerungen des Generalmajors, 207ff.; Werner Hahlweg, Der Diktatfrieden von Brest-Litowsk 1918 und die bolschewistische Weltrevolution (Münster, 1960); Christian Rust, 'Self-Determination at the Beginning of 1918 and the German Reaction', Lithuanian Historical Studies 13 (2008), 43–6.

8. Ottokar Luban, 'Die Massenstreiks fuer Frieden und Demokratie im Ersten Weltkrieg', in Chaja Boebel and Lothar Wentzel (eds), Streiken gegen den Krieg: Die Bedeutung der Massenstreiks in der Metallindustrie vom Januar 1918 (Hamburg, 2008), 11–27.

9. Ernst Haase, Hugo Haase: Sein Leben und Wirken (Berlin, 1929), 157f.

10. Ralf Hoffrogge, Richard Müller: Der Mann hinter der Novemberrevolution (Berlin, 2008).

11. Ibid.

12. Despite his centrality in the German revolution, no major biography on Scheidemann exists. For surveys, see: Manfred Kittel, 'Scheidemann,

Philipp', in *Neue Deutsche Biographie* (Berlin, 2005), vol. 22, 630f.; Christian Gellinek, *Philipp Scheidemann: Gedächtnis und Erinnerung* (Münster, 2006).

13. Wilhelm Keil, *Erlebnisse eines Sozialdemokraten*, vol. 2 (Stuttgart, 1948), 171.

14. Philipp Scheidemann, *Memoiren eines Sozialdemokraten* (Dresden, 1928), vol. 1, 402f.

15. Oleksii Kurayev, *Politika Nimechchini i Avstro-Uhorshchini v Pershii svitovij vijni: Ukrayins'kii napryamok* (Kiev, 2009), 220–46; Wolfdieter Bihl, *Österreich-Ungarn und die Friedensschluesse von Brest-Litovsk* (Vienna, Cologne, and Graz, 1970), 60–2; Caroline Milow, *Die ukrainische Frage 1917–1923 im Spannungsfeld der europäischen Diplomatie* (Wiesbaden, 2002), 110–15; Stephan M. Horak, *The First Treaty of World War I: Ukraine's Treaty with the Central Powers of February 9, 1918* (Boulder, Colo., 1988); Frank Golczewski, *Deutsche und Ukrainer 1914–1939* (Paderborn, 2010), 240–6.

16. Oleh S. Fedyshyn, *Germany's Drive to the East and the Ukrainian Revolution, 1917–1918* (New Brunswick, NJ, 1971); Peter Borowsky, 'Germany's Ukrainian Policy during World War I and the Revolution of 1918–19', in Hans-Joachim Torke and John-Paul Himka (eds), *German–Ukrainian Relations in Historical Perspective* (Edmonton, 1994), 84–94; Golczewski, *Deutsche und Ukrainer*, 289–306; Olavi Arens, 'The Estonian Question at Brest-Litovsk', *Journal of Baltic Studies* 25 (1994), 309; Rust, 'Self-Determination'; Gert von Pistohlkors, *Deutsche Geschichte im Osten Europas: Baltische Länder* (Berlin, 1994), 452–60; Hans-Erich Volkmann, *Die deutsche Baltikumpolitik zwischen Brest-Litowsk und Compiègne* (Cologne and Vienna, 1970).

17. Baumgart, *Deutsche Ostpolitik 1918*, 14f.; Dietmar Neutatz, *Träume und Alpträume: Eine Geschichte Russlands im 20. Jahrhundert* (Munich, 2013), 158–60; Werner Hahlweg, *Der Diktatfrieden von Brest-Litowsk 1918 und die bolschewistische Weltrevolution* (Münster, 1960), 50–2.

18. Leopold Prinz von Bayern, *Leopold Prinz von Bayern, 1846–1930: Aus den Lebenserinnerungen*, ed. Hans-Michael and Ingrid Körner (Regensburg, 1983), 310–19, here 310 (entry of 3 March 1918).

19. Hannes Leidinger and Verena Moritz, *Gefangenschaft, Revolution, Heimkehr: Die Bedeutung der Kriegsgefangenproblematik für die Geschichte des Kommunismus in Mittel- und Osteuropa 1917–1920* (Cologne and Vienna, 2003); Reinhard Nachtigal, *Russland und seine österreichisch-ungarischen Kriegsgefangenen (1914–1918)* (Remshalden, 2003). Alan Rachaminow, *POWs and the Great War: Captivity on the Eastern Front* (Oxford and New York, 2002).

20. On the estimated two million Habsburg PoWs in Russian captivity, see: Nachtigal, *Kriegsgefangenen (1914–1918)*; Lawrence Sondhaus, *World War One: The Global Revolution* (Cambridge and New York, 2011), 421. On Tito in particular: Vladimir Dedijer, *Novi prilozi za biografiju Josipa Broza Tita 1* (Zagreb and Rijeka, 1980), 57–9 (reprint of the original 1953 edition).

21. Scott Stephenson, *The Final Battle: Soldiers of the Western Front and the German Revolution of 1918* (Cambridge and New York, 2009), 4–5; figures

from Richard Bessel, *Germany after the First World War* (Oxford, 1993), 68–74.

22. Max Hoffmann, *Die Aufzeichnungen des Generalmajors Max Hoffmann*, ed. Karl Friedrich Nowak (Berlin, 1929), 214–24, 219 (entry of 19 November 1918).

23. David Kennedy, *Over Here: The First World War and American Society* (Oxford and New York, 1980), 169.

24. Keith Hitchins, *Rumania, 1866–1947* (Oxford and New York, 1994), 273f.

25. Ludendorff, as quoted in Manfred Nebelin, *Ludendorff: Diktator im Ersten Weltkrieg* (Munich, 2010), 404.

26. Diary entry for 31 December 1917, in Albrecht von Thaer, *Generalstabsdienst an der Front und in der OHL: Aus Briefen und Tagebuchaufzeichnungen, 1915–1919* (Göttingen, 1958), 150–1; Alexander Watson, *Ring of Steel: Germany and Austria-Hungary at War, 1914–1918* (London, 2015), 514.

27. Adenauer, as quoted in Hans Peter Schwarz, *Adenauer: Der Aufstieg 1876–1952* (Stuttgart, 1986), 178.

28. Watson, *Ring of Steel*, 514f.

29. Heinz Hagenlücke, *Deutsche Vaterlandspartei: Die nationale Rechte am Ende des Kaiserreichs* (Düsseldorf, 1997).

30. Martin Kitchen, *The Silent Dictatorship: The Politics of the German High Command under Hindenburg and Ludendorff, 1916–1918* (New York, 1976).

31. Nicholas A. Lambert, *Planning Armageddon: British Economic Warfare and the First World War* (Cambridge, Mass., 2012).

32. Avner Offer, *The First World War: An Agrarian Interpretation* (Oxford, 1991), 341; Roger Chickering, *Imperial Germany and the Great War, 1914–1918* (Cambridge, 2004), 41; Charles Paul Vincent, *The Politics of Hunger: The Allied Blockade of Germany, 1915–1919* (Athens, Oh., 1985), 20; Belinda Davis, *Home Fires Burning: Food, Politics, and Everyday Life in World War I Berlin* (Chapel Hill, NC, 2000), 22.

33. Alan Kramer, 'Blockade and Economic Warfare', in Jay Winter (ed.), *Cambridge History of the First World War* (Cambridge, 2014), vol. 2, 460–89, here 470.

34. Kramer, 'Blockade', 473.

35. Volker Ullrich, *Kriegsalltag: Hamburg im Ersten Weltkrieg* (Cologne, 1982), 40.

36. Offer, *First World War*, 28.

37. Kramer, 'Blockade', here 461.

38. As quoted in Watson, *Ring of Steel*, 352.

39. Kramer, 'Blockade', here 461.

40. Jay Winter and Jean-Louis Robert (eds), *Capital Cities at War: Paris, London, Berlin 1914–1919* (Cambridge, 1997), vol. 1, 517.

41. Watson, *Ring of Steel*, 338–9.

42. Ibid.

43. Ibid.

44. Report of Army Command in Karlsruhe, as quoted in Richard Bessel, 'Revolution', in Jay Winter (ed.), *The Cambridge History of the First World War*, vol. 2: *The State* (Cambridge, 2014), 126–44, here 131.

45. Guy Pedroncini, *Les Mutineries de 1917* (3rd edn, Paris, 1996); for a general overview of the crisis of 1917, see: Leonard V. Smith, Stéphane Audoin-Rouzeau and Annette Becker, *France and the Great War* (Cambridge, 2003), 113–45.

46. Christopher Seton-Watson, *Italy from Liberalism to Fascism* (London, 1967), 471.

47. William H. Kautt, *The Anglo-Irish War, 1916–1921: A People's War* (Westport, Conn., and London, 1999).

48. Michael S. Neiberg, *The Second Battle of the Marne* (Bloomington, Ind., 2008), 34; Michael Geyer, *Deutsche Rüstungspolitik 1860–1980* (Frankfurt am Main, 1984), 83–96; Richard Bessel, *Germany after the First World War* (Oxford, 1993), 5. On the transfer of German troops, see Giordan Fong, 'The Movement of German Divisions to the Western Front, Winter 1917–1918', *War in History* 7 (2000), 225–35, here 229–30.

49. Jörn Leonhard, *Die Büchse der Pandora: Geschichte des Ersten Weltkriegs* (Munich, 2014), 805.

50. A very detailed account of the offensive is offered in David T. Zabecki, *The German 1918 Offensives: A Case Study in the Operational Level of War* (New York, 2006), 126–33. For a more concise and recent analysis, see Watson, *Ring of Steel*, 517ff.

51. Ernst Jünger, *In Stahlgewittern: Ein Kriegstagebuch* (24th edn, Berlin, 1942), 244ff. The edited version is not fundamentally different from the original diary entry: Ernst Jünger, *Kriegstagebuch 1914–1918*, ed. Helmuth Kiesel (Stuttgart, 2010), 375ff. (diary entry of 21 March 1918). On Jünger's life, see Helmuth Kiesel, *Ernst Jünger: Die Biographie* (Munich, 2007).

52. Watson, *Ring of Steel*, 519f.; Martin Middlebrook, *The Kaiser's Battle: The First Day of the German Spring Offensive* (London, 1978).

53. J. Paul Harris, *Douglas Haig and the First World War* (Cambridge and New York, 2008), 454–6.

54. Alan Kramer, *Dynamic of Destruction: Culture and Mass Killing in the First World War* (Oxford and New York, 2007), 269–71; Holger Herwig, *The First World War: Germany and Austria-Hungary, 1914–1918* (London, 1997), 400–16. On the overcoming of Franco-British rivalries, see Elizabeth Greenhalgh, *Victory through Coalition: Politics, Command and Supply in Britain and France, 1914–1918* (Cambridge and New York, 2005).

55. Georg Alexander von Müller, *The Kaiser and his Court: The Diaries, Note Books, and Letters of Admiral Alexander von Müller* (London, 1961), 344.

56. Hugenberg as quoted in Nebelin, *Ludendorff*, 414–15.

57. Letter from the Western front by the Social Democrat and trade unionist, Heinrich Aufderstrasse, to Hermann Sachse (1 May 1917), as quoted in

Benjamin Ziemann, 'Enttäuschte Erwartung und kollektive Erschöpfung: Die deutschen Soldaten an der Westfront 1918 auf dem Weg zur Revolution', in Jörg Duppler and Gerhard P. Groß (eds), *Kriegsende 1918: Ereignis, Wirkung, Nachwirkung* (Munich, 1999), 165–82, here 175.

58. Watson, *Ring of Steel*, 520.

59. Zabecki, *German 1918 Offensives*, 139–73; David Stevenson, *With our Backs to the Wall: Victory and Defeat in 1918* (London, 2011), 67.

60. Wilhelm Deist, 'Verdeckter Militärstreik im Kriegsjahr 1918?', in Wolfram Wette (ed.), *Der Krieg des kleinen Mannes: Eine Militärgeschichte von unten* (Munich and Zurich, 1998), 146–67, here 149–50.

61. Alexander Watson, *Enduring the Great War: Combat, Morale and Collapse in the German and British Armies, 1914–1918* (Cambridge and New York, 2008), 181.

62. Zabecki, *German 1918 Offensives*, 184–205; Watson, *Ring of Steel*, 521; Robert Foley, 'From Victory to Defeat: The German Army in 1918', in Ashley Ekins (ed.), *1918: Year of Victory* (Auckland and Wollombi, 2010), 69–88, here 77.

63. Eberhard Kessel (ed.), *Friedrich Meinecke, Werke*, vol. 8: *Autobiographische Schriften* (Stuttgart, 1969), 289–320, here 292.

64. Stevenson, *With our Backs to the Wall*, 78–88.

65. Herwig, *First World War*, 414; Stéphane Audoin-Rouzeau, Annette Becker, and Leonard V. Smith, *France and the Great War, 1914–1918* (Cambridge and New York, 2003), 151; Stevenson, *With our Backs to the Wall*, 345.

66. Stephenson, *Final Battle*, 25.

67. Oliver Haller, 'German Defeat in World War I, Influenza and Postwar Memory', in Klaus Weinhauer, Anthony McElligott, and Kirsten Heinsohn (eds), *Germany 1916–23: A Revolution in Context* (Bielefeld, 2015), 151–80, here 173f. See, too, Eckard Michels, '"Die Spanische Grippe" 1918/19: Verlauf, Folgen und Deutungen in Deutschland im Kontext des Ersten Weltkriegs', *Vierteljahrshefte für Zeitgeschichte* (2010), 1–33; Frieder Bauer and Jörg Vögele, 'Die "Spanische Grippe" in der deutschen Armee 1918: Perspektive der Ärzte und Generäle, *Medizinhistorisches Journal* 48 (2013), 117–52; Howard Phillips and David Killingray (eds), *The Spanish Influenza Pandemic of 1918–19: New Perspectives* (London, 2003).

68. Stephenson, *Final Battle*, 25.

69. For the state of front-line units in the last weeks, see the reports in A. Philipp (ed.), *Die Ursachen des Deutschen Zusammenbruches im Jahre 1918 Zweite Abteilung: Der innere Zusammenbruch*, vol. 6 (Berlin, 1928), 321–86.

70. Bernd Ulrich and Benjamin Ziemann (eds), *Frontalltag im Ersten Weltkrieg: Wahn und Wirklichkeit. Quellen und Dokumente* (Frankfurt am Main, 1994), 94 (report of 4 September 1918).

71. Stevenson, *With our Backs to the Wall*, 112–69.

3 ENDGAME

1. Friederike Krüger and Michael Salewski, 'Die Verantwortung der militärischen Führung deutscher Streitkräfte in den Jahren 1918 und 1945', in Jörg Duppler and Gerhard Paul (eds), Kriegsende 1918: Ereignis, Wirkung, Nachwirkung (Munich, 1999), 377–98, here 390.

2. Bernd Ulrich and Benjamin Ziemann (eds), Frontalltag im Ersten Weltkrieg: Wahn und Wirklichkeit. Quellen und Dokumente (Frankfurt, 1994), doc. 58, 203–4.

3. Manfred Nebelin, Ludendorff: Diktator im Ersten Weltkrieg (Munich, 2010), 423–4. On Hindenburg, see Wolfram Pyta, Hindenburg: Herrschaft zwischen Hohenzollern und Hitler (Munich, 2007).

4. On the battles for Doiran and the commemorations of the First World War in Bulgaria, see Nikolai Vukov, 'The Memory of the Dead and the Dynamics of Forgetting: "Post-Mortem" Interpretations of World War I in Bulgaria', in Oto Luthar (ed.), The Great War and Memory in Central and South Eastern Europe (Leiden, 2016); see also Ivan Petrov, Voynata v Makedonia (1915–1918) (Sofia, 2008); Nikola Nedev and Tsocho Bilyarski, Doyranskata epopeia, 1915–1918 (Sofia, 2009).

5. On the breakthrough at Dobro Pole, see Richard C. Hall, Balkan Breakthrough: The Battle of Dobro Pole 1918 (Bloomington, Ind., 2010); Dimitar Azmanov and Rumen Lechev, 'Probivat na Dobro pole prez sptemvri 1918 godina', Voennoistoricheski sbornik 67 (1998), 154–75.

6. See full details in Bogdan Kesyakov, Prinos kym diplomaticheskata istoriya na Bulgaria (1918–1925): Dogovori, konventsii, spogodbi, protokoli i drugi syglashenia i diplomaticheski aktove s kratki belejki (Sofia, 1925); Petrov, Voynata v Makedonia, 209–11.

7. Eberhard Kessel (ed.), Friedrich Meinecke, Werke, vol. 8: Autobiographische Schriften (Stuttgart, 1969), 305 (diary entry of 27 September 1918).

8. Käthe Kollwitz, Die Tagebücher, ed. Jutta Bohnke-Kollwitz (Berlin, 1989), 374 (diary entry of 1 October 1918), 374.

9. Andrej Mitrović, Serbia's Great War, 1914–1918 (London, 2007), 312–19.

10. Gunther Rothenberg, The Army of Francis Joseph (West Lafayette, Ind., 1997), 212–13.

11. Watson, Ring of Steel, 538.

12. Mark Thompson, The White War: Life and Death on the Italian Front 1915–19 (London, 2009), 344–6; Mark Cornwall, The Undermining of Austria-Hungary: The Battle for Hearts and Minds (Basingstoke, 2000), 287–99.

13. Alexander Watson, Ring of Steel: Germany and Austria-Hungary at War, 1914–1918 (London, 2015), 538.

14. Ibid., 540; Arthur May, The Passing of the Hapsburg Monarchy, vol. 2 (Philadelphia, 1966), 760–3.

15. Rudolf Neck (ed.), Österreich im Jahre 1918: Berichte und Dokumente (Vienna, 1968), 104–13.

16. Quoted in Mario Isenghi and Giorgio Rochat, *La Grande Guerra 1914–1918* (Bologna, 2008), 463–4.

17. Erik-Jan Zürcher, 'The Ottoman Empire and the Armistice of Moudros', in Hugh Cecil and Peter H. Liddle (eds), *At the Eleventh Hour: Reflections, Hopes, and Anxieties at the Closing of the Great War, 1918* (London, 1998), 266–75.

18. Martin Albrecht, *Als deutscher Jude im Ersten Weltkrieg: Der Fabrikant und Offizier Otto Meyer* (Berlin, 2014), 122.

19. Albrecht von Thaer, *Generalstabsdienst an der Front und in der OHL: Aus Briefen und Tagebuchaufzeichnungen, 1915–1919* (Göttingen, 1958), 234 (diary entry for 1 October 1918).

20. Ibid.

21. Herbert Michaelis, Ernst Schraepler, and Günter Scheel (eds), *Ursachen und Folgen*, vol. 2: *Der militärische Zusammenbruch und das Ende des Kaiserreichs* (Berlin, 1959), 319–20 (doc. 365).

22. Wilson's speech to Congress, 11 February 1918, as quoted in Woodrow Wilson, *War and Peace: Presidential Messages, Addresses, and Public Papers (1917–1924)*, ed. Ray Stannard Baker and William E. Dodd (New York, 1927), 177–84, here 180.

23. Harry Rudolph Rudin, *Armistice 1918* (New Haven, 1944), 53–4.

24. Lothar Machtan, *Prinz Max von Baden: Der letzte Kanzler des Kaisers* (Berlin, 2013).

25. Ebert as quoted in Heinrich August Winkler, *Weimar 1918–1933: Die Geschichte der ersten deutschen Demokratie* (Munich, 1993), 22.

26. Heinrich August Winkler, *Age of Catastrophe: A History of the West, 1914–1945* (London and New Haven, 2015), 61–2. On the October reforms, see, most recently, Anthony McElligott, *Rethinking the Weimar Republic: Authority and Authoritarianism, 1916–1936* (London, 2014), 19–26.

27. Rudin, *Armistice 1918*, 53 and 56–80; Watson, *Ring of Steel*, 547–8.

28. Alexander Sedlmaier, *Deutschlandbilder und Deutschlandpolitik: Studien zur Wilson-Administration (1913–1921)* (Stuttgart, 2003), 101. On the exchange of notes between Germany and the United States, see, too, Klaus Schwabe, *Deutsche Revolution und Wilson-Frieden: Die amerikanische und deutsche Friedensstrategie zwischen Ideologie und Machtpolitik 1918/19* (Düsseldorf, 1971), 88–195. Edmund Marhefka (ed.), *Der Waffenstillstand 1918–1919: Das Dokumenten-Material d. Waffenstillstands-Verhandlungen von Compiègne, Spa, Trier und Brüssel*, vol. 1: *Der Waffenstillstandsvertrag von Compiègne und seine Verlängerungen nebst den finanziellen Bestimmungen* (Berlin, 1928), 11.

29. Eberhard Kessel (ed.), *Friedrich Meinecke, Werke*, vol. 8: *Autobiographische Schriften* (Stuttgart, 1969), 306 (diary entry of 3 October 1918).

30. Karl Friedrich Nowak (ed.), *Die Aufzeichnungen des Generalmajors Max Hoffmann* (Berlin, 1929), 214 (entry of 7 October 1918).

31. Klaus Schwabe, *Woodrow Wilson, Revolutionary Germany, and Peacemaking, 1918–1919: Missionary Diplomacy and the Realities of Power* (Chapel Hill, NC, and London, 1985), 47.

32. Ibid., 48.
33. Ibid., 48ff.
34. Marhefka (ed.), *Der Waffenstillstand 1918–1919*, 12.
35. Ibid., 13f.
36. Ibid.
37. Sedlmaier, *Deutschlandbilder*, 217.
38. Bullit Lowry, *Armistice 1918* (Kent, Oh., and London, 1996), 77.
39. Schwabe, *Woodrow Wilson, Revolutionary Germany*, 55ff.
40. Käthe Kollwitz, *Die Tagebücher*, ed. Jutta Bohnke-Kollwitz (Berlin, 1989), 376 (diary entry of 15 October 1918).
41. Marhefka (ed.), *Der Waffenstillstand 1918–1919*, 14f.
42. Sedlmaier, *Deutschlandbilder*, 105.
43. Ibid., 155.
44. Schwabe, *Woodrow Wilson, Revolutionary Germany*, 66.
45. Memorandum by F. K. Lane (23 October 1918), as quoted in Sedlmaier, *Deutschlandbilder*, 105.
46. Schwabe, *Woodrow Wilson, Revolutionary Germany*, 67.
47. Quoted in Rudin, *Armistice 1918*, 173; Watson, *Ring of Steel*, 550–1.
48. Nebelin, *Ludendorff*, 479f.
49. Max Hoffmann, *Die Aufzeichnungen des Generalmajors Max Hoffmann*, ed. Karl Friedrich Nowak (Berlin, 1929), 215 (entry of 8 October 1918).
50. Nebelin, *Ludendorff*, 489ff.; Prince Max von Baden to Wilhelm II, 25 October 1918, in Erich Matthias and Rudolf Morsey, *Die Regierung des Prinzen Max von Baden. Quellen zur Geschichte des Parlamentarismus und der politischen Parteien*, vol. 2 (Düsseldorf, 1962) doc. no. 94.
51. Nebelin, *Ludendorff*, 493.
52. Ibid., 497–8.
53. *Die Aufzeichnungen des Generalmajors Max Hoffmann*, ed. Karl Friedrich Nowak (Berlin, 1929), 216f. (entry of 27 October 1918).
54. Marhefka (ed.), *Der Waffenstillstand 1918–1919*, 17f.
55. Winkler, *Age of Catastrophe*, 61–2; McElligott, *Rethinking the Weimar Republic*, 19–26.
56. Auer as quoted in Joachim Käppner, *1918: Aufstand für die Freiheit. Die Revolution der Besonnenen* (Munich, 2017), 152.
57. Martin Kitchen, *The Silent Dictatorship: The Politics of the German High Command under Hindenburg and Ludendorff, 1916–1918* (New York, 1976). Richard Bessel, 'Revolution', in Jay Winter (ed.), *The Cambridge History of the First World War*, vol. 2 (Cambridge and New York, 2014), 126–44.

4 THE SAILORS' MUTINY

1. Wilhelm Deist, 'Die Politik der Seekriegsleitung und die Rebellion der Flotte Ende Oktober 1918', *Vierteljahrshefte für Zeitgeschichte* 14 (1966), 341–68.

2. Gerhard Groß, 'Eine Frage der Ehre? Die Marineführung und der letzte Flottenvorstoß 1918', in Jörg Duppler and Gerhard P. Groß (eds), *Kriegsende 1918: Ereignis, Wirkung, Nachwirkung* (Munich, 1999), 349–65, here 354–65; Alexander Watson, *Ring of Steel: Germany and Austria-Hungary at War, 1914–1918* (London, 2015), 552.

3. Richard Stumpf, *Warum die Flotte zerbrach: Kriegstagebuch eines christlichen Arbeiters* (Berlin, 1927), 25, as cited in Groß, 'Frage der Ehre?', 349.

4. Dirk Dähnhardt, *Revolution in Kiel* (Neumünster, 1984), 48, on the events of 1917; see also *Das Werk des Untersuchungsausschusses der Verfassungsgebenden Deutschen Nationalversammlung und des Deutschen Reichstages 1919–1928: Verhandlungen, Gutachten, Urkunden*, ed. Walter Schücking et al.; *Die Ursachen des Deutschen Zusammenbruchs im Jahre 1918*, ed. by Albrecht Philipp (Berlin, 1928–9), vol. 9/1 and 2: 'Entschließung und Verhandlungsbericht: Marine und Zusammenbruch', vol. 10/1: 'Gutachten der Sachverständigen Alboldt, Stumpf, v. Trotha zu den Marinevorgängen 1917 und 1918'; vol. 10/2: 'Tagebuch des Matrosen Richard Stumpf'; *Marinestreiks—Meuterei—Revolutionäre Erhebung 1917/1918*, ed. Stephan Huck and Frank Nägler (Munich, 2009).

5. Dähnhardt, *Revolution*, 35 and 48; see, too, Detlef Siegfried, *Das radikale Milieu: Kieler Novemberrevolution, Sozialwissenschaft und Linksradikalismus 1917–1922* (Wiesbaden, 2004).

6. Wilhelm Deist, 'Die Politik der Seekriegsleitung und die Rebellion der Flotte Ende Oktober 1918', *Vierteljahrshefte für Zeitgeschichte* 14 (1966), 341–68, here 347f.

7. Dähnhardt, *Revolution*, 50; Deist, *Politik*, 351; *Quellen zur Geschichte des Parlamentarismus und der politischen Parteien*, vol. 2: 'Die Regierung des Prinzen Max von Baden', ed. E. Matthias and R. Morsey (Düsseldorf, 1962), 220ff.

8. As quoted in Deist, *Politik*, 352.

9. Ibid., 352f.

10. Trotha's 'Überlegungen in ernster Stunde' for Levetzow, 6 October 1918 with a cover letter from 8 October 1918, as quoted in Deist, *Politik*, 352f.

11. Holger H. Herwig, *'Luxury' Fleet: The Imperial German Navy, 1888–1918* (London, 1980), 247 and 250; Watson, *Ring of Steel*, 552.

12. Dähnhardt, *Revolution*, 52; Groß, *Frage*, 351f.

13. On the details of the plan and the discussion regarding its military rationality and the motives of the SKL, see Groß, *Frage*, 351ff.

14. Bernhard Rausch, *Am Springquell der Revolution: Die Kieler Matrosenerhebung* (Kiel, 1918), 7.

15. Dähnhardt, *Revolution*, 52; on the leaflet text, see: Hugo von Waldeyer-Hartz, *Die Meuterei der Hochseeflotte: Ein Beitrag zur Geschichte der Revolution* (Berlin, 1922), 29.

16. Dähnhardt, *Revolution*, 53.

17. 'Sammlung Unruhen in Kiel', BA-MA F4076/64914, as quoted in Dähnhardt, *Revolution*, 54.
18. *Das Werk des Untersuchungsausschusses der Verfassungsgebenden Deutschen Nationalversammlung und des Deutschen Reichstages 1919–1928* (= WUA): *Verhandlungen, Gutachten, Urkunden*, ed. Walter Schücking, Johannes Bell, et al., series 4, *Die Ursachen des Deutschen Zusammenbruchs im Jahre 1918*, ed. Albrecht Philipp (Berlin, 1928–9), vol. 9/1, 486.
19. Dähnhardt, *Revolution*, 54.
20. 'Bericht Konteradmiral Küsel, Eintreffen und Aufenthalt III. Geschwader', BA-MA F 7590/vol.2, as quoted in Dähnhardt, *Revolution*, 55.
21. Lothar Popp, *Ursprung und Entwicklung der Novemberrevolution 1918* (Kiel, 1918), 10.
22. Police report of 2 November 1918, BA-MA Rm 31/v. 2373, fos 10–14, as quoted in Dähnhardt, *Revolution*, 56.
23. Dähnhardt, *Revolution*, 56.
24. Ibid.
25. Popp, *Ursprung*, 11; Dähnhardt, *Revolution*, 57.
26. Hannes Leidinger, 'Der Kieler Aufstand und die deutsche Revolution', in Verena Moritz and Hannes Leidinger (eds), *Die Nacht des Kirpitschnikow: Eine andere Geschichte des Ersten Weltkriegs* (Vienna, 2006), 220–35; Daniel Horn, *Mutiny on the High Seas: Imperial German Naval Mutinies of World War One* (London, 1973), 234–46; Watson, *Ring of Steel*, 553; Dirk Liesemer, *Aufstand der Matrosen: Tagebuch einer Revolution* (Hamburg, 2018); Martin Rackwitz, *Kiel 1918: Revolution. Aufbruch zu Demokratie und Republik* (Kiel, 2018).
27. Dähnhardt, *Revolution*, 58f.
28. 'Kriegstagebuch des Munitionsdepots (Ostufer der Kieler Förde)', in: BA-MA F 3979/63961, as quoted in Dähnhardt, *Revolution*, 60.
29. 'Kriegstagebuch der Kommandatur', BA-MA F. 4077/64921, as quoted in Dähnhardt, *Revolution*, 60.
30. Erich Matthias and Hans Meier-Welcher (eds), *Quellen zur Geschichte des Parlamentarismus und der politischen Parteien*. 2nd ser.: *Militär und Politik: Militär und Innenpolitik im Weltkrieg 1914–1918*, ed. Wilhelm Deist, 2 vols (Düsseldorf, 1970), no. 502, 1361.
31. Philipp Scheidemann, *Der Zusammenbruch* (Berlin, 1921), 190.
32. Wolfram Wette, *Gustav Noske: Eine politische Biographie* (Düsseldorf, 1987), 203; Gustav Noske, *Von Kiel bis Kapp* (Berlin, 1920), 8.
33. 'Kriegstagebuch der Stadtkommandantur', BA-MA RM 3 l/v.2373, fo. 70, as quoted in Dähnhardt, *Revolution*, 62.
34. Dähnhardt, *Revolution*, 63.
35. Popp, *Ursprung*, 14.
36. Dähnhardt, *Revolution*, 64.
37. Souchon Papers, BA-MAN 156/31, as quoted in Dähnhardt, *Revolution*, 65.
38. 'Bericht Steinhäusers über die Ereignisse in der Karlstraße am 3.11.1918', BA-MA RM 31/v. 2373, fos 23f., as quoted in Dähnhardt, *Revolution*, 65.

39. Dähnhardt, *Revolution*, 65. According to Popp's depiction, the procession was shot at without previous warning. Popp, *Ursprung*, 13.
40. Dähnhardt, *Revolution*, 66.
41. 'Kriegstagebuch der Station', BA-MA F 3974a/63919, as quoted in Dähnhardt, *Revolution*, 66.
42. Ibid.
43. Ibid.
44. Popp, *Ursprung*, 16.
45. Dähnhardt, *Revolution*, 82.
46. Ibid., 75.
47. Popp, *Ursprung*, 16; Rausch, *Springquell*, 16.
48. Rausch, *Springquell*, 20.
49. 'Souchon's report of 7 March 1920', BA-MA, F 1660/0, as quoted in Dähnhardt, *Revolution*, 76.
50. Dähnhardt, *Revolution*, 76.
51. Noske, *Kiel bis Kapp*, 10; Conrad Haussmann, *Schlaglichter: Reichstagsbriefe und Aufzeichnungen*, ed. Ulrich Zeller (Frankfurt am Main, 1924), 265; Wette, *Noske*, 203.
52. Noske, *Kiel bis Kapp*, 11.
53. Wette, *Noske*, 206.
54. Ibid.
55. Dähnhardt, *Revolution*, 87; Wette, *Noske*, 208.
56. Noske, *Kiel bis Kapp*, 13.
57. Ibid., 23; Wette, *Noske*, 554.
58. Eberhard Kessel (ed.), *Friedrich Meinecke, Werke*, vol. 8: *Autobiographische Schriften* (Stuttgart, 1969), 309f. (diary entry of 10 November 1918).

5 THE REVOLUTION SPREADS

1. Ulrich Kluge, 'Militärrevolte und Staatsumsturz: Ausbreitung und Konsolidierung der Räteorganisation im rheinisch-westfälischen Industriegebiet', in Reinhard Rürup (ed.), *Arbeiter- und Soldatenräte im rheinisch-westfälischen Industriegebiet* (Wuppertal, 1975), 39–82. More recently, see: Hans-Jörg Czech, Olaf Matthes, and Ortwin Pelc (eds), *Revolution? Revolution! Hamburg 1918/19* (Hamburg, 2018).
2. Hermann Müller, *Die Novemberrevolution: Erinnerungen* (Berlin, 1928), 29.
3. Jan Rüger, *Helgoland. Deutschland, England und ein Felsen in der Nordsee* (Berlin, 2017), 152.
4. On the role of the Home Army in the November Revolution, see Ernst-Heinrich Schmidt, *Heimatheer und Revolution 1918: Die militärischen Gewalten im Heimatgebiet zwischen Oktoberreform und Novemberrevolution* (Stuttgart, 1981).
5. Michael Geyer, 'Zwischen Krieg und Nachkrieg: Die deutsche Revolution 1918/19 im Zeichen blockierter Transnationalität', in Alexander Gallus

(ed.), *Die vergessene Revolution von 1918/19* (Göttingen, 2010), 187–222, here 193–5.

6. Harry Graf Kessler, *Das Tagebuch 1880–1937*, ed. Günter Riederer and Roland Kamzelak, vol. 6 *(Stuttgart, 2006), 619.*

7. Roger Chickering, *Imperial Germany and the Great War, 1914–1918 (2nd edn, Cambridge, 2004)*, 195; *Adam R. Seipp, The Ordeal of Peace: Demobilization and the Urban Experience in Britain and Germany, 1917–1921 (Farnham, 2009).*

8. Hans Beyer, *Die Revolution in Bayern 1918/1919 (East Berlin, 1988)*, 13.

9. Heinrich Hillmayr, 'München und die Revolution 1918/1919', in Karl Bosl (ed.), *Bayern im Umbruch. Die Revolution von 1918, ihre Voraussetzungen, ihr Verlauf und ihre Folgen (Munich and Vienna, 1969)*, 453–504, here 471.

10. Ibid.; Beyer, *Revolution*, 13.

11. Günter Hortzschansky (ed.), *Illustrierte Geschichte der deutschen Novemberrevolution 1918/19* (East Berlin, 1978), 107.

12. Allan Mitchell, *Revolution in Bayern 1918/1919: Die Eisner-Regierung und die Räterepublik* (Munich, 1967), 79; Beyer, *Revolution*, 15.

13. 'Resolution der Theresienwiesen-Versammlung vom 7. November 1918', reprinted in *Münchner Post*, 8 November 1918; also quoted in Beyer, *Revolution*, 161f.

14. Franz Schade, *Kurt Eisner und die bayerische Sozialdemokratie* (Hanover, 1961); Peter Kritzer, *Die bayerische Sozialdemokratie und die bayerische Politik in den Jahren 1918–1923* (Munich, 1969)andBernhard Grau, *Kurt Eisner 1867–1919: Eine Biographie* (Munich, 2001).

15. Mitchell, *Revolution*, 30–55.

16. Ibid.

17. Anthony Read, *The World on Fire: 1919 and the Battle with Bolshevism* (London, 2009), 33–7.

18. Beyer, *Revolution*, 12f.

19. Hillmayr, *München*; Grau, *Eisner*, 344; Mitchell, *Revolution*, 100; David Clay Large, *Where Ghosts Walked: Munich's Road to the Third Reich* (New York, 1997), 78–9; Read, *The World on Fire*, 35.

20. *Dokumente und Materialien zur Geschichte der deutschen Arbeiterbewegung*, second series (East Berlin, 1957), 280.

21. Hilde Kramer, *Rebellin in Munich, Moskau und Berlin: Autobiographie 1901–1924*, ed. Egon Günther (Berlin, 2011), 49.

22. Beyer, *Revolution*, 16; Hillmayr, *München*, 472; Hortzschansky, *Illustrierte Geschichte der deutschen Novemberrevolution*, 107.

23. Felix Fechenbach, *Der Revolutionär Kurt Eisner: Aus persönlichen Erlebnissen* (Berlin, 1929), 42f., as quoted in Hortzschansky, *Illustrierte Geschichte der deutschen Novemberrevolution*, 109.

24. Ulrich Kluge, *Soldatenräte und Revolution: Studien zur Militärpolitik in Deutschland 1918/19* (Göttingen, 1975), 48–56.

25. Rainer Maria Rilke to Clara, 7 November 1918, in Heinrich August Winkler and Alexander Cammann (eds), *Weimar: Ein Lesebuch zur deutschen Geschichte 1918–1933* (Munich, 1997), 44–5.

26. Oswald Spengler, quoted ibid., 57–8.

27. Lothar Machtan, *Die Abdankung: Wie Deutschlands gekrönte Häupter aus der Geschichte fielen* (Berlin, 2008), here 15. See, too, Karina Urbach (ed.), *European Aristocracies and the Radical Right, 1918–1939* (Oxford, 2007). Stephan Malinowski, *Vom König zum Führer: Sozialer Niedergang und politische Radikalisierung im deutschen Adel zwischen Kaiserreich und NS-Staat* (Berlin, 2003), 20–8.

28. On the revolution in Dresden, see Freya Klier, *Dresden 1919: Die Geburt einer neuen Epoche* (Freiburg, 2018). On the revolution in Saxony more generally, see John Ondrovcik '"All the Devils Are Loose": The Radical Revolution in the Saxon Vogtland, 1918–1920' (unpublished Ph.D. thesis, Harvard, 2008).

29. Decie Denholm, 'Eine Australierin in Leipzig: Die heimlichen Briefe der Ethel Cooper 1914–1919', in Bernd Hüppauf (ed.), *Ansichten vom Krieg* (Königstein im Taunus, 1984), 132–52, here 150. On Leipzig during the revolution, see: Werner Bramke and Silvio Reisinger, *Leipzig in der Revolution von 1918/19* (Leipzig, 2009); Silvio Reisinger, 'Die Revolution von 1918/19 in Leipzig', in Ulla Plener (ed.), *Die Novemberrevolution 1918/19 in Deutschland: Für bürgerliche und sozialistische Demokratie. Allgemeine, regionale und biographische Aspekte. Beiträge zum 90. Jahrestag der Revolution* (Berlin, 2009), 163–80.

30. As quoted in: Eberhard Kolb, *Umbrüche deutscher Geschichte 1866/71, 1918/19, 1929/33: Ausgewählte Aufsätze*, ed. Dieter Langewiesche and Klaus Schönhoven (Munich, 1993), 246–7.

31. Oliver Bernhardt, *Alfred Döblin* (Munich, 2007).

32. Alfred Döblin, 'Revolutionstage im Elsaß', *Die Neue Rundschau* 1 (February 1919), 164–72, reprinted in Alfred Döblin, *Schriften zur Politik und Gesellschaft* (Olten and Freiburg im Breisgau, 1972), 59–70, here 60.

33. Ibid., 61f.

34. Ibid., 64.

35. Walter Nojowski, *Victor Klemperer (1881–1960): Romanist—Chronist der Vorhoelle* (Berlin, 2004).

36. Victor Klemperer, *Curriculum Vitae, Erinnerungen 1881–1918*, vol. 2 (Berlin, 1996), 689.

37. Ibid., 690.

38. *Die Aufzeichnungen des Generalmajors Max Hoffmann*, ed. Karl Friedrich Nowak (Berlin, 1929), 214–24, here 218 (entry of 12 November 1918).

39. Klemperer, *Curriculum Vitae*, 703.

40. Max von Baden, *Erinnerungen und Dokumente* (Berlin, 1927), 588. Local studies on some of these events include Martin Gohlke, 'Die Räte in der Revolution 1918/19 in Magedeburg' (unpublished Ph.D. thesis, Oldenburg, 1999); Reinhard Bein, *Braunschweig zwischen rechts und links: Der Freistaat 1918 bis 1930. Materialien zur Landesgeschichte* (Braunschweig, 1991); Reinhold Weber, *Baden und Württemberg 1918/19: Kriegsende—Revolution— Demokratie* (Stuttgart, 2018); Detlef Lehnert (ed.), *Revolution 1918/19 in Norddeutschland* (Berlin, 2018).

41. For a detailed account of the end of the German dynasties, see Lothar Machtan, *Die Abdankung: Wie Deutschlands gekrönte Häupter aus der Geschichte fielen* (Berlin, 2008).

42. Käthe Kollwitz, *Die Tagebücher*, ed. Jutta Bohnke-Kollwitz (Berlin, 1989), 378 (entry of 8 November 1918).

43. Eberhard Kessel (ed.), *Friedrich Meinecke, Werke*, vol. 8: *Autobiographische Schriften* (Stuttgart, 1969), 300.

44. For primary sources on this see Erich Matthias and Rudolf Morsey (eds), *Die Regierung des Prinzen Max von Baden* (Düsseldorf, 1962). For an assessment of the brief period of parliamentary monarchy, see Wolfram Pyta, 'Die Kunst des rechtzeitigen Thronverzichts: Neue Einsichten zur Überlebenschance der parlamentarischen Monarchie in Deutschland im Herbste 1918', in Bernd Sösemann and Patrick Merziger, *Geschichte, Öffentlichkeit, Kommunikation: Festschrift für Bernd Sösemann zum 65. Geburtstag* (Stuttgart, 2010), 363–82.

45. Wolfgang Sauer, 'Das Scheitern der parlamentarischen Monarchie', in Eberhard Kolb, *Vom Kaiserreich zur Weimarer Republik* (Cologne, 1972), 77–102; Alexander Sedlmaier, *Deutschlandbilder und Deutschlandpolitik: Studien zur Wilson-Administration (1913–1921)* (Stuttgart, 2003), 103; Klaus Schwabe, *Deutsche Revolution und Wilson-Frieden: Die amerikanische und deutsche Friedensstrategie zwischen Ideologie und Machtpolitik 1918/19* (Düsseldorf, 1971), 134.

46. Cecil Lamar, *Wilhelm II.*, vol. 2: *Emperor and Exile, 1900–1941* (Chapel Hill, NC, and London, 1996), 286f.

47. Martin Kohlrausch, *Der Monarch im Skandal: Die Logik der Massenmedien und die Transformation der wilhelminischen Monarchie* (Berlin, 2005), 326. There are a number of indications that a staged death-in-action of the monarch (*Königstod*) was considered as a serious option.

48. Baden, *Erinnerungen und Dokumente*, 530.

49. John C. G. Röhl, *Wilhelm II.*, vol. 3: *Der Weg in den Abgrund 1900–1941* (Munich, 2008), 1239; Sedlmaier, *Deutschlandbilder*, 103; Schwabe, *Wilson-Frieden*, 134.

50. 'Bericht Wilhelm Drews über seinen Besuch bei Wilhelm II. an Max von Baden', in Erich Matthias and Rudolf Morsey (eds), *Die Regierung des Prinzen Max von Baden* (Düsseldorf, 1962), doc. no. 115.

51. Wilhelm as quoted in: Röhl, *Wilhelm*, vol. 3, 1242 and 1540, note 225.

52. Alfred Niemann, *Kaiser und Revolution: Die entscheidenden Ereignisse im Großen Hauptquartier im Herbst 1918* (Berlin, 1922), 126.

53. Niemann drew a somewhat more ambivalent picture of the trip, mentioning that some soldiers showed indifference and even hostility towards the Kaiser. Niemann, *Kaiser und Revolution*, 129–31; Alfred Niemann, *Revolution von Oben—Umsturz von unten: Entwicklung und Verlauf der Staatsumwälzung in Deutschland 1914–1918* (Berlin, 1927), 389.

NOTES TO PP. 103–109

54. Baden, *Erinnerungen*, 597.
55. Niemann, *Kaiser und Revolution*, 134; Harry R. Rudin, *Armistice 1918* (New Haven, 1944), 327–9 and 349–51.
56. Groener's testimony in the 1925 'stab-in-the-back trial', as quoted in Christof von Ebbinghaus, *Die Memoiren des Generals von Ebbinghaus* (Stuttgart, 1928), 29.
57. Hünicken, 'Das Frontheer und der 9. November: Erlebnisse eines Regimentskommandeurs in Spa', appendix to Niemann, *Revolution von Oben*, 437–44.
58. Hünicken, 'Das Frontheer', 439; Westarp protocol, in Gerhard A. Ritter, and Susanne Miller (eds), *Die deutsche Revolution 1918–1919: Dokumente* (Hamburg, 1975), 71.
59. Hindenburg's address according to eyewitness accounts of Major Beck and Captain Roedenbeck, reprinted in Kuno Graf Westarp, *Das Ende der Monarchie*, ed. Werner Cnze (Berlin, 1952), 64–5.
60. Westarp, *Das Ende der Monarchie*, 65–6; Hünicken, 'Das Frontheer', 439.
61. Wilhelm Groener, *Lebenserinnerungen: Jugend, Generalstab, Weltkrieg* (Göttingen, 1957), 457–8.
62. Ibid., 438; Röhl, *Wilhelm*, vol. 3, 1244.
63. Groener, *Lebenserinnerungen*, 460.

6 SHOWDOWN IN BERLIN

1. Richard Müller, *Geschichte der deutschen Revolution*, vol. 2: *Die Novemberrevolution* (Berlin, 1974), 10. See, too: Heinrich August Winkler, *Von der Revolution zur Stabilisierung: Arbeiter und Arbeiterbewegung in der Weimarer Republik, 1918 bis 1924* (Berlin, 1984), 45.
2. Adolf Wermuth, *Ein Beamtenleben* (Berlin, 1922), 412.
3. Richard Müller, *Geschichte der deutschen Revolution*, vol. 1: *Vom Kaiserreich zur Republik* (Vienna, 1924; reprint Berlin, 1979), 178f.
4. Müller, *Geschichte der deutschen Revolution*, vol. 2, 12.
5. 'Anordnung General von Linsingens, 7.11.1918', in Gerhard A. Ritter and Susanne Miller (eds), *Die deutsche Revolution 1918–1919: Dokumente* (Hamburg, 1975), 62.
6. Heinrich August Winkler, *Weimar 1918–1933* (Munich, 1993), 29.
7. That at least was von Baden's convincing assessment of the situation. Max von Baden, *Erinnerungen und Dokumente* (Stuttgart, Berlin, and Leipzig, 1927), 579f.
8. Winkler, *Von der Revolution zur Stabilisierung*, 41.
9. Erich Matthias and Rudolf Morsey (eds), *Die Regierung Max von Baden* (Düsseldorf, 1964), 620–7; Baden, *Erinnerungen und Dokumente*, 581.
10. *Vorwärts*, 9 November 1918, morning edition.
11. Winkler, *Von der Revolution zur Stabilisierung*, 42.

12. Emil Barth, *Aus der Werkstatt der Revolution* (Berlin, 1919), 53; Wilhelm Pieck, *Gesammelte Reden und Schriften*, vol. 1 (August 1904–1 January 1919) (East Berlin, 1959), 413ff.; Ritter and Miller, *Revolution*, 64ff.

13. 'Aufruf des Vollzugsauschusses des Arbeiter- und Soldatenrates Berlin vom 8.11.1918', reprinted in Günter Hortzschansky (ed.), *Illustrierte Geschichte der deutschen Novemberrevolution 1918/19* (Berlin (GDR), 1978), 141.

14. 'Flugblatt der Spartakusgruppe, 8.11.1918', reprinted in Hortzschansky (ed.), *Illustrierte Geschichte der deutschen Novemberrevolution*, 140.

15. Barth, *Aus der Werkstatt der Revolution*, 54.

16. Cläre Casper-Derfert, 'Steh auf, Arthur, heute ist Revolution', in Institut für Marxismus-Leninismus beim ZK der SED (ed.), *Vorwärts und nicht vergessen: Erlebnisberichte aktiver Teilnehmer der Novemberrevolution 1918/19* (Berlin (GDR), 1958), 293–300, here 298f.

17. Ingo Materna, '9. November 1918—der erste Tag der Republik: Eine Chronik', *Berlinische Monatsschrift* 4/2000, 140–7, here 141.

18. Müller, *Geschichte der deutschen Revolution*, vol. 2, 11.

19. <http://www.dhm.de/lemo/zeitzeugen/m%C3%BCnsterberg-novemberrevolution-1918> (last accessed 11 January 2018).

20. Winkler, *Von der Revolution zur Stabilisierung*, 42; Hans Adolph, *Otto Wels und die Politik der deutschen Sozialdemokratie 1894–1939: Eine politische Biographie* (Berlin, 1971), 77.

21. Pieck, *Gesammelte Reden und Schriften*, vol. 1, 425f. The same event was described differently by Dittmann. According to him, Ebert, Scheidemann, and Eduard David from the MSPD met with Ledebour, Dittmann, and Ewald Vogtheer from the USPD before the MSPD parliamentary group meeting to discuss the possibilities of forming a shared government. Dittmann and Vogtheer were open to this, whereas Ledebour, who maintained very close relations with the Revolutionary Shop Stewards, rejected the notion 'in the bluntest terms'. See Winkler, *Von der Revolution zur Stabilisierung*, 50.

22. Ernst Troeltsch, *Spektator Briefe: Aufsätze über die deutsche Revolution und die Weltpolitik 1918/22* (Tübingen, 1924), 22f.

23. Winkler, *Von der Revolution zur Stabilisierung*, 45.

24. Müller, *Geschichte der deutschen Revolution*, vol. 2, 10.

25. Hans Adolph, *Otto Wels und die Politik der deutschen Sozialdemokratie 1894–1939: Eine politische Biographie* (Berlin, 1971), 71f.; Winkler, *Von der Revolution zur Stabilisierung*, 46.

26. Joachim Petzold, *Der 9. November 1918 in Berlin: Berliner Arbeiterveteranen berichten über die Vorbereitung der Novemberrevolution und ihren Ausbruch am 9. November 1918 in Berlin* (East Berlin, 1958), 33.

27. Müller, *Geschichte der deutschen Revolution*, vol. 2, 11ff. Materna, '9. November 1918', 141.

28. Aussage Hans Pfeiffers in Petzold, *Der 9. November 1918 in Berlin*, 34.

29. Casper-Derfert, ' "Steh auf, Arthur, heute ist Revolution" ', 300.

30. Sebastian Haffner, *Failure of a Revolution: Germany 1918–1919* (Chicago, 1986), 74.

31. Baden, *Erinnerungen und Dokumente*, vol. 2, 630–1.

32. Reprinted in Wilhelm Stahl (ed.), *Schulthess' Europäischer Geschichtskalender*, 34 (1918), (Munich, 1922), 450f. The translation here is taken from Haffner, *Failure of a Revolution*, 74f.

33. Decie Denholm, 'Eine Australierin in Leipzig: Die heimlichen Briefe der Ethel Cooper 1914–1919', in Bernd Hüppauf (ed.), *Ansichten vom Krieg* (Königstein im Taunus, 1984), 150.

34. Harry Graf Kessler, *Das Tagebuch 1880–1937*, ed. von Roland Kamzelak and Ulrich Ott, vol. 6: *1916–1918* (Stuttgart, 2007), 622–5, here 624.

35. Winkler, *Von der Revolution zur Stabilisierung*, 46f.

36. Materna, *9. November 1918*, 142.

37. Winkler, *Von der Revolution zur Stabilisierung*, 46f.

38. Ibid.

39. Ibid., 39.

40. Bernd Braun, 'Die "Generation Ebert" ', in Bernd Braun and Klaus Schönhoven (eds), *Generationen in der Arbeiterbewegung* (Munich, 2005), 69–86.

41. Robert Gerwarth and John Horne, 'Vectors of Violence: Paramilitarism in Europe after the Great War, 1917–1923', *The Journal of Modern History* 83 (2011), 489–512, here 497.

42. Robert Gerwarth and John Horne, 'Bolshevism as Fantasy: Fear of Revolution and Counter-Revolutionary Violence, 1917–1923', in Robert Gerwarth and John Horne (eds), *War in Peace: Paramilitary Violence in Europe after the Great War* (Oxford, 2012), 40–51, 40ff.

43. Quoted in Mark Jones, *Founding Weimar: Violence and the German Revolution of 1918–1919* (Cambridge, 2016), 10.

44. Robert Gerwarth and Martin Conway, 'Revolution and Counterrevolution', in Donald Bloxham and Robert Gerwarth (eds), *Political Violence in Twentieth-Century Europe* (Cambridge and New York, 2011), 140–75.

45. David Kirby, *A Concise History of Finland* (Cambridge and New York, 2006), 152f.

46. Pertti Haapala and Marko Tikka, 'Revolution, Civil War and Terror in Finland in 1918', in Robert Gerwarth and John Horne (eds), *War in Peace: Paramilitary Violence in Europe after the Great War* (Oxford, 2012), 71–83.

47. On the Finnish Civil War in English: Anthony Upton, *The Finnish Revolution, 1917–18* (Minneapolis, 1980); Risto Alapuro, *State and Revolution in Finland* (Berkeley, 1988); Tuomas Hoppu and Pertti Haapala (eds), *Tampere 1918: A Town in the Civil War* (Tampere, 2010); Jason Lavery, 'Finland 1917–19: Three Conflicts, One Country', *Scandinavian Review* 94 (2006), 6–14; Evan Mawdsley, *The Russian Civil War* (London, 2000), 27–9.

48. Müller, *Geschichte der deutschen Revolution*, vol. 2, 10. *Vorwärts*, 9 November 1918, reprinted in Hortzschansky (ed.), *Illustrierte Geschichte der deutschen Novemberrevolution*, 142.

49. Friedrich Ebert's appeal of 9 November 1918, as printed in Ritter and Miller, *Revolution*, 79f.

50. Philipp Scheidemann, *Der Zusammenbruch* (Berlin, 1921), 173.

51. Scheidemann as quoted in Manfred Jessen-Klingenberg, 'Die Ausrufung der Republik durch Philipp Scheidemann am 9. November 1918', *Geschichte in Wissenschaft und Unterricht* 19 (1968), 649–56, here 653f.

52. Käthe Kollwitz, *Die Tagebücher*, ed. Jutta Bohnke-Kollwitz (Berlin, 1989), 378–9 (entry of 9 November 1918).

53. Dominik Juhnke, Judith Prokasky, and Martin Sabrow: *Mythos der Revolution: Karl Liebknecht, das Berliner Schloss und der 9. November 1918* (Munich, 2018). Niess, *Revolution von 1918/19*, 76.

54. As quoted in 'Karl Liebknecht proklamiert am 09.11.1918 die Sozialistische Republik Deutschland (Auszug)', in Ritter and Miller, *Revolution*, 79.

55. Heinrich August Winkler, *Age of Catastrophe: A History of the West, 1914–1945* (London and New Haven, 2015), 67.

56. Eberhard Kessel (ed.), *Friedrich Meinecke, Werke*, vol. 8: *Autobiographische Schriften* (Stuttgart, 1969), here 310 (diary entry of 11 November 1918).

7 MAKING PEACE IN THE WEST

1. 'Protokoll der Sitzung der Reichsregierung unter Teilnahme von Generalleutnant Groener am 5.11.1918', partly reprinted in Hellmut Otto and Karl Schmiedel, *Der Erste Weltkrieg. Dokumente* (East Berlin, 1977²), 330–4; see, too, Erich Matthias and Rudolf Morsey (eds), *Die Regierung des Prinzen Max von Baden* (Düsseldorf, 1962), 526ff. Matthias Erzberger, *Erlebnisse im Weltkrieg* (Stuttgart and Berlin, 1920), 325f.; Matthias and Morsey (eds), *Die Regierung des Prinzen Max von Baden*, 557.

2. Edmund Marhefka (ed.), *Der Waffenstillstand 1918–1919: Das Dokumenten-Material. Waffenstillstands-Verhandlungen von Compiègne, Spa, Trier und Brüssel*, vol. 1: *Der Waffenstillstandsvertrag von Compiègne und seine Verlängerungen nebst den finanziellen Bestimmungen* (Berlin, 1928), 18f.

3. The following paragraphs are largely based on Erzberger's autobiographical account, written in 1920: Erzberger, *Erlebnisse im Weltkrieg*.

4. Maxime Weygand, as quoted in 'Amis de l'Armistice' (eds), *Der 11. November 1918: Unterzeichnung eines Waffenstillstands im Wald von Compiègne* (Compiègne, n.d.), 5.

5. Ibid.

6. Ibid., 7.

7. Ferdinand Foch, *Mémoire pour servir à l'histoire de la guerre 1914–1918*, vol. 2 (Paris, 1931), 248ff.; Maxime Weygand, *Le onze novembre* (Paris, 1947), 'Amis de l'Armistice' (eds), *Der 11. November 1918*, 9ff.; Erzberger, *Erlebnisse im Weltkrieg*, 330ff.

8. *'Amis de l'Armistice' (eds), Der 11. November 1918*, 9; Erzberger, *Erlebnisse*, 331.
9. Margaret MacMillan, *Peacemakers: Six Months That Changed the World* (London, 2001), 177.
10. Erzberger, *Erlebnisse*, 330.
11. Erzberger, *Erlebnisse*, 332; Bullit Lowry, *Armistice 1918* (Kent, Oh., and London, 1996), 157f.
12. Erzberger, *Erlebnisse*, 333.
13. Marhefka (ed.), *Der Waffenstillstand 1918–1919*, 58f.
14. 'Amis de l'Armistice', *Der 11. November 1918*, 10; Erzberger, *Erlebnisse*, 334; Lowry, *Armistice*, 158.
15. Lowry, *Armistice*, 159.
16. Ibid.
17. Erzberger, *Erlebnisse*, 336.
18. Lowry, *Armistice*, 159f.
19. Marhefka (ed.), *Der Waffenstillstand 1918–1919*, 59.
20. Lowry, *Armistice*, 160.
21. Marhefka (ed.), *Der Waffenstillstand 1918–1919*, 60.
22. Lowry, *Armistice*, 160f.
23. Harry R. Rudin, *Armistice 1918* (New Haven, 1944), 427–32; Alexander Watson, *Ring of Steel: Germany and Austria-Hungary at War, 1914–1918* (London, 2015), 556.
24. Käthe Kollwitz, *Die Tagebücher*, ed. Jutta Bohnke-Kollwitz (Berlin, 1989), 381.
25. Alfred Döblin, 'Revolutionstage im Elsaß', in *Die Neue Rundschau* (February 1919), vol. 1, 164–72, repr. in Alfred Döblin, *Schriften zur Politik und Gesellschaft* (Olten and Freiburg im Breisgau, 1972), 59–70, here 68.
26. Ibid., 69.
27. Prinz Rohan, as quoted in Stephan Malinowski, *Vom König zum Führer: Sozialer Niedergang und politische Radikalisierung im deutschen Adel zwischen Kaiserreich und NS-Staat* (Berlin, 2003), 211.
28. Victor Klemperer, *Man möchte immer weinen und lachen in einem: Revolutionstagebuch 1919* (Berlin, 2015), 26.
29. Klemperer, *Curriculum Vitae*, 708.
30. Ibid., 690.
31. Ibid., 712.

8 CHALLENGES FOR THE YOUNG REPUBLIC

1. Klaus Hock, *Die Gesetzgebung des Rates der Volksbeauftragten* (Pfaffenweiler, 1987); Friedrich-Carl Wachs, *Das Verordnungswerk des Reichsdemobilmachungsamtes* (Frankfurt am Main, 1991); Richard Bessel, *Germany after the First World War* (Oxford, 1993).
2. Statistics from Bessell, *Germany after the First World War*, 5–6, and Willibald Gutsche, Fritz Klein, and Joachim Petzold, *Der Erste Weltkrieg: Ursachen und Verlauf* (Cologne, 1985), 292.

3. On the trauma of defeat and collective memory, see Jay Winter, *Sites of Memory, Sites of Mourning: The Great War in European Cultural History* (Cambridge and New York, 1995); Stefan Goebel, 'Re-Membered and Re-Mobilized: The "Sleeping Dead" in Interwar Germany and Britain', *Journal of Contemporary History* 39 (2004), 487–501; Benjamin Ziemann, *Contested Commemorations: Republican War Veterans and Weimar Political Culture* (Cambridge and New York, 2013); Claudia Siebrecht, *The Aesthetics of Loss: German Women's Art of the First World War* (Oxford and New York, 2013).

4. Bessell, *Germany after the First World War*, 79.

5. Alfred Döblin, 'Revolutionstage im Elsaß', in *Die Neue Rundschau* (February 1919), vol. 1, 164–72, repr. in Alfred Döblin, *Schriften zur Politik und Gesellschaft* (Olten and Freiburg im Breisgau, 1972), vol. 1, 64–72, 70–1.

6. Ernst Willi Hansen, 'Vom Krieg zum Frieden: Probleme der Umstellung nach dem ersten "gesamtgesellschaftlichen" Krieg', in Bernd Wegner (ed.), *Wie Kriege enden: Wege zum Frieden. von der Antike bis zur Gegenwart* (Paderborn, 2002), 163–86.

7. Erich Maria Remarque, *All Quiet on the Western Front*, trans. A. W. Wheen (German original 1928; New York, 1975), 294.

8. Iris von Hoyningen-Huene, *Adel in der Weimarer Republik: Die rechtlich-soziale Situation des reichsdeutschen Adels 1918–1933* (Limburg, 1992), 20–3; Marcus Funck, 'Schock und Chance: Der preußische Militäradel in der Weimarer Republik zwischen Stand und Profession', in Heinz Reif and René Schiller (eds), *Adel und Bürgertum in Deutschland*, vol. 2: *Entwicklungslinien und Wendepunkte im 20. Jahrhundert* (Berlin, 2001), 127–72, here 139–41; Walter Görlitz, *Die Junker, Adel und Bauer im deutschen Osten: Geschichtliche Bilanz von 7 Jahrhunderten* (Glücksburg, 1957), 318–20; Stephan Malinowski, *Vom König zum Führer: Sozialer Niedergang und politische Radikalisierung im deutschen Adel zwischen Kaiserreich und NS-Staat* (Berlin, 2003), 200.

9. The literature on shell shock is now sizeable. See, for example: Paul Frederick Lerner, *Hysterical Men: War, Psychiatry, and the Politics of Trauma in Germany, 1890–1930* (Ithaca, 2003); Ben Shephard, *A War of Nerves: Soldiers and Psychiatrists, 1914–1994* (London, 2002); Robert Whalan, *Bitter Wounds: German Victims of the Great War, 1914–1939* (Ithaca and London, 1984).

10. Vicky Baum, *Menschen im Hotel* (Frankfurt am Main, 1929), 9.

11. Ibid., 307.

12. Käthe Kollwitz, *Die Tagebücher*, ed. Jutta Bohnke-Kollwitz (Berlin, 1989), 389 (entry of 12 December 1918).

13. Scott Stephenson, *The Final Battle: Soldiers of the Western Front and the German Revolution of 1918* (Cambridge, 2009), 3.

14. Heinz Hürten (ed.), *Zwischen Revolution und Kapp-Putsch: Militär und Innenpolitik, 1918–1920* (Düsseldorf, 1977).

15. Albrecht von Thaer, *Generalstabsdienst an der Front und in der O.H.L. Aus Briefen und Tagebuchaufzeichnungen* (Göttingen, 1958), here 274f.

16. Wilhelm Groener, *Lebenserinnerungen: Jugend, Generalstab, Weltkrieg* (Göttingen, 1957), 467f.

17. Ibid., 471f.

18. *Die Aufzeichnungen des Generalmajors Max Hoffmann*, ed. Karl Friedrich Nowak (Berlin, 1929), 219 (entry of 21 November 1918).

19. Susanne Rouette, 'Frauenerwerbsarbeit in Demobilisierung und Inflation 1918–1923: Struktur und Entwicklung des Arbeitsmarktes in Berlin', in Klaus Tenfelde (ed.), *Arbeiter im 20. Jahrhundert* (Stuttgart, 1991), 32–65.

20. Ute Daniel, *The War from Within: German Working-Class Women in the First World War* (Oxford, 1997).

21. Helen Boak, *Women in the Weimar Republic* (Manchester, 2013), 20.

22. Henriette Fürth, *Die deutschen Frauen im Kriege* (Tübingen, 1917). See, too, Angelika Eppele, *Henriette Fürth und die Frauenbewegung im deutschen Kaiserreich: Eine Sozialbiographie* (Pfaffenweiler, 1999); Laurie Marhoefer, 'Degeneration, Sexual Freedom, and the Politics of the Weimar Republic, 1918–1933', *German Studies Review* 34 (2011), 529–50.

23. Helga Grebing, *Frauen in der deutschen Revolution 1918/19* (Heidelberg, 1994), 26. Renate Bridenthal and Claudia Koonz, 'Beyond *Kinder, Küche, Kirche*: Weimar Women in Politics and Work', in Renate Bridenthal et al. (eds), *When Biology Became Destiny: Women in Weimar and Nazi Germany* (New York, 1984), 33–65.

24. Gerald D. Feldman, *The Great Disorder: Politics, Economics, and Society in the German Inflation, 1914–1924* (New York, 1993); Harold James, 'The Weimar Economy', in Anthony McElligott (ed.), *Weimar Germany* (Oxford, 2009), 102–26, here 108–9; Theo Balderston, *Economics and Politics in the Weimar Republic* (London, 2002), 34–60; Stephen B. Webb, *Hyperinflation and Stabilization in Weimar Germany* (Oxford, 1989).

25. James, 'Weimar Economy', 110.

26. Knut Borchardt, *Perspectives on Modern German Economic History and Policy* (Cambridge, 1991); Feldman, *Great Disorder*, 837–9.

27. Gerald D. Feldman, 'Das deutsche Unternehmertum zwischen Krieg und Revolution: Die Entstehung des Stinnes-Legien-Abkommens', in Feldman, *Vom Weltkrieg zur Weltwirtschaftskrise: Studien zur deutschen Wirtschafts- und Sozialgeschichte 1914–1932* (Göttingen, 1984), 100–27. Gerald D. Feldman and Irmgard Steinisch, *Industrie und Gewerkschaften 1918–1924: Die überforderte Zentralarbeitsgemeinschaft* (Stuttgart, 1985), 135–7.

28. 'Bekanntmachung des Rats der Volksbeauftragten vom 15. 11. 1918', as printed in Gerhard Ritter and Susanne Miller (eds), *Die deutsche Revolution 1918–1919: Dokumente* (Frankfurt am Main, 1983), 229. On Ebert's role in the revolution, see Walther Mühlhausen, *Friedrich Ebert 1871–1925: Reichspräsident in der Weimarer Republik* (Bonn, 2006), 150–64.

29. Martin Buber (ed.), *Gustav Landauer: Sein Lebensgang in Briefen*, 2 vols (Frankfurt am Main, 1929), vol. 2, 296.

30. On subjectivity and the German Revolution, see Moritz Föllmer, 'The Unscripted Revolution: Male Subjectivities in Germany, 1918–19', *Past & Present* 240 (2018), 161–92.

9 FIGHTING RADICALIZATION

1. *Heinrich August Winkler, Von der Revolution zur Stabilisierung: Arbeiter und Arbeiterbewegung in der Weimarer Republik, 1918 bis 1924 (Berlin, 1984)*, 122–3; *Heinrich August Winkler, Weimar 1918–1933: Die Geschichte der ersten deutschen Demokratie (Munich, 1993)*, 58.

2. *On Karl Liebknecht, see Helmut Trotnow, Karl Liebknecht: Eine Politische Biographie (Cologne, 1980); Heinz Wohlgemuth, Karl Liebknecht: Eine Biographie (East Berlin, 1975); Annelies Laschitza and Elke Keller, Karl Liebknecht: Eine Biographie in Dokumenten (East Berlin, 1982); Annelies Laschitza, Die Liebknechts: Karl und Sophie, Politik und Familie (Berlin, 2009); Anthony Read, The World on Fire: 1919 and the Battle with Bolshevism (London, 2009)*, 29.

3. *Read, World on Fire*, 29. Mark Jones, '*Violence and Politics in the German Revolution, 1918–19*' (Dissertation, European University Institute, 2011), 91.

4. *On Radek's life, see Wolf-Dietrich Gutjahr, Revolution muss sein: Karl Radek—Die Biographie (Cologne, Weimar, and Vienna, 2012)*.

5. *Radek as quoted in Gutjahr, Revolution muss sein*, 333.

6. *Peter Nettl, Rosa Luxemburg (Frankfurt am Main, 1968), 67 (on her deformation); Annelies Laschitza, Im Lebensrausch, trotz alledem. Rosa Luxemburg: Eine Biographie (Berlin, 1996/2002), 25; Jason Schulman (ed.), Rosa Luxemburg: Her Life and Legacy (New York, 2013); Mathilde Jacob, Rosa Luxemburg: An Intimate Portrait (London, 2000); Read, World on Fire, 29f.*

7. *Rosa Luxemburg, Die Russische Revolution: Eine kritische Wuerdigung (first written in 1917; Berlin, 1922)*, 113–14.

8. *Ibid.*, 109.

9. *Laschitza, Rosa Luxemburg*, 584.

10. Rosa Luxemburg to Clara Zetkin, 18 November 1918, in Georg Adler, Peter Hudis, and Annelies Laschitza (eds), *The Letters of Rosa Luxemburg* (London and New York, 2011), 480.

11. Rosa Luxemburg, *Gesammelte Werke*, vol. 4: *August 1914–Januar 1919* (East Berlin, 1974), 399; Karl Egon Lönne (ed.), *Die Weimarer Republik, 1918–1933: Quellen zum politischen Denken der Deutschen im 19. und 20. Jahrhundert* (Darmstadt, 2002), 79–82.

12. Martin Buber (ed.), *Gustav Landauer: Sein Lebensgang in Briefen*, 2 vols (Frankfurt am Main, 1929), 336.

13. Max Cohen, 'Rede für die Nationalversammlung vor dem Allgemeinen Kongress der Arbeiter- und Soldatenräte', 19 December 1918, in Peter Wende (ed.), *Politische Reden III, 1914–1945* (Berlin, 1990), 97–121 See, too: Weitz, Weimar, 29-30.

14. Ibid., 109 (italics in the original).

15. Ernst Däumig, 'Rede gegen die Nationalversammlung vor dem Allgemeinen Kongress der Arbeiter- und Soldatenräte', 19 December 1918, in *Politische Reden III*, 122–41, quotation 122 (italics in the original).

16. Ulrich Kluge, *Soldatenräte und Revolution: Studien zur Militärpolitik in Deutschland 1918/19* (Göttingen, 1975), 241–3; Winkler, *Von der Revolution*, 109–10; Scott Stephenson, *The Final Battle: Soldiers of the Western Front and the German Revolution of 1918* (Cambridge and New York, 2009), 262–71. On violence in this phase of the revolution, see Jones, 'Violence and Politics', 177–96.

17. Käthe Kollwitz, *Die Tagebücher*, ed. Jutta Bohnke-Kollwitz (Berlin, 1989), 390–1 (entry of 24 December 1918).

18. Eduard Bernstein, *Die deutsche Revolution*, vol. 1: *Ihr Ursprung, ihr Verlauf und ihr Werk* (Berlin, 1921), 131–5; Winkler, *Von der Revolution*, 120.

19. David W. Morgan, *The Socialist Left and the German Revolution: A History of the German Independent Social Democratic Party, 1917–1922* (Ithaca, 1976), 213–40.

20. Mark Jones, *Founding Weimar: Violence and the German Revolution of 1918–1919* (Cambridge and New York, 2016), 173ff.

21. Winkler, *Weimar*, 58.

22. Liebknecht as quoted in Jones, *Founding Weimar*, 177–8.

23. Harry Graf Kessler, *Das Tagebuch 1880–1937*, ed. von Roland Kamzelak and Ulrich Ott, vol. 7: 1919–1923 (Stuttgart, 2007), 52.

24. Kollwitz, *Tagebücher*, 396 (entry of 5 January 1919).

25. Ibid., 397 (entry of 6 January 1919).

26. Betty Scholem to Gershom Scholem, 7 January 1919, in Itta Shedletzky and Thomas Sparr (eds), *Betty Scholem—Gershom Scholem, Mutter und Sohn im Briefwechsel 1917–1946* (Munich, 1989), 30–1.

27. Betty Scholem to Gershom Scholem, 13 January 1919, ibid., 32–3.

28. Winkler, *Von der Revolution*, 122.

29. Gustav Noske, *Von Kiel bis Kapp: Zur Geschichte der deutschen Revolution* (Berlin, 1920), 66–7.

30. Scheidemann, as quoted in Jones, *Founding Weimar*, 185.

31. Ibid.

32. Andreas Wirsching, *Vom Weltkrieg zum Bürgerkrieg: Politischer Extremismus in Deutschland und Frankreich 1918–1933/39. Berlin und Paris im Vergleich* (Munich, 1999), 134; Winkler, *Von der Revolution*, 124; Noske, *Von Kiel bis Kapp*, 68.

33. On the *Freikorps*, see Hagen Schulze, *Freikorps und Republik, 1918–1920* (Boppard am Rhein, 1969); Hannsjoachim W. Koch, *Der deutsche Bürgerkrieg: Eine Geschichte der deutschen und österreichischen Freikorps 1918–1923* (Berlin, 1978). Wolfram Wette, *Gustav Noske: Eine politische Biographie* (Düsseldorf, 1987). Bernhard Sauer, 'Freikorps und Antisemitismus', *Zeitschrift für Geschichtswissenschaft* 56 (2008), 5–29; Klaus Theweleit,

Männerphantasien, 2 vols (Frankfurt am Main, 1977); Rüdiger Bergien, 'Republikschützer oder Terroristen? Die Freikorpsbewegung in Deutschland nach dem Ersten Weltkrieg', *Militärgeschichte* (2008), 14–17; Rüdiger Bergien, *Die bellizistische Republik: Wehrkonsens und Wehrhaftmachung in Deutschland, 1918–1933* (Munich, 2012), 64–9.

34. Ernst Rüdiger Starhemberg, 'Aufzeichnungen des Fürsten Ernst Rüdiger Starhemberg im Winter 1938/39 in Saint Gervais in Frankreich', in Nachlass Starhemberg, Oberösterreichisches Landesarchiv Linz, 26.

35. Robert Gerwarth, 'The Central European Counter-Revolution: Paramilitary Violence in Germany, Austria and Hungary after the Great War', *Past & Present* 200 (2008), 175–209.

36. Ibid.

37. On the gender dimension, see Theweleit, *Maennerphantasien*.

38. James D. Steakley, *The Homosexual Emancipation Movement in* Germany (New York, 1975); John C. Fout, 'Sexual Politics in Wilhelmine Germany: The Male Gender Crisis, Moral Purity, and Homophobia', *Journal of the History of Sexuality* 2 (1992), 388–421. Kathleen Canning, 'Das Geschlecht der Revolution: Stimmrecht und Staatsbürgertum 1918/1919', in Alexander Gallus (ed.), *Die vergessene Revolution von 1918/19* (Göttingen, 2010) 84–116.

39. Jens Dobler, 'Zensur von Büchern und Zeitschriften mit homosexueller Thematik in der Weimarer Republik', *Invertito: Jahrbuch für die Geschichte der Homosexualitäten* 2 (2000), 83–104.

40. Magnus Hirschfeld, 'Die Homosexualität', in Leo Schidrowitz (ed.), *Sittengeschichte des Lasters* (Vienna, 1927), 310, quoted in James D. Steakley, *The Homosexual Emancipation Movement in Germany* (Salem, NH, 1993), 78. More recently: Laurie Marhoefer, *Sex and the Weimar Republic: German Homosexual Emancipation and the Rise of the Nazis* (Toronto, 2015).

41. Jürgen Reulecke, *'Ich möchte einer werden so wie die…': Männerbünde im 20. Jahrhundert* (Frankfurt am Main, 2001), 89ff.

42. Ernst von Salomon, *Die Geächteten* (Berlin, 1923), 10–11. On the autobiographical *Freikorps* literature, see, in particular, Matthias Sprenger, *Landsknechte auf dem Weg ins Dritte Reich? Zu Genese und Wandel des Freikorps-Mythos* (Paderborn, 2008).

43. Quoted in Richard Evans, *The Coming of the Third Reich* (London, 2003), vol. 1, 69.

44. Joseph Roth, *Das Spinnennetz* (first serialized in 1923, first book edition: Cologne and Berlin, 1967), 6.

45. Friedrich Wilhelm Heinz, *Sprengstoff* (Berlin, 1930), 7.

46. Boris Barth, *Dolchstoßlegenden und politische Disintegration: Das Trauma der deutschen Niederlage im Ersten Weltkrieg* (Düsseldorf, 2003). See also Gerd Krumeich, 'Die Dolchstoß-Legende', in Étienne François and Hagen Schulze (eds), *Deutsche Erinnerungsorte* (Munich, 2001), vol. 1, 585–99; Wolfgang Schivelbusch, *Die Kultur der Niederlage: Der amerikanische Süden 1865, Frankreich 1871, Deutschland 1918* (Berlin, 2001), 203–47.

47. 'Kriegsübersicht für November', in *Die Baracke. Zeitschrift des Kriegsgefangenenlagers Bando*, 15 December 1918 (11/64), 184. On the Bandō camp, which offered very liberal rules for its inmates, see Mahon Murphy, *Colonial Captivity during the First World War: Internment and the Fall of the German Empire, 1914–1919* (Cambridge, 2017).

48. Manfred von Killinger, *Der Klabautermann: Eine Lebensgeschichte* (3rd edn, Munich, 1936), 263. On Killinger, see Bert Wawrzinek, *Manfred von Killinger (1886–1944): Ein politischer Soldat zwischen Freikorps und Auswaertigem Amt* (Preussisch Oldendorf, 2004).

49. Volker Ullrich, *Die Revolution von 1918/19* (Munich, 2016), 72.

50. On Steinbrink: Helga Grebing, *Frauen in der deutschen Revolution 1918/19* (Heidelberg, 1994), 6.

51. See the report of the Prussian parliament in *Sammlung der Drucksachen der Verfassunggebenden Preußischen Landesversammlung, Tagung 1919/21*, vol. 15 (Berlin, 1921), 7705; see, too, Dieter Baudis and Hermann Roth, 'Berliner Opfer der Novemberrevolution 1918/19', *Jahrbuch für Wirtschaftsgeschichte* (1968), 73–149, here 79.

52. Kollwitz, *Die Tagebücher*, 396 (entry of 12 January 1919), 110.

53. Eberhard Kessel (ed.), *Friedrich Meinecke, Werke*, vol. 8: *Autobiographische Schriften* (Stuttgart, 1969), 289–320, 313–14.

54. Rosa Luxemburg, 'Versäumte Pflichten', *Rote Fahne*, 8 January 1919.

55. Karl Liebknecht, *Ausgewählte Reden, Briefe und Aufsätze* (East Berlin, 1952), 526–30.

56. Rosa Luxemburg, *Politische Schriften,* ed. Ossip K. Flechtheim (Frankfurt am Main, 1975), vol. 3, here 209.

57. On the discovery and arrest see Klaus Gietinger, *Eine Leiche im Landwehrkanal: Die Ermordnung Rosa Luxemburgs* (Hamburg, 2008), 18. On Pabst, see Klaus Gietinger, *Der Konterrevolutionär: Waldemar Pabst—eine deutsche Karriere* (Hamburg, 2009).

58. Gietinger, *Leiche*, 66.

59. On the treatment of Liebknecht, see the summary of evidence contained in BA-MA Ph8v/2 Bl. 206–20: 'Schriftsatz in der Untersuchungsache gegen von Pflugk-Harttung und Genossen. Berlin, den 15 März 1919' and further Bl. 221–7. I am grateful to Mark Jones for providing these references.

60. For the description of how Luxemburg was murdered in the Tiergarten (as told to Wiezsäcker by Pflugk-Harttung the following day): Leonidas E. Hill (ed.), *Die Wiezsäcker-Papiere 1900–1934* (Berlin, 1982), 325; see, too, Gietinger, *Leiche*, 37 and 134 (annexe document 1). See further the file contained in BA-MA Ph8v/10, esp. Bl. 1–3, 'Das Geständnis. Otto Runge, 22 Jan. 1921'. See, too, the older, but still very good, account by John Peter Nettl, *Rosa Luxemburg* (Oxford, 1966).

61. Kollwitz, *Tagebücher*, 401–2 (entry of 25 January 1919).

62. On Rathenau and his assassination, see Martin Sabrow, *Die verdrängte Verschwörung: Der Rathenaumord und die deutsche Gegenrevolution* (Frankfurt

am Main, 1999); ShulamitVolkov, *Walter Rathenau:Weimar's Fallen Statesman* (New Haven, 2012) On Scheidemann's time as mayor of Kassel, see: Walther Mühlhausen, *'Das große Ganze im Auge behalten': Philipp Scheidemann als Oberbürgermeister von Kassel (1920–1925)* (Marburg, 2011).

63. Tânia Puschnerat, *Clara Zetkin: Bürgerlichkeit und Marxismus. Eine Biographie* (Essen, 2003).

64. 'Protokoll über die Verhandlungen des ausserordentlichen Parteitages vom 2. bis 6. März 1919 in Berlin', in *Protokolle der Unabhängigen Sozialdemokratischen Partei Deutschlands*, vol. 1: 1917–1919 (Glashütten im Taunus, 1975), 140.

10 THE TRIUMPH OF LIBERALISM

1. Heinrich August Winkler, *Weimar 1918–1933: Die Geschichte der ersten deutschen Demokratie* (Munich, 1993), 69.

2. 'Verordnung des Rats der Volksbeauftragten über die Wahlen zur Verfassunggebenden Deutschen Nationalversammlung (Reichswahlgesetz) vom 30.11.1918', in Gerhard A. Ritter and Susanne Miller (eds), *Die deutsche Revolution 1918–1919: Dokumente* (Hamburg, 1975), 369–71; Siegfried Heimann, *Der Preußische Landtag 1899–1947: Eine politische Geschichte* (Berlin, 2011), 266f. Gisela Bock, *Geschlechtergeschichten der Neuzeit: Ideen, Politik, Praxis* (Göttingen, 2014), 230ff.

3. Ritter and Miller, *Die deutsche Revolution*, 104.

4. Ina Hochreuther, *Frauen im Parlament: Südwestdeutsche Parlamentarierinnen von 1919 bis heute* (Stuttgart, 2002), 73.

5. Christiane Streubel, *Radikale Nationalistinnen: Agitation und Programmatik rechter Frauen in der Weimarer Republik* (Frankfurt am Main and New York, 2006).

6. Adele Schreiber, *Revolution und Frauenwahlrecht: Frauen! Lernt wählen!* (Berlin, 1919), 14–15; Hans-Ulrich Wehler, *Deutsche Gesellschafts-geschichte*, vol. 4: *Vom Beginn des Ersten Weltkrieges bis zur Gründung der beiden deutschen Staaten 1914–1949* (Munich, 2003), 232f.

7. Helga Grebing, *Frauen in der deutschen Revolution 1918/19* (Heidelberg, 1994), 17–18.

8. Christl Wickert, *Unsere Erwaehlten: Sozialdemokratische Frauen im Deutschen Reichstag und im Preussischen Landtag 1919 bis 1932*, 2 vols (Göttingen, 1986), vol. 2, 64–9.

9. Heidemarie Lauterer, *Parliamentarierinnen in Deutschland 1918/19–1949* (Königstein im Taunus, 2002).

10. Verhandlungen der verfassunggebenden Deutschen Nationalversammlung (NV) vol. 326. Stenographische Berichte (Berlin, 1920), 177D.

11. Grebing, *Frauen*, 15.

12. Lothar Albertin, *Liberalismus und Demokratie am Anfang der Weimarer Republik: Eine vergleichende Analyse der Deutschen Demokratischen Partei und*

der Deutschen Volkspartei (Düsseldorf, 1972); Ernst Portner, *Die Verfassungspolitik der Liberalen 1919: Ein Beitrag zur Deutung der Weimarer Reichsverfassung* (Bonn, 1973); Rudolf Morsey, *Die Deutsche Zentrumspartei 1917–1923* (Bonn, 1966), 196–245; Wolfgang Luthardt, *Sozialdemokratische Verfassungstheorie in der Weimarer Republik* (Opladen, 1986); Sigrid Vestring, *Die Mehrheitssozialdemokratie und die Entstehung der Reichsverfassung von Weimar 1918/1919* (Münster, 1987).

13. Heiko Holste, *Warum Weimar? Wie Deutschlands erste Republik zu ihrem Geburtsort kam* (Vienna, 2017).

14. Käthe Kollwitz, *Die Tagebücher*, ed. Jutta Bohnke-Kollwitz (Berlin, 1989), 406 (entry of 6 February 1919).

15. Friedrich Ebert, *Rede zur Eröffnung der Verfassunggebenden Nationalversammlung*, 6 February 1919, in Peter Wende (ed.), *Politische Reden III, 1914–1945* (Frankfurt am Main, 1990), 244–53.

16. Ibid., 246 (italics in the original).

17. Ibid.

18. Stanley Suval, *The Anschluß Question in Germany and Austria in the Weimar Era: A Study of Nationalism in Germany and Austria 1918–1932* (Baltimore and London, 1974).

19. 'Gesetz über die Staats- und Regierungsform Deutsch-Österreichs', in Ernst R. Huber, *Deutsche Verfassungsgeschichte seit 1789*, vol. 5: *Weltkrieg, Revolution und Reichserneuerung 1914–1919* (Stuttgart, 1978), 1175. See, too, Otto Bauer, *Die österreichische Revolution* (Vienna, 1923), 143.

20. Erich Matthias and Susanne Miller (eds), *Die Regierung der Volksbeauftragten 1918/19*, 2 vols (Düsseldorf, 1969), vol. 1, 45.

21. See: Susanne Miller, 'Das Ringen um "die einzige großdeutsche Republik": Die Sozialdemokratie in Österreich und im Deutschen Reich zur Anschlußfrage 1918/19', *Archiv für Sozialgeschichte* 11 (1971), 1–68.

22. *Berliner Tageblatt*, 10 November 1918, morning edition; Max Weber, 'Deutschlands künftige Staatsform' (November 1918), in Weber, *Gesammelte politische Schriften*, 2nd edn, ed. J. Winckelmann (Tübingen, 1958), 436–71, here 441.

23. Wilhelm Heile, 'Der deutsche Neubau', *Die Hilfe* 24 (1918), 559f.

24. Elisabeth Fehrenbach, 'Die Reichsgründung in der deutschen Geschichtsschreibung', in Theodor Schieder and Ernst Deuerlein (eds), *Reichsgründung 1870/71: Tatsachen, Kontroversen, Interpretationen* (Stuttgart, 1970), 259–90, here 261.

25. Hermann Oncken, 'Die Wiedergeburt der großdeutschen Idee', in Oncken, *Nation und Geschichte: Reden und Aufsätze 1919–1935* (Berlin, 1935), 45–70, here 61. The essay was first published in *Österreichische Rundschau* 63 (1920), 97–114.

26. Ibid., 64.

27. Suval, *Anschluss Question*, 9ff.; see also Dieter Fricke et al. (eds), *Lexikon zur Parteiengeschichte: Die bürgerlichen und kleinbürgerlichen Parteien und*

Verbände in Deutschland (1789–1945), 4 vols (Leipzig, 1983–6), here vol. 3, 566ff. On public opinion see, among others, Duane P. Myers, *Germany and the Question of Austrian Anschluss 1918–1922* (New Haven, 1968).

28. *Berliner Tageblatt*, 4 February 1919, morning edition.
29. Stanley Suval, 'Overcoming Kleindeutschland: The Politics of Historical Mythmaking in the Weimar Republic', *Central European History* 2 (1969), 312–30, here 321.
30. NV, 24 February 1919, vol. 326, 292. Preuß's constitutional draft was published in *Deutscher Reichs- und Preußischer Staatsanzeiger*, 20 January 1919.
31. Gerhard Anschütz (ed.), *Die Verfassung des Deutschen Reiches vom 11. August 1919* (2nd edn, Berlin, 1921), 30 (Art. 2) and 119f. (Art. 61).
32. Fritz Klein, 'Between Compiègne and Versailles: The Germans on the Way from a Misunderstood Defeat to an Unwanted Peace', in Manfred F. Boemeke et al. (eds), *The Treaty of Versailles: A Reassessment after 75 Years* (Cambridge and New York, 1998), 203–20.
33. *Treaty of Peace between the Allied and Associated Powers and Germany* (London, 1925), 51. The wording is almost identical with that of Article 88 in the Treaty of Saint-Germain. See: *Der Staatsvertrag von St. Germain* (Vienna, 1919), 58.
34. Grebing, *Frauen*, 22; Ute Frevert, *Women in German History: From Bourgeois Emancipation to Sexual Liberation* (Oxford, 1989).
35. Cornelie Usborne, *Cultures of Abortion in Weimar Germany* (New York and Oxford, 2007).
36. Helen Boak, *Women in the Weimar Republic* (Manchester, 2013), 212.
37. Ibid., 292.
38. Enno Eimers, *Das Verhältnis von Preußen und Reich in den ersten Jahren der Weimarer Republik 1918–1923* (Berlin, 1969); Wolfgang Benz, *Süddeutschland in der Weimarer Republik: Ein Beitrag zur deutschen Innenpolitik 1918–1923* (Berlin, 1970); Gerhard Schulz, *Zwischen Demokratie und Diktatur: Verfassungspolitik und Reichsreform in der Weimarer Republik*, vol. 1: *Die Periode der Konsolidierung und der Revision des Bismarckschen Reichsaufbaus 1919–1930* (2nd edn, Berlin, 1987). Manfred Peter Heimers, *Unitarismus und süddeutsches Selbstbewußtsein: Weimarer Koalition und SPD in Baden in der Eichsreformdiskussion 1918–1933* (Düsseldorf, 1992); Waldemar Besson, *Württemberg und die deutsche Staatskrise 1928–1933: Eine Studie zur Auflösung der Weimarer Republik* (Stuttgart, 1959); Ulrich Reuling, 'Reichsreform und Landesgechichte: Thüringen und Hessen in der Länderneugliederungsdiskussion der Weimarer Republik', in *Aspekte thüringisch-hessischer Geschichte* (Marburg, 1992), 257–308; Franz Menges, *Reichsreform und Finanzpolitik: Die Aushöhlung der Eigenstaatlichkeit Bayerns auf finanzpolitischem Wege in der Zeit der Weimarer Republik* (Berlin, 1971).
39. Eberhard Schanbacher, *Parlamentarische Wahlen und Wahlsystem in der Weimarer Republik* (Düsseldorf, 1982).

40. Article 48 long featured prominently in the debate about Weimar's alleged birth defects because it enabled the President to rule by decree in case of an emergency. Ludwig Richter, 'Die Vorgeschichte des Art. 48 der Weimarer Reichsverfassung', *Der Staat* 37 (1998), 1–26; Ludwig Richter, 'Reichspräsident und Ausnahmegewalt: Die Genese des Art. 48 in den Beratungen der Weimarer Nationalversammlung', *Der Staat* 37 (1998), 221–47; Ludwig Richter 'Notverordnungsrecht', in Eberhard Kolb (ed.), *Friedrich Ebert als Reichspräsident: Amtsführung und Amtsverständnis* (Munich, 1997), 250–7.

41. Sebastian Ullrich, 'Mehr als Schall und Rauch: Der Streit um den Namen der ersten deutschen Demokratie 1918–1949', in Moritz Völlmer and Rüdiger Graf, *Die 'Krise' der Weimarer Republik: Zur Kritik eines Deutungsmusters* (Frankfurt am Main, 2005), 187–207, here 199.

42. Christoph Gusy, 'Die Grundrechte in der Weimarer Republik', *Zeitschrift für neuere Rechtsgeschichte* 15 (1993), 163–83.

43. NV, vol. 7, 353.

44. James Sheehan, *Where Have All the Soldiers Gone? The Transformation of Modern Europe* (New York, 2008), 94.

45. Kollwitz, *Tagebücher*, 392–3 (entry of 31 December 1918).

46. Kathleen Canning, 'The Politics of Symbols, Semantics, and Sentiments in the Weimar Republic', *Central European History* 43 (2010), 567–80.

47. Andreas Wirsching and Jürgen Eder (eds), *Vernunftrepublikanismus in der Weimarer Republik: Politik, Literatur, Wissenschaft* (Stuttgart, 2008).

48. Hermann Müller, *Die November-Revolution: Erinnerungen* (Berlin, 1928), 7.

49. Christian Welzbacher, *Der Reichskunstwart: Kulturpolitik und Staatsinszenierung in der Weimarer Republik 1918–1933* (Weimar, 2010).

II DEMOCRACY BESIEGED

1. Quoted in Andreas Wirsching, *Vom Weltkrieg zum Bürgerkrieg? Politischer Extremismus in Deutschland und Frankreich 1918–1933/39* (Munich, 1999), 134. See, too, Dietmar Lange, *Massenstreik und Schießbefehl: Generalstreik und Märzkämpfe in Berlin 1919* (Berlin, 2012).

2. Mark Jones, *Founding Weimar: Violence and the German Revolution of 1918–1919* (Cambridge and New York, 2016), 136ff.

3. Heinrich August Winkler, *Von der Revolution zur Stabilisierung: Arbeiter und Arbeiterbewegung in der Weimarer Republik, 1918 bis 1924* (Berlin, 1984), 171–82; Jones, *Founding Weimar*, 136–72.

4. Allan Mitchell, *Revolution in Bavaria 1918/19: The Eisner Regime and the Soviet Republic* (Princeton, 1965), 171–2; Freya Eisner, *Kurt Eisner: Die Politik des libertären Sozialismus* (Frankfurt am Main, 1979), 175–80.

5. Holger Herwig, 'Clio Deceived: Patriotic Self-Censorship in Germany after the Great War', *International Security* 12 (1987), 5–22, quotation on p. 9.

6. Bernhard Grau, *Kurt Eisner 1867–1919: Eine Biographie* (Munich, 2001), 397ff.

7. Alois Schmid (ed.), *Handbuch der bayerischen Geschichte*, vol. 4.2: *Das neue Bayern von 1800 bis zur Gegenwart* (2nd rev. edn, Munich, 2007), 742.

8. *Leopold Prinz von Bayern, 1846–1930: Aus den Lebenserinnerungen*, ed. Hans-Michael and Ingrid Körner (Regensburg, 1983), 314.

9. Susanne Miller, *Die Bürde der Macht: Die deutsche Sozialdemokratie 1918–1920* (Düsseldorf, 1978), 457; Grau, *Eisner*, 439; Hans von Pranckh, *Der Prozeß gegen den Grafen Anton Arco-Valley, der den bayerischen Ministerpräsidenten Kurt Eisner erschossen hat* (Munich, 1920).

10. Allan Mitchell, *Revolution in Bavaria 1918–19: The Eisner Regime and the Soviet Republic* (Princeton, 1965), 271; Heinrich August Winkler, *Weimar 1918–1933: Die Geschichte der ersten deutschen Demokratie* (Munich, 1993), 77; Pranckh, *Der Prozeß gegen den Grafen Anton Arco-Valley*.

11. Wilhelm Böhm, *Im Kreuzfeuer zweier Revolutionen* (Munich, 1924), 297; Wolfgang Maderthaner, 'Utopian Perspectives and Political Restraint: The Austrian Revolution in the Context of Central European Conflicts', in Günter Bischof, Fritz Plasser, and Peter Berger (eds), *From Empire to Republic: Post World War I Austria* (Innsbruck, 2010), 52–66, here 58.

12. Victor Klemperer, *Man möchte immer weinen und lachen in einem: Revolutionstagebuch 1919* (Berlin, 2015), 89.

13. Mühsam as quoted in Anthony Read, *The World on Fire: 1919 and the Battle with Bolshevism* (London, 2009), 151.

14. Read, *World on Fire*, 152.

15. Quoted in Richard M. Watt, *The Kings Depart: The German Revolution and Treaty of Versailles 1918–19* (New York, 1968), 364. Hans Beyer, *Von der Novemberrevolution zur Räterepublik in München* (East Berlin, 1957), 77–8.

16. Martin Buber (ed.), *Gustav Landauer: Sein Lebensgang in Briefen*, 2 vols (Frankfurt am Main, 1929), here vol. 2, 413–14.

17. Klemperer, *Revolutionstagebuch 1919*, 113 and 134

18. Ibid., 24.

19. Zinoviev, as quoted in David J. Mitchell, *1919: Red Mirage* (London, 1970), 165.

20. Thomas Mann, *Diaries 1919–1939*, trans. Richard and Clare Winston (London, 1983), 44 (entry for 7 April 1919). See, too, Ralf Höller, *Das Wintermärchen: Schriftsteller erzählen die bayerische Revolution und die Münchner Räterepublik 1918/1919* (Berlin, 2017).

21. Lansing as quoted in Alan Sharp, 'The New Diplomacy and the New Europe', in Nicholas Doumanis, *The Oxford Handbook of Europe 1914–1945* (Oxford and New York, 2016).

22. On the flight to Bamberg see Wolfram Wette, *Gustav Noske: Eine politische Biographie* (Düsseldorf, 1987), 431. On the events of Palm Sunday, see Heinrich Hillmayr, *Roter und Weißer Terror in Bayern nach 1918* (Munich, 1974), 43; Wette, *Noske*, 434; Mitchell, *Revolution in Bavaria*, 316–17.

23. Mitchell, *Revolution in Bavaria*, 304–31.

24. Watt, *The Kings Depart*, 366–8. For a more recent account, see Martin H. Geyer, *Verkehrte Welt: Revolution, Inflation und Modern München 1914–1924* (Kritische Studien zur Geschichtswissenschaft, 128) (Göttingen, 1998).

25. Ernst Toller, *I was a German: The Autobiography of Ernst Toller* (New York, 1934), 180–9; Mitchell, *Revolution in Bavaria*, 320.

26. Wolfgang Zorn, *Geschichte Bayerns im 20. Jahrhundert* (Munich, 1986), 194.

27. Read, *World on Fire*, 154; Allan Mitchell, *Revolution in Bavaria*, 322.

28. Mitchell, *Revolution in Bavaria*, 322; Read, *World on Fire*, 155.

29. On these rumours, see Jones, *Founding Weimar*, 286–23; Hillmayr, *Roter und Weißer Terror in Bayern*, 136–7.

30. As quoted in Wette, *Noske*, 440.

31. Hermann Gilbhard, *Die Thule-Gesellschaft: Vom okkulten Mummenschanz zum Hakenkreuz* (Munich, 1994), 116; Detlev Rose, *Die Thule-Gesellschaft: Legende—Mythos—Wirklichkeit* (3rd edn, Tübingen, 2017), 58–66.

32. A reproduction of the photographs can be found in Rudolf Herz and Dirk Halfbrodt, *Revolution und Fotografie: München 1918/19* (Berlin, 1988), 183–92. Quotation from *Bayerischer Kurier* 3–4 May 1919, as cited in Herz and Halfbrodt, *Revolution und Fotografie*, 184. For the context, see Geyer, *Verkehrte Welt*.

33. Hillmayr, *Roter und Weißer Terror*, 108–10.

34. Klemperer, *Revolutionstagebuch 1919*, 168.

35. Buber (ed.) *Landauer*, vol. 2, 394.

36. Jones, *Founding Weimar*, 286.

37. Manfred von Killinger, *Der Klabautermann: Eine Lebensgeschichte* (3rd edn, Munich, 1936), 13ff. and 52f.

38. Mitchell, *Revolution in Bavaria*, 331, fn 51.

39. As quoted in Wolfgang Niess, *Die Revolution von 1918/19: Der wahre Beginn unserer Demokratie* (Berlin et al., 2017), 383.

40. Thomas Mann, *Thomas Mann: Tagebücher 1918–1921*, ed. Peter de Mendelsohn (Frankfurt am Main, 1979), 218.

41. For a detailed discussion of how the political atmosphere in post-war Munich shaped Hitler, see Thomas Weber, *Becoming Hitler: The Making of a Nazi* (Oxford, 2017).

12 UNDERMINING WEIMAR

1. David Lloyd George, *The Truth About the Peace Treaties*, 2 vols (London, 1938), vol. 1, 565; Margaret MacMillan, *Peacemakers: Six Months That Changed the World* (London, 2001), 5.

2. MacMillan, *Peacemakers*, 7; on the Fiume crisis: ibid., 302–21.

3. Bruno Cabanes, *La Victoire endeuillée: la sortie de guerre des soldats français (1918–1920)* (Paris, 2004).

4. Robert E. Bunselmeyer, *The Cost of War 1914–1919: British Economic War Aims and the Origins of Reparation* (Hamden, Conn., 1975), 141; MacMillan, *Peacemakers*, 100; David Reynolds, *The Long Shadow: The Great War and the Twentieth Century* (London, 2013), 93; Heinrich August Winkler, *Age of Catastrophe: A History of the West, 1914–1945* (London and New Haven, 2015), 125.

5. Leonard V. Smith, 'The Wilsonian Challenge to International Law', *The Journal of the History of International Law* 13 (2011), 179–208. See also Leonard V. Smith, 'Les États-Unis et l'échec d'une seconde mobilisation', in Stéphane Audoin-Rouzeau and Christophe Prochasson (eds), *Sortir de la Guerre de 14–18* (Paris, 2008), 69–91. Manfred F. Boemeke, 'Woodrow Wilson's Image of Germany, the War-Guilt Question and the Treaty of Versailles', in Gerald D. Feldman and Elisabeth Glaser (eds), *The Treaty of Versailles: A Reassessment after 75 Years* (Cambridge and New York, 1998), 603–14. See, too, Alexander Sedlmaier, *Deutschlandbilder und Deutschlandpolitik: Studien zur Wilson-Administration (1913–1921)* (Stuttgart, 2003).

6. Leonard V. Smith, 'Empires at the Paris Peace Conference', in Robert Gerwarth and Erez Manela (eds), *Empires at War, 1911–1923* (Oxford, 2014), 254–76.

7. Adam Tooze, *The Deluge: The Great War and the Re-Making of Global Order* (London, 2014).

8. See, in particular, Manfred F. Boemeke, Gerald D. Feldman, and Elisabeth Glaser (eds), *The Treaty of Versailles: A Reassessment after 75 Years* (Cambridge and New York, 1998); David A. Andelman, *A Shattered Peace: Versailles 1919 and the Price We Pay Today* (Hoboken, NJ, 2008); MacMillan, *Peacemakers*; Alan Sharp, *The Versailles Settlement: Peacemaking after the First World War, 1919–1923* (2nd edn, London, 2008). Most recently: Eckart Conze, *Die grosse Illusion: Versailles und die Neuordnung der Welt* (Munich, 2018).

9. MacMillan, *Peacemakers*, 470.

10. Ibid., 470–1.

11. Quoted ibid., 474.

12. Ibid., 475; Erich Eyck, *A History of the Weimar Republic*, vol. 1: *From the Collapse of the Empire to Hindenburg's Election* (German original 1954; Cambridge, Mass., 1964), 92–5.

13. Laird Boswell, 'From Liberation to Purge Trials in the "Mythic Provinces": Recasting French Identities in Alsace and Lorraine, 1918–1920', *French Historical Studies* 23 (2000), 129–62, here 141.

14. Alan Sharp, 'The Paris Peace Conference and its Consequences', in *1914–1918-online. International Encyclopedia of the First World War.* <https://encyclopedia.1914-1918-online.net/article/the_paris_peace_conference_and_its_consequences> (last accessed 3 March 2018).

15. MacMillan, *Peacemakers*, 217.

16. Gotthold Rhode, 'Das Deutschtum in Posen und Pommerellen in der Zeit der Weimarer Republik', in Senatskommission für das Studium des

Deutschtums im Osten an der Rheinischen Friedrich-Wilhelms-Universität Bonn, *Studien zum Deutschtum im Osten* (Cologne and Graz, 1966), 99. Other estimates are higher. See Richard Blanke, *Orphans of Versailles: The Germans in Western Poland, 1918–1939* (Lexington, Ky, 1993), 32–4.

17. On Upper Silesia, see James E. Bjork, *Neither German nor Pole: Catholicism and National Indifference in a Central European Borderland, 1890–1922* (Ann Arbor, 2008); T. Hunt Tooley, 'German Political Violence and the Border Plebiscite in Upper Silesia, 1919–1921', *Central European History* 21 (1988), 56–98 and T. Hunt Tooley, *National Identity and Weimar Germany: Upper Silesia and the Eastern Border, 1918–22* (Lincoln, Neb., and London, 1997). See, too, Tim K. Wilson, 'The Polish-German Ethnic Dispute in Upper Silesia, 1918–1922: A Reply to Tooley', *Canadian Review of Studies in Nationalism* 32 (2005), 1–26.

18. MacMillan, *Peacemakers*, 230.

19. Waldemar Grosch, *Deutsche und polnische Propaganda während der Volksabstimmung in Oberschlesien 1919–1921* (Dortmund, 2003).

20. Britain and France divided German Kamerun (Cameroon) and Togoland. Belgium gained Ruanda-Urundi in north-western German East Africa, German South-West Africa (Namibia) was taken under mandate by South Africa. In the Pacific, Japan gained Germany's islands north of the equator (the Marshall Islands, the Caroline Islands, the Marianas, the Palau Islands) and Kiautschou in China. German Samoa was assigned to New Zealand; German New Guinea, the Bismarck Archipelago, and Nauru to Australia. Sharp, *Versailles*, 109–38.

21. Smith, 'Empires at the Paris Peace Conference', 262 and 265.

22. On the mandate system, see Susan Pedersen, 'The Meaning of the Mandates System: An Argument', *Geschichte und Gesellschaft* 32 (2006), 1–23; Susan Pedersen, *The Guardians: The League of Nations and the Crisis of Empire* (Oxford and New York, 2015), 17–44. See, too Nadine Méouchy and Peter Sluglett (eds), *The British and French Mandates in Comparative Perspective* (Leiden, 2004); and David K. Fieldhouse, *Western Imperialism in the Middle East, 1914–1958* (Oxford and New York, 2006), 3–20; see, too, Lutz Raphael, *Imperiale Gewalt und Mobilisierte Nation: Europa 1914–1945* (Munich, 2011), 74–5.

23. MacMillan, *Peacemakers*; Boemeke et al., *The Treaty*, 11–20; Zara Steiner, 'The Treaty of Versailles Revisited', in Michael Dockrill and John Fisher (eds), *The Paris Peace Conference 1919: Peace without Victory?* (Basingstoke, 2001), 13–33; Mark Mazower, 'Two Cheers for Versailles', *History Today* 49 (1999); Alan Sharp, *Consequences of Peace. The Versailles Settlement: Aftermath and Legacy 1919–2010* (London, 2010), 1–40; Sally Marks, 'Mistakes and Myths: The Allies, Germany and the Versailles Treaty, 1918–1921', *Journal of Modern History* 85 (2013), 632–59.

24. See, for example, David Andelman, *A Shattered Peace: Versailles 1919 and the Price We Pay Today* (Hoboken, NJ, 2008); Norman Graebner and Edward

Bennett, *The Versailles Treaty and its Legacy: The Failure of the Wilsonian Vision* (Cambridge and New York, 2011).

25. Aviel Roshwald, *Ethnic Nationalism and the Fall of Empires: Central Europe, Russia and the Middle East, 1914–1923* (London, 2001).

26. On this, see the introduction and chapter contributions to Robert Gerwarth and Erez Manela (eds), *Empires at War, 1911–1923* (Oxford, 2014); on the German case in particular, see Annemarie H. Sammartino, *The Impossible Border: Germany and the East, 1914–1922* (Ithaca, NY, 2010); Vejas G. Liulevicius, 'Der Osten als apokalyptischer Raum: Deutsche Fronterfahrungen im und nach dem Ersten Weltkrieg', in Gregor Thum (ed.), *Traumland Osten: Deutsche Bilder vom östlichen Europa im 20. Jahrhundert* (Göttingen, 2006), 47–65.

27. Ian Kershaw, *To Hell and Back: Europe, 1914–1949* (London, 2015), 122.

28. Wolfgang Elz, 'Versailles und Weimar', *Aus Politik und Zeitgeschichte* 50/1 (2008), 31–8.

29. Sally Marks, 'The Myths of Reparations', *Central European History* 11 (1978), 231–9; Niall Ferguson, *The Pity of War: Explaining World War I* (London, 1998), 399–432. The London Schedule of Payments was also to be revised twice, in 1924 (Dawes Plan) and 1929 (Young Plan) before being temporarily suspended during the Great Depression. When Hitler came to power, he cancelled all further payments. Between 1919 and 1932, Germany paid just over 20 billion Marks (out of 50 billion Gold Marks agreed on in 1921 as A and B bonds) in reparations. See Boemeke et al., *The Treaty*, 424.

30. Richard Evans, *The Coming of the Third Reich* (London, 2003), 65; Alan Sharp, 'The Paris Peace Conference and its Consequences', in: *1914–1918-online. International Encyclopedia of the First World War*, MacMillan, *Peacemakers*, 186.

31. Andreas Krause, *Scapa Flow: Die Selbstversenkung der Wilhelminischen Flotte* (Berlin, 1999).

32. Verhandlungen der verfassunggebenden Deutschen Nationalversammlung. Stenographische Berichte (Berlin, 1920), vol. 327, 1082–3.

33. Ibid., 1084.

34. Arthur Graf von Posadowsky-Wehner, 'Gegen die Unterzeichnung des Friedensvertrages', 22 June 1919, in *Stenographische Berichte*, vol. 327, 1120–5.

35. Alexander Watson, *Ring of Steel: Germany and Austria-Hungary at War, 1914–1918* (London, 2015), 561; MacMillan, *Peacemakers*, 475–81.

36. Quoted in Peter Longerich, *Deutschland 1918–1933: Die Weimarer Republik. Handbuch zur Geschichte* (Hanover, 1995), 99.

37. Sharp, *Versailles*, 37–9.

38. Stéphane Audoin-Rouzeau, 'Die Delegation der "Gueules cassées" in Versailles am 28. Juni 1919', in Gerd Krumeich et al. (eds), *Versailles 1919: Ziele, Wirkung, Wahrnehmung* (Essen, 2001), 280–7.

39. Edward M. House, *The Intimate Papers of Colonel House Arranged as a Narrative by Charles Seymour* (Boston and New York, 1926–8), here vol. 4, 487.

40. As quoted in Bruno Cabanes, '1919: Aftermath', in Jay Winter (ed.), *Cambridge History of the First World War*, vol. 1, 172–98.

41. Evans, *Coming of the Third Reich*, 66.

42. Winkler, *Age of Catastrophe*, 888.

43. John Maynard Keynes, *The Economic Consequences of the Peace* (London, 1919).

44. Elz, 'Versailles und Weimar', 33.

45. On the Treaty of Saint-Germain, see Nina Almond and Ralph Haswell Lutz (eds), *The Treaty of St. Germain: A Documentary History of its Territorial and Political Clauses* (Stanford, Calif., 1935); Isabella Ackerl and Rudolf Neck (eds), *Saint-Germain 1919: Protokoll des Symposiums am 29. und 30. Mai 1979 in Wien* (Vienna, 1989); Fritz Fellner, 'Der Vertrag von St. Germain', in Erika Weinzierl and Kurt Skalnik (eds), *Österreich 1918–1938*, vol. 1 (Graz, 1983), 85–106; Lorenz Mikoletzky, 'Saint-Germain und Karl Renner: Eine Republik wird diktiert', in Helmut Konrad and Wolfgang Maderthaner (eds), *Das Werden der Ersten Republik . . . der Rest ist Österreich* (Vienna, 2008), vol. 1, 179–86. Erich Zöllner, *Geschichte Österreichs: Von den Anfängen bis zur Gegenwart* (8th edn, Vienna, 1990), 499.

46. S. W. Gould, 'Austrian Attitudes toward Anschluss: October 1918– September 1919', *Journal of Modern History* 22 (1950), 220–31; Walter Rauscher, 'Die Republikgründungen 1918 und 1945', in Klaus Koch, Walter Rauscher, Arnold Suppan, and Elisabeth Vyslonzil (eds), *Außenpolitische Dokumente der Republik Österreich 1918–1938*, special vol.: *Von Saint-Germain zum Belvedere: Österreich und Europa 1919–1955* (Vienna and Munich, 2007), 9–24. On the Anschluss debate in Germany, see Robert Gerwarth, 'Republik und Reichsgründung: Bismarcks klein-deutsche Lösung im Meinungsstreit der ersten deutschen Demokratie', in Heinrich August Winkler (ed.), *Griff nach der Deutungsmacht: Zur Geschichte der Geschichtspolitik in Deutschland* (Göttingen, 2004), 115–33.

47. Ivan T. Berend, *Decades of Crisis: Central and Eastern Europe before World War II* (Berkeley, Los Angeles, and London, 1998), 224–6.

48. *Vorwärts*, 18 March 1919.

49. *Die Tradition* 1 (1919), 19f.

50. *Kreuzzeitung*, 7 September 1919.

51. Verhandlungen der verfassunggebenden Deutschen Nationalversammlung (NV), 22 June 1919, vol. 327 (Berlin, 1920), 1117.

52. Evans, *Coming of the Third Reich*, 62f; Gerwarth, 'Republik und Reichsgründung'.

53. For a general account of the effects of Trianon, see Robert Evans, 'The Successor States', in Robert Gerwarth (ed.), *Twisted Paths: Europe 1914–45* (Oxford and New York, 2007), 210–36; Raymond Pearson, 'Hungary: A State Truncated, a Nation Dismembered', in Seamus Dunn and T. G. Fraser,

Europe and Ethnicity: World War I and Contemporary Ethnic Conflict (London and New York, 1996), 88–109, here 95–6. Ignác Romsics, *A trianoni békeszerződés* (Budapest, 2008); Dániel Ballabás, *Trianon 90 év távlatából: Konferenciák, műhelybeszélgetések* (Eger, 2011).

54. Berend, *Decades of Crisis*, 224–6.
55. Georgi P. Genov, *Bulgaria and the Treaty of Neuilly* (Sofia, 1935), 31. MacMillan, *Peacemakers*, 248–50.
56. Richard J. Crampton, *Aleksandur Stamboliiski: Bulgaria* (Chicago, 2009), 75–109. Nejiski Mir, *Vojna enciklopedija* (Belgrade, 1973), 19.
57. MacMillan, *Peacemakers*, 151.
58. Ibid.
59. Doncho Daskalov, *1923: Sadbonosni resheniya isabitiya* (Sofia, 1983), 23.
60. Theodora Dragostinova, 'Competing Priorities, Ambiguous Loyalties: Challenges of Socioeconomic Adaptation and National Inclusion of the Interwar Bulgarian Refugees', *Nationalities Papers* 34 (2006), 549–74, here 553. For a detailed early analysis and insightful interpretation of the refugee crisis in interwar Bulgaria, see Dimitar Popnikolov, *Balgarite ot Trakiya i spogodbite na Balgaria s Gartsia i Turtsia* (Sofia, 1928).
61. For details of the social and economic difficulties with the accommodation of refugees after the First World War in Bulgaria, see Georgi Dimitrov, *Nastanyavane i ozemlyavane na balgarskite bezhantsi*, (Blagoevgrad, 1985); Karl Hitilov, *Selskostopanskoto nastanyavane na bezhantsite 1927–1932* (Sofia, 1932).
62. Letter of Alexander Stambolijski to Georges Clemenceau, 22 November 1919. See Tsocho Bilyarski and Grigorov Nikola (eds), *Nyoiskiyat pogrom i terorat na bulgarite: Sbornik dokumenti i materiali* (Sofia, 2009), 312.
63. Erik Jan Zürcher, 'The Ottoman Empire and the Armistice of Moudros', in Hugh Cecil and Peter H. Liddle (eds), *At the Eleventh Hour: Reflections, Hopes, and Anxieties at the Closing of the Great War, 1918* (London, 1998), 266–75.
64. Quoted in George Goldberg, *The Peace to End Peace: The Paris Peace Conference of 1919* (London, 1970), 196.
65. Michael A. Reynolds, 'Ottoman-Russian Struggle for Eastern Anatolia and the Caucasus, 1908–1918: Identity, Ideology and the Geopolitics of World Order', Ph.D. thesis (Princeton, 2003), 377. From a nationalist perspective, see Justin McCarthy, *Death and Exile: The Ethnic Cleansing of Ottoman Muslims 1821–1922* (Princeton, 2004), 198–200; Salahi Sonyel, *The Great War and the Tragedy of Anatolia: Turks and Armenians in the Maelstrom of Major Powers* (Ankara, 2000), 161–3.
66. Gingeras Ryan, *Fall of the Sultanate: The Great War and the End of the Ottoman Empire 1908–1922* (Oxford, 2016), 255.
67. A. E. Montgomery, 'The Making of the Treaty of Sevres of 10 August 1920', *The Historical Journal* 15 (1972), 775–87.

68. Hasan Kayali, 'The Struggle for Independence', in Reşat Kasaba (ed.), *The Cambridge History of Turkey*, vol. 4: *Turkey in the Modern World* (Cambridge and New York, 2008), 118ff.

69. Ibid.; Smith, 'Empires at the Paris Peace Conference'. See, too, Paul C. Helmreich, *From Paris to Sèvres: The Partition of the Ottoman Empire at the Paris Peace Conference of 1919–1920* (Columbus, Oh., 1974).

70. Gerd Krumeich et al., *Versailles 1919: Ziele, Wirkung, Wahrnehmung* (Essen, 2001).

71. Henryk Batowski, 'Nationale Konflikte bei der Entstehung der Nachfolgestaaten', in Richard Georg Plaschka and Karlheinz Mack (eds), *Die Auflösung des Habsburgerreiches: Zusammenbruch und Neuorientierung im Donauraum* (Munich, 1970), 338–49.

72. Dudley Kirk, *Europe's Population in the Interwar Years* (New York, 1946); Pearson, 'Hungary', 98–9. István I. Mócsy, *The Effects of World War I: The Uprooted: Hungarian Refugees and their Impact on Hungary's Domestic Politics, 1918–1921* (New York, 1983), 10.

73. Hannah Arendt, *Elemente und Ursprünge totaler Herrschaft* (Frankfurt am Main, 1955), 260; on this general theme, see also Karen Barkey and Mark von Hagen (eds), *After Empires: Multiethnic Societies and Nation-Building. The Soviet Union, and the Russian, Ottoman, and Habsburg Empires* (Boulder, Colo., 1997), and Smith, 'Empires at the Paris Peace Conference', in Gerwarth and Manela (eds), *Empires at War*, 254–76.

74. Norman Davies, *Microcosm: A Portrait of a Central European City* (London, 2003), 337.

75. Ibid., 389–90.

76. As Michael Mann has pointed out, those who in addition lost their homes as frontiers moved at the conflict's end were six times overrepresented among Holocaust perpetrators. Michael Mann, *The Dark Side of Democracy: Explaining Ethnic Cleansing* (Cambridge, 2005), 223–8.

77. See Mark Mazower, *Hitler's Empire: How the Nazis Ruled Europe* (New York, 2008).

78. Statistics according to M. C. Kaser and E. A. Radice (eds), *The Economic History of Eastern Europe, 1919–1975*, vol. 1 (Oxford, 1985), 25. See also the detailed discussion of the issue in Alexander Victor Prusin, *The Lands Between: Conflict in the East European Borderlands, 1870–1992* (Oxford, 2010), 11–124.

79. Mark Levene, *The Crisis of Genocide*, vol. 1: *Devastation: The European Rimlands 1912–1938* (Oxford, 2016), 230–40.

80. For the text, see 'Treaty of Peace between the United States of America, the British Empire, France, Italy, and Japan and Poland', *American Journal of International Law* 13, Supplement, Official Documents (1919), 423–40. Carole Fink, 'The Minorities Question at the Paris Peace Conference: The Polish Minority Treaty, June 28, 1919', in Manfred Boemeke, Gerald

    Feldman, and Elisabeth Glaser (eds), *The Treaty of Versailles: A Reassessment after 75 Years* (Cambridge, 1998), 249–74.

81. Fink, 'The Minorities Question'.

82. Jaroslav Kucera, *Minderheit im Nationalstaat: Die Sprachenfrage in den tschechisch-deutschen Beziehungen 1918–1938* (Munich, 1999), 307.

83. Carole Fink, *Defending the Rights of Others: The Great Powers, the Jews, and International Minority Protection* (New York, 2004), 260; Zara Steiner, *The Lights that Failed: European International History 1919–1933* (Oxford and New York, 2005), 86.

84. On revisionism, see the following collection of essays: Marina Cattaruzza, Stefan Dyroff, and Dieter Langewiesche (eds), *Territorial Revisionism and the Allies of Germany in the Second World War: Goals, Expectations, Practices* (New York and Oxford, 2012).

85. Jerzy Borzęcki, 'German Anti-Semitism à la Polonaise: A Report on Poznanian Troops' Abuse of Belarusian Jews in 1919', *East European Politics and Societies and Cultures* 26 (2012), 693–707.

86. Arnold Zweig, *Das ostjüdische Antlitz* (Berlin, 1920), 9–11.

87. Victor Klemperer, *Curriculum Vitae, Erinnerungen 1881—1918*, vol. 2, 687–712 (Berlin, 1996), 686–7.

88. Steven E. Aschheim, *Brothers and Strangers: The East European Jew in German and German-Jewish Consciousness, 1800–1923* (Madison, 1982).

89. Trude Maurer, *Ostjuden in Deutschland, 1918–1933* (Hamburg, 1990).

90. Lina Heydrich, *Leben mit einem Kriegsverbrecher* (Pfaffenhofen, 1976), 42f.

91. Alfred Rosenberg, 'Die russisch-jüdische Revolution', *Auf gut Deutsch*, 24 May 1919.

92. Norman Cohn, *Warrant for Genocide: The Myth of the Jewish World-Conspiracy and the Protocols of the Elders of Zion* (New York, 1966).

93. Marc Raeff, *Russia Abroad: A Cultural History of the Russian Emigration, 1919–1939* (Oxford and New York, 1990). On France: Catherine Goussef, *L'Exil russe: la fabrique du réfugié apatride (1920–1939)* (Paris, 2008). On Prague: Catherine Andreyev and Ivan Savicky, *Russia Abroad: Prague and the Russian Diaspora 1918–1938* (New Haven and London, 2004).

94. Robert C. Williams, *Culture in Exile: Russian Emigrés in Germany, 1881–1941* (Ithaca, NY, 1972), 114; Fritz Mierau, *Russen in Berlin, 1918–1933* (Berlin, 1988), 298; Karl Schlögel (ed.), *Chronik russischen Lebens in Deutschland, 1918 bis 1941* (Berlin, 1999).

EPILOGUE

1. Johannes Erger, *Der Kapp-Lüttwitz-Putsch: Ein Beitrag zur deutschen Innenpolitik, 1919–20* (Düsseldorf, 1967); Erwin Könnemann and Gerhard Schulze (eds), *Der Kapp-Lüttwitz-Putsch: Dokumente* (Munich, 2002); Anthony Read, *The World on Fire: 1919 and the Battle with Bolshevism* (London, 2009), 319f.

2. Read, *World on Fire*, 320.

3. Rüdiger Bergien, *Die bellizistische Republik: Wehrkonsens und "Wehrhaftmachung" in Deutschland 1918–1933* (Munich, 2012); Peter Keller, 'Die Wehrmacht der deutschen Republik ist die Reichswehr': Die deutsche Armee 1918–1921 (Paderborn, 2014); William Mulligan, *The Creation of the Modern German Army: General Walther Reinhardt and the Weimar Republic, 1914–1930* (New York, 2005).

4. Könnemann and Schulze (eds), *Kapp-Lüttwitz-Putsch*.

5. Read, *World on Fire*, 321.

6. Harry Graf Kessler, *Das Tagebuch 1880–1937*, ed. von Roland Kamzelak and Ulrich Ott, vol. 7: 1919–1923 (Stuttgart, Klaus Tenfelde, 'Bürgerkrieg im Ruhrgebiet 1918–1920', in Karl-Peter Ellerbrock (ed.), *Erster Weltkrieg, Bürgerkrieg und Ruhrbesetzung. Dortmund und das Ruhrgebiet 1914/18–1924* (Dortmund, 2010), 19–66.2007), 294 (diary entry of 19 March 1920).

7. Ibid., 295 (diary entry of 20 March 1920).

8. Klaus Tenfelde, 'Bürgerkrieg im Ruhrgebiet 1918–1920', in Karl-Peter Ellerbrock (ed.), *Erster Weltkrieg, Bürgerkrieg und Ruhrbesetzung. Dortmund und das Ruhrgebiet 1914/18–1924* (Dortmund, 2010), 19–66.

9. Max Zeller, as quoted in Nigel H. Jones, *Hitler's Heralds: The Story of the Freikorps 1918–1923* (London, 1987), 50.

10. Read, *World on Fire*, 323.

11. Christian Leitzbach, *Matthias Erzberger: Ein kritischer Beobachter des Wilhelminischen Reiches 1895–1914* (Frankfurt am Main, 1998); Martin Sabrow, *Die verdrängte Verschwörung: Der Rathenau-Mord und die deutsche Gegenrevolution* (Frankfurt am Main, 1999).

12. The murder of Erzberger was part of a wider culture of political violence, notably—but not exclusively—on the far Right. For statistics, see Emil J. Gumbel, *Vier Jahre politischer Mord* (Berlin, 1924), 73–5.

13. Anselm Döring-Manteuffel, 'Der politische Mord als Anschlag auf die Demokratie: Das Attentat auf Walther Rathenau', in Georg Schild and Anton Schindling (eds), *Politische Morde in der Geschichte: Von der Antike bis zur Gegenwart* (Paderborn, 2012), 113–28; Sabrow, *Rathenau-Mord*.

14. On the Organization Consul, responsible for these acts of terrorism, see in particular the files in the Institut für Zeitgeschichte (Munich), Fa 163/1 and MA 14412. See, too, Sabrow, *Rathenau-Mord*.

15. *Verhandlungen des Reichstags: Stenographische Berichte*, 24 June 1922, p. 8037 (D)-8039 (B).

16. Christoph Gusy, *Weimar—die wehrlose Republik? Verfassungsschutzrecht und Verfassungsschutz in der Weimarer Republik* (Tübingen, 1991); Gotthard Jasper, *Der Schutz der Republik. Studien zur staatlichen Sicherung der Demokratie in der Weimarer Republik 1922–1930* (Tübingen, 1963).

17. Christine Hikel, 'Unsichere Republik? Terrorismus und politischer Mord in der Weimarer Republik und der BRD', *ZfAS*, special issue 1 (2011), 125–49.

18. Verhandlungen des Reichstags, 1. Wahlperiode, Stenographische Berichte, 235. Sitzung, 24/6/1922, p. 8037 (B).

19. Wolfgang Wehler, 'Der Staatsgerichtshof für das Deutsche Reich: Die politische Rolle der Verfassungsgerichtsbarkeit in der Zeit der Weimarer Republik', unpublished Ph.D. thesis, Bonn, 1979.

20. Christian Welzbacher, *Der Reichskunstwart: Kulturpolitik und Staatsinszenierung in der Weimarer Republik 1918–1933* (Weimar, 2010).

21. Martin H. Geyer, *Verkehrte Welt: Revolution, Inflation und Modern München 1914–1924* (Kritische Studien zur Geschichtswissenschaft, 128) (Göttingen, 1998), 112–17.

22. Thomas Weber, *Hitler's First War: Adolf Hitler, the Men of the List Regiment, and the First World War* (Oxford and New York, 2010).

23. Othmar Plöckinger, *Unter Soldaten und Agitatoren: Hitlers prägende Jahre im deutschen Militär 1918–1920* (Paderborn, 2013).

24. Peter Longerich, *Hitler: Biographie* (Munich, 2015); Thomas Weber, *Wie Adolf Hitler zum Nazi wurde: Vom unpolitischen Soldaten zum Autor von Mein Kampf* (Berlin, 2016).

25. Ernst Deuerlein (ed.), *Der Hitler-Putsch: Bayerische Dokumente zum 8./9. November 1923* (Stuttgart, 1962); Hans Mommsen, 'Hitler und der 9. November 1923', in Johannes Willms (ed.), *Der 9. November: Fünf Essays zur deutschen Geschichte* (Munich, 1995), 33–48.

26. Harald Jentsch, *Die KPD und der 'deutsche Oktober' 1923* (Rostock, 2005); Bernhard B. Bayerlein et al. (eds), *Deutscher Oktober 1923: Ein Revolutionsplan und sein Scheitern* (Berlin, 2003).

27. Richard Evans, *The Coming of the Third Reich* (London, 2003), 104; Gerald D. Feldman, *The Great Disorder: Politics, Economics, and Society in the German Inflation, 1914–1924* (New York, 1993), 5 (table 1). For the Ruhr occupation, see Conan Fischer, *The Ruhr Crisis 1923–1924* (Oxford, 2003); Hermann J. Rupieper, *The Cuno Government and Reparations 1922–1923: Politics and Economics* (The Hague, 1979); and Klaus Schwabe (ed.), *Die Ruhrkrise 1923: Wendepunkt der internationalen Beziehungen nach dem Ersten Weltkrieg* (Paderborn, 1985).

28. Bruce Kent, *The Spoils of War: The Politics, Economics, and Diplomacy of Reparations 1918–1932* (Oxford, 2011), 245–8.

29. Ibid., 778–93.

30. Ibid., 754–835.

31. Kurt Tucholsky published this poem under one of his pseudonyms, 'Theobald Tiger', in *Die Weltbühne*, 5 November 1929, 710.

Picture Acknowledgements

Bibliography

NEWSPAPERS AND MAGAZINES

Die Baracke: Zeitschrift des Kriegsgefangenenlagers Bando, Bayerischer Kurier, Berliner Tageblatt, Deutscher Reichs-und Preußischer Staatsanzeiger, Kreuzzeitung, Rote Fahne, The Times, Die Tradition: Wochenschrift der Vereinigten Vaterländischen Verbände Deutschlands, Vorwärts

SOURCE COLLECTIONS AND MEMOIRS

Albrecht, Martin, *Als deutscher Jude im Ersten Weltkrieg: Der Fabrikant und Offizier Otto Meyer*, ed. Andreas Meyer, Berlin, be.bra verlag, 2014.

Amis de l'Armistice (ed.), *Der 11. November 1918: Unterzeichnung eines Waffenstillstands im Wald von Compiègne*, Compiègne, Imprimerie Bourson, undated.

Arbeitskreis verdienter Gewerkschaftsveteranen beim Bundesvorstand des FDGB (ed.), *Erinnerungen von Veteranen der deutschen Gewerkschaftsbewegung an die Novemberrevolution*, 2nd edn, Berlin (GDR), Tribüne, 1960.

Baden, Max von, *Erinnerungen und Dokumente*, Stuttgart, Berlin, and Leipzig, Deutsche Verlags-Anstalt, 1927.

Baker, Ray Stannard, and William E. Dodded (eds), *Woodrow Wilson, War and Peace: Presidential Messages, Addresses, and Public Papers (1917–1924)*, New York, Harper, 1927.

Balla, Erich, *Landsknechte wurden wir: Abenteuer aus dem Baltikum*, Berlin, Kolk, 1932.

Barth, Emil, *Aus der Werkstatt der Revolution*, Berlin, Hoffmann, 1919.

Bauer, Otto, *Die österreichische Revolution*, Vienna, Volksbuchhandlung, 1923.

Bernstein, Eduard, *Die Voraussetzungen des Sozialismus und die Aufgaben der Sozialdemokratie*, Stuttgart, Dietz, 1899.

Bernstein, Eduard, *Die deutsche Revolution*, vol. 1: *Ihr Ursprung, ihr Verlauf und ihr Werk*, Berlin, Verlag Gesellschaft und Erziehung, 1921.

Bilyarski, Tsocho, and Grigorov Nikola (eds), *Nyoiskiyat pogrom i terorat na bulgarite: Sbornik dokumenti i materiali*, Sofia, Aniko, 2009.

Bischoff, Josef, *Die letzte Front: Geschichte der Eisernen Division*, Berlin, Schützen-Verlag, 1935.

Böhm, Wilhelm, *Im Kreuzfeuer zweier Revolutionen*, Munich, Verlag für Kulturpolitik, 1924.

Cohen, Max, 'Rede für die Nationalversammlung vor dem Allgemeinen Kongress der Arbeiter- und Soldatenräte', 19 December 1918, in Peter Wende (ed.), *Politische Reden III, 1914–1945*, Berlin, Deutscher Klassiker Verlag, 1990, 97–121.

Däumig, Ernst, 'Rede gegen die Nationalversammlung vor dem Allgemeinen Kongress der Arbeiter- und Soldatenräte', 19 December 1918, in Peter Wende (ed.), *Politische Reden III, 1914–1945*, Frankfurt am Main, Deutscher Klassiker Verlag, 1990, 122–41.

Dehmel, Richard, *Zwischen Volk und Menschheit: Kriegstagebuch*, Berlin, Fischer, 1919.

Deppe, Ludwig, *Mit Lettow-Vorbeck durch Ostafrika*, Berlin, Scherl, 1921.

Deuerlein, Ernst (ed.), *Der Hitler-Putsch: Bayerische Dokumente zum 8./9. November 1923*, Stuttgart, Deutsche Verlags-Anstalt, 1962.

Döblin, Alfred, 'Revolutionstage im Elsaß', in *Die Neue Rundschau* (February 1919), vol. 1, 164–72, reprinted in Alfred Döblin, *Schriften zur Politik und Gesellschaft*, Olten and Freiburg im Breisgau, Walter, 1972, 59–70.

Ebbinghaus, Christof von, *Die Memoiren des Generals von Ebbinghaus*, Stuttgart, Berger, 1928.

Ebert, Friedrich, *Rede zur Eröffnung der Verfassunggebenden Nationalversammlung*, 6 February 1919, in Peter Wende (ed.), *Politische Reden III, 1914–1945*, Frankfurt am Main, Deutscher Klassiker Verlag, 1990, 244–53.

Einstein, Albert, *Einstein Papers*, vol. 7: *The Berlin Years: Writings, 1918–1921*, Princeton, Princeton University Press, 1998.

Erzberger, Matthias, *Erlebnisse im Weltkrieg*, Stuttgart and Berlin, Deutsche Verlags Anstalt, 1920.

Fendall, Charles Pearce, *The East African Force 1915–1919: An Unofficial Record of its Creation and Fighting Career*, London, Witherby, 1921.

Foch, Ferdinand, *Mémoire pour servir à l'histoire de la guerre 1914–1918*, vol. 2, Paris, Librairie Pion, 1931.

Foerster, Wolfgang (ed.), *Kämpfer an vergessenen Fronten*, Berlin, Deutsche Buchvertriebsstelle, 1931.

Goltz, Rüdiger von der, *Meine Sendung in Finnland und im Baltikum*, Leipzig, K. F. Koehler, 1920.

Groener, Wilhelm, *Lebenserinnerungen: Jugend, Generalstab, Weltkrieg*, Göttingen, Vandenhoeck & Ruprecht, 1957.

Heinz, Friedrich Wilhelm, *Sprengstoff*, Berlin, Frundsberg-Verlag, 1930.

Hendrick, Burton J., *The Life and Letters of Walter Hines Page*, vol. 3, Garden City, NY, Doubleday, Page & Co., 1925.

Heydrich, Lina, *Leben mit einem Kriegsverbrecher*, Pfaffenhofen, Ludwig, 1976.

Heymann, Lida Gustava, and Anita Augspurg, *Erlebtes—Erschautes: Deutsche Frauen kämpften für Freiheit, Recht und Frieden 1850–1950*, ed. Margit Twellmann, Frankfurt am Main, Helmer, 1992.

Hill, Leonidas E. (ed.), *Die Weizsäcker-Papiere 1900–1934*, Berlin, Propyläen, 1982.

Hitilov, Karl, *Selskostopanskoto nastanyavane na bezhantsite 1927–1932*, Sofia, Glavna direktsiya na bezhantsite, 1932.

Hitler, Adolf, *Mein Kampf: Eine kritische Edition*, ed. Christian Hartmann, Thomas Vordermayer, Othmar Plöckinger, and Roman Töppel, Berlin and Munich, Institut für Zeitgeschichte, 2016.

Höss, Rudolf, *Kommandant in Auschwitz: Autobiographische Aufzeichnungen*, ed. Martin Broszat, Stuttgart, Deutsche Verlags-Anstalt, 1958.

House, Edward M., *The Intimate Papers of Colonel House Arranged as a Narrative by Charles Seymour*, Boston and New York, Houghton Mifflin Company, 1926–8.

Institut für Marxismus-Leninismus beim Zentralkomitee der SED (ed.), *Dokumente und Materialien zur Geschichte der deutschen Arbeiterbewegung*, 2nd ser., Berlin (GDR), Dietz, 1957.

Institut für Marxismus-Leninismus beim Zentralkomitee der SED (ed.), *Vorwärts und nicht vergessen: Erlebnisberichte aktiver Teilnehmer der Novemberrevolution 1918/19*, Berlin (GDR), Dietz, 1958.

Institut für Marxismus-Leninismus beim Zentralkomitee der SED (ed.), *Wladimir Iljitsch Lenin. Werke*, vol. 23: August 1916–March 1917, 7th edn, Berlin (GDR), Dietz, 1975.

Jünger, Ernst, *In Stahlgewittern: Ein Kriegstagebuch*, Berlin, Verlag Mittler & Sohn, 1942.

Jünger, Ernst, *Kriegstagebuch 1914–1918*, ed. Helmuth Kiesel, Stuttgart, Klett-Cotta, 2010.

Kessel, Eberhard (ed.), *Friedrich Meinecke, Werke*, vol. 8: *Autobiographische Schriften*, Stuttgart, K. F. Koehler Verlag, 1969.

Kessler, Harry Graf, *Das Tagebuch 1880–1937*, ed. Roland Kamzelak and Ulrich Ott, vol. 6: *1916–1918*, vol. 7: *1919–1923*, Stuttgart, Klett-Cotta, 2007.

Kesyakov, Bogdan, *Prinos kym diplomaticheskata istoriya na Bulgaria (1918–1925): Dogovori, konventsii, spogodbi, protokoli i drugi syglashenia i diplomaticheski aktove s kratki belejki*, Sofia, Pečatnica Rodopi, 1925.

Keynes, John Maynard, *The Economic Consequences of the Peace*, London, Macmillan, 1919.

Killinger, Manfred von, *Der Klabautermann: Eine Lebensgeschichte*, 3rd edn, Munich, Eher, 1936.

Klemperer, Victor, *Curriculum Vitae: Erinnerungen 1881–1918*, vol. 2, Berlin, Rütten & Loening, 1996.

Klemperer, Victor, *Man möchte immer weinen und lachen in einem: Revolutionstagebuch 1919*, Berlin, Aufbau-Verlag, 2015.

Köhl, Franz, *Der Kampf um Deutsch-Ostafrika 1914–1918*, Berlin, Kameradschaft, 1920.

Kollwitz, Käthe, *Die Tagebücher*, ed. Jutta Bohnke-Kollwitz, Berlin, Siedler, 1989.

Körner, Hans-Michael, and Ingrid Körner (eds), *Leopold Prinz von Bayern, 1846–1930: Aus den Lebenserinnerungen*, Regensburg, Pustet, 1983.

Kramer, Hilde, *Rebellin in Munich, Moskau und Berlin: Autobiographie 1901–1924*, ed. Egon Günther, Berlin, Basisdruck, 2011.

Kühlmann, Richard von, *Erinnerungen*, Heidelberg, Lambert Schneider, 1948.

Lafontaine, Oskar, 'Rede auf dem Parteitag in Cottbus am 24./25. Mai 2008', <https://archiv2017.dielinke.de/fileadmin/download/disput/2008/disput_juni2008.pdf> (last accessed 22 November 2017).

Lettow-Vorbeck, Paul von, *Meine Erinnerungen an Ostafrika*, Leipzig, K. F. Koehler, 1920.

Linket, Arthur S. (ed.), *The Papers of Woodrow Wilson*, vol. 40 (20 November 1916–23 January 1917), Princeton, Princeton University Press, 1982.

Lloyd George, David, *The Truth about the Peace Treaties*, 2 vols, London, Victor Gollancz, 1938.

Lönne, Karl Egon (ed.), *Die Weimarer Republik, 1918–1933: Quellen zum politischen Denken der Deutschen im 19. und 20. Jahrhundert*, Darmstadt, Wissenschaftliche Buchgesellschaft, 2002.

Luxemburg, Rosa, *Gesammelte Werke*, vol. 4: *August 1914–Januar 1919*, Berlin (GDR), Dietz, 1974.

Luxemburg, Rosa, *Politische Schriften*, ed. Ossip K. Flechtheim, Frankfurt am Main, Europäische Verlagsanstalt, 1975.

Mann, Thomas, *Tagebücher 1918–1921*, ed. Peter de Mendelssohn, paperback edition, Frankfurt am Main, Fischer, 2003.

Marhefka, Edmund (ed.), *Der Waffenstillstand 1918–1919: Das Dokumenten-Material. Waffenstillstands-Verhandlungen von Compiègne, Spa, Trier und Brüssel*, vol. 1: *Der Waffenstillstandsvertrag von Compiègne und seine Verlängerungen nebst den finanziellen Bestimmungen*, Berlin, Deutsche Verlagsgesellschaft für Politik und Geschichte, 1928.

Marx-Engels-Lenin-Institut beim ZK der SED (ed.), Karl Liebknecht, *Ausgewählte Reden, Briefe und Aufsätze*, Berlin (GDR), Dietz, 1952.

Matthias, Erich, and Hans Meier-Welcher (eds), *Quellen zur Geschichte des Parlamentarismus und der politischen Parteien*. 2nd ser.: *Militär und Politik*: *Militär und Innenpolitik im Weltkrieg 1914–1918*, ed. Wilhelm Deist, 2 vols, Düsseldorf, Droste, 1970.

Matthias, Erich, and Susanne Miller (eds), *Die Regierung der Volksbeauftragten 1918/19*, 2 vols, Düsseldorf, Droste, 1969.

Matthias, Erich, and Rudolf Morsey (eds), *Quellen zur Geschichte des Parlamentarismus und der politischen Parteien*, vol. 2: *Die Regierung des Prinzen Max von Baden*, Düsseldorf, Droste, 1962.

Meinecke, Friedrich, *Die Deutsche Katastrophe*, Wiesbaden, Brockhaus, 1947.

Michaelis, Herbert, Ernst Schraepler, and Günter Scheel (eds), *Ursachen und Folgen*, vol. 2: *Der militärische Zusammenbruch und das Ende des Kaiserreichs*, Berlin, Wendler, 1959.

Müller, Hermann, *Die Novemberrevolution: Erinnerungen*, Berlin, Der Bücherkreis, 1928.

Müller, Richard, *Geschichte der deutschen Revolution*, vol. 1: *Vom Kaiserreich zur Republik*, Vienna, 1924; repr. Berlin, Olle und Wolter, 1979.

Müller, Richard, *Geschichte der deutschen Revolution*, vol. 2: *Die Novemberrevolution*, Berlin, Olle und Wolter, 1974.

Neck, Rudolf (ed.), *Österreich im Jahre 1918: Berichte und Dokumente*, Vienna, Verlag für Geschichte und Politik, 1968.

Niemann, Alfred, *Revolution von Oben—Umsturz von unten: Entwicklung und Verlauf der Staatsumwälzung in Deutschland 1914–1918*, Berlin, Verlag für Kulturpolitik, 1927.

Noske, Gustav, *Von Kiel bis Kapp: Zur Geschichte der deutschen Revolution*, Berlin, Verlag für Politik und Wirtschaft, 1920.

Oncken, Hermann, 'Die Wiedergeburt der großdeutschen Idee', in Oncken, *Nation und Geschichte: Reden und Aufsätze 1919–1935*, Berlin, Grote'sche Verlagsbuchhandlung, 1935, 45–70. [First published in *Österreichische Rundschau* 63 (1920), 97–114.]

Otto, Hellmut, and Karl Schmiedel, *Der Erste Weltkrieg: Dokumente*, 2nd edn, Berlin (GDR), Militärverlag, 1977.

Pieck, Wilhelm, *Gesammelte Reden und Schriften*, vol. 1: *August 1904–1. Januar 1919*, Berlin (GDR), Dietz, 1959.

Popp, Lothar, *Ursprung und Entwicklung der Novemberrevolution 1918*, Kiel, Hermann Behrens, 1918.

Protokoll über die Verhandlungen des Parteitages der Sozialdemokratischen Partei Deutschlands, abgehalten zu Mannheim vom 23. bis 29. September 1906 sowie Bericht über die 4. Frauenkonferenz am 22. und 23. September 1906 in Mannheim 1906, Berlin, Buchhandlung Vorwärts, 1906.

Rausch, Bernhard, *Am Springquell der Revolution: Die Kieler Matrosenerhebung*, Kiel, Haase, 1918.

Remarque, Erich Maria, *Im Westen nichts Neues*, Cologne, Kiepenheuer & Witsch, 2010.

Riddell, George A. Baron, *Lord Riddell's Intimate Diary of the Peace Conference and After, 1918–1923*, London, Gollancz, 1933.

Riezler, Kurt, *Tagebücher, Aufsätze, Dokumente*, Göttingen, Vandenhoeck & Ruprecht, 2008.

Ritter, Gerhard A., and Susanne Miller (eds), *Die deutsche Revolution 1918–1919: Dokumente*, Hamburg, Hoffmann und Campe, 1975.

Rosenberg, Alfred, 'Die russisch-jüdische Revolution', *Auf gut Deutsch* 1 (1919), 120–4 (21 February 1919).

Rosenberg, Alfred, *Dreißig Novemberköpfe*, Munich, Kampfverlag, 1927.

Roth, Joseph, *Das Spinnennetz*, Cologne and Berlin, Kiepenheuer & Witsch, 1967.

Ruckteschell, Walter von, 'Der Feldzug in Ostafrika', in Paul von Lettow-Vorbeck (ed.), *Um Vaterland und Kolonie: Ein Weckruf an die deutsche Nation*, Berlin-Lichterfelde, Bermühler, 1919.

Salomon, Ernst von, *Die Geächteten*, Berlin, Rowohlt, 1923.

Sammlung der Drucksachen der Verfassunggebenden Preußischen Landesversammlung, Tagung 1919/21, vol. 15, Berlin, Preussische Verlags Anstalt, 1921.

Samson-Himmelstjerna, Alfred von, 'Meine Erinnerungen an die Landwehrzeit', Herder Institut, Marburg, n.d., DSHI 120 BR BLW 9.

Scheidemann, Philipp, *Der Zusammenbruch*, Berlin, Verlag für Sozialwissenschaft, 1921.

Schnee, Heinrich, *Deutsch-Ostafrika im Weltkriege: Wie wir lebten und kämpften*, Leipzig, Quelle & Meyer, 1919.

Schreiber, Adele, *Revolution und Frauenwahlrecht: Frauen! Lernt wählen!*, Berlin, Arbeitsgemeinschaft für staatsbürgerliche und wirtschaftliche Bildung, 1919.

Shedletzky, Itta, and Thomas Sparr (eds), *Betty Scholem—Gershom Scholem: Mutter und Sohn im Briefwechsel 1917–1946*, Munich, C. H. Beck, 1989.

Der Staatsvertrag von St. Germain, Vienna, Österreichische Staatsdruckerei, 1919.

Stahl, Wilhelm (ed.), *Schulthess' Europäischer Geschichtskalender*, 34 (1918), Munich, C. H. Beck, 1922.

Stampfer, Friedrich, *Die 14 Jahre der Ersten Deutschen Republik*, Offenbach, Drott, 1947.

Starhemberg, Ernst Rüdiger, 'Aufzeichnungen des Fürsten Ernst Rüdiger Starhemberg im Winter 1938/39 in Saint Gervais in Frankreich', in Nachlass Starhemberg, Oberösterreichisches Landesarchiv Linz.

Toller, Ernst, *I was a German: The Autobiography of Ernst Toller*, New York, Morrow, 1934.

Treaty of Peace between the Allied and Associated Powers and Germany, London, H. M. Stationery Office, 1925.

'Treaty of Peace between the United States of America, the British Empire, France, Italy, and Japan and Poland', *American Journal of International Law* 13, Supplement, Official Documents (1919), 423–40.

Troeltsch, Ernst, *Spektator-Briefe: Aufsätze über die deutsche Revolution und die Weltpolitik 1918/22*, Tübingen, Mohr, 1924.

Verhandlungen der verfassunggebenden Deutschen Nationalversammlung: Stenographische Berichte, vol. 327, Berlin, Norddeutsche Buchdruckerei und Verlags-Anstalt, 1920.

Die Verfassung des Deutschen Reiches vom 11. August 1919, ed. Gerhard Anschütz, 2nd edn, Berlin, Stilke, 1921.

Weber, Max, 'Deutschlands künftige Staatsform' (November 1918), in Weber, *Gesammelte politische Schriften*, 2nd edn, ed. J. Winckelmann, Tübingen, J. C. B. Mohr, 1958, 436–71.

Wenig, Richard, *Kriegs-Safari: Erlebnisse und Eindrücke auf den Zügen Lettow-Vorbecks durch das östliche Afrika*, Berlin, Scherl, 1920.

Das Werk des Untersuchungsausschusses der Verfassungsgebenden Deutschen Nationalversammlung und des Deutschen Reichstages 1919–1928. Verhandlungen, Gutachten, Urkunden, ed. Walter Schücking; series 4, *Die Ursachen des deutschen Zusammenbruchs im Jahre 1918*, Berlin, Deutsche Verlagsgesellschaft für Politik und Geschichte, 1928.

Wermuth, Adolf, *Ein Beamtenleben*, Berlin, Scherl, 1922.

Westarp, Kuno Graf von, *Das Ende der Monarchie am 9. November 1918*, ed. Werner Conze, Berlin, Helmut Rauschenbusch Verlag, 1952.

Wilson, Woodrow, *The War Addresses of Woodrow Wilson*, with an introduction and notes by Arthur Roy Leonard, Boston, Ginn, 1918.

Weygand, Maxime, *Le onze Novembre*, Paris, Flammarion, 1947.

Yourcenar, Marguerite, *Le coup de grâce*, Paris, Gallimard, 1939.

Zweig, Arnold, *Das ostjüdische Antlitz*, Berlin, Welt-Verlag, 1920.

SECONDARY LITERATURE

Ackerl, Isabella, and Rudolf Neck (eds), *Saint-Germain 1919: Protokoll des Symposiums am 29. und 30. Mai 1979 in Wien*, Vienna, Verlag für Geschichte und Politik, 1989.

Adolph, Hans, *Otto Wels und die Politik der deutschen Sozialdemokratie 1894–1939: Eine politische Biographie*, Berlin, de Gruyter, 1971.

Afflerbach, Holger, *Falkenhayn: Politisches Denken und Handeln im Kaiserreich*, Munich, Oldenbourg, 1994.

Alapuro, Risto, *State and Revolution in Finland*, Berkeley, University of California Press, 1988.

Albertin, Lothar, *Liberalismus und Demokratie am Anfang der Weimarer Republik: Eine vergleichende Analyse der Deutschen Demokratischen Partei und der Deutschen Volkspartei*, Düsseldorf, Droste, 1972.

Albrecht, Günther (ed.), *Erlebte Geschichte von Zeitgenossen gesehen und geschildert. Erster Teil: Vom Kaiserreich zur Weimarer Republik*, Berlin (GDR), Verlag der Nation, 1967.

Albrecht, Willy, Friedhelm Boll, Beatrix W. Bouvier, Rosemarie Leuschen-Seppel, and Michael Schneider, 'Frauenfrage und deutsche Sozialdemokratie vom Ende des 19. Jahrhunderts bis zum Beginn der zwanziger Jahre', *Archiv für Sozialgeschichte* 19 (1979), 459–510.

Almond, Nina, and Ralph Haswell Lutz (eds), *The Treaty of St. Germain: A Documentary History of its Territorial and Political Clauses*, Stanford, Calif., Stanford University Press, 1935.

Alpern, Engel Barbara, 'Not by Bread Alone: Subsistence Riots in Russia during World War I', *Journal of Modern History* 69 (1997), 696–721.

Altrichter, Helmut, *Rußland 1917: Ein Land auf der Suche nach sich selbst*, Paderborn, Schöningh, 1997.

Andelman, David A., *A Shattered Peace: Versailles 1919 and the Price We Pay Today*, Hoboken, NJ, J. Wiley, 2008.

Andreyev, Catherine, and Ivan Savicky, *Russia Abroad: Prague and the Russian Diaspora 1918–1938*, New Haven and London, Yale University Press, 2004.

Arendt, Hannah, *Elemente und Ursprünge totaler Herrschaft*, Frankfurt am Main, Europäische Verlagsanstalt, 1955.

Arens, Olavi, 'The Estonian Question at Brest-Litovsk', *Journal of Baltic Studies* 25 (1994), 305–30.

Ascher, Harvey, 'The Kornilov Affair: A Reinterpretation', *Russian Review* 29 (1970), 235–52.

Aschheim, Steven E., *Brothers and Strangers: The East European Jew in German and German-Jewish Consciousness, 1800–1923*, Madison, Wis., University of Wisconsin Press, 1982.

Audoin-Rouzeau, Stéphane, 'Die Delegation der "Gueulescassées" in Versailles am 28. Juni 1919', in Gerd Krumeich (ed.), *Versailles 1919: Ziele, Wirkung, Wahrnehmung*, Essen, Klartext-Verlag, 2001, 280–7.

Audoin-Rouzeau, Stéphane, Annette Becker, and Leonard V. Smith, *France and the Great War, 1914–1918*, Cambridge and New York, Cambridge University Press, 2003.

Azmanov, Dimitar, and Rumen Lechev, 'Probivat na Dobropole prezsptemvri 1918g odina', *Voenno-istoricheski sbornik* 67 (1998), 154–75.

Babík, Milan, *Statecraft and Salvation: Wilsonian Liberal Internationalism as Secularized Eschatology*, Waco, Baylor University Press, 2013.

Balke, Friedrich, and Benno Wagner (eds), *Vom Nutzen und Nachteil historischer Vergleiche: Der Fall Bonn–Weimar*, Frankfurt am Main, Campus, 1997.

Balkelis, Tomas, 'Turning Citizens into Soldiers: Baltic Paramilitary Movements after the Great War', in Robert Gerwarth and John Horne (eds), *War in Peace: Paramilitary Violence in Europe after the Great War*, Oxford, Oxford University Press, 2012, 126–44.

Ball, Alan, 'Building a New State and Society: NEP, 1921–1928', in Ronald Grigor Suny (ed.), *The Cambridge History of Russia*, vol. 3, Cambridge, Cambridge University Press, 2006, 168–91.

Ballabás, Dániel, *Trianon 90 évtávlatából: Konferenciák, műhelybeszélgetések*, Cheb, Líceum, Kiadó, 2011.

Barker, Ernest, *The Submerged Nationalities of the German Empire*, Oxford, Clarendon Press, 1915.

Barkey, Karen, and Mark von Hagen (eds), *After Empires: Multiethnic Societies and Nation-Building. The Soviet Union, and the Russian, Ottoman, and Habsburg Empires*, Boulder, Colo., Westview Press, 1997.

Baron, Nick, and Peter Gatrell, 'Population Displacement, State-Building and Social Identity in the Lands of the Former Russian Empire, 1917–1923', *Kritika: Explorations in Russian and Eurasian History* 4 (2003), 51–100.

Barth, Boris, *Dolchstoßlegenden und politische Desintegration: Das Trauma der deutschen Niederlage im Ersten Weltkrieg*, Düsseldorf, Droste, 2003.

Batowski, Henryk, 'Nationale Konflikte bei der Entstehung der Nachfolgestaaten', in Richard Georg Plaschka and Karlheinz Mack (eds), *Die Auflösung des Habsburgerreiches: Zusammenbruch und Neuorientierung im Donauraum*, Munich, Oldenbourg, 1970, 338–49.

Baudis, Dieter, and Hermann Roth, 'Berliner Opfer der Novemberrevolution 1918/19', *Jahrbuch für Wirtschaftsgeschichte* (1968), 73–149.

Bauer, Frieder, and Jörg Vögele, 'Die "Spanische Grippe" in der deutschen Armee 1918: Perspektive der Ärzte und Generäle', *Medizinhistorisches Journal* 48 (2013), 117–52.

Baumgart, Winfried, *Deutsche Ostpolitik 1918: Von Brest-Litovsk bis zum Ende des Ersten Weltkriegs*, Vienna and Munich, Oldenbourg, 1966.

Bayerlein, Bernhard B., et al. (eds), *Deutscher Oktober 1923: Ein Revolutionsplan und sein Scheitern*, Berlin, Aufbau-Verlag, 2003.

Becker, Winfried, *Frederic von Rosenberg (1874–1937): Diplomat vom späten Kaiserreich bis zum Dritten Reich, Außenminister der Weimarer Republik*, Göttingen, Vandenhoeck & Ruprecht, 2011.

Bein, Reinhard, *Braunschweig zwischen rechts und links: Der Freistaat 1918 bis 1930. Materialien zur Landesgeschichte*, Braunschweig, Döring-Druck, 1991.

Benbow, Mark, *Leading Them to the Promised Land: Woodrow Wilson, Covenant Theology, and the Mexican Revolutions, 1913–1915*, Kent, Oh., Kent State University Press, 2010.

Bendikowski, Tillmann, *1914: Zwischen Begeisterung und Angst—wie Deutsche den Kriegsbeginn erlebten*, Munich, C. Bertelsmann Verlag, 2014.

Benz, Wolfgang, *Süddeutschland in der Weimarer Republik: Ein Beitrag zur deutschen Innenpolitik 1918–1923*, Berlin, Duncker & Humblot, 1970.

Berend, Ivan T., *Decades of Crisis: Central and Eastern Europe before World War II*, Berkeley, Los Angeles, and London, University of California Press, 1998.

Bergien, Rüdiger, 'Republikschützer oder Terroristen? Die Freikorpsbewegung in Deutschland nach dem Ersten Weltkrieg', *Militärgeschichte* 3 (2008), 15–17.

Bergien, Rüdiger, *Die bellizistische Republik: Wehrkonsens und 'Wehrhaftmachung' in Deutschland, 1918–1933*, Munich, Oldenbourg, 2012.

Bernhardt, Oliver, *Alfred Döblin*, Munich, Deutscher Taschenbuch-Verlag, 2007.

Bessel, Richard, *Germany after the First World War*, Oxford, Clarendon Press, 1993.

Bessel, Richard, 'Revolution', in Jay Winter (ed.), *The Cambridge History of the First World War*, vol. 2, Cambridge and New York, Cambridge University Press, 2014.

Besson, Waldemar, *Württemberg und die deutsche Staatskrise 1928–1933: Eine Studie zur Auflösung der Weimarer Republik*, Stuttgart, Deutsche Verlags-Anstalt, 1959.

Beyer, Hans, *Die Revolution in Bayern 1918/1919*, Berlin (GDR), Deutscher Verlag der Wissenschaften, 1988.

Bieber, Hans-Joachim, *Bürgertum in der Revolution*, Hamburg, Christians, 1992.

Bihl, Wolfdieter, *Österreich-Ungarn und die Friedensschlüße von Brest-Litovsk*, Vienna, Cologne, and Graz, Böhlau, 1970.

Bjork, James E., *Neither German nor Pole: Catholicism and National Indifference in a Central European Borderland, 1890–1922*, Ann Arbor, University of Michigan Press, 2008.

Blanke, Richard, *Orphans of Versailles: The Germans in Western Poland, 1918–1939*, Lexington, University Press of Kentucky, 1993.

Boak, Helen, *Women in the Weimar Republic*, Manchester, 2013.

Boebel, Chaja, and Lothar Wentzel (eds), *Streiken gegen den Krieg: Die Bedeutung der Massenstreiks in der Metallindustrie vom Januar 1918*, Hamburg, VSA, 2008.

Boell, Ludwig, *Die Operationen in Ostafrika. Weltkrieg 1914–1918*, Hamburg, Dachert, 1951.

Boell, Ludwig, 'Der Waffenstillstand 1918 und die ostafrikanische Schutztruppe: Eine Berichtigung', *Wehrwissenschaftliche Rundschau* 14 (1964), 324–36.

Boemeke, Manfred F., 'Woodrow Wilson's Image of Germany, the War-Guilt Question and the Treaty of Versailles', in Boemeke, Gerald D. Feldman, and Elisabeth Glaser (eds), *The Treaty of Versailles: A Reassessment after 75 Years*, Cambridge and New York, Cambridge University Press, 1998, 603–14.

Boemeke, Manfred F., Gerald D. Feldman, and Elisabeth Glaser (eds), *The Treaty of Versailles: A Reassessment after 75 Years*, Cambridge and New York, Cambridge University Press, 1998.

Boghardt, Thomas, *The Zimmermann Telegram: Intelligence, Diplomacy and America's Entry into World War I*, Annapolis, Md, Naval Institute Press, 2012.

Borowsky, Peter, 'Germany's Ukrainian Policy during World War I and the Revolution of 1918–19', in Hans-Joachim Torke and John-Paul Himka (eds), *German–Ukrainian Relations in Historical Perspective*, Edmonton, Canadian Institute of Ukrainian Studies Press, 1994, 84–94.

Borzęcki, Jerzy, 'German Anti Semitism à la Polonaise: A Report on Poznanian Troops' Abuse of Belarusian Jews in 1919', *East European Politics and Societies and Cultures* 26 (2012), 693–707.

Boswell, Laird, 'From Liberation to Purge Trials in the "Mythic Provinces": Recasting French Identities in Alsace and Lorraine, 1918–1920', *French Historical Studies* 23 (2000), 129–62.

Bramke, Werner, and Silvio Reisinger, *Leipzig in der Revolution von 1918/19*, Leipzig, Leipziger Universitäts-Verlag, 2009.

Braun, Bernd, 'Die "Generation Ebert"', in Braun and Klaus Schönhoven (eds), *Generationen in der Arbeiterbewegung*, Munich, Oldenbourg, 2005, 69–86.

Browder, Robert Paul, and Alexander F. Kerensky (eds), *The Russian Provisional Government 1917: Documents*, 3 vols, Stanford, Calif., Stanford University Press, 1961.

Buber, Martin (ed.), *Gustav Landauer: Sein Lebensgang in Briefen*, 2 vols, Frankfurt am Main, Rütten & Loening, 1929.

Bührer, Tanja, *Die Kaiserliche Schutztruppe für Deutsch-Ostafrika: Koloniale Sicherheitspolitik und transkulturelle Kriegführung, 1885 bis 1918*, Munich, Oldenbourg, 2011.

Bunselmeyer, Robert E., *The Cost of War 1914–1919: British Economic War Aims and the Origins of Reparation*, Hamden, Conn., Archon Books, 1975.

Burleigh, Michael, *The Third Reich: A New History*, London, Macmillan, 2001.

Büttner, Ursula, *Weimar: Die überforderte Republik 1918–1933*, Stuttgart, Klett-Cotta, 2008.

Cabanes, Bruno, *La victoire en deuillée: la sortie de guerre des soldats français (1918–1920)*, Paris, Seuil, 2004.

Cabanes, Bruno, '1919: Aftermath', in Jay Winter (ed.), *Cambridge History of the First World War*, vol. 1, Cambridge and New York, Cambridge University Press, 2014, 172–98.

Calvert, Peter, *A Study of Revolution*, Oxford, Clarendon Press, 1970.

Canning, Kathleen, ' "Sexual Crisis," the Writing of Citizenship, and the State of Emergency in Germany, 1917–1922', in Alf Lüdtke and Michael Wildt (eds), *Staats-Gewalt: Ausnahmezustand und Sicherheitsregimes. Historische Perspektiven*, Göttingen, Wallstein Verlag, 2008, 167–213.

Canning, Kathleen, 'The Politics of Symbols, Semantics, and Sentiments in the Weimar Republic', *Central European History* 43 (2010), 567–80.

Canning, Kathleen, Kerstin Barndt, and Kristin McGuire (eds), *Weimar Publics/Weimar Subject: Rethinking the Political Culture of Germany in the 1920s*, New York, Berghahn Books, 2010.

Carrère D'Encausse, Hélène, *Lenin: Revolution and Power*, New York and London, Longman Higher Education, 1982.

Carsten, Frances L., *Revolution in Central Europe 1918–19*, London, Maurice Temple Smith, 1972.

Casper-Derfert, Cläre, 'Steh auf, Arthur, heute ist Revolution', in Institut für Marxismus-Leninismus beim Zentralkomitee der SED (ed.), *Vorwärts und nicht vergessen: Erlebnisberichte aktiver Teilnehmer der Novemberrevolution 1918/1919*, Berlin (GDR), Dietz, 1960, 293–300.

Cattaruzza, Marina, Stefan Dyroff, and Dieter Langewiesche (eds), *Territorial Revisionism and the Allies of Germany in the Second World War: Goals, Expectations, Practices*, New York and Oxford, Berghahn Books, 2012.

Chernev, Borislav, *Twilight of Empire: The Brest-Litovsk Conference and the Remaking of East-Central Europe, 1917–1918*, Toronto, University of Toronto Press, 2017.

Chickering, Roger, *We Men Who Feel Most German: A Cultural Study of the Pan-German League, 1886–1914*, London, HarperCollins, 1984.

Chickering, Roger, *Imperial Germany and the Great War, 1914–1918*, Cambridge, Cambridge University Press, 2004.

Cipriano Venzon, Anne (ed.), *The United States in the First World War: An Encyclopedia*, New York and London, Garland, 1995.

Cohn, Norman, *Warrant for Genocide: The Myth of the Jewish World-Conspiracy and the Protocols of the Elders of Zion*, New York, Harper & Row, 1966.

Connor, James E. (ed.), *Lenin on Politics and Revolution: Selected Writings*, Indianapolis, Pegasus, 1968.

Conrad, Sebastian, and Jürgen Osterhammel (eds), *Das Kaiserreich transnational: Deutschland in der Welt, 1971–1914*, Göttingen, Vandenhoeck & Ruprecht, 2006.

Conze, Eckart, *Die grosse Illusion: Versailles und die Neuordnung der Welt*, Munich, Siedler Verlag, 2018.

Cornwall, Mark, *The Undermining of Austria-Hungary: The Battle for Hearts and Minds*, Basingstoke, Macmillan, 2000.

Crampton, Richard J., *Aleksandur Stamboliiski: Bulgaria*, Chicago and London, Haus Publishing, 2009.

Czech, Hans-Jörg, Olaf Matthes, and Ortwin Pelc (eds), *Revolution? Revolution! Hamburg 1918/19*, Hamburg, Wachholtz, 2018.

Dähnhardt, Dirk, *Revolution in Kiel*, Neumünster, Wachholtz, 1984.

Daly, Mary E. (ed.), *Roger Casement in Irish and World History*, Dublin, Royal Irish Academy, 2005.

Daniel, Ute, *The War from Within: German Working-Class Women in the First World War*, Oxford, Berg Publishers, 1997.

Daskalov, Doncho, *1923: Sadbonosni resheniya isabitiya*, Sofia, BZNS, 1983.

Davies, Norman, *Microcosm: A Portrait of a Central European City*, London, Pimlico, 2003.

Davis, Belinda, *Home Fires Burning: Food, Politics, and Everyday Life in World War I Berlin*, Chapel Hill, NC, University of North Carolina Press, 2000.

Dedijer, Vladimir, *Novi priloziza biografiju Josipa Broza Tita 1*, Zagreb and Rijeka, Liburnija, 1980 (reprint).

Deist, Wilhelm, 'Die Politik der Seekriegsleitung und die Rebellion der Flotte Ende Oktober 1918', *Vierteljahrshefte für Zeitgeschichte* 14 (1966), 341–68.

Deist, Wilhelm, 'Verdeckter Militärstreik im Kriegsjahr 1918?', in Wolfram Wette (ed.), *Der Krieg des kleinen Mannes: Eine Militärgeschichte von unten*, Munich and Zurich, Piper, 1995, 146–67.

Denholm, Decie, 'Eine Australierin in Leipzig: Die heimlichen Briefe der Ethel Cooper 1914–1919', in Bernd Hüppauf (ed.), *Ansichten vom Krieg*, Königstein im Taunus, Athenäum, 1984, 132–52.

Deutscher, Isaac, *The Prophet Armed: Trotsky, 1879–1921*, Oxford, Oxford University Press, 1954.

Dimitrov, Georgi, *Nastanyavane i ozemlyavane na balgarskite bezhantsi*, Blagoewgrad, VPI, 1985.

Doerries, Reinhard R., *Prelude to the Easter Rising: Sir Roger Casement in Imperial Germany*, London and Portland, Ore., Frank Cass, 2000.

Dowe, Dieter, and Peter-Christian Witt, *Friedrich Ebert 1871–1925: Vom Arbeiterführer zum Reichspräsidenten*, Bonn, Forschungsinstitut der Friedrich-Ebert-Stiftung, Historisches Forschungszentrum, 1995.

Drabkin, Jakov S., *Die Novemberrevolution in Deutschland*, Berlin (GDR), Deutscher Verlag der Wissenschaften, 1968.

Dragostinova, Theodora, 'Competing Priorities, Ambiguous Loyalties: Challenges of Socioeconomic Adaptation and National Inclusion of the Interwar Bulgarian Refugees', *Nationalities Papers* 3/4 (2006), 549–74.

Dragostinova, Theodora, *Between Two Motherlands: Nationality and Emigration among the Greeks of Bulgaria, 1900–1949*, Ithaca, NY, Cornell University Press, 2011.

Eimers, Enno, *Das Verhältnis von Preußen und Reich in den ersten Jahren der Weimarer Republik 1918–1923*, Berlin, Duncker & Humblot, 1969.

Eley, Geoff, and James Retallack (eds), *Wilhelminism and its Legacies: German Modernities, Imperialism, and the Meaning of Reform, 1890–1930: Essays for Hartmut Pogge von Strandmann*, Oxford, Berghahn Books, 2003.

Eley, Geoff, Jennifer L. Jenkin, and Tracie Matysik (eds), *German Modernities from Wilhelm to Weimar: A Contest of Futures*, London, Bloomsbury Academic, 2016.

Elz, Wolfgang, 'Versailles und Weimar', *Aus Politik und Zeitgeschichte* 50/1 (2008), 31–8.

Engelmann, Dieter, and Horst Naumann, *Hugo Haase: Lebensweg und politisches Vermächtnis eines streitbaren Sozialisten*, Berlin, Edition Neue Wege, 1999.

Erdmann, Karl Dietrich, 'Die Geschichte der Weimarer Republik als Problem der Wissenschaft', *Vierteljahrshefte für Zeitgeschichte* 3 (1955), 1–19.

Erger, Johannes, *Der Kapp-Lüttwitz-Putsch: Ein Beitrag zur deutschen Innenpolitik, 1919–20*, Düsseldorf, Droste, 1967.

Evans, Richard, *The Coming of the Third Reich*, London, Penguin, 2003.

Eyck, Erich, *Geschichte der Weimarer Republik*, vol. 1: *Vom Zusammenbruch des Kaisertums bis zur Wahl Hindenburgs*, Zurich, Rentsch, 1954.

Eyck, Erich, *Geschichte der Weimarer Republik*, vol. 2: *Von der Konferenz von Locarno bis zu Hitlers Machtübernahme*, Zurich, Rentsch, 1956.

Fedyshyn, Oleh S., *Germany's Drive to the East and the Ukrainian Revolution, 1917–1918*, New Brunswick, NJ, Rutgers University Press, 1971.

Fehrenbach, Elisabeth, 'Die Reichsgründung in der deutschen Geschichtsschreibung', in Theodor Schieder and Ernst Deuerlein (eds), *Reichsgründung 1870/71: Tatsachen, Kontroversen, Interpretationen*, Stuttgart, Seewald, 1970.

Feldman, Gerald D., 'Das deutsche Unternehmertum zwischen Krieg und Revolution: Die Entstehung des Stinnes-Legien-Abkommens', in Feldman, *Vom Weltkrieg zur Weltwirtschaftskrise: Studien zur deutschen Wirtschafts- und Sozialgeschichte 1914–1932*, Göttingen, Vandenhoeck & Ruprecht, 1984.

Feldman, Gerald D., *The Great Disorder: Politics, Economics, and Society in the German Inflation, 1914–1924*, New York, Oxford University Press, 1993.

Feldman, Gerald D., and Irmgard Steinisch, *Industrie und Gewerkschaften 1918–1924: Die überforderte Zentralarbeitsgemeinschaft*, Stuttgart, Deutsche Verlags-Anstalt, 1985.

Fellner, Fritz, 'Der Vertrag von St. Germain', in Erika Weinzierl and Kurt Skalnik (eds), *Österreich 1918–1938*, vol. l, Graz, Styria, 1983, 85–106.

Ferguson, Niall, *The Pity of War: Explaining World War I*, London, Allen Lane, 1998.

Ferro, Marc, *October 1917: A Social History of the Russian Revolution*, London, Routledge & Kegan Paul, 1980.

Fieldhouse, David K., *Western Imperialism in the Middle East, 1914–1958*, Oxford and New York, Oxford University Press, 2006.

Figes, Orlando, *Peasant Russia, Civil War: The Volga Countryside in Revolution, 1917–21*, Oxford and New York, Clarendon Press, 1989.

Figes, Orlando, *Die Tragödie eines Volkes: Die Epoche der russischen Revolution 1891 bis 1924*, Berlin, Berlin-Verlag, 1998.

Fink, Carole, 'The Minorities Question at the Paris Peace Conference: The Polish Minority Treaty, June 28, 1919', in Manfred Boemeke, Gerald Feldman, and Elisabeth Glaser (eds), *The Treaty of Versailles: A Reassessment after 75 Years*, Cambridge, Cambridge University Press, 1998.

Fink, Carole, *Defending the Rights of Others: The Great Powers, the Jews, and International Minority Protection*, New York, Cambridge University Press, 2004.

Foley, Robert, 'From Victory to Defeat: The German Army in 1918', in Ashley Ekins (ed.), *1918: Year of Victory*, Auckland and Wollombi, Exisle, 2010.

Föllmer, Moritz, 'The Unscripted Revolution: Male Subjectivities in Germany, 1918–19', *Past & Present* 240 (2018), 161–92.

Föllmer, Moritz, and Rüdiger Graf (eds), *Die 'Krise' der Weimarer Republik: Zur Kritik eines Deutungsmusters*, Frankfurt am Main, Campus, 2005.

Fong, Giordan, 'The Movement of German Divisions to the Western Front, Winter 1917–1918', *War in History* 7 (2000), 225–35.

Fricke, Dieter, et al. (eds), *Lexikon zur Parteiengeschichte: Die bürgerlichen und kleinbürgerlichen Parteien und Verbände in Deutschland (1789–1945)*, 4 vols, Leipzig, Bibliographisches Institut, 1983–6.

Friedensburg, Ferdinand, *Die Weimarer Republik*, 2nd edn, Berlin, Hanover, Norddeutsche Verlags-Anstalt, 1957.

Fritzsche, Peter, 'Historical Time and Future Experience in Postwar Germany', in Wolfgang Hardtwig (ed.), *Ordnungen in der Krise: Zur politischen Kulturgeschichte Deutschlands 1900–1933*, Munich, Oldenbourg, 2007, 141–64.

Führer, Karl Christian, Jürgen Mittag, and Axel Schildt (eds), *Revolution und Arbeiterbewegung in Deutschland 1918–1920*, Essen, Klartext Verlag, 2013.

Funck, Marcus, 'Schock und Chance: Der preußische Militäradel in der Weimarer Republik zwischen Stand und Profession', in Heinz Reif and René Schiller (eds), *Adel und Bürgertum in Deutschland*, vol. 2: *Entwicklungslinien und Wendepunkte im 20. Jahrhundert*, Berlin, Akademie-Verlag, 2001, 127 –72.

Gallus, Alexander, *Die vergessene Revolution von 1918/19*, Göttingen, Vandenhoeck & Ruprecht, 2010.

Gatrell, Peter, *A Whole Empire Walking: Refugees in Russia during World War I*, Bloomington, Ind., Indiana University Press, 1999.

Gatrell, Peter, *Russia's First World War, 1914–1917: A Social and Economic History*, London, Routledge, 2005.

Gautschi, Willi, *Lenin als Emigrant in der Schweiz*, Zurich, Benziger, 1973.

Gellinek, Christian, *Philipp Scheidemann: Gedächtnis und Erinnerung*, Münster, Waxmann, 2006.

Genov, Georgi P., *Bulgaria and the Treaty of Neuilly*, Sofia, Danov & Co., 1935.

Gentile, Emilio, *The Sacralization of Politics in Fascist Italy*, Cambridge, Mass., Harvard University Press, 1996.

Georg, Kreis, *Insel der unsicheren Geborgenheit: Die Schweiz in den Kriegsjahren 1914–1918*, Zurich, Verlag Neue Zürcher Zeitung, 2014.

Ģērmanis, Uldis, *Oberst Vācietis und die lettischen Schützen im Weltkrieg und in der Oktoberrevolution*, Stockholm, Almqvist & Wiksell, 1974.

Gerwarth, Robert, 'Republik und Reichsgründung: Bismarcks kleindeutsche Lösung im Meinungsstreit der ersten deutschen Demokratie', in Heinrich August Winkler (ed.), *Griff nach der Deutungsmacht: Zur Geschichte der Geschichtspolitik in Deutschland*, Göttingen, Wallstein-Verlag, 2004, 115–33.

Gerwarth, Robert, 'The Central European Counter-Revolution: Paramilitary Violence in Germany, Austria and Hungary after the Great War', *Past & Present* 200 (2008), 175–209.

Gerwarth, Robert, *The Vanquished: Why the First World War Failed to End*, London, Allen Lane, 2016.

Gerwarth, Robert and Martin Conway, 'Revolution and Counterrevolution', in Donald Bloxham and Robert Gerwarth (eds), *Political Violence in Twentieth-Century Europe*, Cambridge and New York, Cambridge University Press, 2011, 140–75.

Gerwarth, Robert and Dominik Geppert (eds), *Wilhelmine Germany and Edwardian Britain: Essays on Cultural Affinity*, Oxford and New York, Oxford University Press, 2008.

Gerwarth, Robert and John Horne, 'Vectors of Violence: Paramilitarism in Europe after the Great War, 1917–1923', *The Journal of Modern History* 83 (2011), 489–512.

Gerwarth, Robert and John Horne, 'Bolshevism as Fantasy: Fear of Revolution and Counter-Revolutionary Violence, 1917–1923', in Robert Gerwarth and John Horne (eds), *War in Peace: Paramilitary Violence in Europe after the Great War*, Oxford, Oxford University Press, 2012, 40–51.

Gerwarth, Robert and Erez Manela (eds), *Empires at War, 1911–1923*, Oxford, Oxford University Press, 2014.

Geyer, Martin H., *Verkehrte Welt: Revolution, Inflation und Moderne: München 1914–1924* (Kritische Studien zur Geschichtswissenschaft, 128), Göttingen, Vandenhoeck & Ruprecht, 1998.

Geyer, Martin H., 'Die Gleichzeitigkeit des Ungleichzeitigen: Zeitsemantik und die Suche nach Gegenwart in der Weimarer Republik', in Wolfgang Hardtwig (ed.), *Utopie und politische Herrschaft im Europa der Zwischenkriegszeit*, Munich, Oldenbourg, 2003, 75–100.

Geyer, Michael, *Deutsche Rüstungspolitik 1860–1980*, Frankfurt am Main, Suhrkamp, 1984.

Geyer, Michael, 'Zwischen Krieg und Nachkrieg: Die deutsche Revolution 1918/19 im Zeichen blockierter Transnationalität', in Alexander Gallus (ed.), *Die vergessene Revolution von 1918/19*, Göttingen, Vandenhoeck & Ruprecht, 2010, 187–222.

Gietinger, Klaus, *Eine Leiche im Landwehrkanal: Die Ermordung Rosa Luxemburgs*, Hamburg, Nautilus, 2008.

Gietinger, Klaus, *Der Konterrevolutionär: Waldemar Pabst—eine deutsche Karriere*, Hamburg, Nautilus, 2009.

Gilbhard, Hermann, *Die Thule-Gesellschaft: Vom okkulten Mummenschanz zum Hakenkreuz*, Munich, Kiessling, 1994.

Gill, Graeme J., *Peasants and Government in the Russian Revolution*, London, Macmillan, 1979.

Gingeras, Ryan, *Fall of the Sultanate: The Great War and the End of the Ottoman Empire 1908–1922*, Oxford, Oxford University Press, 2016.

Glenny, Michael, and Norman Stone, *The Other Russia: The Experience of Exile*, London, Faber and Faber, 1990.

Glenny, Misha, *The Balkans, 1804–1999: Nationalism, War and the Great Powers*, London, Granta Books, 1999.

Goebel, Stefan, 'Re-Membered and Re-Mobilized: The "Sleeping Dead" in Interwar Germany and Britain', *Journal of Contemporary History* 39 (2004), 487–501.

Gohlke, Martin, 'Die Räte in der Revolution 1918/19 in Magdeburg' (unpublished Ph.D. thesis, Oldenburg, 1999).

Golczewski, Frank, *Deutsche und Ukrainer*, Paderborn, Schöningh, 2010.

Goldberg, George, *The Peace to End Peace: The Paris Peace Conference of 1919*, London, Pitman, 1970.

Görlitz, Walter, *Die Junker, Adel und Bauer im deutschen Osten: Geschichtliche Bilanz von 7 Jahrhunderten*, Glücksburg, Starke, 1957.

Gosewinkel, Dieter, *Einbürgern und Ausschließen: Die Nationalisierung der Staatsangehörigkeit vom Deutschen Bund bis zur Bundesrepublik Deutschland*, Göttingen, Vandenhoeck & Ruprecht, 2001.

Gould, S. W., 'Austrian Attitudes toward Anschluss: October 1918–September 1919', *Journal of Modern History* 22 (1950), 220–31.

Goussef, Catherine, *L'exil russe: la fabrique du réfugié apatride (1920–1939)*, Paris, CNRS Édition, 2008.

Graebner, Norman, and Edward Bennett, *The Versailles Treaty and its Legacy: The Failure of the Wilsonian Vision*, Cambridge and New York, Cambridge University Press, 2011.

Graf, Rüdiger, 'Optimismus und Pessimismus in der Krise: Der politisch-kulturelle Diskurs in der Weimarer Republik', in Wolfgang Hardtwig (ed.), *Ordnungen in der Krise: Zur politischen Kulturgeschichte Deutschlands 1900–1933*, Munich, Oldenbourg, 2007, 115–40.

Grau, Bernhard, *Kurt Eisner 1867–1919: Eine Biographie*, Munich, C. H. Beck, 2001.

Grebing, Helga, *Frauen in der deutschen Revolution 1918/19*, Heidelberg, Stiftung Reichspräsident-Friedrich-Ebert-Gedenkstätte, 1994.

Greenhalgh, Elizabeth, *Victory through Coalition: Politics, Command and Supply in Britain and France, 1914–1918*, Cambridge and New York, Cambridge University Press, 2005.

Grosch, Waldemar, *Deutsche und polnische Propaganda während der Volksabstimmung in Oberschlesien 1919–1921*, Dortmund, Forschungsstelle Ostmitteleuropa, 2002.

Groß, Gerhard, 'Eine Frage der Ehre? Die Marineführung und der letzte Flottenvorstoß 1918', in Jörg Duppler and Gerhard P. Groß (eds), *Kriegsende 1918: Ereignis, Wirkung, Nachwirkung*, Munich, Oldenbourg, 1999.

Gueslin, Julien, 'Riga, de la métropole russe à la capitale de la Lettonie 1915–1919', in Philippe Chassaigne and Jean-Marc Largeaud (eds), *Villes en guerre (1914–1945)*, Paris, Colin, 2004, 185–95.

Gumbrecht, Hans Ulrich, *1926: Living on the Edge of Time*, Cambridge, Mass., Harvard University Press, 1997.

Gusy, Christoph, 'Die Grundrechte in der Weimarer Republik', *Zeitschrift für neuere Rechtsgeschichte* 15 (1993), 163–83.

Gusy, Christoph (ed.), *Weimars langer Schatten: 'Weimar' als Argument nach 1945*, Baden-Baden, Nomos Verlags-Gesellschaft, 2003.

Gutjahr, Wolf-Dietrich, *Revolution muss sein: Karl Radek—Die Biographie*, Cologne, Weimar, and Vienna, Böhlau, 2012.

Gutsche, Willibald, Fritz Klein, and Joachim Petzold, *Der Erste Weltkrieg: Ursachen und Verlauf*, Cologne, Pahl-Rugenstein, 1985.

Haapala, Pertti, and Marko Tikka, 'Revolution, Civil War and Terror in Finland in 1918', in Robert Gerwarth and John Horne (eds), *War in Peace: Paramilitary Violence in Europe after the Great War*, Oxford, Oxford University Press, 2012, 71–83.

Haase, Ernst, *Hugo Haase: Sein Leben und Wirken*, Berlin, J. J. Ottens, 1929.

Haffner, Sebastian, *Die verratene Revolution: Deutschland 1918/19*, Bern, Munich, and Vienna, Scherz, 1969.

Hagen, Mark von, *War in a European Borderland: Occupations and Occupation Plans in Galicia and Ukraine, 1914–1918*, Seattle, University of Washington Press, 2007.

Hagenlücke, Heinz, *Deutsche Vaterlandspartei: Die nationale Rechte am Ende des Kaiserreichs*, Düsseldorf, Droste, 1997.

Hahlweg, Werner, *Der Diktatfrieden von Brest-Litowsk 1918 und die bolschewistische Weltrevolution*, Münster, Aschendorff, 1960.

Hall, Richard C., *Balkan Breakthrough: The Battle of Dobro Pole 1918*, Bloomington, Ind., Indiana University Press, 2010.

Haller, Oliver, 'German Defeat in World War I, Influenza and Postwar Memory', in Klaus Weinhauer, Anthony McElligott, and Kirsten Heinsohn (eds), *Germany 1916–23: A Revolution in Context*, Bielefeld, Transcript, 2015, 151–80.

Hampe, Karl, *Kriegstagebuch 1914–1919*, ed. Folker Reichert and Eike Wolgast, Munich, Oldenbourg, 2007.

Hardtwig, Wolfgang, *Ordnungen in der Krise: Zur politischen Kulturgeschichte Deutschlands 1900–1933*, Munich, Oldenbourg, 2007.

Harris, J. Paul, *Douglas Haig and the First World War*, Cambridge and New York, Cambridge University Press, 2008.

Hasegawa, Tsuyoshi, 'The February Revolution', in Edward Acton, Vladimir Cherniaev, and William G. Rosenberg (eds), *Critical Companion to the Russian Revolution 1914–1921*, London, Arnold, 1997, 48–61.

Haupt, Georges, *Socialism and the Great War: The Collapse of the Second International*, Oxford, Clarendon Press, 1972.

Haussmann, Conrad, *Schlaglichter: Reichstagsbriefe und Aufzeichnungen*, ed. Ulrich Zeller, Frankfurt am Main, Frankfurter Societäts-Druckerei, 1924.

Hawkins, Nigel, *The Starvation Blockades: Naval Blockades of World War I*, Barnsley, Seaforth Publishing, 2002.

Heimers, Manfred Peter, *Unitarismus und süddeutsches Selbstbewußtsein: Weimarer Koalition und SPD in Baden in der Reichsreformdiskussion 1918–1933*, Düsseldorf, Droste, 1992.

Helbig, Rolf, Wilhelm Langbein, and Lothar Zymara, 'Beiträge zur Lage des weiblichen Proletariats und dessen aktive Einbeziehung in den Kampf der deutschen Arbeiterklasse gegen Imperialismus, Militarismus und Krieg in der dritten Hauptperiode der Geschichte der deutschen Arbeiterbewegung', unpubl. graduate thesis, Leipzig, 1973.

Helmreich, Paul C., *From Paris to Sèvres: The Partition of the Ottoman Empire at the Paris Peace Conference of 1919–1920*, Columbus, Oh., Ohio State University Press, 1974.

Hermens, Ferdinand, *Mehrheitswahlrecht oder Verhältniswahlrecht?*, Berlin, Duncker & Humblot, 1949.

Hervé, Florence, *Geschichte der deutschen Frauenbewegung*, Cologne, Papyrossa, 1995.

Herwig, Holger H., *'Luxury' Fleet: The Imperial German Navy, 1888–1918*, London, Allen & Unwin, 1980.

Herwig, Holger, 'Clio Deceived: Patriotic Self-Censorship in Germany after the Great War', *International Security* 12 (1987), 5–22.

Herwig, Holger, *The First World War: Germany and Austria-Hungary, 1914–1918*, London, Arnold, 1997.

Herz, Rudolf, and Dirk Halfbrodt, *Revolution und Fotografie: München 1918/19*, Berlin, Nishen, 1988, 183–92.

Hiden, John, *The Baltic States and Weimar Ostpolitik*, Cambridge and New York, Cambridge University Press, 1987.

Hiden, John, and Martyn Housden, *Neighbours or Enemies? Germans, the Baltic, and Beyond*, Amsterdam and New York, Rodopi, 2008.

Hildebrand, Klaus, *Das vergangene Reich: Deutsche Außenpolitik von Bismarck bis Hitler 1871–1945*, Stuttgart, Deutsche Verlags-Anstalt, 1995.

Hildermeier, Manfred, *Geschichte der Sowjetunion 1917–1991: Entstehung und Niedergang des ersten sozialistischen Staates*, Munich, C. H. Beck, 1998.

Hillmayr, Heinrich, 'Munich und die Revolution 1918/1919', in Karl Bosl (ed.), *Bayern im Umbruch: Die Revolution von 1918, ihre Voraussetzungen, ihr Verlauf und ihre Folgen*, Munich and Vienna, Oldenbourg, 1969.

Hillmayr, Heinrich, *Roter und Weißer Terror in Bayern nach 1918*, Munich, Nusser, 1974.

Hobsbawm, Eric J., 'Revolution', in Roy Porter and Mikulas Teich (eds), *Revolution in History*, Cambridge, Cambridge University Press, 1986.

Hock, Klaus, *Die Gesetzgebung des Rates der Volksbeauftragten*, Pfaffenweiler, Centaurus-Verlagsgesellschaft, 1987.

Hoffrogge, Ralf, *Richard Müller: Der Mann hinter der Novemberrevolution*, Berlin, Dietz, 2008.

Holquist, Peter, *Making War, Forging Revolution: Russia's Continuum of Crisis*, Cambridge, Mass., Harvard University Press, 2002.

Holquist, Peter, 'Violent Russia, Deadly Marxism? Russia in the Epoch of Violence, 1905–21', *Kritika: Explorations in Russian and Eurasian History* 4 (2003), 627–52.

Holste, Heiko, *Warum Weimar? Wie Deutschlands erste Republik zu ihrem Geburtsort kam*, Vienna, Böhlau, 2018.

Höpp, Gerhard, *Muslime in der Mark: Als Kriegsgefangene und Internierte in Wünsdorf und Zossen, 1914–1924*, Berlin, Das Arabische Buch, 1997.

Hoppu, Tuomas, and Pertti Haapala (eds), *Tampere 1918: A Town in the Civil War*, Tampere, Museum Centre Vapriikki, 2010.

Horak, Stephan M., *The First Treaty of World War I: Ukraine's Treaty with the Central Powers of February 9, 1918*, Boulder, Colo., Columbia University Press, 1988.

Horn, Daniel, *Mutiny on the High Seas: Imperial German Naval Mutinies of World War One*, London, Frewin, 1973.

Hortzschansky, Günter (ed.), *Illustrierte Geschichte der deutschen Novemberrevolution 1918/19*, Berlin (GDR), Dietz, 1978.

Howard, N. P., 'The Social and Political Consequences of the Allied Food Blockade of Germany, 1918–19', *German History* 11 (1993), 161–88.

Hoyningen-Huene, Iris von, *Adel in der Weimarer Republik: Die rechtlich-soziale Situation des reichsdeutschen Adels 1918–1933*, Limburg, C. A. Starke Verlag, 1992.

Huber, Ernst R., *Deutsche Verfassungsgeschichte seit 1789*, vol. 5: *Weltkrieg, Revolution und Reichserneuerung 1914–1919*, Stuttgart, Kohlhammer, 1978.

Huck, Stephan, and Frank Nägler (eds), *Marinestreiks-Meuterei Revolutionäre Erhebung 1917/1918*, Munich, Oldenbourg, 2009.

Hürten, Heinz (ed.), *Zwischen Revolution und Kapp-Putsch: Militär und Innenpolitik, 1918–1920*, Düsseldorf, Droste, 1977.

Isnenghi, Mario, and Giorgio Rochat, *La Grande Guerra 1914–1918*, Bologna, Società ed. il Mulino, 2008.

Jacob, Mathilde, *Rosa Luxemburg: An Intimate Portrait*, London, Lawrence & Wishart, 2000.

James, Harold, 'The Weimar Economy', in Anthony McElligott (ed.), *Weimar Germany*, Oxford, Oxford University Press, 2009, 102–26.

Janz, Oliver, *14: Der Grosse Krieg* (Frankfurt am Main, 2013).

Jefferies, Matthew, *Imperial Culture in Germany, 1871–1918*, Houndmills and New York, Macmillan, 2003.

Jentsch, Harald, *Die KPD und der 'Deutsche Oktober' 1923*, Rostock, Koch, 2005.

Jessen-Klingenberg, Manfred, 'Die Ausrufung der Republik durch Philipp Scheidemann am 9. November 1918', *Geschichte in Wissenschaft und Unterricht* 19 (1968), 649–56.

Jones, Mark, 'Violence and Politics in the German Revolution, 1918–19', Dissertation, European University Institute, 2011.

Jones, Mark, *Founding Weimar: Violence and the German Revolution of 1918–1919*, Cambridge and New York, Cambridge University Press, 2016.

Jones, Nigel H., *Hitler's Heralds: The Story of the Freikorps 1918–1923*, London, Murray, 1987.

Juhnke, Dominik, Judith Prokasky, and Martin Sabrow, *Mythos der Revolution: Karl Liebknecht, das Berliner Schloss und der 9. November 1918*, Munich, Carl Hanser Verlag, 2018.

Käppner, Joachim, *1918: Aufstand für die Freiheit. Die Revolution der Besonnenen*, Munich, Piper, 2017.

Kasekamp, Andres, *A History of the Baltic States*, New York, Palgrave, 2010.

Kaser, M. C., and E. A. Radice (eds), *The Economic History of Eastern Europe, 1919–1975*, vol. 1, Oxford, Clarendon Press, 1985.

Katkov, George, *The Kornilov Affair: Kerensky and the Breakup of the Russian Army*, London and New York, Longman, 1980.

Katz, Friedrich, *The Secret War in Mexico: Europe, the United States, and the Mexican Revolution*, Chicago, University of Chicago Press, 1981.

Kautt, William H., *The Anglo-Irish War, 1916–1921: A People's War*, Westport, Conn., and London, Praeger, 1999.

Kayali, Hasan, 'The Struggle for Independence', in Reşat Kasaba (ed.), *The Cambridge History of Turkey*, vol. 4: *Turkey in the Modern World*, Cambridge and New York, Cambridge University Press, 2008.

Keene, Jennifer D., 'The United States', in John Horne (ed.), *Companion to World War I*, Malden, Mass., Wiley-Blackwell, 2010, 508–23.

Keller, Peter, *'Die Wehrmacht der deutschen Republik ist die Reichswehr': Die deutsche Armee 1918–1921*, Paderborn, Schöningh, 2014.

Kellogg, Michael, *The Russian Roots of Nazism: White Russians and the Making of National Socialism, 1917–1945*, Cambridge and New York, Cambridge University Press, 2005.

Kennedy, David, *Over Here: The First World War and American Society*, Oxford and New York, Oxford University Press, 1980.

Kent, Bruce, *The Spoils of War: The Politics, Economics, and Diplomacy of Reparations 1918–1932*, Oxford, Clarendon Press, 2011.

Kershaw, Ian, *Höllensturz: Europa von 1914–1949*, Munich, Deutsche Verlags-Anstalt, 2017.

Kiesel, Helmuth, *Ernst Jünger: Die Biographie*, Munich, Siedler, 2007.

Kirby, David, *A Concise History of Finland*, Cambridge and New York, Cambridge University Press, 2006.

Kirk, Dudley, *Europe's Population in the Interwar Years*, New York, Gordon & Breach, 1967.

Kitchen, Martin, *The Silent Dictatorship: The Politics of the German High Command under Hindenburg and Ludendorff, 1916–1918*, New York, Croom Helm, 1976.

Kittel, Manfred, 'Scheidemann, Philipp', in *Neue Deutsche Biographie*, vol. 22, Berlin, Duncker & Humblot, 2005, 630f.

Klein, Fritz, 'Between Compiègne and Versailles: The Germans on the Way from a Misunderstood Defeat to an Unwanted Peace', in Manfred F. Boemeke et al. (eds), *The Treaty of Versailles: A Reassessment after 75 Years*, Cambridge and New York, Cambridge University Press, 1998, 203–20.

Klier, Freya, *Dresden 1919: Die Geburt einer neuen Epoche*, Freiburg, Verlag Herder, 2018.

Kluge, Ulrich, 'Militärrevolte und Staatsumsturz: Ausbreitung und Konsolidierung der Räteorganisation im rheinisch-westfälischen Industriegebiet', in Reinhard Rürup (ed.), *Arbeiter- und Soldatenräte im rheinisch-westfälischen Industriegebiet*, Wuppertal, Hammer, 1975, 39–82.

Kluge, Ulrich, *Soldatenräte und Revolution: Studien zur Militärpolitik in Deutschland 1918/19*, Göttingen, Vandenhoeck & Ruprecht, 1975.

Knock, Thomas J., *To End All Wars: Woodrow Wilson and the Quest for a New World Order*, New York, Oxford University Press, 1992.

Koch, Hannsjoachim W., *Der deutsche Bürgerkrieg: Eine Geschichte der deutschen und österreichischen Freikorps 1918–1923*, Berlin, Ullstein, 1978.

Koch-Baumgarten, Sigrid, *Aufstand der Avantgarde: Die Märzaktion der KPD 1921*, Cologne, Campus, 1986.

Koehl, Robert Lewis, 'Colonialism inside Germany: 1886–1918', *The Journal of Modern History* 25 (1953), 255–72.

Koenen, Gerd, *Der Russland-Komplex: Die Deutschen und der Osten, 1900–1945*, Munich, C. H. Beck, 2005.

Kohlrausch, Martin, *Der Monarch im Skandal: Die Logik der Massenmedien und die Transformation der wilhelminischen Monarchie*, Berlin, Akademie-Verlag, 2005.

Kolb, Eberhard, *Die Arbeiterräte in der deutschen Innenpolitik 1918/19*, 2nd edn, Düsseldorf, Ullstein, 1978.

Kolb, Eberhard, '1918/19: Die steckengebliebene Revolution', in Carola Stern und Heinrich A. Winkler (eds), *Wendepunkte deutscher Geschichte 1848–1990*, reprint, Frankfurt am Main, Fischer, 2001, 100–25.

Kolb, Eberhard, *Die Weimarer Republik*, Munich, Oldenbourg, 2002.

König, Wolfgang, *Wilhelm II. und die Moderne: Der Kaiser und die technisch-industrielle Welt*, Paderborn, Schöningh, 2007.

Könnemann, Erwin, and Gerhard Schulze (eds), *Der Kapp-Lüttwitz-Putsch: Dokumente*, Munich, Olzog, 2002.

Kopp, Kristin, 'Gray Zones: On the Inclusion of "Poland" in the Study of German Colonialism', in Michael Perraudin and Jürgen Zimmerer (eds), *German Colonialism and National Identity*, New York and London, Routledge, 2011, 33–42.

Kozuchowski, Adam, *The Afterlife of Austria-Hungary: The Image of the Habsburg Monarchy in Interwar Europe*, Pittsburgh, University of Pittsburgh Press, 2013.

Kramer, Alan, 'Wackes at War: Alsace-Lorraine and the Failure of German National Mobilization, 1914–1918', in John Horne (ed.), *State, Society and Mobilization in Europe during the First World War*, Cambridge, Cambridge University Press, 1997, 110–21.

Kramer, Alan, *Dynamic of Destruction: Culture and Mass Killing in the First World War*, Oxford and New York, Oxford University Press, 2007.

Kramer, Alan, 'Deportationen', in Gerhard Hirschfeld, Gerd Krumeich, and Irina Renz (eds.), *Enzyklopädie Erster Weltkrieg*, Paderborn, Schöningh, 2009, 434–5.

Kramer, Alan, 'Blockade and Economic Warfare', in Jay Winter (ed.), *Cambridge History of the First World War*, vol. 2, Cambridge, Cambridge University Press, 2014, 460–89.

Krause, Andreas, *Scapa Flow: Die Selbstversenkung der Wilhelminischen Flotte*, Berlin, Ullstein, 1999.

Kritzer, Peter, *Die bayerische Sozialdemokratie und die bayerische Politik in den Jahren 1918–1923*, Munich, Stadtarchiv, 1969.

Kroll, Frank-Lothar, *Geburt der Moderne: Politik, Gesellschaft und Kultur vor dem Ersten Weltkrieg*, Berlin, Be.bra-Verlag, 2013.

Krüger, Friederike, and Michael Salewski, 'Die Verantwortung der militärischen Führung deutscher Streitkräfte in den Jahren 1918 und 1945', in Jörg Duppler and Gerhard Paul (eds), *Kriegsende 1918: Ereignis, Wirkung, Nachwirkung*, Munich, Oldenbourg, 1999, 377–98.

Krüger, Fritz Konrad, *Government and Politics of the German Empire*, London, World Book Company, 1915.

Krumeich, Gerd, 'Die Dolchstoß-Legende', in Étienne François and Hagen Schulze (eds), *Deutsche Erinnerungsorte*, vol. 1, Munich, C. H. Beck, 2001, 585–99.

Krumeich, Gerd (ed.), *Versailles 1919: Ziele, Wirkung, Wahrnehmung*, Essen, Klartext, 2001.

Kucera, Jaroslav, *Minderheit im Nationalstaat: Die Sprachenfrage in den tschechisch-deutschen Beziehungen 1918–1938*, Munich, Oldenbourg, 1999.

Lademacher, Horst (ed.), *Die Zimmerwalder Bewegung: Protokolle und Korrespondenz*, 2 vols, Paris and The Hague, Mouton, 1967.

Lamar, Cecil, *Wilhelm II.*, vol. 2: *Emperor and Exile, 1900–1941*, Chapel Hill and London, University of North Carolina Press, 1996.

Lambert, Nicholas A., *Planning Armageddon: British Economic Warfare and the First World War*, Cambridge, Mass., Harvard University Press, 2012.

Lange, Dietmar, *Massenstreik und Schießbefehl: Generalstreik und Märzkämpfe in Berlin 1919*, Berlin, Edition Assemblage, 2012.

Large, David Clay, *Where Ghosts Walked: Munich's Road to the Third Reich*, New York, Norton, 1997.

Laschitza, Annelies, *Im Lebensrausch, trotz alledem. Rosa Luxemburg: Eine Biographie*, Berlin, Aufbau, 1996.

Laschitza, Annelies, *Die Liebknechts: Karl und Sophie, Politik und Familie*, Berlin, Aufbau, 2009.

Laschitza, Annelies, and Elke Keller, *Karl Liebknecht: Eine Biographie in Dokumenten*, Berlin (GDR), Dietz, 1982.

Lavery, Jason, 'Finland 1917–19: Three Conflicts, One Country', *Scandinavian Review* 94 (2006), 6–14.

Lehnert, Detlef, *Sozialdemokratie und Novemberrevolution: Die Neuordnungsdebatte 1918/19 in der politischen Publizistik von SPD und USPD*, Frankfurt am Main, Campus, 1983.

Lehnert, Detlef (ed.), *Revolution 1918/19 in Norddeutschland*, Berlin, Metropol-Verlag, 2018.

Leidinger, Hannes, 'Der Kieler Aufstand und die deutsche Revolution', in Verena Moritz and Hannes Leidinger (eds), *Die Nacht des Kirpitschnikow: Eine andere Geschichte des Ersten Weltkriegs*, Vienna, Deuticke, 2006.

Leidinger, Hannes, and Verena Moritz, *Gefangenschaft, Revolution: Heimkehr. Die Bedeutung der Kriegsgefangenenproblematik für die Geschichte des Kommunismus in Mittel- und Osteuropa 1917–1920*, Cologne and Vienna, Böhlau, 2003.

Leonhard, Jörn, *Die Büchse der Pandora: Geschichte des Ersten Weltkriegs*, Munich, C. H. Beck, 2014.

Lerner, Paul Frederick, *Hysterical Men: War, Psychiatry, and the Politics of Trauma in Germany, 1890–1930*, Ithaca, NY, Cornell University Press, 2003.

Levene, Mark, *The Crisis of Genocide*, vol. 1: *Devastation: The European Rimlands 1912–1938*, Oxford, Oxford University Press, 2016.

Liesemer, Dirk, *Aufstand der Matrosen: Tagebuch einer Revolution*, Hamburg, Mare Verlag, 2018.

Lieven, Dominic, *Nicholas II. Emperor of All the Russias*, London, Murray, 1994.

Lincoln, W. Bruce, *Passage through Armageddon: The Russians in War and Revolution*, New York, Simon & Schuster, 1986.

Liulevicius, Vejas G., *War Land on the Eastern Front: Culture, National Identity and German Occupation in World War I*, Cambridge and New York, Cambridge University Press, 2000.

Liulevicius, Vejas G., 'Der Osten als apokalyptischer Raum: Deutsche Fronterfahrungen im und nach dem Ersten Weltkrieg', in Gregor Thum (ed.), *Traumland Osten: Deutsche Bilder vom östlichen Europa im 20. Jahrhundert*, Göttingen, Vandenhoeck & Ruprecht, 2006, 47–65.

Lohr, Eric, *Nationalizing the Russian Empire: The Campaign against Enemy Aliens during World War I*, Cambridge, Mass., Harvard University Press, 2003.

Longerich, Peter, *Deutschland 1918–1933: Die Weimarer Republik. Handbuch zur Geschichte*, Hanover, Fackelträger-Verlag, 1995.

Longerich, Peter, *Hitler: Biographie*, Munich, Siedler, 2015.

Lösche, Peter, *Der Bolschewismus im Urteil der deutschen Sozialdemokratie 1903–1920*, Berlin, Colloquium-Verlag, 1967.

Lowry, Bullit, *Armistice 1918*, Kent, Oh., and London, Kent State University Press, 1996.

Luban, Ottokar, 'Die Massenstreiks für Frieden und Demokratie im Ersten Weltkrieg', in Chaja Boebel and Lothar Wentzel (eds), *Streiken gegen den Krieg: Die Bedeutung der Massenstreiks in der Metallindustrie vom Januar 1918*, Hamburg, VSA-Verlag, 2008, 11–27.

Lüdke, Tilman, *Jihad made in Germany: Ottoman and German Propaganda and Intelligence Operations in the First World War*, Münster, Lit, 2005, 117–25.

Luebke, Frederick C., *Bonds of Loyalty: German Americans and World War I*, DeKalb, Ill., Northern Illinois University Press, 1974.

Luthardt, Wolfgang, *Sozialdemokratische Verfassungstheorie in der Weimarer Republik*, Opladen, Westdeutscher Verlag, 1986.

Luther, Karl-Heinz, 'Die nachrevolutionären Machtkämpfe in Berlin, November 1918 bis März 1919', *Jahrbuch für Geschichte Mittel- und Ostdeutschlands* 8 (1959), 187–222.

Lutz, Raphael, *Imperiale Gewalt und mobilisierte Nation: Europa 1914–1945*, Munich, C. H. Beck, 2011.

McCarthy, Justin, *Death and Exile: The Ethnic Cleansing of Ottoman Muslims 1821–1922*, Princeton, Darwin Press, 2004.

McElligott, Anthony (ed.), *Weimar Germany*, Oxford and New York, Oxford University Press, 2011.

McElligott, Anthony, *Rethinking the Weimar Republic: Authority and Authoritarianism, 1916–1936*, London, Bloomsbury, 2014.

McElligott, Anthony, and Kirsten Heinsohn (eds), *Germany 1916–23: A Revolution in Context*, Bielefeld, transcript Verlag, 2015.

Machtan, Lothar, *Die Abdankung: Wie Deutschlands gekrönte Häupter aus der Geschichte fielen*, Berlin, Propyläen, 2008.

Machtan, Lothar, *Prinz Max von Baden: Der letzte Kanzler des Kaisers*, Berlin, Suhrkamp, 2013.

McMeekin, Sean, *History's Greatest Heist: The Looting of Russia by the Bolsheviks*, London and New Haven, Yale University Press, 2009.

MacMillan, Margaret, *Peacemakers: Six Months That Changed the World*, London, John Murray, 2001.

Maderthaner, Wolfgang, 'Utopian Perspectives and Political Restraint: The Austrian Revolution in the Context of Central European Conflicts', in Günter Bischof, Fritz Plasser, and Peter Berger (eds), *From Empire to Republic: Post World War I Austria*, Innsbruck, Innsbruck University Press, 2010, 52–66.

Malinowski, Stephan, *Vom König zum Führer: Sozialer Niedergang und politische Radikalisierung im deutschen Adel zwischen Kaiserreich und NS-Staat*, Berlin, Akademie, 2003.

Mann, Michael, *The Dark Side of Democracy: Explaining Ethnic Cleansing*, Cambridge, Cambridge University Press, 2005.

Mark, Rudolf A., *Krieg an fernen Fronten: Die Deutschen in Zentralasien und am Hindukusch 1914–1924*, Paderborn, Schöningh, 2013.

Marks, Sally, 'The Myths of Reparations', *Central European History* 11 (1978), 231–9.

Marks, Sally, 'Mistakes and Myths: The Allies, Germany and the Versailles Treaty, 1918–1921', *Journal of Modern History* 85 (2013), 632–59.

Materna, Ingo, '9. November 1918—der erste Tag der Republik: Eine Chronik', *Berlinische Monatsschrift* 4 (2000), 139–46.

Matthias, Erich, *Die deutsche Sozialdemokratie und der Osten*, Tübingen, Arbeitsgemeinschaft für Osteuropaforschung, 1954.

Matthias, Erich, *Zwischen Räten und Geheimräten: Die deutsche Revolutionsregierung 1918/19*, Düsseldorf, Droste, 1970.

Maurer, Trude, *Ostjuden in Deutschland, 1918–1933*, Hamburg, Christians, 1990.

Mawdsley, Evan, *The Russian Civil War*, Edinburgh, Birlinn, 2000.

May, Arthur, *The Passing of the Hapsburg Monarchy*, vol. 2, Philadelphia, University of Pennsylvania Press, 1966.

Mazower, Mark, *Dark Continent: Europe's Twentieth Century*, New York, Knopf, 1999.

Mazower, Mark, 'Two Cheers for Versailles', *History Today* 49 (1999), 8–14.

Mazower, Mark, *Hitler's Empire: How the Nazis Ruled Europe*, New York, Penguin Press, 2008.

Melzer, Liane, *Die Gesetzgebung des Rats der Volksbeauftragten (1918/19): Entstehungsgeschichte und Weitergeltung*, Frankfurt am Main, Peter Lang, 1988.

Menges, Franz, *Reichsreform und Finanzpolitik: Die Aushöhlung der Eigenstaatlichkeit Bayerns auf finanzpolitischem Wege in der Zeit der Weimarer Republik*, Berlin, Duncker & Humblot, 1971.

Méouchy, Nadine, and Peter Sluglett (eds), *The British and French Mandates in Comparative Perspective*, Leiden, Brill, 2004.

Merridale, Catherine, *Lenin on the Train*, London, Allen Lane, 2016.

Michels, Eckard, '*Der Held von Deutsch-Ostafrika': Paul von Lettow-Vorbeck. Ein preußischer Kolonialoffizier*, Paderborn, Schöningh, 2008.

Michels, Eckard, '"Die Spanische Grippe" 1918/19: Verlauf, Folgen und Deutungen in Deutschland im Kontext des Ersten Weltkriegs', *Vierteljahrshefte für Zeitgeschichte* 58 (2010), 1–33.

Middlebrook, Martin, *The Kaiser's Battle: The First Day of the German Spring Offensive*, London, Allen Lane, 1978.

Mierau, Fritz, *Russen in Berlin, 1918–1933*, Berlin, Quadriga, 1988.

Mikoletzky, Lorenz, 'Saint-Germain und Karl Renner: Eine Republik wird diktiert', in Helmut Konrad and Wolfgang Maderthaner (eds), *Das Werden der Ersten Republik...der Rest ist Österreich*, vol. 1, Vienna, Gerold, 2008, 179–86.

Miller, Susanne, 'Das Ringen um "die einzige großdeutsche Republik": Die Sozialdemokratie in Österreich und im Deutschen Reich zur Anschlußfrage 1918/19', *Archiv für Sozialgeschichte* 11 (1971), 1–68.

Miller, Susanne, *Burgfrieden und Klassenkampf: Die deutsche Sozialdemokratie im Ersten Weltkrieg*, Düsseldorf, Droste, 1974.

Miller, Susanne, *Die Bürde der Macht: Die deutsche Sozialdemokratie 1918–1920*, Düsseldorf, Droste, 1978.

Miller, Susanne, and Gerhard A. Ritter, 'Die November-Revolution im Herbst 1918 im Erleben und Urteil der Zeitgenossen', *Aus Politik und Zeitgeschichte* 18 (1968), 3–40.

Milow, Caroline, *Die ukrainische Frage 1917–1923 im Spannungsfeld der europäischen Diplomatie*, Wiesbaden, Harrassowitz, 2002.

Mitchell, Allan, *Revolution in Bayern 1918/1919: Die Eisner-Regierung und die Räterepublik*, Munich, C. H. Beck, 1967.

Mitchell, David J., *1919: Red Mirage*, London, Cape, 1970.

Mitrović, Andrej, *Serbia's Great War, 1914–1918*, London, Hurst, 2007.

Mócsy, István, *The Effects of World War I: The Uprooted: Hungarian Refugees and their Impact on Hungary's Domestic Politics, 1918–1921*, New York, Columbia University Press, 1983.

Mommsen, Hans, 'Hitler und der 9. November 1923', in Johannes Willms (ed.), *Der 9. November: Fünf Essays zur deutschen Geschichte*, Munich, C. H. Beck, 1995, 33–48.

Montgomery, A. E., 'The Making of the Treaty of Sevres of 10 August 1920', *The Historical Journal* 15 (1972), 775–87.

Morgan, David W., *The Socialist Left and the German Revolution: A History of the German Independent Social Democratic Party, 1917–1922*, Ithaca, NY, Cornell University Press, 1976.

Morsey, Rudolf, *Die Deutsche Zentrumspartei 1917–1923*, Düsseldorf, Droste, 1966.

Mosley, Leonard, *Duel for Kilimanjaro: The East African Campaign 1914–1918*, London, Weidenfeld and Nicolson, 1963.

Moyd, Michelle ' "We don't want to die for nothing": *askari* at War in German East Africa', in Santanu Das (ed.), *Race, Empire and First World War Writing*, Cambridge, Cambridge University Press, 2011, 90–107.

Moyd, Michelle, *Violent Intermediaries: African Soldiers, Conquest, and Everyday Colonialism in German East Africa*, Athens, Oh., Ohio University Press, 2014.

Mühlhausen, Walter, 'Die Zimmerwalder Bewegung', in Gerhard Hirschfeldt, Gerd Krumeich, and Irina Renz (eds), *Enzyklopädie Erster Weltkrieg*, Paderborn, Schöningh, 2004.

Mühlhausen, Walther, *Friedrich Ebert 1871–1925: Reichspräsident in der Weimarer Republik*, Bonn, Dietz, 2006.

Mühlhausen, Walther, *'Das große Ganze im Auge behalten': Philipp Scheidemann als Oberbürgermeister von Kassel (1920–1925)*, Marburg, Historische Kommission für Hessen, 2011.

Müller, Georg Alexander von, *The Kaiser and his Court: The Diaries, Note Books, and Letters of Admiral Alexander von Müller*, London, Macdonald, 1961.

Müller, Sven O., and Cornelius Torp (eds), *Das Deutsche Kaiserreich in der Kontroverse*, Göttingen, Vandenhoeck & Ruprecht, 2009.

Mulligan, William, *The Creation of the Modern German Army: General Walther Reinhardt and the Weimar Republic, 1914–1930*, New York, Berghahn, 2005.

Murphy, Mahon, *Colonial Captivity during the First World War: Internment and the Fall of the German Empire, 1914–1919*, Cambridge, Cambridge University Press, 2017.

Myers, Duane P., *Germany and the Question of Austrian Anschluss 1918–1922*, New Haven, Yale University Press, 1968.

Nachtigal, Reinhard, *Russland und seine österreichisch-ungarischen Kriegsgefangenen (1914–1918)*, Remshalden, Greiner, 2003.

Nebelin, Manfred, *Ludendorff: Diktator im Ersten Weltkrieg*, Munich, Siedler, 2010.

Neiberg, Michael S., *The Second Battle of the Marne*, Bloomington, Ind., Indiana University Press, 2008.

Nettl, John Peter, *Rosa Luxemburg*, Oxford, Oxford University Press, 1968.

Neutatz, Dietmar, *Träume und Alpträume: Eine Geschichte Russlands im 20. Jahrhundert*, Munich, C. H. Beck, 2013.

Niemann, Alfred, *Kaiser und Revolution: Die entscheidenden Ereignisse im Großen Hauptquartier im Herbst 1918*, Berlin, Verlag für Kulturpolitik, 1928.

Niess, Wolfgang, *Die Revolution von 1918/19: Der wahre Beginn unserer Demokratie*, Berlin et al., Europa Verlag, 2017.

Nivet, Philippe, *Les réfugiés français de la Grande Guerre, 1914–1920: les 'boches du nord'*, Paris, Institut de Stratégie Comparée, 2004.

Nojowski, Walter, *Victor Klemperer (1881–1960): Romanist–Chronist der Vorhölle*, Berlin, Hentrich und Hentrich, 2004.

Nowak, Karl Friedrich (ed.), *Die Aufzeichnungen des Generalmajors Max Hoffmann*, Berlin, Verlag für Kulturpolitik, 1929.

Oertzen, Peter von, 'Die großen Streiks der Ruhrbergarbeiterschaft im Frühjahr 1919', *Vierteljahrshefte für Zeitgeschichte* 6 (1958), 231–62.

Oertzen, Peter von, *Betriebsräte in der Novemberrevolution: Eine politikwissenschaftliche Untersuchung über Ideengehalt und Struktur der betrieblichen und wirtschaftlichen Arbeiterräte in der deutschen Revolution 1918/1919*, 2nd edn, Berlin, Dietz, 1976.

Offer, Avner, *The First World War: An Agrarian Interpretation*, Oxford, Oxford University Press, 1991.

Ondrovcik, John, '"All the Devils Are Loose": The Radical Revolution in the Saxon Vogtland, 1918–1920' (unpublished Ph.D. thesis, Harvard, 2008).

Osborne, Eric W., *Britain's Economic Blockade of Germany, 1914–1919*, London and New York, Cass, 2004.

Pearson, Raymond, 'Hungary: A State Truncated, a Nation Dismembered', in Seamus Dunn and T. G. Fraser, *Europe and Ethnicity: World War I and Contemporary Ethnic Conflict*, London and New York, Routledge, 1996, 88–109.

Pedersen, Susan, 'The Meaning of the Mandates System: An Argument', *Geschichte und Gesellschaft* 32 (2006), 1–23.

Pedersen, Susan, *The Guardians: The League of Nations and the Crisis of Empire*, Oxford and New York, Oxford University Press, 2015.

Pedroncini, Guy, *Les Mutineries de 1917*, 3rd edn, Paris, 1996.

Petrov, Ivan, *Voynata v Makedonia (1915–1918)*, Sofia, SEMARŠ, 2008.

Petzold, Joachim, *Der 9. November 1918 in Berlin: Berliner Arbeiterveteranen berichten über die Vorbereitung der Novemberrevolution und ihren Ausbruch am 9. November 1918 in Berlin*, Berlin (GDR), Bezirksleitung der SED Groß-Berlin, 1958.

Phillips, Howard, and David Killingray (eds), *The Spanish Influenza Pandemic of 1918–19: New Perspectives*, London and New York, Routledge, 2003.

Pipes, Richard, *The Russian Revolution 1899–1919*, London, Harvill, 1997.

Pistohlkors, Gert von (ed.), *Deutsche Geschichte im Osten Europas: Baltische Länder*, Berlin, Siedler, 1994.

Plakans, Andrejs, *The Latvians*, Stanford, Calif., Hoover Institution Press, 1995.

Plakans, Andrejs, *A Concise History of the Baltic States*, Cambridge and New York, Cambridge University Press, 2011.

Plöckinger, Othmar, *Unter Soldaten und Agitatoren: Hitlers prägende Jahre im deutschen Militär 1918–1920*, Paderborn, Schöningh, 2013.

Plowman, Matthew, 'Irish Republicans and the Indo-German Conspiracy of World War I', *New Hibernia Review* 7 (2003), 81–105.

Poljakov, Jurij Aleksandrovič, and Valentina Borisovna Žiromskaja (eds), *Naselenie Rossii v XX veke*, vol. 1: *1900–1939*, Moscow, ROSSPĖN, 2000.

Portner, Ernst, *Die Verfassungspolitik der Liberalen 1919: Ein Beitrag zur Deutung der Weimarer Reichsverfassung*, Bonn, Röhrscheid, 1973.

Pourchier-Plasseraud, Suzanne, 'Riga 1905–2005: A City with Conflicting Identities', *Nordost-Archiv* 15 (2006), 175–94.

Pranckh, Hans von, *Der Prozeß gegen den Grafen Anton Arco-Valley, der den bayerischen Ministerpräsidenten Kurt Eisner erschossen hat*, Munich, Lehmann, 1920.

Priestland, David, *The Red Flag: A History of Communism*, New York, Grove, 2009.

Prusin, Alexander Victor, *The Lands Between: Conflict in the East European Borderlands, 1870–1992*, Oxford, Oxford University Press, 2010.

Purseigle, Pierre, '"A Wave on to our Shores": The Exile and Resettlement of Refugees from the Western Front, 1914–1918', *Contemporary European History* 16 (2007), 427–44.

Pyta, Wolfram, *Hindenburg: Herrschaft zwischen Hohenzollern und Hitler*, Munich, Siedler, 2007.

Pyta, Wolfram, 'Die Kunst des rechtzeitigen Thronverzichts: Neue Einsichten zur Überlebenschance der parlamentarischen Monarchie in Deutschland im Herbst 1918', in Bernd Sösemann and Patrick Merziger, *Geschichte, Öffentlichkeit, Kommunikation: Festschrift für Bernd Sösemann zum 65. Geburtstag*, Stuttgart, Steiner, 2010.

Rabinowitch, Alexander, *The Bolsheviks in Power: The First Year of Soviet Rule in Petrograd*, Bloomington, Ind., Indiana University Press, 2007.

Rachaminow, Alan, *POWs and the Great War: Captivity on the Eastern Front*, Oxford and New York, Berg, 2002.

Rackwitz, Martin, *Kiel 1918: Revolution. Aufbruch zu Demokratie und Republik*, Kiel, Wachholtz, 2018.

Raeff, Marc, *Russia Abroad: A Cultural History of the Russian Emigration, 1919–1939*, Oxford and New York, Oxford University Press, 1990.

Raleigh, Donald J., *Experiencing Russia's Civil War: Politics, Society and Revolutionary Culture in Saratov, 1917–1922*, Princeton, Princeton University Press, 2002.

Raleigh, Donald J., 'The Russian Civil War 1917–1922', in Ronald Grigor Suny (ed.), *The Cambridge History of Russia*, vol. 3, Cambridge, Cambridge University Press, 2006, 140–67.

Rappaport, Helen, *Conspirator: Lenin in Exile*, New York, Basic Books, 2010.

Rauch, Georg von, *The Baltic States: The Years of Independence: Estonia, Latvia, Lithuania, 1917–1940*, Berkeley, Calif., University of California Press, 1974.

Rauscher, Walter, 'Die Republikgründungen 1918 und 1945', in Klaus Koch, Walter Rauscher, Arnold Suppan, and Elisabeth Vyslonzil (eds), *Außenpolitische Dokumente der Republik Österreich 1918–1938, Sonderband, Von Saint-Germain zum Belvedere: Österreich und Europa 1919–1955*, Vienna and Munich, Verlag für Geschichte und Politik, 2007, 9–24.

Raymond, Boris, and David R. Jones, *The Russian Diaspora 1917–1941*, Lanham, Md, Scarecrow Press, 2000.

Read, Anthony, *The World on Fire: 1919 and the Battle with Bolshevism*, London, Pimlico, 2009.

Read, Christopher, *From Tsar to Soviets: The Russian People and their Revolution, 1917–1921*, Oxford and New York, Oxford University Press, 1996.

Read, Christopher, *Lenin: A Revolutionary Life*, London and New York, Routledge, 2005.

Reisinger, Silvio, 'Die Revolution von 1918/19 in Leipzig', in Ulla Plener (ed.), *Die Novemberrevolution 1918/19 in Deutschland: Für bürgerliche und sozialistische Demokratie. Allgemeine, regionale und biographische Aspekte. Beiträge zum 90. Jahrestag der Revolution*, Berlin, Dietz, 2009, 163–80.

Reulecke, Jürgen, *'Ich möchte einer werden so wie die…': Männerbünde im 20. Jahrhundert*, Frankfurt am Main, Campus, 2001.

Reuling, Ulrich, 'Reichsreform und Landesgeschichte: Thüringen und Hessen in der Länderneugliederungsdiskussion der Weimarer Republik', in Michael Gockel (ed.), *Aspekte thüringisch-hessischer Geschichte*, Marburg, Hessisches Landesamt für Geschichtliche Landeskunde, 1992, 257–308.

Reynolds, David, *The Long Shadow: The Great War and the Twentieth Century*, London, Simon & Schuster, 2013.

Reynolds, Michael A., 'Ottoman–Russian Struggle for Eastern Anatolia and the Caucasus, 1908–1918: Identity, Ideology and the Geopolitics of World Order', Thesis, Princeton, 2003.

Rhode, Gotthold, 'Das Deutschtum in Posen und Pommerellen in der Zeit der Weimarer Republik', in Senatskommission für das Studium des Deutschtums im Osten an der Rheinischen Friedrich-Wilhelms-Universität Bonn (ed.), *Studien zum Deutschtum im Osten*, Cologne and Graz, Böhlau, 1966, 88–132.

Riasanovsky, Nicholas, and Mark Steinberg, *A History of Russia*, New York, Oxford University Press, 2005.

Richter, Ludwig, 'Notverordnungsrecht', in Eberhard Kolb (ed.), *Friedrich Ebert als Reichspräsident: Amtsführung und Amtsverständnis*, Munich, Oldenbourg, 1997, 250–7.

Richter, Ludwig, 'Reichspräsident und Ausnahmegewalt: Die Genese des Art. 48 in den Beratungen der Weimarer Nationalversammlung', *Der Staat* 37 (1998), 221–47.

Richter, Ludwig, 'Die Vorgeschichte des Art. 48 der Weimarer Reichsverfassung', *Der Staat* 37 (1998), 1–26.

Ritter, Gerhard A. (ed.), *Geschichte der Arbeiter und Arbeiterbewegung in Deutschland seit dem Ende des 18. Jahrhunderts*, vol. 6, Berlin and Bonn, Dietz, 1985.

Rogger, Hans, *Russia in the Age of Modernisation and Revolution 1881–1917*, London, Longman, 1997.

Röhl, John C. G., *Wilhelm II.: Der Weg in den Abgrund, 1900–1941*, Munich, C. H. Beck, 2008.

Rose, Detlev, *Die Thule-Gesellschaft: Legende—Mythos—Wirklichkeit*, 3rd edn, Tübingen, Grabert, 2017.

Rosenberg, Arthur, *Entstehung und Geschichte der Weimarer Republik*, Frankfurt am Main, Europäische Verlagsanstalt, 1955.

Rosenberg, William G., *The Liberals in the Russian Revolution: The Constitutional Democratic Party, 1917–1921*, Princeton, Princeton University Press, 1974.

Roshwald, Aviel, *Ethnic Nationalism and the Fall of Empires: Central Europe, Russia and the Middle East, 1914–1923*, London, Routledge, 2001.

Rossfeld, Roman, Thomas Buomberger, and Patrick Kury (eds), *14/18: Die Schweiz und der Große Krieg*, Baden, Hier und Jetzt, 2014.

Rothenberg, Gunther, *The Army of Francis Joseph*, West Lafayette, Ind., Purdue University Press, 1976.

Rubenstein, Joshua, *Leon Trotsky: A Revolutionary's Life*, New Haven and London, Yale University Press, 2011.

Rudin, Harry R., *Armistice 1918*, New Haven, Yale University Press, 1944.

Rüger, Jan, *Helgoland: Deutschland, England und ein Felsen in der Nordsee*, Berlin, Propyläen, 2017.

Rürup, Reinhard, *Probleme der Revolution in Deutschland 1918/19*, Wiesbaden, Steiner, 1968.

Rürup, Reinhard, 'Problems of the German Revolution 1918–19', *Journal of Contemporary History* 3 (1968), 109–35.

Rürup, Reinhard (ed.), *Arbeiter- und Soldatenräte im rheinisch-westfälischen Industriegebiet: Studien zur Geschichte der Revolution 1918/19*, Wuppertal, Hammer, 1975.

Rust, Christian, 'Self-Determination at the Beginning of 1918 and the German Reaction', *Lithuanian Historical Studies* 13 (2008), 43–6.

Sabrow, Martin, *Die verdrängte Verschwörung: Der Rathenau-Mord und die deutsche Gegenrevolution*, Frankfurt am Main, Fischer, 1999.

Sammartino, Annemarie H., *The Impossible Border: Germany and the East, 1914–1922*, Ithaca, NY, Cornell University Press, 2010.

Sanborn, Joshua A., *Drafting the Russian Nation: Military Conscription, Total War, and Mass Politics, 1905–1925*, DeKalb, Northern Illinois University Press, 2003.

Sanborn, Joshua A., 'Unsettling the Empire: Violent Migrations and Social Disaster in Russia during World War I', *The Journal of Modern History* 77 (2005), 290–324.

Sanborn, Joshua, *Imperial Apocalypse: The Great War and the Destruction of the Russian Empire*, Oxford and New York, Oxford University Press, 2014.

Sauer, Bernhard, 'Vom "Mythos eines ewigen Soldatentums": Der Feldzug deutscher Freikorps im Baltikum im Jahre 1919', *Zeitschrift für Geschichtswissenschaft* 43 (1995), 869–902.

Sauer, Bernhard, 'Freikorps und Antisemitismus', *Zeitschrift für Geschichtswissenschaft* 56 (2008), 5–29.

Sauer, Wolfgang, 'Das Scheitern der parlamentarischen Monarchie', in Eberhard Kolb (ed.), *Vom Kaiserreich zur Weimarer Republik*, Cologne, Kiepenheuer und Witsch, 1972.

Schade, Franz, *Kurt Eisner und die bayerische Sozialdemokratie*, Hanover, Verlag für Literatur und Zeitgeschehen, 1961.

Schanbacher, Eberhard, *Parlamentarische Wahlen und Wahlsystem in der Weimarer Republik*, Düsseldorf, Droste, 1982.

Schieder, Wolfgang, 'Die Umbrüche von 1918, 1933, 1945 und 1989 als Wendepunkte deutscher Geschichte', in Dietrich Papenfuß and Wolfgang Schieder (eds), *Deutsche Umbrüche im 20. Jahrhundert*, Cologne, Weimar, and Vienna, Böhlau, 2000, 3–18.

Schivelbusch, Wolfgang, *Die Kultur der Niederlage: Der amerikanische Süden 1865, Frankreich 1871, Deutschland 1918*, Berlin, Fest, 2001.

Schlögel, Karl (ed.), *Chronik russischen Lebens in Deutschland, 1918 bis 1941*, Berlin, De Gruyter, 1999.

Schmidt, Ernst-Heinrich, *Heimatheer und Revolution: Die militärischen Gewalten im Heimatgebiet zwischen Oktoberreform und Novemberrevolution*, Stuttgart, Deutsche Verlags-Anstalt, 1981.

Schöler, Uli, and Thilo Scholle (eds), *Weltkrieg. Spaltung. Revolution: Sozialdemokratie 1916–1922*, Bonn, Dietz, 2018.

Schröder, Joachim, *Die U-Boote des Kaisers: Die Geschichte des deutschen U-Boot-Krieges gegen Großbritannien im Ersten Weltkrieg*, Bonn, Bernard und Graefe, 2003.

Schulman, Jason (ed.), *Rosa Luxemburg: Her Life and Legacy*, New York, Palgrave Macmillan, 2013.

Schulz, Gerhard, *Zwischen Demokratie und Diktatur: Verfassungspolitik und Reichsreform in der Weimarer Republik*, vol. 1: *Die Periode der Konsolidierung und der Revision des Bismarckschen Reichsaufbaus 1919–1930*, Berlin, de Gruyter, 1987.

Schulze, Hagen, *Freikorps und Republik, 1918–1920*, Boppard am Rhein, Boldt, 1969.

Schwabe, Klaus, *Deutsche Revolution und Wilson-Frieden: Die amerikanische und deutsche Friedensstrategie zwischen Ideologie und Machtpolitik 1918/19*, Düsseldorf, Droste, 1971.

Schwarz, Hans Peter, *Adenauer: Der Aufstieg 1876–1952*, Stuttgart, Deutsche Verlags-Anstalt, 1986.

Schwarzschild, Leopold, *Von Krieg zu Krieg*, Amsterdam, Querido-Verlag, 1947.

Sedlmaier, Alexander, *Deutschlandbilder und Deutschlandpolitik: Studien zur Wilson-Administration (1913–1921)*, Stuttgart, Steiner, 2003.

Seipp, Adam R., *The Ordeal of Peace: Demobilization and the Urban Experience in Britain and Germany, 1917–1921*, Farnham, Ashgate, 2009.

Service, Robert, *Lenin: A Biography*, London, Macmillan, 2000.

Service, Robert, *Comrades! World History of Communism*, Cambridge, Mass., Harvard University Press, 2007.

Service, Robert, *Trotsky: A Biography*, Cambridge, Mass., Belknap Press of Harvard University Press, 2009.

Seton-Watson, Christopher, *Italy from Liberalism to Fascism*, London, Methuen, 1967.

Sharp, Alan, *The Versailles Settlement: Peacemaking after the First World War, 1919–1923*, 2nd edn, London, Palgrave Macmillan, 2008.

Sharp, Alan, *Consequences of Peace. The Versailles Settlement: Aftermath and Legacy 1919–2010*, London, Haus, 2010.

Sharp, Alan, 'The Paris Peace Conference and its Consequences', in <https://encyclopedia.1914-1918-online.net/article/the_paris_peace_conference_and_its_consequences>.

Sharp, Alan, 'The New Diplomacy and the New Europe', in Nicholas Doumanis (ed.), *The Oxford Handbook of Europe 1914–1945*, Oxford and New York, Oxford University Press, 2016, 119–37.

Sheehan, James, *Where Have All the Soldiers Gone? The Transformation of Modern Europe*, Boston et al., Houghton Mifflin, 2008.

Shephard, Ben, *A War of Nerves: Soldiers and Psychiatrists, 1914–1994*, London, Pimlico, 2002.

Siebrecht, Claudia, *The Aesthetics of Loss: German Women's Art of the First World War*, Oxford and New York, Oxford University Press, 2013.

Siegfried, Detlef, *Das radikale Milieu: Kieler Novemberrevolution, Sozialwissenschaft und Linksradikalismus 1917–1922*, Wiesbaden, Deutscher Universitäts-Verlag, 2004.

Smith, Douglas, *Former People: The Final Days of the Russian Aristocracy*, New York, Farrar, Straus and Giroux, 2012.

Smith, Jeffrey R., *A People's War: Germany's Political Revolution, 1913–1918*, Lanham, Md, University Press of America, 2007.

Smith, Leonard V., 'Les États-Unis et l'échec d'une seconde mobilisation', in Stéphane Audoin-Rouzeau and Christophe Prochasson (eds), *Sortir de la grande guerre: le monde et l'après-1918*, Paris, Éditions Tallandier, 2008, 69–91.

Smith, Leonard V., 'The Wilsonian Challenge to International Law', *The Journal of the History of International Law* 13 (2011), 179–208.

Smith, Leonard V., 'Empires at the Paris Peace Conference', in Robert Gerwarth and Erez Manela (eds), *Empires at War, 1911–1923*, Oxford, Oxford University Press, 2014, 254–76.

Smith, Leonard V, *Sovereignty at the Paris Peace Conference of 1919*, Oxford, Oxford University Press, 2018.

Smith, Leonard V., Stéphane Audoin-Rouzeau, and Annette Becker, *France and the Great War*, Cambridge, Cambridge University Press, 2003.

Smith, Stephen, *The Russian Revolution: A Very Short Introduction*, Oxford and New York, Oxford University Press, 2002.

Snyder, Timothy, *The Reconstruction of Nations: Poland, Ukraine, Lithuania, Belarus, 1569–1999*, New Haven and London, Yale University Press, 2004.

Sondhaus, Lawrence, *World War One: The Global Revolution*, Cambridge and New York, Cambridge University Press, 2011.

Sondhaus, Lawrence, *The Great War at Sea: A Naval History of the First World War*, Cambridge, Cambridge University Press, 2014.

Sondhaus, Lawrence, *German Submarine Warfare in World War I: The Onset of Total War at Sea*, Lanham, Md, Rowman & Littlefield, 2017.

Sonyel, Salahi R., *The Great War and the Tragedy of Anatolia: Turks and Armenians in the Maelstrom of Major Powers*, Ankara, Turkish Historical Society Printing House, 2000.

Sprenger, Matthias, *Landsknechte auf dem Weg ins Dritte Reich? Zu Genese und Wandel des Freikorps-Mythos*, Paderborn, Schöningh, 2008.

Steakley, James D., *The Homosexual Emancipation Movement in Germany*, New York, Arno Press, 1975.

Steiner, Zara, 'The Treaty of Versailles Revisited', in Michael Dockrill and John Fisher (eds), *The Paris Peace Conference 1919: Peace without Victory?*, Basingstoke, Palgrave, 2001, 13–33.

Steiner, Zara, *The Lights that Failed: European International History 1919–1933*, Oxford and New York, Oxford University Press, 2005.

Stephenson, Scott, *The Final Battle: Soldiers of the Western Front and the German Revolution of 1918*, Cambridge and New York, Cambridge University Press, 2009.

Stevenson, David, *With our Backs to the Wall: Victory and Defeat in 1918*, London, Allen Lane, 2011.

Stevenson, David, *1917: War, Peace, and Revolution*, Oxford, Oxford University Press, 2017.

Stone, Norman, *The Eastern Front 1914–1917*, London, Hodder and Stoughton, 1975.

Strachan, Hew, *The First World War in Africa*, Oxford, Oxford University Press, 2004.

Straub, Eberhard, *Albert Ballin: Der Reeder des Kaisers*, Berlin, Siedler, 2001.

Straub, Eberhard, *Kaiser Wilhelm II. In der Politik seiner Zeit: Die Erfindung des Reiches aus dem Geist der Moderne*, Berlin, Landtverlag, 2008.

Sullivan, Charles L., 'The 1919 German Campaign in the Baltic: The Final Phase', in Stanley Vardys and Romuald Misiunas, *The Baltic States in Peace and War, 1917–1945*, University Park, Pa., Pennsylvania State University Press, 1978, 31–42.

Suny, Ronald G., 'Toward a Social History of the October Revolution', *American Historical Review* 88 (1983), 31–52.

Suval, Stanley, 'Overcoming Kleindeutschland: The Politics of Historical Mythmaking in the Weimar Republic', *Central European History*, 2 (1969), 312–30.

Suval, Stanley, *The Anschluß Question in Germany and Austria in the Weimar Era: A Study of Nationalism in Germany and Austria 1918–1932*, Baltimore and London, Johns Hopkins University Press, 1974.

Suzzi Valli, Roberta, 'The Myth of Squadrismo in the Fascist Regime', *Journal for Contemporary History* 35 (2000), 131–50.

Swain, Geoffrey, *Trotsky and the Russian Revolution*, London and New York, Routledge, 2014.

Tachjian, Vahé, *La France en Cilicie et en Haute-Mésopotamie: aux confins de la Turquie, de la Syrie et de l'Irak, 1919–1933*, Paris, Édition Karthala, 2004.

Tasca, Angelo, *La naissance du fascism*, Paris, Gallimard, 1938.

Thaer, Albrecht von, *Generalstabsdienst an der Front und in der OHL: Aus Briefen und Tagebuchaufzeichnungen, 1915–1919*, Göttingen, Vandenhoeck & Ruprecht, 1958.

Ther, Philipp, 'Deutsche Geschichte als imperiale Geschichte: Polen, slawophone Minderheiten und das Kaiserreich als kontinentales Empire', in Sebastian Conrad and Jürgen Osterhammel (eds), *Das Kaiserreich transnational: Deutschland in der Welt, 1871–1914*, 2nd edn, Göttingen, Vandenhoeck & Ruprecht, 2006, 129–48.

Theweleit, Klaus, *Männerphantasien*, 2 vols, Frankfurt am Main, Verlag Roter Stern, 1977.

Thompson, Mark, *The White War: Life and Death on the Italian Front 1915–19*, London, Faber and Faber, 2009.

Thorsen, Niels Aage, *The Political Thought of Woodrow Wilson*, Princeton, Princeton University Press, 1988.

Thum, Gregor, 'Mythische Landschaften: Das Bild vom deutschen Osten und die Zäsuren des 20. Jahrhunderts', in Thum (ed.), *Traumland Osten: Deutsche Bilder vom östlichen Europa im 20. Jahrhundert*, Göttingen, Vandenhoeck & Ruprecht, 2006, 181–212.

Thum, Gregor (ed.), *Traumland Osten: Deutsche Bilder vom östlichen Europa im 20. Jahrhundert*, Göttingen, Vandenhoeck & Ruprecht, 2006.

Tooley, Terry Hunt, 'German Political Violence and the Border Plebiscite in Upper Silesia, 1919–1921', *Central European History* 21 (1988), 56–98.

Tooley, Terry Hunt, *National Identity and Weimar Germany: Upper Silesia and the Eastern Border, 1918–22*, Lincoln and London, University of Nebraska Press, 1997.

Tooze, Adam, *Sintflut: Die Neuordnung der Welt 1916–1931*, Munich, Siedler, 2015.

Tormin, Walter, *Zwischen Rätediktatur und sozialer Demokratie: Die Geschichte der Rätebewegung in der deutschen Revolution 1918/19*, Düsseldorf, Droste, 1959.

Traxel, Richard, *Crusader Nation: The United States in Peace and the Great War 1898–1920*, New York, Knopf, 2006.

Trippe, Christian F., *Konservative Verfassungspolitik 1918–1923: Die DNVP als Opposition in Reich und Ländern*, Düsseldorf, Droste, 1995.

Trotnow, Helmut, *Karl Liebknecht: Eine Politische Biographie*, Cologne, Kiepenheuer & Witsch, 1980.

Tuchman, Barbara W., *The Zimmermann Telegram*, New York, Viking Press, 1958.

Tuchman, Barbara W., *August 1914*, Bern, Munich, and Vienna, Scherz, 1960.

Ullrich, Sebastian, 'Mehr als Schall und Rauch: Der Streit um den Namen der ersten deutschen Demokratie 1918–1949', in Moritz Völlmer and Rüdiger Graf, *Die 'Krise' der Weimarer Republik: Zur Kritik eines Deutungsmusters*, Frankfurt am Main, Campus, 2005, 187–207.

Ullrich, Sebastian, *Der Weimar-Komplex: Das Scheitern der ersten deutschen Demokratie und die politische Kultur der frühen Bundesrepublik 1945–1959*, Göttingen, Wallstein, 2009.

Ullrich, Volker, *Kriegsalltag: Hamburg im Ersten Weltkrieg*, Cologne, Prometh Verlag, 1982.

Ullrich, Volker, 'Kriegsalltag: Zur inneren Revolutionierung der Wilhelminischen Gesellschaft', in Wolfgang Michalka (ed.), *Der Erste Weltkrieg: Wirkung—Wahrnehmung—Analyse*, Weyarn, Seehamer, 1997, 603–21.

Ullrich, Volker, *Die Revolution von 1918/19*, Munich, C. H. Beck, 2016.

Ulrich, Bernd, and Benjamin Ziemann (eds), *Frontalltag im Ersten Weltkrieg: Wahn und Wirklichkeit. Quellen und Dokumente*, Frankfurt am Main, Fischer, 1994.

Upton, Anthony, *The Finnish Revolution, 1917–1918*, Minneapolis, University of Minnesota Press, 1980.

Urbach, Karina (ed.), *European Aristocracies and the Radical Right, 1918–1939*, Oxford, Oxford University Press, 2007.

Verhey, Jeffrey, *The Spirit of 1914: Militarism, Myth, and Mobilization in Germany*, Cambridge, Cambridge University Press, 2000.

Vestring, Sigrid, *Die Mehrheitssozialdemokratie und die Entstehung der Reichsverfassung von Weimar 1918/1919*, Münster, Lit, 1987.

Vincent, Charles Paul, *The Politics of Hunger: The Allied Blockade of Germany, 1915–1919*, Athens, Oh., Ohio University Press, 1985.

Vivarelli, Roberto, *Storia delle origini del fascism: l'Italia dalla grande Guerra alla marcia su Roma*, Bologna, Società editrice il Mulino, 2012.

Volkmann, Hans-Erich, *Die deutsche Baltikumpolitik zwischen Brest-Litovsk und Compiègne*, Cologne and Vienna, Böhlau, 1970.

Volkov, Shulamit, *Walter Rathenau: Weimar's Fallen Statesman*, New Haven, Yale University Press, 2012.

Völlmer, Moritz, and Rüdiger Graf (eds), *Die 'Krise' der Weimarer Republik: Zur Kritik eines Deutungsmusters*, Frankfurt am Main, Campus, 2005.

Vukov, Nikolai, 'The Memory of the Dead and the Dynamics of Forgetting: 'Post-Mortem' Interpretations of World War I in Bulgaria', in Oto Luthar (ed.), *The Great War and Memory in Central and South Eastern Europe*, Leiden, Brill, 2016.

Wachs, Friedrich-Carl, *Das Verordnungswerk des Reichsdemobilmachungsamtes*, Frankfurt am Main, Lang, 1991.

Wade, Rex A., *The Russian Revolution, 1917*, Cambridge and New York, Cambridge University Press, 2000.

Wade, Rex A., 'The October Revolution, the Constituent Assembly, and the End of the Russian Revolution', in Ian D. Thatcher, *Reinterpreting Revolutionary Russia: Essays in Honor of James D. White*, Basingstoke, Palgrave Macmillan, 2006, 72–85.

Waite, Robert G. L., *Vanguard of Nazism: The Free Corps Movement in Postwar Germany, 1918–1923*, Cambridge, Mass., Harvard University Press, 1952.

Waldeyer-Hartz, Hugo von, *Die Meuterei der Hochseeflotte: Ein Beitrag zur Geschichte der Revolution*, Berlin, Universitas, 1922.

Walker, Christopher J., *Armenia: The Survival of a Nation,* 2nd edn, London, St Martin's Press, 1990.

Watson, Alexander, *Enduring the Great War: Combat, Morale and Collapse in the German and British Armies, 1914–1918*, Cambridge and New York, Cambridge University Press, 2008.

Watson, Alexander, 'Fighting for Another Fatherland: The Polish Minority in the German Army, 1914–1918', *The English Historical Review* 126 (2011), 1137–66.

Watson, Alexander, *Ring of Steel: Germany and Austria-Hungary at War, 1914–1918*, London, Penguin, 2015.

Watt, Richard M., *The Kings Depart: The German Revolution and Treaty of Versailles 1918–19*, New York, Simon & Schuster, 1968.

Wawrzinek, Bert, *Manfred von Killinger (1886–1944): Ein politischer Soldat zwischen Freikorps und Auswärtigem Amt*, Preußisch Oldendorf, Deutsche Verlags-Gesellschaft, 2004.

Weber, Reinhold, *Baden und Württemberg 1918/19: Kriegsende—Revolution—Demokratie*, Stuttgart, Landeszentrale für politische Bildung Baden-Württemberg, 2018.

Weber, Thomas, *Hitler's First War: Adolf Hitler, the Men of the List Regiment, and the First World War*, Oxford and New York, Oxford University Press, 2010.

Weber, Thomas, *Becoming Hitler: The Making of a Nazi*, Oxford, Oxford University Press, 2017.

Weitz, Eric, *Weimar Germany: Promise and Tragedy*, Princeton, Princeton University Press, 2007.

Wette, Wolfram, *Gustav Noske: Eine politische Biographie*, Düsseldorf, Droste, 1987.

Whalan, Robert, *Bitter Wounds: German Victims of the Great War, 1914–1939*, Ithaca, NY, and London, 1984.

Wheeler-Bennett, John, *Brest-Litovsk: The Forgotten Peace. March 1918*, London, W. W. Norton & Co. Inc., 1938.

White, James D., 'National Communism and World Revolution: The Political Consequences of German Military Withdrawal from the Baltic Area in 1918–19', *Europe–Asia Studies* 8 (1994), 1349–69.

Wickert, Christl, *Unsere Erwählten: Sozialdemokratische Frauen im Deutschen Reichstag und im Preußischen Landtag 1919 bis 1932*, vol. 2, Göttingen, Sovec, 1986.

Wiel, Jerome aan de, *The Irish Factor 1899–1919: Ireland's Strategic and Diplomatic Importance for Foreign Powers*, Dublin, Irish Academic Press, 2008.

Wildman, Allan K., *The End of the Russian Imperial Army: The Old Army and the Soldiers' Revolt, March to April 1917*, Princeton, Princeton University Press, 1980.

Wildman, Allan K., *The End of the Russian Imperial Army II: The Road to Soviet Power and Peace*, Princeton, Princeton University Press, 1987.

Williams, Robert C., *Culture in Exile: Russian Emigrés in Germany, 1881–1941*, Ithaca, NY, Cornell University Press, 1972.

Wilson, Tim K., 'The Polish–German Ethnic Dispute in Upper Silesia, 1918–1922: A Reply to Tooley', *Canadian Review of Studies in Nationalism* 32 (2005), 1–26.

Winkler, Heinrich August, *Die Sozialdemokratie und die Revolution von 1918/19: Ein Rückblick nach sechzig Jahren*, Berlin, Dietz, 1979.

Winkler, Heinrich August, *Von der Revolution zur Stabilisierung: Arbeiter und Arbeiterbewegung in der Weimarer Republik, 1918 bis 1924*, Berlin, Dietz, 1984.

Winkler, Heinrich August, *Weimar 1918–1933: Die Geschichte der ersten deutschen Demokratie*, Munich, C. H. Beck, 1993.

Winkler, Heinrich August, *Age of Catastrophe: A History of the West, 1914–1945*, London and New Haven, Yale University Press, 2015.

Winkler, Heinrich August, and Alexander Cammann (eds), *Weimar: Ein Lesebuch zur deutschen Geschichte 1918–1933*, Munich, C. H. Beck, 1997.

Winter, Jay, *Sites of Memory, Sites of Mourning: The Great War in European Cultural History*, Cambridge and New York, Cambridge University Press, 1995.

Winter, Jay, and Jean-Louis Robert (eds), *Capital Cities at War: Paris, London, Berlin 1914–1919*, Cambridge, Cambridge University Press, 1997.

Wirsching, Andreas, *Vom Weltkrieg zum Bürgerkrieg: Politischer Extremismus in Deutschland und Frankreich 1918–1933/39. Berlin und Paris im Vergleich*, Munich, Oldenbourg, 1999.

Wirsching, Andreas, and Jürgen Eder (eds), *Vernunftrepublikanismus in der Weimarer Republik: Politik, Literatur, Wissenschaft*, Stuttgart, Steiner, 2008.

Wohlgemuth, Heinz, *Karl Liebknecht: Eine Biographie*, Berlin (GDR), Dietz, 1975.

Wollstein, Günter, *Theobald von Bethmann Hollweg: Letzter Erbe Bismarcks, erstes Opfer der Dolchstoßlegende*, Göttingen, Muster-Schmidt, 1995.

Zabecki, David T., *The German 1918 Offensives: A Case Study in the Operational Level of War*, New York, Routledge, 2006.

Ziemann, Benjamin, 'Enttäuschte Erwartung und kollektive Erschöpfung: Die deutschen Soldaten an der Westfront 1918 auf dem Weg zur Revolution', in Jörg Duppler and Gerhard P. Groß (eds), Kriegsende 1918: Ereignis, Wirkung, Nachwirkung, Munich, Oldenbourg, 1999, 165–82.

Ziemann, Benjamin, 'The German Revolution in 1918/1919: Romance, Tragedy or Satire?', unpublished lecture given at conference: 'Approaching Revolutions', University of Virginia, 25–7 March 2010.

Ziemann, Benjamin, Contested Commemorations: Republican War Veterans and Weimar Political Culture, Cambridge and New York, Cambridge University Press, 2013.

Zöllner, Erich, Geschichte Österreichs: Von den Anfängen bis zur Gegenwart, 8th edn, Vienna, Böhlau, 1990.

Zorn, Wolfgang, Bayerns Geschichte im 20. Jahrhundert: Von der Monarchie zum Bundesland, Munich, C. H. Beck, 1986.

Zürcher, Erik Jan, 'The Ottoman Empire and the Armistice of Moudros', in Hugh Cecil and Peter H. Liddle (eds), At the Eleventh Hour: Reflections, Hopes, and Anxieties at the Closing of the Great War, 1918, London, Leo Cooper, 1998, 266–75.

Zürcher, Erik Jan, Turkey: A Modern History, London and New York, Tauris, 2004.

Index

Note: Figures are indicated by an italic "*f*", and notes are indicated by "n" following the page numbers.

For the benefit of digital users, indexed terms that span two pages (e.g., 52–53) may, on occasion, appear on only one of those pages.